Introduction to Theology

Revised Edition

Owen C. Thomas

MOREHOUSE PUBLISHING
WILTON, CONNECTICUT

The author wishes to thank the following for permission to reproduce copyrighted material: F. W. Dillistone, for *The Significance of the Cross,* published by the Westminster Press (Philadelphia), copyright © 1944; Harper and Row (New York), for *In the End God,* by John A. T. Robinson, copyright © 1968; Charles Scribner's Sons (New York), for *God Was in Christ,* by D. M. Baillie, copyright © 1948, for *Psychotherapy and a Christian View of Man,* by David E. Roberts, copyright © 1950; and for *Paul Tillich and the Christian Message,* by George H. Tavard, copyright © 1962; The University of Chicago Press for *Systematic Theology,* Vol. I and Vol. III, by Paul Tillich, copyright © 1951 and 1963 respectively; and The Westminster Press, for *The Divine Imperative,* by Emile Brunner, copyright © MCMXLVII by L. Jenkins.

The biblical quotations are from the Revised Standard Version of the Bible, copyrighted © 1946 and 1952.

Morehouse Publishing
78 Danbury Road
Wilton, Connecticut 06897

ISBN 0-8192-1319-5

Library of Congress Catalog Card Number 82-61890

Printed in the United States of America
by BSC Litho
Harrisburg, PA

Second Printing

Preface

This book is a revision of material originally written for an introductory course in theology at the Episcopal Theologicial School (now the Episcopal Divinity School) and published in 1973. The revisions consist mainly of expansions and additions to take account of theological writings and developments since the early seventies, especially in process, liberation and feminist theology.

The purpose of this book is not to develop a system of theology but rather to introduce beginning students to the study of theology. Therefore, the chapters usually take the form of a definition of the topic, a summary of contemporary discussion, a survey of its basis in the Bible and of its treatment in Christian hisory, and an attempt at reinterpretation.

I want to express my gratitude to certain peoiple who have helped me in various ways in the prepararion of this revised edition: Professor Gabriel Fackre of Andover-Newton Theological School for much bibliographical help; Professor Robert D. Hughes III of the School of Theology of the University of the South for several valuable suggestions, especially in regard to chapter 18; and to Miss Frances Ricker of the Episcopal Divinity School for a great deal of patient and expert secretarial help.

O. C. Thomas
Arlington, Massachusetts
July, 1982

Contents

1

Introduction

Before we begin to dig into the details of systematic theology, we should remind ourselves that what we are talking about is not a structure of abstract theoretical propositions but the story of the Bible, the concrete, dramatic story of God and the people of God, the history of Israel, old and new, seen as the events in which God is revealed for our salvation. This is the story of the creation, the rebellion of humanity, the election and covenant with Israel, the crisis of the coming of the Messiah, the reconciliation of God and humanity in the new covenant, the birth of the new Israel as God's instrument in the divine mission to the world, and the gift of the Spirit as the promise of the final fulfillment. The Christian gospel and the Christian faith are this kind of thing, and Christian theology is the attempt to understand and interpret this story of what God has done.

Nature and Necessity of Theology

Systematic or dogmatic theology is the methodical investigation and interpretation of the content of Christian faith. It is the orderly clarification and explanation of what is affirmed in the Christian message. Theology is an activity or function of the Christian church carried out by members of the church. It is the church reflecting on the basis of its existence and the content of its message. The church has to reflect on its faith and message in every age, so that it can interpret and present them in a way that can be understood in each new period. If the church tries too hard to make its message relevant, it may lose its message and become simply a sanctification of the culture around it. But it may also be so concerned to maintain the purity of its message that it becomes unintelligible to the contemporary age. So the task of theology or the theological task of the church is to interpret its faith and message so that they can be understood and affirmed in each new age.

To put this in another way, the church has a mission to speak about God to the world. It uses language about God in all of its activities, in worship, preaching, instruction, social action and pastoral care. The function and task of theology is to test, criticize and revise the language which the Church uses about God, to test it by its norm, namely, God's self-disclosure to which testimony is given in the Bible. This testing is necessary because the church's language about God is fallible and can fall into error and confusion. Furthermore, the church's understanding of God and the gospel is always being expanded and deepened. Finally, human language itself is constantly changing in meaning and thus must be regularly revised in order to maintain a continuity of meaning. Thus theology is not a luxury or an academic game for those specially inclined but something necessary in the life of the church.

It is sometimes objected that theology moves away from the directness and simplicity of faith and tends to get lost in subtle distinctions, arid definitions, abstract conceptions, and hair-splitting analysis. It is objected that the gospel calls us to active love and faithful obedience rather than to intellectual reflection. It is objected that theology tends to make true doctrine the object of faith rather than God. It is objected that theology arouses controversies which divide the church. And it is objected that the Bible contains little if any theology in the sense defined above.

It is true that theology is not of the essence of the church, that it is possible to be a Christian without theology, that theology is not necessary for salvation. Why then is it necessary in the life of the church? First, it is necessary in order to determine what is essential to the Christian faith and message and what is not essential, what is central and what is peripheral. In a word, theology is necessary in order to determine what is and what is not part of Christian faith. Misunderstandings and distortions of Christian faith arise in the church, and it becomes necessary to distinguish true doctrine from false. The only thing which saved the church from Gnosticism, Arianism, Apollinarianism, and so forth, was hard theological work.

Secondly, after preaching there must be teaching in the church, catechetical instruction, explaining what the Christian faith means and requires. This may raise further questions which must be answered carefully. The simplest kind of teaching, even of the youngest children, is full of theological content. There are several references in the New Testament to the necessity of teaching and teachers.

Thirdly, the Bible as the main source and standard of Christian teaching is not uniform. It does not present a simple unity of teaching but rather a multiplicity of different approaches which must be resolved by critical reflection, by theological work. This may be considered to be the domain of biblical scholars rather than theologians, but the former have been rather reticent about the task of presenting a consensus of the theology of the Bible. In any case the division of labor is one of expediency rather than essential distinction. Furthermore, the thought categories of the Bible must be translated into the thought categories of the present. Our understanding of ourselves, our language and concepts, the issues we face, and the questions we raise about Christian faith change from age to age. We cannot require modern people to return to the thought world of the first century nor can we present the thought world of the Bible untranslated. The work of theology is essentially translation.

Fourthly, the Christian message which is based on the Bible must be distinguished from the scientific picture of the world of the first century. The geology, biology and historiography of the Bible have no authority for us and must be distinguished from the faith testimony of the Bible. Bultmann has raised this issue in a new way in our day and thus pointed up the necessity of theology again.

The first objection mentioned above that theology moves away from the directness of faith toward abstract conceptions is valid and correct. We can see this process taking place in the Bible. At Caesarea Philippi Peter says to Jesus, "You are the Christ." This is direct personal confrontation and encounter, the immediacy and spontaneous response of faith. In his sermon on the day of Pentecost he says, "He is Lord and Christ." This is preaching, giving testimony, and it is one step removed from the immediacy of personal encounter which is indicated by the use of the third in place of the second person. This is the beginning of the movement in the direction of theology. It is no longer a spontaneous response but involves some reflection. The next step is the answering of questions arising from the preaching, then baptismal and catechetical instruction, then the training of teachers, and finally the work of theologians. The greater clarity and precision of concepts is gained only at the cost of moving away from the immediacy of conscious personal relationship to God. It is not possible to worship and to think critically about the object of worship at the same time, but both are necessary to the life of faith. William Temple writes: "For the fullest practice of . . . the Christian religion, the two sides must be held together as closely as possible. An uncritical surrender will involve an unsanctified intellect; while an unsurrendered criticism will be incapable of worship."[1] Theology serves faith through critical clarification, but there is a danger that the critical reflective temper may replace rather than serve the humble openness and expectancy before God. Emil Brunner offers a parable: chemists analyze food for its nourishing value. The food they use is no longer useful for nourishment but their work serves the aim of nourishment.

This can be put in another way. Faith can be defined as the right relationship of a person to God, a relationship of grateful trust and obedience. Thus faith necessarily involves a measure of understanding of the object of faith. Otherwise it would be completely blind or unconscious and thus not faith. Faith seeks greater understanding of God, greater comprehension and clarity, because it involves the impulse toward the giving of testimony, toward communication, both within the community of faith and to the world outside. Theology is a continuation of this inherent movement of faith toward understanding and greater clarity in its comprehension of its object, God. Theology is the unfolding and elaboration, the explication and clarification of the understanding which is essentially involved in faith. As Anselm put it, theology is *fides quaerens intellectum,* faith seeking understanding. Anselm's friends asked him for proofs of doctrine, and he writes in *Cur Deus Homo?*, "This they ask, not for the sake of attaining to faith by means of reason, but that they may be gladdened by understanding and meditating on those things which they believe" (I,1). Thus it is faith itself which seeks greater understanding in theology. Theologians have faith, stand in the community of faith, and their work serves the faith of the community. So theology is faith moving to a level of clearer and more comprehensive understanding. Bultmann writes, "It is of decisive importance that theological thoughts be conceived and explicated as thoughts of faith, that is, as thoughts in which faith's understanding of God, the world, and man is unfolding itself. . . . Theological propositions—even those of the New Testament—can never be the object of faith; they can only be the explication of the understanding which is inherent in faith itself."[2]

From what has been said it becomes clear that theology is *normative* and not merely descriptive. Some theologians have maintained that the only purpose of theology is to describe the faith of the church, to draw up a coherent consensus of Christian faith. This is the implication of such a book as Horton's *Christian Theology: An Ecumenical Approach* which is an attempt to describe the contemporary Christian consensus. Nor is theology simply the combination and commentary on the dogmatic tradition in the form of creeds, conciliar decisions, and confessions, which is what theology has often been in the Roman Catholic Church. Nor is theology a historical report on the consensus in some special classical period, such as the early church, the Reformation, or the seventeenth century Anglican divines. These are historical and not systematic theological studies. Neither is theology simply a personal statement of faith on the part of the theologian, although this seems to be the tendency among some contemporary theologians.

Theology is normative in the sense of attempting to determine what is the true Christian faith, to distinguish true doctrine from false doctrine, to determine what is and what is not part of Christian faith. Thus one of the functions of theology is to scrutinize, criticize, and if necessary reform the church's formulations of its faith in creeds, conciliar decisions, and confessions.

Theology and Philosophy

I have elaborated my views on the relation of theology, philosophy and philosophy of religion in my book *William Temple's Philosophy of Religion*.[3] My thesis in brief is that theology and philosophy are parallel enterprises. More specifically, Christian theology is a species of the genus philosophy. Philosophy in its constructive function is the attempt to organize and interpret the data of human experience in the light of some key-category or organizing principle, such as matter in motion, nature, life, organism, process, mind or spirit. The key-category or organizing principle is chosen by a decision which is analogous to the decision of faith, and the first task of the constructive philosopher is to analyze and clarify this key-category. Theology as we have defined it is the analysis and clarification of the key-category or organizing principle of Christian faith, namely, God as manifest in the testimony of the Bible. Then the larger task of theology, usually called Christian philosophy, is the interpretation of the data of human experience in the light of the Christian key-category. The parallel character of theology and philosophy has been obscured recently by the fact that theology has tended to ignore its larger task and philosophy its constructive function, and by the fact that theology has often neglected its critical function, that is, its responsibility to be clear and precise in its concepts and propositions. But there are hopeful signs that these lacks are beginning to be overcome.

Thus the relation of theology to philosophy should be considered in terms of the relation of theology to various philosophies. This is the relation between different world views, some of which are near to each other, some of which overlap, and some of which contradict each other. Theologians are free to make use of any concepts, analysis, or arguments of any philosophy which is of help to them in their task. They do this to some extent simply in the use of language. But there is a danger that concepts imported from another philosophy may distort rather than clarify the meaning of the Christian faith, and in any case no philosophical conclusions can be normative per se for theology.

One part of the larger task of theology and of the constructive function of philosophy is the interpretation of the phenomenon of religion. This is the *philosophy of religion*. Thus there will be a Christian philosophy of religion and a philosophy of religion corresponding to each of the different philosophical world views.

Theology and Science

Some theologians, such as J. Baillie and A. Richardson, claim that theology is one of the special sciences comparable to psychology or sociology, because it applies the empirical scientific method to its special area of investigation, namely, the biblical events or the contemporary church. It will be clear from the above that I disagree with this suggestion. A particular science is the investigation and interpretation of a limited body of facts. It is essentially descriptive rather than normative and is not concerned with the larger context of its purview, with questions of value, or with existential or religious questions about the ultimate origin and destiny of the universe or humanity. Theology is, to be sure, concerned in the first instance with a limited body of facts, namely, the biblical events, but it is concerned not simply to describe them but to ascertain their significance as the key-category or organizing principle of the Christian world view. Furthermore, theology is normative rather than descriptive, deals with the existential or religious questions, and is concerned in its larger task to interpret all areas of human experience, including science, in the light of the biblical revelation.

Theology cannot interfere or intervene with any of the areas of the special sciences or prejudge any of their investigations, nor can any scientific conclusions be decisive for theology. Paul Tillich has made this point in the following way: "Theology has no right and no obligation to prejudice a physical or historical, sociological or psychological, inquiry. And no result of such an inquiry can be directly productive or disastrous for theology." "Knowledge of revelation cannot interfere with ordinary knowledge. Likewise, ordinary knowledge cannot interfere with knowledge of revelation. There is no scientific theory which is more favorable to the truth of revelation than any other theory. It is disastrous for theology if theologians prefer one scientific view to others on theological grounds."[4] This is obviously a systematic and not a historical statement. Historically theology has attempted to prejudice scientific inquiries and has considered certain scientific conclusions to be either destructive or supportive to theology. Tillich is simply suggesting that this was a theological error. This means, for example, that the debate over the "big bang" versus the "steady state" theories of the universe cannot be decisive for the Christian doctrine of creation, and that psychoanalytic findings can neither support nor undercut the Christian doctrine of sin.[5]

This point is clearer in the case of the natural sciences than it is in the case of the human or social sciences, because the relation between theology and the human sciences is considerably more complex. Psychology, for example, while not decisive for theological formulations, can give concrete specification and documentation for the psychic side of the various aspects of the theological doctrine of humanity.[6]

Although science cannot be decisive for theology, religion including Christianity can be studied scientifically by the human sciences. Thus we have the psychology, sociology, anthropology and history of religion. The aim of these sciences will be to establish religion as a special category of culture, to determine its structure and to classify its various forms and elements. Then philosophers and theologians will use the results of the scientific investigation of religion to develop their philosophies of religion.

While not a special science, theology can be called scientific in the general (German) sense in which philosophy can be called scientific, because it follows an orderly method, aims at precise definitions, clear concepts, strict logicality, and coherence of its statements. Karl Barth calls theology a science, because like the other sciences it is a human effort after a definite object of knowledge and follows a consistent method. But since the meaning of "scientific" in English is considerably narrower, it is probably better to call theology systematic rather than scientific.

Reason and Logic in Theology

This issue is important today, because we often hear it said that the Christian gospel transcends reason or that it is somehow impious or spiritually dangerous to try to think carefully and precisely about God.

Let us define reason as the human capacity (1) to receive, sort out, interpret, and understand experience, (2) to generalize on experience or to conceive general principles or laws of experience, (3) to relate ideas consistently and purposively as in logic and mathematics, including the drawing of inferences from premises, (4) to develop means to ends, and (5) to evaluate, judge and choose among various ends and values.

In the first place, human reason is active in the receiving of God's self-disclosure in a way analogous to its activity in the receiving of human self-disclosure. This means that the knowledge of God given in revelation is rational in the sense that it does not bypass or destroy the structure and activity of the mind. Secondly, reason is active in the work of theology, in analyzing and reflecting on the testimony to and interpretation of revelation in the Bible and the history of Christian theology.

Now in what ways is theology rational? Tillich supplies us with a handy outline here. He suggests that theology is rational in three senses: it has semantic, logical and methodological rationality.[7]

Semantic rationality. Theologians should attempt to use words carefully and precisely. They should try to define their terms clearly and use them consistently. This does not mean that they should try to develop a univocal language, that is, a simple language with no connotations as in mathematics, but that they should try to elaborate the various connotations of their terms, clarify them, and show how they are related to each other. (The problem of the nature of theological language will be treated below.)

Logical rationality. Theologians should not allow simple logical contradictions, since these can have no meaning. But theology does recognize and use something which has usually been called paradox or dialectical tension. This phenomenon appears in various places in theology and for various reasons.

First there is the literal meaning of the word paradox, namely, that which is against the accepted opinion, that which is astounding, that which transcends all human expectations. The best example of it is the incarnation, which D. Baillie and Tillich describe as the central paradox of Christian faith. This is "what no eye has seen, nor ear heard, nor the heart of man conceived, what God has prepared for those who love him" (1 Cor. 2:9). This does not mean that the incarnation is nonsense or that we can say nothing about it in meaningful statements. Otherwise we could never preach or have a doctrine of the incarnation.

Secondly, in various parts of theology and in some degree in all parts, there arise seeming or apparent contradictions. We seem to have to make apparently contradictory statements in order to say what we believe we must say about God. This appears in the doctrine of the incarnation when we assert that Christ was both fully human and fully divine. D. Baillie gives as other examples the doctrines of creation and providence and explains that there is a similar paradoxical situation whenever we claim that God is the ultimate source of anything in our experience.[8] The doctrine of providence asserts that the world is a network of natural and human causes and that God is in control of the world process; that an event can be understood as having a natural or human causal explanation *and* can be seen as a providential event, an act of God, at the same time.

The same paradoxical situation is seen in the assertion of divine omniscience of foreknowledge and human freedom, in the assertion of the universality and inevitability of sin and human responsibility, and in the assertion of the presence of divine grace and human freedom in one human act. "I worked harder than any of them, though it was not I, but the grace of God which is with me" (1 Cor. 15:10).

One reason for the appearance of these paradoxical statements lies in the finite character of all human language. All language is primarily finite in its reference, limited to the context of space and time. All words have their direct and primary reference to the finite elements of our experience. Thus language cannot be applied to any reality which transcends our finite experience without becoming indirect, symbolic, figurative, meta-phorical, or analogical. Thus when we apply our language to God, apparent contradictions begin to appear.

Another reason for the appearance of seeming contradictions in theo-logical statements is that in theology we have to think and speak about God in a way that is not fully possible. Because God is the absolute subject who is always present and confronting us, we can know God only in a personal relationship and we cannot say anything *about* God which is not said *to* God. Thus the only proper way to use language about God is to address God personally. Augustine begins his *Confessions* with praise of God: "Great are thou, O Lord, and greatly to be praised." Anselm begins his *Proslogium* with a prayer: "Come thou now, O Lord, my God, teach my heart where and how it may seek thee, where and how it may find thee." Martin Buber states that properly speaking God cannot be expressed but only addressed. We can find an analogy to the impropriety of speaking *about* God in the sense of inappropriateness we feel in speaking *about* other people in their presence. The difference is that our fellow human beings are not always present, and having bodies they can be treated properly as objects in some circumstances, whereas God is always present and is never simply an object. In theology we have to forsake the mode of direct address, of prayer, and attempt to conceptualize God, to speak about God. So we may expect that our statements will get diffracted into propositions which seem contradictory and must be balanced by each other in order to express the truth we are aiming at. D. Baillie has a parable of this. Making correct statements about God is like trying to draw a map of the world on a flat surface. The latter is impossible without a certain degree of falsification. In order to get a correct picture two projections must be compared which contradict each other to some extent at every point. But when they are used to correct each other, the proper spherical relation-ships are presented.

Methodological rationality. In so far as theology is scientific in the general sense and aims at clarity and comprehensiveness, it must follow a consis-tent method and aim at an orderly presentation. Thus the final result will be a theological system, a totality of consistent assertions. The theological system will not be complete or closed nor will it restrict change or cut off further research. It will not be a rigid or deductive system in the sense of a complete structure built upon or deduced from a fundamental principle or set of axioms like the Euclidian geometry, because the activity of God cannot be condensed or summarized in such a way. If it is objected that the Christian gospel cannot be captured in any kind of system but bursts through any human attempt at formulation, then it must be asked that the meaning of these statements be given as clearly and precisely as possible and that the reasons for them be stated as consistently and coherently as possible, that is, as systematically as possible. The demand for as much clarity and consistency as possible in theology cannot be refused or avoided without giving up one of the fundamental purposes of theology.[9]

Because of the systematic character of theology, all parts and statements are dependent upon each other. As Tillich puts it, the parts of theology form a circle. When you treat any part of theology including the introduction you must assume all the other parts. A theological system cannot be built up piece by piece inductively or deductively. You cannot climb into the theological circle inductively or deductively; you must jump. And it does not make much difference where you begin. The order in which you take up the topics is expedient rather than necessary. In a way the most existential place to begin would be with the doctrine of the Church. Calvin begins with the problem of the knowledge of God, Schleiermacher with the doctrines of the church and creation, and Barth with the doctrine of the word of God. Traditionally there are four main topics or *loci* in theology: God (trinity, revelation), creation (providence, humanity), reconciliation (sin, Christology, church), redemption (eschatology). This order is expedient in that the active subject of the topics is treated first, and then the other topics follow in the dramatic order in which they are presented in the Bible.

Theological Language

The question of the nature and function of religious and theological language has been at the center of theological and philosophical discussion in this century. Especially is this the case in the response to the challenges of analytical philosophy. The crucial problems in regard to theological language are its very possibility, its relation to other kinds of language, and its typical characteristics.

Can we speak about God? We have noted a certain inappropriateness in speaking about God rather than to God. But beyond this there have been religious traditions in which it has been asserted that it is not possible to talk about God at all. The mystic has sometimes said that God is ineffable, that the divine being is incapable of being expressed in words. The tradition of negative theology has asserted that we can say of God only what God is not. But the main stream of the biblical and Christian tradition has always affirmed that it is possible to speak about God.

Religious and theological language about God lies on a spectrum or continuum. At one end is the language of the immediate response of faith, which is marked by vivid image, dramatic metaphor, and poetic symbol. At the other end is the language of systematic theology, which is marked (hopefully) by clarity, precision, consistency and coherence. In between lie various mixtures of these two extremes in the form of liturgies, catechisms and creeds. This is a real continuum without any radical breaks. As has been noted above, theology is not something radically different from immediate expressions of faith. Theology is the unfolding and clarification of the understanding which is already essentially involved in faith itself.

What is the relation of theological language to ordinary everyday language? In the first place theology uses ordinary language. Although it has developed its own technical vocabulary, it does not use a sacred or revealed language which has no meaning outside the context of theology. But in the second place it uses ordinary language in an extraordinary way. I.T. Ramsey in his book *Religious Language* has analyzed the various ways in which theology uses ordinary language in logically odd ways in order to speak about God. As has been suggested above, all language is primarily finite in its reference, limited to the context of space and time. All words have their direct and primary reference to the finite elements of our experience. If this language were applied directly or univocally to God, then God could be understood only as a finite object. This is the case of naive anthropomorphism. On the other hand, if we were to assert that when we apply certain terms to God, such as love, father and creator, we are using them in an altogether different sense from that in which we use them about humanity, then we have thereby emptied them of all meaning and would be asserting nothing about God. This is known as the equivocal use of terms.

Traditional Christian theology has taken a middle way between the univocal and equivocal use of language about God, namely the analogical use. An analogy is the application of a term to two objects in which there is a correspondence between the two objects in some characteristics implied by the term but not in all. If there were a correspondence in all characteristics implied by the term, the term would be used univocally. If there were a correspondence in no characteristics of the term, the term would be used equivocally. Thus when the term "love" is applied analogically to God, there is asserted a correspondence between God and humanity in some but not all of the characteristics of the term "love" in its primary or direct sense. The work of systematic theology is to analyze and specify which of the characteristics of a term are being applied to God and which are not.

The possibility of speaking of God by the way of analogy is based on the premise that there is some likeness, similarity, or correspondence between God and the world. This assumption has been stated classically in the doctrine of the *analogia entis,* the analogy of being between God and the world. Denial of the doctrine of the *analogia entis* necessarily involves a denial of the possibility of speaking about God at all.[10]

The necessity for the analogical use of language in speaking of God lies in the fact that God is not a finite object in the world but transcends the world as its creator. This is the main point at which debate has raged over theological language, especially in response to the challenge of analytical philosophy. The two main issues here are the meaning of transcendence and the ways in which theological language can refer to transcendent reality. Some analytical theologians have denied that the concept of transcendent reality has any meaning or that theological statements refer to transcendent reality. (Hare, Braithwaite, MacIntyre, Miles, Van Buren.)[11] They assert that faith is non-cognitive, that theological statements do not refer to states of affairs, that is, to transcendent reality. This solution would seem, however, to reduce Christian faith to a naturalistic humanism centered on the figure of Jesus. Other analytical theologians have shown that it is possible to speak meaningfully of transcendent reality and have analyzed the ways in which theological language can do this. (Hick, Wilson, Crombie, Ramsey.)

The most radical and fundamental challenge to the meaning of theological assertions has come from the analytical philosophers who claim that a statement about a state of affairs is meaningful only if it can be verified or falsified in some way. Many of them go on to claim that since theological statements can be neither verified or falsified, they are meaningless. (Ayer, Flew.) One way out of this dilemma, as we have noted above, is to deny that theological statements are cognitive or refer to states of affairs and to assert that they are statements of commitment or conviction or moral recommendations. This would seem, however, to give up the fundamental character of Christian faith as testifying to the reality of God. The only solution would seem to be to meet the challenge head-on and to affirm that theological statements can be verified or falsified in religious experience understood as the whole experience of the faithful person which may be focused in special moments of awareness.[12]

Theology as Confessional and Ecumenical

Before one is ordained in the Episcopal Church, one must subscribe to the following declaration: ". . . I do solemnly engage to conform to the Doctrine . . . of the Protestant Episcopal Church in the United States of America" (*Constitution*, Art. VIII). This refers primarily to preaching and teaching rather than to theological thinking and writing, but it points to the fact that theologians live and work in a particular part of the Christian church. They cannot withdraw from the visible church and seek a platform in the unity of some invisible church which transcends the division of the church, and from there expound a universal Christian faith. To be sure, theologians aim at the true Christian faith rather than a description of what Episcopalians believe or should believe. But they must begin from where they are in some particular Christian tradition and ecclesiastical jurisdiction. So in these chapters reference will be made to the various elements in the tradition of the Episcopal Church, such as the Articles of Religion, the Catechism and *The Book of Common Prayer.*

But since theologians aim to determine the true Christian faith and not simply some classical statement of Anglicanism, for example, their theology must be ecumenical as well as confessional. The great new fact about Christian theology in the second half of the twentieth century is that it is carried on in ecumenical perspective, as a result of the work of the World Council of Churches and the second Vatican Council. The theologian must be open to learn from all the traditions of the church, because no one has all the truth and each one probably has a grasp of some facet of the truth which has escaped the others. We must begin from where we are, but then we are free to learn from any theologian in any tradition.

Organization of Theology

Theology in the broad sense can be divided into four parts: biblical, historical, systematic and practical. Biblical theology is the expounding of the meaning of the Bible in its parts and as a whole. It is the foundation of the church's preaching, teaching, worship and action. It includes textual and higher criticism, the exegesis of the separate books, the analysis of recurrent themes, and it culminates in the elaboration of the theological consensus of the Bible.[13]

Historical theology is the study of the ways in which the church has interpreted the Bible and Christian faith and lived them out in the various periods of Christian history. (See the section on tradition in chapter 3.)

Systematic or dogmatic theology has been defined above as the explication of the content of the Christian faith and the testing of the church's language about God in the light of its norm. It includes apologetics and ethics which are separated off only for expedient reasons.[14]

Practical theology is the study of the norms and principles of the practice of the church and its members. It begins with the doctrine of the church and asks what the church must do in order to fulfill its being, in order to be the church, both what is essential and necessary and what is expedient. It includes homiletics, liturgics, education, pastoral, care, and so forth.[15]

Theological Method

As has been suggested above, because theology is scientific in the general sense and aims at clarity, consistency and comprehensiveness, it must follow a specific method or way of accomplishing its purposes. This method cannot be something independent of Christian faith but must be part of the theological circle and thus dependent upon the other parts of theology.

Method in theology can mean several different but closely connected things. It can mean the general way in which systematic theologians go about producing their systems, their starting points and procedures. (See, for example, Tillich's method of correlation.) It can mean the way in which theologians go about determining whether or not a particular statement is part of the Christian faith. It can refer to the procedure by which any Christians go about resolving theological issues which are presented to them.

Some theologians are quite explicit about their method, while the method of others can be determined only by analysis of how they actually proceed. Among classic systematic theologians those who have been most explicit about their method are Schleiermacher and to a lesser extent Aquinas and Melanchthon. Among recent and systematic theologians only Tillich and Tracy have been quite explicit about their methods. Barth writes about his method at some length, but the result is quite general and consists in following the traditional *loci* and in the rule that the theologian must remain open to the Word of God.

Historically the method of theology has been derived from the motivations and purposes of theology. The first theological writings were polemical in character dealing both with distortions of Christian faith within the church and with attack from outside. The Gnostics presented their interpretation of Christian faith and were refuted by Irenaeus in his *Against the Heresies*. The pagan Middle Platonist Celsus attacked Christian faith and was answered by Origen in his *Against Celsus*. The method of these early polemical theological writings was in general to take up the distortions or attacks point by point in the order given by the opponent or in some other logical order. The specific method followed in responding to each point was logical analysis for inconsistencies, appeal to Scripture, and appeal to the "rule of faith" as an orthodox summary outline of Scripture and apostolic faith. Later, of course, appeal was made to creeds, councils, confessions, and "the fathers."

A second purpose of theology was doctrinal instruction of new members. This was the purpose of Irenaeus' *Demonstration of the Apostolic Preaching*, the catechetical works of Cyril and Gregory of Nyssa, and Augustine's *Enchiridion*. This developed naturally into the treatment of more speculative issues, as in Origen's *De Principiis* and Thomas' *Summa Theologiae*. The method in these works was quite various including commenting on the topics in the rule of faith and discussing traditional questions of dispute in theology.

A third purpose and method which can be discerned in the history of theology is the summary and development of the fundamental ideas of the Bible. This can be seen in Augustine's *On Christian Doctrine* and especially in Melanchthon's *Loci Communes* and Calvin's *Institutes*. But perhaps the majority of theological writing has been occasional and monographic, letters, essays, sermons, tracts, and so forth, addressed to some particular issue. Today this takes the form of journal articles.

An important question to keep in mind in reading theological works is the authors' methods. What do they say about their methods? How do they go about the development of their system? How do they deal with each particular issue? In this book the overall method will be that of commenting on the traditional *loci* or topics of theology. Within each topic the method in most cases will include a survey of the biblical consensus, a survey of the issues raised on this topic in the history of theology, and an attempt to restate the topic in the light of contemporary issues and discussion.

The type of theological reflection that most of us will be called upon to do is not the development of a theological system but rather the resolving of specific issues and problems. These questions may be of a variety of types: (1) an issue which might confront Christians in their life or work, (2) an issue confronting the church at large either in its communal life or in its relation to the world, or (3) a personal issue of understanding, affirming, doubting, or denying some element in Christian faith.[16]

Now how can a theological question be distinguished from any other question? A theological question is one involving the understanding or interpretation of some element in Christian faith or one involving a decision as to whether or not some assertion is a valid part of Christian faith. A question is theological if it inquires about God, or the world or part of it in relation to God. Scientific, empirical, or historical questions are not theological, although the interpretation of a biblical or historical text may enter into the resolution of a theological question. In other words a theological question is one in which the resolution involves a judgment about God or the relation of God to the world.

Tillich suggests another way of distinguishing theological issues from other kinds of issues. Paraphrasing his first formal criterion of theology, a theological issue is one that concerns us ultimately. Only those issues are theological which deal with something which can become a matter of ultimate concern for us.[17] This distinguishes theological issues from issues of preliminary concern, but preliminary concerns can become the subject of theological issues if they are the vehicle or bearer of ultimate concern. Some issues may be a mixture of theological and other elements. Whether or not a particular issue is theological in whole or in part will have to be determined in each case.

What is the method for dealing with specific theological questions? First, it is necessary to be sure that it is a theological question and not a historical, empirical, psychological or strategic question. This may involve separating the theological question out from the other types of questions. Secondly, the question must be interpreted and clarified. This will involve the clarification of key terms in order to remove ambiguities and misleading connotations. For example, if the term "necessary" appears in the question, it is important to make clear whether it is understood logically, morally, practically, legally, canonically, psychologically, scientifically, hypothetically, or theologically.[18] Clarification and interpretation may be summarized by rephrasing the question.

Thirdly, it is usually helpful to list the various possible answers to the question. For example, if the question inquires about the relation between two things, then it will help to explore the following possible relations: identity, independence (no significant relation), complementarity (two aspects of the same reality), causality, inclusion (class membership), exclusion or contradiction. Fourthly, in order to proceed with the question it is necessary to make a judgment as to one's theological criterion or norm. This is discussed in chapter 3.

Fifthly, there are then three ways to proceed. You can select one possible answer and argue for it by giving the appropriate grounds or reasons. You can assess each possible answer and choose the one for which the grounds are strongest. Or you can consult your theological norm, for example, the Bible, to see which possible answer it supports the most strongly.

Finally, if you should adopt the theological norm outlined in chapter 3, you may proceed in the following way. Investigate whether the question is addressed directly or indirectly by any biblical author or consensus of biblical authors. To check the results of this or when the results are unclear or nil, you should investigate the tradition of the church, especially in the form of creeds, councils, confessions, liturgies and theological writings to see if the question is addressed by any of them. The use of the Bible and the tradition will require you to "translate" the meaning of the texts into language which is intelligible today. This is a very complex process requiring theological imagination and creativity. You can get an idea of how this might be done by consulting contemporary theologians on the question at hand.[19]

Questions for Discussion

1. *What is the relation between (a) understanding a theological assertion, (b) deciding that it is true, (c) deciding it is an essential element in Christian faith, and (d) affirming or believing it? Are b, c and d identical? What would you make of the situation in which your decision in regard to some particular theological assertion was positive in c and negative in b or d?*

2. *What is the relation and difference between believing in God and believing that God exists?*

3. *Is it important to be as clear as possible on what we believe and why we believe it? Why? What is the relation of this to the Christian life? Is it in any way dangerous, wrong, or impious to analyze what we mean by the term "God," for example?*

4. *Is it true in any sense to say that God or Christian salvation is beyond our comprehension or cannot be grasped or expressed in rational concepts? If so, what problems does this pose for theology?*

5. *What is the relation of language to reality in the case of theology?*

6. *Would it be possible for a non-Christian to do Christian theology?*

7. *If philosophy is our attempt to understand our experience, and if theology is the clarification of Christian faith, how can they be "parallel enterprises?" (p. 5).*

8. *If science is the best avenue to the knowledge of reality, and if theology should be completely open to science, how is it that no scientific conclusion can be decisive for theology? (p. 6).*

9. *Does "the Christian faith" (p. 1) refer to the faith which we believe (fides quae creditur) or to the faith by which we believe (fides qua creditur)? What is the relation between them?*

10. *Assuming that theology deals primarily with the cognitive (intellectual) use of language, what place if any is there for the emotive (affectional) and conative (ethical) uses of language in theology? Should they be excluded from theology? If theological judgments are affected by all three levels of human nature, to what extent can we expect to reach theological agreement by discourse on the cognitive level alone? What is the significance of agreement on one level along with disagreement on another?*

11. *What is the relation of theology to life and/or experience?*

12. *Are there any situations in the lives of Christians or the church in which theological reflection is absolutely necessary and unavoidable? If so specify. If not, are there any situations in which it is helpful? Give examples.*

13. *How would you distinguish a theological assertion from any other kind of assertion (scientific, historical, moral)? Are there some theological assertions which are also historical or scientific?*

14. *Are there affirmations in Christian faith which are true but not essential or necessary for salvation?*

2

Revelation

The most important critical question which can be raised about Christian faith is this: How do you know what you claim to know about God, humanity and the world? The theological answer to this question is contained in the doctrine of revelation. (We will see that each doctrine can be considered to be the theological answer to some real question which can be raised in different forms and on different levels by those inside and outside the church.)

In this chapter I will be presenting a theological consensus which includes the majority of contemporary theologians, especially those standing in traditions associated with the World Council of Churches. It is a part of a consensus which came into being after the victory of neo-orthodoxy over the older liberal theology in the second quarter of this century. But in the third quarter of this century this whole consensus has begun to be criticized across the board by theologians influenced by Bultmann, Tillich, Bonhoeffer, and analytical and process philosophy. The last area of this consensus to be criticized has been the basis of the whole, namely, the doctrine of revelation. But in the past two years this too has begun to be subjected to radical scrutiny.[1] I will take up the various points of criticism in the process of presenting the consensus.

Revelation is the basis and content of Christian faith. Apart from God's self-revelation there would be no knowledge of God and no Christian faith. And what God has revealed about the godhead constitutes the content of Christian faith. Thus the word "revelation" refers to both the act of revealing and the content of what is revealed. Confusion can be avoided if this dual meaning of the word is kept in mind in the following discussion.

The basis of the possibility of revelation is the personal nature of God. God is self-revealed to us as personal in a way analogous to human personhood, and we perceive that it is only because God is personal that God could be revealed to us. Although aspects of the subhuman world can be said to "reveal" themselves to us, nothing sub-personal can reveal itself in the way that a person can. (In chapter 5 we will investigate why we say God is personal and what we mean by this.) Thus Brunner can assert that personhood and the capacity to reveal oneself or the fact that one can be known only through self disclosure are identical concepts.

Therefore the most illuminating analogy for understanding revelation is the realm of human personal relationships. Revelation is a matter of the personal God in self-disclosure to human persons, rendering the divine reality accessible to a personal relationship. However, this is still an analogy and not an identity since none of the finite elements of human personhood can be applied to God. Furthermore, it is not simply a matter of our knowing human personhood and applying this analogically to God. Historically it has been rather the reverse; we have come to understand the full meaning of human personhood only through the self-disclosure of the personal God and through the human attempt to understand this revelation in the doctrine of the trinity. This we can call theomorphism, the tendency to define humanity in the image of God rather than vice versa. J. V. Langmead Casserley writes, "It is significant that the conception of divine personality thus preceded in time the conception of human personality. Human thought has an inveterate tendency always to conceive man in God's image."[2]

This emphasis on the personal in the doctrine of revelation and in theology generally is part of an important movement in modern philosophy and theology which began shortly after World War I. This movement involved a new understanding of how we gain knowledge of other persons. It is traceable to the work of Kierkegaard in the last century and today is especially associated with the writings of Martin Buber. John Baillie has traced the history of this movement and its theological implications in his book *Our Knowledge of God*.[3] The traditional interpretation of our knowledge of other persons was that it was an inference based on sense perception and self-knowledge. The newer understanding of knowledge of other persons is that it is a unique type of knowledge not reducible to anything else. In fact personal knowledge is genetically prior to self-knowledge and to sense perception of objects in the world.[4]

Now let us use the analogy of human personal relations to clarify the idea of God's revelation. A person (*A*) reveals herself to another person (*B*) by words and acts which express her character, attitudes, convictions, plans, hopes, fears, and loves. *A*'s self-disclosure is constituted by the history of her meetings and encounters with *B*. *B* must be open to *A*'s self-disclosure and must receive it in trust that it is an honest and authentic self-revelation. *B* can come to know *A* only if *A* freely chooses to open herself up to *B*. *B* cannot coerce *A* into revealing herself. *B* can learn a lot about *A* against *A*'s will or without her co-operation. *B* can subject to an intensive investigation and analysis by means of the various sciences: physics, chemistry, biology, psychology, sociology, and history. (In the human sciences there will be various degrees of dependence upon the willingness of the object of study to reveal herself.) But even at the conclusion of such a thorough investigation *B* would not be able to say of *A* in the fullest personal sense, "I know her." Finally, even if *A* reveals herself fully to *B*, there will be depths of the selfhood of *A* which will remain mysterious to *B*.

Now let us apply this analysis of human personal self-disclosure to our knowledge of God. God reveals the divine reality to us by words and acts which express the divine nature, attitudes, plans and loves. God's self-disclosure, is constituted by the history of the divine meetings and encounters with us in history, especially the history of Israel, old and new. We must be open to God's self-disclosure and must receive it in trust and faith. We can come to know God only if God freely chooses to reveal the godhead to us. We may be able to learn something about God through empirical investigation of the world or of our own experience, in the way that art critics may learn something about painters by examining their works. But as this is not yet personal knowledge of the painter, so it is not yet personal knowledge of God. Finally, even if God is self-revealed to us, there will be depths of the being of God which will remain mysterious to us.

The limitations of this analogy lie primarily in the finitude and bodily character of the human person who is being revealed. God is not finite in the sense of being an object in space and time. God is "without body, parts, or passions" (Articles of Religion, I). Some theologians have asserted that God is related to the world or to Jesus or to the Church in ways which are analogous to the ways in which persons are related to their bodies. But in any case God's words and acts are not manifest immediately to us but are mediated through the words of prophets and through events in human history which are perceived by faith to be the words and acts of God. Another limitation of the analogy is that human persons in their self-disclosure can deceive through ignorance and sin. But neither of these possibilities can be affirmed to God.

Thus the knowledge of God which we receive through revelation is not the kind of knowledge we could gain in any other way. We can gain unlimited knowledge about the world, but God is not part of the world. God transcends the world as its creator, and thus God stands outside the realm in which independent human knowledge can move. The corollary of this is that revelation does not give knowledge which can also be gained by scientific investigation. The Bible, which is the history of Israel interpreted as the locus of God's self-disclosure, does not give us authoritative knowledge in the fields of geology, astronomy, biology, anthropology, psychology, or sociology. Revelation cannot come into conflict with these sciences, because it does not give knowledge which is on the same level with the sciences.[5] There is a possibility of conflict between revelation and the conclusions of the human sciences in so far as the latter must use views of humanity which are on the theological or philosophical level in order to arrive at their final interpretations.[6] Thus we cannot know God by science, nor can we gain scientific knowledge through God's self-revelation.

Furthermore there are qualitative differences between the knowledge received in revelation and in human personal self-disclosure on the one hand and the knowledge we receive in any other way, especially scientific knowledge, on the other. Scientific knowledge depends upon the initiative of the knower, whereas revelation depends upon the initiative of the (logical) object of knowledge. Scientific knowledge requires disinterestedness and the abstraction from personal concerns, whereas revelation involves exactly the opposite. In scientific knowledge we become the masters of what we know, but in revelation God becomes the master or Lord of us. Scientific knowledge adds to my store of knowledge about the world, but knowledge of revelation does not do this but rather changes me. Ordinary knowledge by itself does not create community and may isolate, but the aim of knowledge of revelation is to create community with God and neighbor.

The use of the analogy of human knowledge of other persons is one of the points at which the doctrine of revelation is being criticized today. Downing attacks this analogy as unsuitable for clarifying the nature of our knowledge of God. Human knowledge of other persons is "objectively shaped by physical contact with the Other, and empirically verifiable from moment to moment by the accuracy of conscious and unconscious forecasts of moods and wishes."[7] Therefore Downing concludes that we do not have this kind of knowledge of God, and he suggests as a better analogy that of a "pen-friend" which involves others' impressions of the friend qualified by the friend's letters.[8] Downing's book is a helpful critique of excesses in the application of the analogy of personal knowledge, but this analogy still seems to be closest to the biblical view of our knowledge of God.

Natural and Revealed Theology

The view of revelation presented above and in the rest of this lecture is new in its explicit statement since the nineteenth century. The view generally held before the nineteenth century in all of Christendom was quite different. This traditional view of revelation was based on the traditional view of the Bible, namely, that it was dictated word by word by the Holy Spirit, that it was verbally inspired and thus inerrant and infallible. This was the view which the primitive church inherited from Judaism in regard to the Old Testament and which was soon applied to the New

Testament. In this traditional view revelation is the supernatural communication of truths about God from God to humanity in propositional form. These truths are the statements found in the Bible. Thus the Bible was seen as a source-book of divine truths which could not otherwise be attained by the unaided human reason. The supernatural origin and infallibility of these truths was attested by the miracles which accompanied the events described and by the miraculous power of the prophets to predict events which came to pass centuries after their time. So from the time of the canonization of the New Testament up to the eighteenth century, revelation generally meant the communication of truths about God through the verbal inspiration of Scripture. And faith meant assent to this true doctrine.

So the usage developed of speaking of truths of revelation and contrasting them with truths of reason to which unaided human reason could attain apart from revelation. This was the basis of the distinction between natural theology and revealed theology which was elaborated fully in the Middle Ages and most clearly by Aquinas. *Natural theology* consists of truths about God, God's existence, and certain divine attributes, which are attainable by the unaided reason of any person, Christian or pagan. In his *Summa Contra Gentiles* Aquinas asserts that the following can be demonstrated by the unaided human reason: the existence of God as unmoved mover, first cause, and intelligent governor of the universe; that God is eternal, necessary, pure actuality, incorporeal, simple, one, perfect, good, infinite, intelligent; that God has knowledge which is immediate and intuitive, that all things are eternally present to God, that God has no passions; the immortality of the soul, the freedom of the will, and the existence of angels.

Revealed theology consists of those truths about God which, although not contrary to reason, cannot be attained by the human reason alone but which can be known only through the divine revelation in the Bible, such as the incarnation and the trinity. This distinction between natural and revealed theology was generally accepted up until the eighteenth century, but now it has disappeared outside official Roman Catholic theology and Neo-Thomism.

What is wrong with this distinction? First, it derives from an erroneous view of the authority of Scripture, namely, the theory of verbal inspiration, which was undercut by the historical critical study of the Bible in the eighteenth and nineteenth centuries. This theory of verbal inspiration and of revelation as the communication of propositional truths from God to humanity does not fit the facts of the Bible. It makes the words of the Bible the locus of revelation rather than the events described in the Bible. The words of the Bible are the record of events and the interpretation of them as events in which God is acting. Faith or the reception of revelation in the

Bible is clearly not the acceptance of supernaturally communicated propositions but rather trust in and obedience to the living God who confronts humanity in the events of the Bible. As Temple puts it "There are truths of revelation, that is to say, propositions which express the results of correct thinking concerning revelation; but they are not themselves directly revealed.... What is offered to man's apprehension in any specific revelation is not truth concerning God but the living God himself." [9]

This is another point at which Downing criticizes the contemporary doctrine of revelation. The main thesis of his book is that in the Bible it is not God who is revealed but rather information about God, that is, God's plan, will, love, power, glory, righteousness, salvation and the obedience God requires. Personal knowledge of God is referred to the eschaton. His argument seems to involve a good deal of strained exegesis. For example, all biblical references to personal knowledge of God are ascribed to the influence of Gnosticism. His distinction between knowledge about God and knowledge of God is not very clear. Knowledge of other persons would seem always to involve a complex mixture of both these types of knowledge. Downing's assertion that no personal knowledge of God is referred to in the Bible seems odd in the light of his further assertion that the fulfillment of our relation to God will involve full personal knowledge of God. He makes the valuable point that Hebrew words for knowledge are much less intellectualistic than English words. Again his work serves as a valuable corrective to extreme claims of personal knowledge of God in the doctrine of revelation. Pannenberg also denies a direct self-revelation of God in the Bible and affirms that God is known only indirectly through divine acts in history.

The second difficulty with the traditional distinction of natural and revealed theology is that the arguments in the scholastic natural theology are not rigorous and conclusive, as they are claimed to be. They have received damaging criticism from many philosophers. Kant pointed out that they ignore the finite character of human reason and thus are invalid. Tillich asserts that you cannot argue rigorously from the world to God, and that the arguments are the expressions of the question of God implied in human finitude. Casserley suggests that the arguments are exhibitions of the intellectual fruitfulness, adequacy and illuminative power of Christian theism in making sense of our experience of the world. Brunner states that the arguments are really rationalized versions of the Christian doctrine of creation which can be known only by God's self-disclosure, and that when the arguments are severed from Christian faith they tend to dissolve into pantheism or deism.

In general the authors of the arguments were not brought to faith by the arguments, and although the arguments may be illuminating and impressive, they are not convincing. You cannot climb into the theological circle by rigorous deductive or inductive argument. The authors of the arguments came to know God in some other way, through God's self-disclosure. So the result is that natural theology is as much based on revelation as is revealed theology. But because of the traditional distinction, the attributes of God which have been held to be proven by natural theology have been isolated from the influence of the Christian revelation and have thus been retained in sub-Christian or pre-Christian form and not incorporated into the organic unity of Christian faith. Natural theology claims that a part of theology is outside the theological circle. Thus the arguments claim to prove the existence of a first cause, a prime mover, a necessary being, a highest being, and so forth, but the relation of these concepts to the Christian God is highly questionable.

A third difficulty with the idea of natural theology is that it seems to assume a static view of human nature. Innate moral and religious ideas are brought to consciousness by the unaided exercise of reason upon the individual's experience. A more historical view of humanity would hold that these ideas are not innate but rather the result of God's dealings and communion with humanity. John Baillie writes: "Our conclusion must therefore be that such moral and spiritual knowledge as may in any one period of human history seem to have become an inherent part of human nature, and so to be an 'unaided' natural knowledge, is actually the blessed fruit of God's personal and historical dealings with man's soul, and so in the last resort also a revealed knowledge." [10]

In summary, our criticism of the natural theology-revealed theology distinction is that the concept of revealed theology involves an unbiblical view of revelation, that natural theology is as much based on revelation as revealed theology, and that its formulation suffers from not making clear this basis in revelation. Recent attempts to rehabilitate natural theology are really concerned with Christian philosophy or apologetics rather than with natural theology as defined above.[11]

The Liberal View of Revelation

The destruction of the traditional view of revelation came about historically as the result of three factors: the anti-rationalist tendency of romanticism, pietism, and the liberal theology of the last century; the change in the view of human nature from the static view involving innate moral and religious ideas to the dynamic view in which human nature is molded by historical and cultural influences; and the application of the methods of literary and historical criticism to the Bible. The result was what Alan Richardson has called "the greatest revolution that has ever taken place in the history of Christian thought." [12]

The view of revelation which first took the place of the traditional view in the last century and which prevailed through the first quarter of this century is usually known as the liberal view of revelation. Here revelation is essentially the human discovery of universal religious truth which is accessible to all people but which has been discovered most fully by the great religious geniuses of the world, such as Buddha, Confucius, Moham-med, Socrates, the prophets of Israel, and especially Jesus. The supreme religious value of the Bible lies in the fact that it records the lives, religious experience, and teaching of the greatest religious geniuses. In all the great world religions there are analogies on a lower level of all the Christian doctrines, but Christianity, when it is purged of all its nonessential theo-logical trappings, represents the highest manifestation that has yet ap-peared of the universal religious consciousness of mankind. And the core of this is the ethical teaching of Jesus when it is stripped of primitive theological accretions. This is the pure essence of religion which appears in various forms more or less distorted in all the religions of the world. The biblical emphasis on unique acts of divine revelation is simply the giving of concrete illustrations of universal religious truths which could be grasped by the unsophisticated mind more easily than the universal truths of which they were examples.

This is the liberal alternative to the traditional view of revelation, and it has been almost entirely swept away by the neo-orthodox movement (also called neo-Reformation, dialectical, or crisis theology) which is a return to the themes of the Reformers in the light of the critical approach to the Bible, and which was ushered in by Karl Barth after the first World War.

What is wrong with the liberal view of revelation? First of all, as in the case of the traditional view, it does not make sense of the Bible and other religions. Revelation is pictured in the Bible not as human discovery but as God seeking out people to confront them, for example, God seeking Adam in the Garden, Ps. 139, and the parables of the lost sheep and the lost coin. What is discovered or revealed is not universal religious truth but the living God. The comparative study of religion has determined that there is no such thing as the essence of religion which is found in differ-ent forms in each of the world religions, that there are radical differences between the religions, and that these differences are more significant than anything they might have in common. The message of the Bible is not the religious experience of religious geniuses but the holy love of the living God who judges and saves sinful humanity. The so-called theological trappings of Christianity are at the very center and not the periphery of Christian faith. The revelation attested in the Bible is not simply the best yet nor the concrete illustration for the slow of mind, but the once-for-all self-disclosure of the eternal God.

If the traditional and liberal views of revelation are inadequate, we need a new interpretation of revelation which will do justice to the Bible, to the fact suggested by both the traditional and the liberal views that there is some knowledge of God apart from the biblical revelation, and to the uniqueness of Christian revelation, as the judgment and fulfillment of religion. In place of the natural theology-revealed theology distinction and rather than the liberal alternative, the majority of contemporary theologians are agreed on substituting the concepts of general and special revelation.

General Revelation

General revelation (sometimes called original or universal revelation) is God's self-disclosure in the creation and in the moral consciousness of humanity. Some theologians would add to this definition God's self disclosure in the course of history and in human reason. Special revelation refers to God's self-disclosure in the events recorded and interpreted in the Bible. General revelation is like studying the works of an artist, while special revelation is, like meeting the artist in person.

If God is the personal creator, if all creation is the manifestation of God's will, then the creation will involve to a certain extent a self-disclosure of God. The creature bears the impress of the will and purpose and thus the nature of the creator. If humanity is created in the image of God, and if God is always present to all people, their moral experience (and perhaps their reason) will reflect their origin and relation to God. If God is the Lord of history and effects the divine judgments and carries out the divine purposes in history, then the course of history will involve to some extent a self-disclosure of God's will and purpose. Thus as J. Baillie has suggested in the above quotation, the fundamental religious and moral ideas in any age are the result of general revelation and not innate aspects of human nature or conclusions of the unaided human reason.

There are three approaches to general revelation in the Bible: prehistorical myth, faith in God as creator, and analysis of the religion and ethics of the pagans. In the Noachic covenant of Genesis 8 God is revealed to and makes a covenant with all humanity. The patriarchal and mosaic covenants are made with people who are already in covenant with God. The prophets seem to be aware that all people stand in a relation to God which involves moral responsibility. This approach, however, is a very minor one in the Bible.[13]

The approach through faith in God as creator is seen in the Old Testament most clearly in Psalm 19:1-4. The clearest statement in the New Testament is in Romans 1:18ff. God has manifested the invisible divine nature, the eternal divine power and deity in the creation. This is the basis of Paul's interpretation of pagan religion as idolatry; it is the sinful distortion of God's revelation in the creation (See Acts 14:17, Jn. 1:1-9).

God's self-disclosure is manifest not only in the religion of the pagans but also in their moral awareness. Several passages in the New Testament imply that pagan gentiles know the law of God and can distinguish correctly between right and wrong (Rom. 1:32, 12:17, 13:1-4, 1 Pet. 2:12-14). Paul sums this up in Romans 2:14-16.

Building on the doctrine of general revelation in the Bible, the view that human nature is constituted by its relation to God, and the doctrine that God is present in grace and demand to all people, several contemporary theologians, including Brunner, J. Baillie, Farmer, Richardson and Rahner have gone on to assert that all of human experience and activity evidences the presence and self disclosure of God. The phenomenon of conscience, the moral commitment of the humanist, the scientist's devotion to truth, and the artist's dedication to beauty are interpreted as their response to the presence and demand of God in general revelation. This is an example of Christian philosophy, the attempt to interpret the various areas of human experience from the point of view of Christian faith. The questions raised by this approach are extremely important for the theology of the mission of the church. The Christian's approach to the "natural man" will depend upon the theological understanding of the "natural man's" relation to God.[14]

The limitations of general revelation are that it is relatively non-historical, impersonal and inadequate. The revelation of the power and trustworthiness of God in the regularities of nature is perfect in its way but it is not very revealing of God. Personal reality is disclosed most fully in historical activity in the face of unusual circumstances rather than in some kind of uniform activity. General revelation is relatively non-historical in that it is not given in and through particular historical events in the sense of the encounter of persons and institutions. It is relatively impersonal in that it does not involve conscious personal confrontation with God. General revelation is also inadequate in that it is always misunderstood, distorted, and misinterpreted in polytheism, pantheism, deism or mysticism. Richardson, Tillich and Brunner suggest that general revelation may save society from falling into chaos but that it is not sufficient to save in the theological sense of reconciling humanity to God.

General revelation can be seen for what it really is only from the point of view of special revelation. Special revelation is both the judgment upon the reception of general revelation and its true fulfillment, since it fully reveals the God who is partially revealed in general revelation. Thus special revelation is not simply an addition to general revelation (as is suggested in the natural-revealed theology distinction) nor is it simply a concrete illustration of general revelation (as is suggested in the liberal view of revelation). However, general revelation is the presupposition of special revelation, because apart from general revelation humanity would not be responsible before God; we could not be addressed as sinners and called to repent. Paul asserts that it is because of God's revelation in the creation that the pagan gentiles are "without excuse" in their ignorance of God (Rom. 1:20, 2:1). It is on this basis that they can be addressed as sinners and called to repent.[15] Tillich suggests that without the symbols and religious experience created by general revelation, the special revelation could not have been received.[16] But he does not explain why the general revelation did not require a similar preparation. The question has sometimes been raised as to why God is revealed in general revelation if it is not sufficient for salvation. Paul's implication in Romans 1: 19f is that apart from sin God's revelation in the creation would have been sufficient for human fulfillment.[17]

Special Revelation

Special revelation is God's self-disclosure in the history of Israel, old and new, that is, in the events recorded and interpreted in the Bible culminating in Christ. Personal reality is more fully revealed in unusual situations and actions than in uniform and regular activity. The main source of unusual and critical situations for a personal being is the free actions of other personal agents. That is, personality is more fully revealed in dealing with persons than with things. Thus it might be expected that the most fully revealing area of God's activity will be human history. But why is the history of Israel any more revealing of God than the history of any other nation? The answer from Israel is that God has chosen Israel for this purpose so that she may become a witness to God before the nations of the world. As to why Israel rather than some other nation was chosen, there is no answer except the mystery of the divine choosing. But it is clearly not because Israel possessed any special aptitude for this vocation, such as greatness, or religious sensitivity. Seen from an external point of view the history of Israel is not unusual or extraordinary. It is simply the story of a small nation of the Near East during a period of the clash of empires. What distinguishes the history of Israel from that of any other nation is the unique interpretation placed upon it from within Israel. Thus special revelation consists of event plus interpretation. Temple defines it as "the coincidence of divinely guided events and minds divinely illuminated to interpret those events."[18] Revelation has objective and subjective sides, an objective event and a human perception of this event and interpretation of it as an act of God.

This concept of revelation in and through history has been criticized by

Barr and Pannenberg in the works mentioned above. Barr points out that there is great diversity in the understanding of the nature of history among those who affirm this concept. He also suggests that there are substantial areas of the Old Testament which do not fit in with the idea that revelation through history is the fundamental motif of Old Testament thought (for example, the Wisdom Literature). He asserts that although the idea of revelation through history expresses an important element in the Bible, it is not a biblical category and that other strands of biblical material should be considered as well, such as direct verbal communication between God and humanity. "Direct communication from God to man has fully as much claim to be called the core of the tradition as has revelation through events in history."[19] This is an important criticism of the concept of revelation in and through history, but the latter still seems to be the main emphasis of the biblical authors. Pannenberg goes to the other extreme and identifies the revelation with the historical events (see p. 32).

The two basic forms of the special revelation in the Old Testament are the acts and words of God seen, heard and interpreted by the prophets, both former and latter, that is, both the historians and the prophets in the narrower sense. Thus events in the history of Israel are seen as the acts of God and so interpreted, and the interpretation, being given by divine inspiration, is understood as the words of God. "The word of the Lord came to the prophet, and he said, 'Thus says the Lord . . .'"

The Old Testament is primarily a book of interpreted history, because its authors saw the hand of God in the events of their history (see Deut. 11:2-7, Ps. 77:11-15). Psalms 105 and 106 are summaries of the history of Israel told as the story of the acts of God. The greatest of these acts is God's deliverance of Israel from bondage in Egypt which becomes the basis of the covenant and the law. God's acts of mercy and judgment are interpreted by God's words, the words of the prophets whom God inspires (Amos 3:7). But also the word itself becomes an act which determines history (Hos. 6:5, Jer. 1:9f; 5:14, 23:29, Ps. 33:9). In this combination of act and word God reveals the divine self, the divine name which means God's very person, and the divine face which means God's gracious presence. But in revealing this God also reveals God's plan and purpose for Israel, God's relation to humanity and the world, the divine judgment and salvation, and God's requirement of repentance and obedience. But the revelation in the Old Testament is incomplete; it ends with a promise; it looks forward in hope to a future fulfillment of revelation. There are many symbols of this hope, and one of them is that of the agent through whom God will bring about the fulfillment. The relation of the revelation of the Old Testament to that of the New Testament is one of promise and fulfillment, preparation and realization (Heb. l:lf, 1 Pet. 1:10-12, 2 Cor. 1:20, Lk. 24:27).

The special revelation in the New Testament takes the form of the union of word and act in the person of Jesus. Temple suggests that this makes sense since the personal God can be revealed adequately and fully only in and through the life of a person, and human persons can fully understand only that which is personal. Jesus is the union of the act of God and the word of God (1 Cor. 1:24, Jn. 1:14). In the case of the prophets the one who speaks is different from the one who ultimately gives the message and from the content of the message, that is, the one who is spoken about. But in the case of Jesus, speaker, ultimate giver of the message, and the content of the message are one. The prophets speak not on their own authority but with an authority derived from their message and its author, but Jesus speaks with his own authority and not like the scribes. (This raises many questions which will be dealt with in the chapter on Christology.) Thus the concept of the word of God is transformed and gains a new meaning. It means no longer speech from God mediated by the prophets but the very personal presence of God. Now the word of God is not simply something which is heard but the one who is seen, touched, and encountered (1 Jn. 1:1). So Christ is the fulness of the revelation of God (Jn. 14:9). However, the New Testament lays as much if not more emphasis on Christ's work of establishing the Kingdom, reconciliation, and atonement as on Christ's work of revelation. However, revelation and salvation are inseparable, two sides of the same coin.

But if revelation is the coincidence of event and interpretation, how can God be revealed as creator and final judge? These are "events" which could not be present to any prophet or apostle. The passages about creation and eschatology in the Bible do not derive from any speculation about the beginning and end of history but from the revelation of God's lordship over Israel in the present. God is made known as Lord of Israel's present history, before being known as creator and final judge. And since God is the Lord of present history, God must be the Lord of nature as the stage of history and its origin and also Lord of the goal or end of history. Thus in the New Testament Christ is understood as God's agent in creation and in judgment at the end of history.

It has been stated above that besides an objective side in divinely guided event, revelation has a subjective side in the interpretation of the event by a divinely illumined mind. Revelation can be received only if God the Holy Spirit illumines the mind ("heart"), only through the inner testimony of the Spirit (1 Cor. 12:3, 2:9f, Mt. 16:18, Jn. 6:44, 15:26). Revelation is received by faith which is a gift of the Spirit (1 Cor. 12:9). This gives us our basic definition of *faith*. Faith is the receiving of God's self-revelation and the relationship to God established by this, namely, communion with God involving knowledge of and trust in God. Thus faith is not the acceptance of divinely revealed truths, assent to theological doctrines because they are found in the Bible or taught by the church. These ideas of faith are based on the traditional view of revelation as the giving of truths or doctrine about God. Here again the analogy of human personal relations is illuminating. Faith is like the receiving of the self-disclosure of another person and thus coming into a relation of personal communion involving knowledge of and trust in this person. It is not like accepting the statement of a reliable authority about this person. More generally in the Bible faith means grateful, confident and steadfast reliance upon the trustworthiness, faithfulness, and all-sufficiency of God, which leads to obedience. Faith is the opposite of sin (Rom. 14:23) which is the breaking of communion with God, failure to trust God, and the suppression of the knowledge of God, (Rom. 1 :18f) which leads to disobedience.

Pannenberg denies that the reception of revelation depends upon faith and the illumination of the Holy Spirit. Because he identifies revelation and history, he asserts that revelation is given objectively in the historical events and can be perceived by anyone who looks in the right place. Revelation is perceived by reason in historical investigation, because knowledge of revelation is the same as historical knowledge. Knowledge of revelation is not the product but the presupposition of faith. Faith is based on rational historical knowledge of revelation. This view seems to be quite different from the understanding of the reception of revelation in the Bible.

Gilkey and Dilley have mounted a radical criticism of the conception of God's revelation in divine acts. (See references above.) They admit that this is an accurate representation of the Bible, but they claim that since the cosmology of the Bible has been superseded by that of modern science, it is now impossible to understand the acts of God as interventions in the natural order. Thus we now use the concept "act of God" not in the univocal sense in which it is used in the Bible (that is, in the same sense in which we speak about human acts) but in some analogical sense. But the problem is that we are not able to specify that to which the analogy points. We now understand the Bible no longer as a description of the acts of God but as a statement of Israel's faith in the acts of God, which acts call no longer be understood as Israel understood them. If the outward aspect of the Exodus event was indistinguishable from other similar events and if it involved a real act of God, then we must specify what this is, or else the concept of act of God is void of meaning. The alternatives are liberal and existentialist views of the action of God which limit it to our inner life, and the traditional orthodox view which asserts God's intervention in the natural order. Gilkey's and Dilley's point is that many contemporary theologians claim to have avoided these alternatives but in fact have not specified a viable third way. Many of the problems raised by Gilkey and Dilley will be taken up in the chapter on providence. Various attempts have been made to specify such a third way, and they will be explored in that chapter.

Recent interpretations of the doctrine of revelation drawing on the philosophical and anthropological explorations of thinkers such as Langer, Ricoeur and Eliade have stressed and elaborated the fundamental role played in the revelatory process by imagination and symbol. From this point of view the uniqueness of human beings consists in their imaginative capacity to create symbols to express their longings, fears and the meaning of their lives. It is this symbol-creating capacity which is brought fully into play in the reception and response to divine revelation. Symbols mediate participatory and transforming knowledge, focus and elicit commitment, and introduce us to realms of knowledge which are inaccessible to discursive thought.

The revelation of God is always mediated through parts of the creation which are thus understood symbolically: cosmic or historical events, personages, artifacts, words, myths and parables. Then the Bible can be seen as the product of the creative human imagination in its symbolmaking capacity under the inspiration of the Holy Spirit.[20]

Dependent or Continuing Revelation

We have discussed how the prophets and apostles and the communities of the Old Testament and the New Testament came to know God. But how did people in later ages come to know God? How do we come to know God today? The answer again is by God's self-revelation. God continues to be revealed today in general revelation in the ways described above. God continues to be revealed in special revelation in two main ways: through the testimony of the prophets and apostles recorded in the Bible and through the testimony of the church in its preaching, sacraments, teaching, common life, and action in the world. This is called dependent revelation because it is dependent on God's revelation once for all in the biblical events culminating in Christ. The Bible is the first written deposit of the reception of the original special revelation in the events of the history of Israel, old and new. (See chapter 3 for a detailed analysis of this statement.) So no one comes to Christian faith today except on the basis of the original special revelation. This does not mean that a person must read the Bible in order to become a Christian, but it does mean that one cannot become a Christian, that is, receive God's special revelation, apart from some event, preaching, teaching, conversation, or reading, which is ultimately dependent upon the Bible. In a word God does not produce Christians today directly without any mediation. God may approach them in and through the various areas of their experience mentioned above in connection with general revelation. But God does not approach us today in special revelation apart from some human activity which is ultimately dependent upon the Bible. The reason for this is simply that Christian faith is based on a revelation of God in history. Herbert H. Farmer has made this point in the following way:

> It is theoretically conceivable that all the sacred books of Hinduism, and every Hindu, might be utterly destroyed, and yet substantially the same religion reappear. It is not very likely; but it is not a self-contradictory idea. Indeed it would fit harmoniously into the Hindu scheme of thought to suppose that if Hinduism vanished today it would reappear tomorrow, fifty years, a thousand years hence. But were all Christian records and all Christians extirpated, Christianity could not recur again. In its recurrence without a preacher, without a witness, it would flatly contradict all that it had always claimed to be. To put it paradoxically, in happening again it would show that it had never, according to its own definition of itself, happened at all.[21]

This means incidentally that you cannot convert people to Christian faith by loving them or by the example of a Christ-like life alone. At some point there must be testimony to the historical events as the revealing and saving acts of God.

Since each new generation which receives the special revelation of God stands in a new and different cultural situation with new assumptions, language, concerns, problems, strengths and weaknesses, the reception of the revelation will vary, will bring out new aspects and emphases of the original special revelation, and thus will enlarge the church's understanding of it. This new and deeper understanding of the original revelation is tradition in its various forms of creeds, conciliar decisions, confessions, and theological works (see chapter 3). But the church does not expect a new original revelation which would radically alter or take the place of the biblical revelation and thus replace Christian faith with some other faith.

But the fact that the continuing special revelation today is dependent upon the original special revelation does not make it any less a real self-disclosure of God to us in the present. In this continuing or dependent revelation we meet God in Christ through the Spirit just as really and truly as did the apostles, but this meeting is mediated to us by the testimony of the apostles recorded in the Bible and commented on, proclaimed, taught, and reenacted by the church.[22] We are in exactly the same situation as the apostles as far as the reality and the basic content of the revelation is concerned. The difference is the way in which the revelation is given: by the words and acts of Christ in the case of the apostles, and by the apostles' testimony to the words and acts of Christ in our case. The objective side of revelation for us is the event of reading the Bible, hearing a sermon, participating in a sacrament, or hearing the testimony of a Christian, but the subjective side is the same for us as for the apostles. For both it is received by faith and the inner testimony of the Spirit.

Preaching

The above discussion of dependent revelation constitutes the theological basis of preaching. Preaching is one of the two main ways in which dependent or continuing revelation can take place. It is one of the main ways in which God is made known and people can come to know God today, the other being the sacraments (see 1 Thess. 2:13, 1 Cor. 1:21, Lk. 10:16). Therefore preaching is essentially a repeating of the prophetic and apostolic testimony to God in Christ in such a way that it can be received and understood today. It is essentially a translation, interpretation, explanation, and application of this testimony. This means that preaching is essentially exposition and application of some passage of the Bible. It may be that skilled and experienced preachers who have made the message of the Bible their own can expound and apply the biblical testimony without expounding and applying a particular passage, but it is significant that the greatest preachers in the history of the Church almost always began with a particular passage.[23]

Final Revelation

When the main term for revelation in the New Testament (*apokalupsis*) is used in a special theological sense, it refers to a future revelation which is the fulfillment or completion of special revelation. This is referred to as the revelation, appearing, presence, or coming of Christ in glory (1 Cor. 1:7, 2 Thess. 1:7, 2:8, 1 Pet. 1:5, 7, 13, 4:13, Titus 2:13, Mt. 24:30). The special revelation culminating in Christ was still veiled in the sense that it could be perceived only by faith through the inner testimony of the Holy Spirit. In the final revelation all will perceive God in Christ. Paul describes the contrast by stating that in the Christian life his knowledge of God is imperfect, that his vision of God is dim, that he walks by faith and not by sight, but that in the final revelation he will know God fully, that he will see God "face to face" (1 Cor. 13:12, 2 Cor. 5:7). These are symbols of the assertion that the fulfillment and completion of God's self-revelation is yet to come. This element of Christian faith will be taken up in our discussion of eschatology in chapter 16.

We have discussed four modes of God's revelation: the general revelation in the creation and in moral experience, the special revelation in the events of the Bible, the dependent or continuing revelation in and through the history of the church, and the final revelation. But these modes of revelation form a unity and the principle of this unity is Christ: Christ is the agent in creation, the culmination of the special revelation attested in the Bible, the one to whom testimony is given in the history of the church, and the one whose coming constitutes the final revelation. The reason for this is that Christ as God the Son is God in self-revelation. This will be analyzed in detail in chapter 4 on the trinity.

The Test of Revelation

How can we know that revelation is really the revelation of God? This is a question which has two sides or can mean two different things. On the one hand it can mean, within the context of the Christian faith and church how do we go about determining what is true revelation and what is not? This question is the subject of chapter 3. Briefly, there cannot be any external or a priori criteria for the truth of revelation. If there were, we would not need the revelation. "The truth of revelation is not dependent on criteria which are not themselves revelatory. Knowledge of revelation, like ordinary knowledge, must be judged by its own implicit criteria."[24]

On the other hand this question can mean, how does the individual, when confronted by the Christian claim to a revelation of God, go about deciding whether or not this claim is true? This is the question of how one goes about making judgments in the realm of ultimate concern, religion and philosophy. The only criteria are very general: inner consistency, coherence with everything else we know to be true about reality, the capacity to illuminate or make sense of all of one's experience and effectiveness in our lives.[25] This is what Tillich calls "experiential verification."[26] This is the question of how one decides whether or not to become a Christian. It is prior to the question above of how one does theology.

Questions for Discussion

1. *How can we recognize revelation as the revelation of God? Is it because we have previous knowledge of God? If so, and if this is previous knowledge of God is based on general revelation, then how can we recognize the general revelation as the revelation of God? In other words, can God be recognized as God in revelation unless we have some previous knowledge of God?*

2. *Which comes first, faith or revelation? Do we need faith to perceive revelation as revelation, or do we need revelation in order to have faith?*

3. *"I cannot say that I know God personally. I believe that God is, that God created me, loves me and demands my obedience, and I trust in God's all-sufficiency for me. But I do not know God in the way that I know my friend. Am I Christian? Have I received revelation of God? If so, how can we say that revelation gives personal knowledge of God?" Discuss.*

4. *If God is the most real reality and is present in every time and place, how is it that we can know nothing of God except that God actively reveal the divine reality to us?*

5. *Does God's revelation in the creation involve an active self-disclosure in the present, or is it simply a revelation in the sense that the creation is the result of God's creative will, that is, on the analogy of the revelation of artists in their works? Is not God's general revelation in the creation and in moral experience and history more a matter of our reflection on our experience than the active self-disclosure of God?*

6. *What is the relation of knowledge about God to knowledge of God? Does the latter include the former? Does not the former when approaching completeness become indistinguishable from the latter? If our knowledge of God is really only knowledge about God (see question 3), then could not revelation be understood in the traditional sense as the disclosure of truths about God?*

7. *Is knowledge of God (knowing God), as distinct from knowledge about God, necessary to the Christian life?*

8. *If all knowledge and truth constitute a unity, how can it be that theological knowledge and truth derived from revelation can never conflict or overlap with scientific knowledge or truth?*

9. *Do we become Christians through receiving God's special revelation by faith which is a gift of the Holy Spirit? Or do we become Christians by being drawn into the Christian fellowship, moved by Christian worship, persuaded by Christian apologetics, and convinced by the illuminative power of Christian teaching? What is the relation between these two ways?*

10. *Is not prayer, rather than preaching and sacraments, the best way to get to know God? Does it involve revelation?*

11. *If faith is a gift of the Spirit, are people responsible for their faith or unfaith?*

12. *"It is sometimes said that revelation is self-authenticating and cannot be judged by any external criteria (for example, consistency, appropriate evidence, coherence). But this makes a claim to revelation circular and question-begging and supplies no reasonable grounds for accepting it as revelation." Discuss.*

13. *Is the biblical testimony primarily to God in self-revelation or to God as acting to judge and save?*

14. *If there is no universal essence of religion (p. 26), how can religion be defined?*

3

Authority

The problem of authority in the realm of religion is very complex, because of the great confusion which reigns in the language used. One will often find Christian theologians writing about the authority of the gospel, the Bible, the church, tradition, and experience very emphatically but very confusedly. So it is an important task of theology to try to overcome this confusion and to clarify the terms and the meanings involved here.

The problem of authority in Christian faith can refer to any of the following questions:

1. How can we know about the historical origins of Christian faith? (historical authority)

2. How can we know what is true Christian faith? How can we determine what is and what is not part of the content of Christian faith? (theological authority)

3. How can we know what we ought to do as Christians? Who can properly claim my total allegiance and commitment? (ethical and moral authority)

4. How can we determine what we must do or else? Who can force me to do something? (political authority)

5. How can we determine what we must believe and do in order to be a member of the church? Who determines this? (disciplinary authority of the church)

In this chapter we are concerned only with 2. (1 is investigated by historical research, 3 and 4 in Christian ethics, and 5 in canon law.) The problem of authority arises in theology, because theology is a normative and not simply a descriptive discipline. The problem of authority is, in the face of the multiplicity of testimony in the Bible and the history of the church, how can we go about determining the true Christian faith, the (theological) truth about God, humanity, and the world. By what standard, criterion, or norm can we decide whether or not a particular statement or doctrine is a valid part of Christian faith? The criterion cannot be external or prior to Christian faith but must be internal to or implicit in it. That is, the theological criterion cannot be, for example, the prevailing philosophical point of view, or the universal and perennial mystical intuition.

There have been four main answers to the problem of theological authority which I believe to be erroneous:

1. True Christian faith is what is taught literally in the Bible (biblical literalism).

2. True Christian faith is what is pronounced by the infallible spokesman of the church (papal infallibility).

3. True Christian faith is what is verified by the consensus of Christian religious experience (religious empiricism).

4. True Christian faith is the consensus of what is believed "everywhere, always, and by all" (Vincentian canon).

Biblical Literalism

This is the view that the words and statements of the Bible are infallibly inspired and inerrant. The early church took over from Judaism the view of the Old Testament as directly inspired by God (2 Tim 3:16). In Hellenistic minds this inspiration came to be understood at God's dictation in which the rational and critical faculties of the writers were in abeyance or superseded. The biblical authors are pictured as flutes, lyres, or pens in the hand of God. This view came to be applied to the New Testament and was the generally accepted view until the eighteenth century with some outstanding exceptions, such as Luther. It was never radically denied and thus never became the subject of general debate in the church. Furthermore this literalism was softened and modified in practice by the widespread use of the allegorical method of interpretation and by common sense which prevented the doctrine of verbal inspiration from being elaborated in absurd detail. This view hardened into what we may call fundamentalism only after the critical issue had been raised by the historical study of the Bible in the eighteenth and nineteenth centuries.

In the last few decades, however, a heated debate has arisen among conservative or evangelical Christians over the nature of the inerrancy of the Bible. A spectrum of views on this issue has emerged which stretches all the way from a rigid view of verbal inspiration and total inerrancy to something close to the view of Karl Barth who was very critical of inerrancy.[1]

What is wrong with this view? First, it does not fit the facts of the biblical record. The divine inspiration of prophets and apostles does not supersede but rather heightens their faculties. Infallible inspiration is not the way in which God is presented as dealing with people in the Bible. This view makes the Bible itself the revelation rather than the inspired human witness and testimony to revelation. To deny the human and thus fallible element in the

Bible is to commit the docetic or monophysite heresy in regard to the Bible. "The Church must develop its doctrine of the Scriptures on the same lines as the doctrine of the two natures (of Christ)."[2] Secondly, in this view the Bible tends to become an authority in matters of scientific investigation and thus sets up an intolerable tension between Christian faith and modern science. Thirdly, this view tends to put all parts of the Bible on the same level of authority. Finally, this view is incomplete as a norm of doctrine. The Bible may be inerrant, but its true meaning is still not clear and must be determined by an interpreter. Unless the revelation in Scripture is not only infallibly true but also unmistakably clear, the theory does not fulfill its purpose of giving an absolute norm of true doctrine. Thus this view moves logically on to the second view of theological authority, the infallible interpreter of the infallible Scripture.

Papal Infallibility

The first Vatican Council of 1870 defined papal infallibility in the following way:

> The Roman Pontiff, when he speaks ex cathedra, that is, when in discharge of the office of Pastor and Doctor of all Christians, by virtue of his supreme Apostolic authority he defines a doctrine regarding faith or morals to be held by the Universal Church, by the divine assistance promised to him in blessed Peter, is possessed of that infallibility with which the divine Redeemer willed that His Church should be endowed for defining doctrine regarding faith or morals: and that therefore such definitions of the Roman Pontiff are irreformable of themselves, and not from the consent of the Church.[3]

This definition was confirmed as the second Vatican Council (1963-65), but infallibility was also attributed to the church as a whole and to the bishops and councils in union with the pope.[4] Roman Catholic theologians base this doctrine on various New Testament passages such as Mt. 16:18f, Lk. 22:32, and Jn. 21:15-18, but no collection of texts can bear the weight of such a theory even granting biblical inerrancy. Moreover on the basis of the Christian view of humanity, we must affirm that liability to error is a permanent and ineradicable condition of human life in this world. It is conceivable that the "divine Redeemer" willed papal infallibility, but in the absence of any evidence for such a claim it must be denied.

Furthermore, we must make the same point about this view as we did about biblical literalism. The purpose of a claim of infallibility is apparently to offer certainty of truth in regard to the content of Christian faith. Thus a statement by a putatively infallible spokesperson must be unmistakably

clear or else be infallibly interpreted by someone. Neither of these conditions is fulfilled in the case of papal infallibility. Moreover, the decision to
accept the claim to infallibility is inevitably an act of individual judgment,
which may be correct but cannot be known to be infallible. Thus the
apparent purpose of a claim of infallibility to offer certainty of truth cannot
be fulfilled.

It is important to note, however, that papal infallibility is a particular form
of a doctrine held quite generally in all periods of church history, namely,
the doctrine of the indefectibility of the church, that is, that the church will
not completely lose the true content of Christian faith or fall permanently
into fundamental error. The doctrine of papal infallibility is a particular
form of this doctrine in that it defines the way in which indefectibility is
carried out. The above criticisms of papal infallibility do not apply to the
doctrine of the indefectibility of the church. Another version of the latter
appears in the Vincentian Canon. Küng has argued against the traditional
interpretation of infallibility and for the doctrine of the indefectibility of the
church.[5]

Religious Empiricism

This view makes the Christian religious consciousness or experience the
criterion of what is true Christian doctrine. Schleiermacher formulated this
answer to the question of theological authority most clearly for the modern
period. "Christian doctrines are accounts of the Christian religious affec-
tions set forth in speech." "We shall exhaust the whole compass of Christian
doctrine if we consider the facts of the religious self-consciousness. . . ."[6] An
increasing number of theologians is appealing to experience as the norm
of theology.[7]

The problem with this view is that it requires some criterion for distinguishing authentic Christian experience from inauthentic, from other
types of religious experience, and from the whole of experience in general.
But such a criterion cannot be derived solely from experience but must be
brought to it. Thus this criterion and not the experience is the final
authority. This criterion is usually derived from the particular religious
experience of the theologian in question. This is in fact exactly what
Schleiermacher did. Therefore we must assert that Christian experience is
not the norm of theology but rather the means by which we receive any
norm. "Experience is not the source from which the contents of systematic
theology are taken but the medium through which they are existentially
received."[8] Or as P. T. Forsyth has put it, "Nothing can be an authority for us
which is not experienced, but the experience is not the authority."

Vincentian Canon

This view on the problem of theological authority was stated classically by

Vincent of Lerins in his *Commonitory* of 434:

> In the Catholic Church itself, all possible care must be taken, that we
> hold that faith which has been believed everywhere, always, and by all.
> For that is truly and in the strictest sense "Catholic," which, as the name
> itself and the reason of the thing declare, comprehends all universally.
> This rule we shall observe if we follow universality, antiquity, and
> consent (of priests and doctors) (ch. II).

According to this view the true Christian doctrine is the consensus of that
which is held most universally at the present time and in the history of the
church.

The first difficulty with this view is that it subtly turns a descriptive judgment into a normative judgment; the description of the universal consensus becomes the norm of true doctrine. The hidden assumption is that the
universal consensus will in fact always be true doctrine. But this requires a
special doctrine of the church, namely, that God will always bring it about
that the universal consensus of the church is the truth. This is another form
of the doctrine of the indefectibility of the church, namely, that the indefectibility is assured in such a way that the historical and contemporary consensus of the church will always represent the true content of Christian faith.
It may be that the church is indefectible in the sense that it will not lose the
Christian faith entirely, yet it is certainly possible that a majority of the
church may be in heresy at any one time. This was clearly the view of the
Reformers.

Another problem for this view is that there may be no universal consensus on certain issues. For example, it may be the case that the church is
divided about equally on the issue of papal infallibility both in its history and
today. Then the principle of universality would be of no help, and the issue
would have to be resolved on other grounds. Although universality cannot
be a criterion of theological truth, it may be of useful principle for assessing
the weight of tradition on some particular issue. This is in fact what Vincent
had in mind, because the context of his "Canon" indicates that it is to be
applied when there is disagreement over the meaning of the Bible.

Supremacy of Scripture

The solution to the problem of theological authority which is presented
in the remainder of this chapter is the general consensus of contemporary
theologians in the traditions associated with the World Council of Churches,
i.e. the consensus of non-Roman Catholic, non-fundamentalist, non-liberal
theologians. (This is said not as an argument for this view but simply to place
it in the contemporary scene.) In this consensus the criterion of true
Christian doctrine, of what is and what is not a valid part of Christian faith,

is the revelation of God to which testimony is given in the Bible.[9]

The aim of theology is to express the reality of God and God's relation to the world. But as we have seen in chapter 2, the only way we can know anything about the reality of God and God's relation to the world is in divine revelation. So the ultimate norm of theology is God's revelation. But we do not have this revelation in itself. We know of this revelation in the first instance only through the testimony of those who first received it, the prophets and apostles. What we have in the Bible is not directly the testimony of these prophets and apostles but the first written deposit of their testimony to the revelation. Thus the Bible is not the ultimate norm of theology but rather the secondary, instrumental, or formal norm, which mediates the ultimate norm to us. But although secondary or instrumental it precedes in authority the infallible spokesman of the church, the consensus of Christian experience, and the testimony of tradition.

Why is the Bible the highest court of appeal in theology? God's revelation must be received in order to be revelation, and the reception of revelation is the completion of the event of revelation. Thus the original receivers of the special revelation culminating in Christ participate in the original event of revelation and thus hold a unique position in comparison to later receivers. Without the response of the original receivers, the events would not have been revelatory. Later receivers of the revelation are dependent for their own reception of revelation upon the testimony of the original receivers. We do not have the original testimony of the first receivers which was mostly oral, but we do have in the Bible the first written deposit of this original testimony which thus becomes the means of all later dependent revelation.

> The Bible, however, is the basic source of systematic theology because it is the original document about the events on which the Christian church is founded. . . . The documentary character of the Bible is identical with the fact that it contains the original witness of those who participated in the revealing events. Their participation was their response to the happenings which became revealing events through this response. . . . Since there is no revelation unless there is someone who receives it as revelation, the act of reception is a part of the event itself. The Bible is both original event and original document; it witnesses to that of which it is a part.[10]

Parts of the New Testament are probably secondary, that is, already dependent upon the original testimony, and parts of the oral tradition of the original testimony of the first receivers may not have been committed to writing. (See diagram on p. 47.) But those latter parts which remained oral even after the first century cannot be compared in authority to the main New Testament writings because oral tradition is distorted and expanded by legendary material more rapidly than is written tradition. Furthermore Papias, investigating the oral tradition in the first half of the second century, could discover very little of any importance apart from the canonical gospels.[11] This problem will be analyzed further in the section on the canon.

Because we have rejected the theory of the literal inerrancy of the Bible, it is clear that not all parts of the Bible testify to God's revelation with equal clarity and fidelity. And we have to say that some parts probably do not testify to it at all. The Old Testament and the New Testament do not testify with equal clarity to the fullness of God's revelation, and the same kind of distinction can be made within the New Testament and within books of the New Testament.

This raises the problem of how we use the Bible as our secondary or instrumental norm of theology, of how we decide between different parts, authors, or themes of the Bible when their testimony to revelation differs. The only possible answer is a circular one. We must judge the various parts of the Bible in the light of what we perceive to be the central message or consensus of the Bible, in the light of what we perceive to be God's revelation in Christ. This is circular, because the norm by which the various parts of the Bible is judged is the ultimate norm, namely, God's revelation. But we have this norm not directly but only by means of the testimony of the Bible. The church must listen expectantly to the whole Bible and then make a decision as to what it believes to be the central message or main witness of the Bible. Then the church must return to the whole Bible and on the basis of this decision determine which parts of the Bible bear witness most fully, clearly, and faithfully to God's revelation. An analogy of this process is the method of successive approximations in mathematics in which a preliminary answer to a problem is used in a second solution of the problem in order to get a more precise answer, and so forth.

But of course the church's decision about the central message of the Bible is never made *de novo*. It is always guided provisionally by tradition in the form of creeds, conciliar decisions, and confessions. However, these guides themselves must always be kept under the judgment of the central message of the Bible.

So it is only through the Bible that we can receive and discern the norm by which we can judge and criticize the Bible. We are bound to the Bible as the means by which we apprehend the norm of theology, but we are not bound absolutely to the Bible as the ultimate authority in itself.

Thus there is no legalistic or immutable authority in theology, but only the living authority of God in self-revelation which is mediated by the Bible and apprehended by the church under the guidance of the Holy Spirit. After the Reformation when the principle of the supremacy of the Bible was being developed and refined, the authority of the Bible was interpreted in a legalistic way because it was believe to be literally inerrant. But this tendency has been completely undercut by the historical-critical approach to the Bible. This has made clear not only the distance between the Bible and the events to which it testifies but also the distance between the thought-world of the first century and that of the twentieth century. The historical approach aims to determine what the original authors meant in their own terms and in their own day. The task of systematic theology is not simply to repeat this meaning or the consensus of the meanings of the biblical authors but to attempt to express this meaning in terms of the problems and thought-world of the present. "Theology, perhaps, comes closest to material agreement with the biblical witnesses when it seriously takes up the questions of its own time in order to express in relation to them what the biblical writers attested in the language and conceptual framework of their time." [12]

Now the question can be raised as to the criterion by which we decide the question of theological authority in favor of the supremacy of the Bible. How do we decide whether or not this doctrine is true, a valid part of Christian faith? Because of the circular nature of Christian theology, the only criterion by which questions about the theological norm can be resolved is their coherence with the understanding of Christian faith already being affirmed and in particular the doctrine of revelation. Thus we decide this question on the basis of the way in which revelation is understood in the Bible. This is in fact what we have just done. By looking at how revelation is understood in the Bible, we have concluded that biblical literalism, papal infallibility, Christian experience, and universality are inadequate as theological criteria. And we have decided that this criterion can be gained only by looking at the first written deposit of the testimony of those who first received the revelation. In other words, the Bible gives indirect testimony to itself as the secondary or instrumental norm of theology. This is certainly circular but not in the vicious sense of assuming what you are attempting to prove, but in the sense of the theological circle, that is, in the sense that in the work of theology we have to assume the whole content of the Christian faith in order to criticize and reformulate it.

That the Bible gives indirect testimony to itself can be seen, for example, in the understanding of apostleship in the New Testament. The apostles are those in the first instance chosen by Jesus, taught by him, sent out by him to preach and to represent him, and then witnesses of his resurrection commissioned to bear witness to him (Mk. 3:14, Lk 10:16, Acts 1:21, Mt. 10:40, 16:18). Furthermore, the New Testament writings represent themselves as the writings of the apostles or the teaching of the apostles as transmitted by their associates. This, of course, does not determine their authorship but only how they were understood by their authors and the early church. Thus in the concept of apostleship the New Testament writings represent themselves implicitly as the first written deposit of the original testimony of those who first received the revelation of God in Christ and therefore as the secondary norm in determining the content of Christian faith. A similar analysis can be made of the concept of prophet in the Old Testament.[13]

The Canon of Scripture

Now it becomes clear why we have a canon of Scripture rather than a continuing library of Christian writings. Because the first written deposit of the testimony of those who first received the revelation of God is unique in that it participates in the original event of revelation, and because all later testimony is based on it and dependent on it, it can be distinguished from all later testimony as its norm. Because Christian faith is based on certain historical events and the testimony of those who perceived in these events the revelation of God, this firsthand testimony or its first written deposit is crucial to the maintenance of Christian faith and thus has a unique authority. So the necessity of the canon of Scripture is based on the distinction between the original testimony and all later testimony which is dependent on it.

But because it is often extremely difficult to distinguish the first written deposit of the original testimony from the written deposit of testimony which is dependent upon this, and because, as has been stated above, some parts of the Bible witness more clearly and faithfully to the revelation of God than others, it becomes clear that the canon has a central core and a periphery. At the center is the first written deposit of the original testimony to revelation which bears witness clearly and faithfully to the revelation of God. At the periphery are the writings about which this judgment would be doubtful if not negative. These relationships can be diagrammed in the following way for the New Testament:

In this diagram the area between the two wavy lines represents the material in the New Testament. Area A´ represents that part of the first written deposit of the original testimony which did not get into the New Testament. (Some logia of Jesus in the apocryphal gospels and elsewhere? Parts of the epistles of Ignatius or the Shepherd of Hermas?) Area B´ represents that part of the New Testament which is not part of the first written deposit of the original testimony to revelation (Pastoral Epistles, 2 Peter, Jude?). As the diagram indicates, there is probably a lot more of B´ in the New Testament than there is A´ outside it.

Furthermore, since the church determined the limits of the canon, and since no decision of the church is infallible (see Article XXI), the canon is still open in principle and may be altered by the church. But this is obviously not a practical possibility because of both the division of the church and the universal agreement that the early church made a sound decision in regard to the New Testament. However, there is considerable disagreement in regard to the Old Testament, especially in relation to the status of the Apocrypha.[14]

Although the formal alteration of the limits of the canon is not a practical possibility (or need) today, the actual or practical limits of the canon are modified in every age. As indicated above, the church in every period makes a decision about which parts of the Bible bear witness most fully, clearly, and faithfully to God's revelation. This is not a formal decision but rather an informal one carried out by theologians and implicitly by the teachers and preachers of the church. For example, Luther concentrated on John and Romans and tended to ignore Hebrews and James. The liberal Protestant theologians emphasized the Synoptic gospels and tended to ignore the Pauline epistles, whereas the neo-orthodox theologians tended to do exactly the opposite. Bultmann's practical canon emphasizes the Pauline and Johannine literature but excludes Luke-Acts. The liberation theologians emphasize the Book of Exodus and certain New Testament passages, such as Luke 4.

It is sometimes suggested that since the church existed before the New Testament and determined its limits, the theological authority of the church is above that of the Bible. This is true in the sense that the church is free to alter the canon, but if it alters it radically it would lose the Christian faith and cease to be the church. The authority of Cod's revelation is above the authority of the church, and the former is mediated to the church only through the Bible. So the church in setting up the canon decided to subordinate its authority to that of the Bible.

What has been said so far applies most clearly to the New Testament. What about the Old Testament? What was said about the revelation in the Old Testament in chapter 2 is relevant here. The coming of Christ is the climax of a larger event or series of events which can be described from the point of view of Christian faith as God's action in revelation to judge and save the people of God. The Old Testament is the history of Israel seen as involving the words and acts of God, which is the necessary preparation for the revelation in Christ, which in turn presupposes this preparation and which could not have been received or understood apart from it. The whole Bible can thus be seen as the history of Israel, old and new, understood as the locus of God's action in revelation and salvation. If the center of the Bible is the testimony to God in Christ, then the Old Testament is this testimony in the form of promise, preparation, and expectation, whereas the New Testament is this testimony in the form of fulfillment and realization. C. H. Dodd has demonstrated that the first element of the primitive apostolic preaching was the affirmation that Old Testament prophecy had been fulfilled. W. Vischer has suggested that the Bible is composed of two semicircles of witness, one pointing to a future event and one pointing to a past event whose final fulfillment is still future.[15]

It has been suggested that the essential difference between writings inside and outside the canon is that those inside constitute the first written deposit of the original testimony to God's revelation whereas those outside are dependent upon this testimony. Sometimes the difference has been stated in terms of *inspiration*: those inside are inspired by God the Holy Spirit and those outside are not. This view was originally associated with the view of the Bible as literally inspired by the Holy Spirit, but it has been asserted in modern times apart from this view. But the record of the Bible and Christian history indicates that the inspiration of the prophets, apostles and biblical authors is not different in kind from that of Christian prophets and teachers in every age. (Nor is it different in kind from the inspiration of prophets of other religions, great philosophers, artists, scientists and political leaders.) In other words the biblical books were not written in any manner generically different from that of later Christian writings. The receiving of revelation by prophets and apostles was enabled by the illumination of the Holy Spirit, but the same pertains to the receiving of God's revelation in later ages on the basis of the testimony of the prophets and apostles. So the category of inspiration is not adequate for distinguishing the canonical literature from other writings.[16]

How is this understanding of the canon of Scripture related to the results of the historical study of the formation of the canon? The standards which the early church applied in determining canonicity were authorship by an apostle or an associate of an apostle, accordance with the consensus of received doctrine (the rule of faith), wide usage in the church, address to the whole church, a unified message, and antiquity. Most of these principles were both erroneously applied and also rationalizations after the fact. The church knew intuitively which writings it wanted in the canon, that is, which writings bore the clearest and fullest testimony to Christ, produced authentic Christian conversion, Christian life, and the fruit of the Spirit, the "demonstration of the Spirit and power" (1 Cor. 2:4). So the church worked out principles by which these writings would be included and others excluded. And the fundamental decision here was not made in church councils or by bishops. "The organized church as such did not create the Canon; it recognized the Canon which had already been created. . . . For it goes without saying that the Church, understood as the entire body of believers, created the Canon. But this Canon grew, in fact, from the bottom upwards, in the communities, among the believers, and only later was officially legitimatized from the top."[17] Much is often made in histories of the formation of the canon of the fact that there was still disagreement about the limits of the canon down into the fifth and sixth centuries. But this is very misleading since 85 percent of the canon of the New Testament was in fact universally agreed upon by the end of the second century.[18] This historical picture of the development of the canon of Scripture complements the theological view suggested above that the church determined the limits of the canon on the basis of its understanding of the central message of the Bible. A similar view of the development of the canon is offered by Guthrie. His point is that it was the church's experience of the thankful recital in the liturgy of the acts of God in the history of Israel culminating in Christ that was the means by which it received its identity as the people of God, and that this was in fact the working norm by which the church judged the various Christian writings of the first and second centuries.[19]

The Apocrypha

The one area of the canon in which there is significant disagreement among the churches today is the Apocrypha. The Roman Catholic, Greek Orthodox, Russian Orthodox, Reformed, Lutheran and Anglican churches all have different canons in regard to the Apocrypha. Anglicanism holds an ambiguous or even contradictory attitude toward the Apocrypha. Several of the readings in the lectionary of *The Book of Common Prayer* are taken from the Apocrypha. These lessons are read in the same way as those from the Old Testament, that is, as though they were canonical Scripture. And yet Article VI states that the church does "not apply them to establish any doctrine." It is clear from Articles VI, VIII, XX, XXI and XXII that canonicity means the basis for "establishing" or "proof" of doctrine. Thus the Apocrypha is definitely non-canonical. Article VI does state that the church reads the Apocrypha "for example of life and instruction of manners (*mores*)." But this is apparently something less than the establishment of fundamental

Christian ethical principles which would be integrally related to doctrine. Thus there is a contradiction between the practice and the theory of Anglicanism in regard to the Apocrypha.

This raises the question of whether or not the Apocrypha should be in the canon. It would seem that on the grounds of canonicity developed in this chapter, a good case can be made that the Apocrypha should be in the canon. The apocryphal books are at least in part a history of Israel during the intertestamental period interpreted as involving the activity and revelation of God. It constitutes the immediate background of and preparation for the New Testament. Furthermore the Apocrypha, although its exact limits have varied, has been affirmed as canonical during three-quarters of the history of the church, and since the sixteenth century it has been considered fully canonical by the majority of the church.

Tradition

The term tradition has several meanings in theology. It can mean the apostolic tradition which is the original response to the revelation in Christ. Some authors suggest that since apostolic tradition in this sense precedes the New Testament writings, it has an authority above them. But since the New Testament is the first written deposit of this apostolic tradition, this tradition is available only in the New Testament and is not simply to be equated with the earliest layers of tradition in the New Testament. The earliest traditions probably did not contain the full original response to the revelation.

Tradition can also mean what the Roman Catholic Church calls the secret tradition, namely, that part of the apostolic tradition which was not committed to writing, but was handed down orally by the apostolic bishops. There is no historical foundation for the existence of such a tradition.

Tradition in this chapter is understood to mean the written deposit of the church's continuing attempt under the guidance of the Holy Spirit to enter more deeply into the meaning of God's revelation attested in the Bible. Tradition in this sense takes the form of creeds, conciliar decisions, confessions of faith, liturgies, and theological writings.

Why is tradition in this latter sense necessary to the life of the church? Since it is theology which produces tradition in its various forms, tradition is necessary for the same reasons that theology is necessary (see chapter 1). Tradition attempts to determine the central message of the Bible in the face of its multiplicity, to distinguish what is essential from what is peripheral in Christian faith, to distinguish true doctrine from false, and to guide the teaching function of the church. Tradition helps to maintain the unity of the church by supplying a common basis for preaching and teaching, for example, in the creeds. The church has to settle doctrinal controversies and disputes when the Bible is not decisive or must be interpreted, and the results of such decisions constitute part of tradition. Tradition in any period is the church's attempt to express the Christian faith in terms of the assumptions and problems of that period. So by examining the church's tradition in various periods we can get an idea of what is permanent and essential and what is transient and peripheral in Christian faith.

One of the main forms of tradition is *dogma*. Dogma is official teaching, those doctrines explicitly formulated by duly constituted authority in the church. Dogma does not cover the whole of Christian doctrine but only certain points which became the subject of debate and were determined by church authorities such as the early church councils. These councils enunciated dogma in the area of the trinity and christology but not on the atonement or the church, for example. Besides being official teaching, dogma is also a legal enactment acceptance of which may be used to determine membership in the church or in the official ministry of the church.

Article XXI states that councils "may err, and sometimes have erred" in their dogmatic pronouncements, and that these have no authority unless they are "taken" (*desumpta*, chosen, selected) out of the Bible. It is one of the main tasks of theology (which produces tradition) to examine and criticize the dogma of the church in the light of theological norm. Dogma has certain dangers connected with it. There is the tendency to make dogma absolute and irreformable. There is also a tendency to set up dogma as the object of faith, to make faith essentially assent to dogma. Finally the necessary disciplinary authority of the church may be used to curb the freedom of theologians to investigate and criticize the dogma of the church. The experience of Bishops J. A. T. Robinson and J. A. Pike has shown that this tendency is not dead.

What is the relation of the theological authority of the Bible to that of tradition? This issue is at the heart of the recent Protestant-Roman Catholic dialogue. The Council of Trent declared in 1564:

> Seeing clearly that this truth and discipline [of the Gospel promulgated by Christ] are contained in the written books [of the Bible], and the un-written traditions which, received by the Apostles from the mouth of Christ himself, or from the Apostles themselves, the Holy Ghost dictating, have come down even unto us, transmitted as it were from hand to hand: (the Synod) following the examples of the orthodox Fathers, receives and venerates with an equal affection of piety and reverence, all the books both of the Old and of the New Testament—seeing that

one God is the author of both—as also the said traditions, as well those appertaining to faith as to morals, as having been dictated, either by Christ's own word of mouth, or by the Holy Ghost, and preserved in the Catholic Church by a continuous succession.[20]

The "unwritten traditions" refers to extra-biblical oral tradition which is presumably committed to writing from time to time in various papal declarations. This statement does not mean that the gospel is fully contained in both the Bible and tradition, but that the gospel is contained partly in the Bible and partly in tradition. Thus the Bible does not contain "all things necessary to salvation" (Article VI) but must be supplemented by tradition. In other words the supremacy of Scripture is undercut and the church is freed from the theological criterion of the first written deposit of the original testimony to the revelation. Some contemporary Roman Catholic theologians, notably Geiselmann and Tavard, have denied the above interpretation of Trent and affirmed that it means that the gospel is fully contained in both the Bible and tradition. Although they are clearly wrong historically, their work constitutes a hopeful development of Roman Catholic theology in this area.[21]

It is clear from what has been said above that the theological authority of the Bible is superior to that of tradition, that where the Bible and tradition are in conflict, the Bible must prevail. But since tradition is essentially the church's growing understanding of the testimony of the Bible, such a conflict would amount to a failure on the part of the church in its theological task.

How then is tradition to be used in the task of theology? In the work of interpreting the biblical testimony we must first hear how the church has understood the Bible in the past. Barth suggests that this attitude toward tradition follows from the inner meaning of the Fifth Commandment. The same kind of obedience is required toward the church's tradition, toward the elders of the church, as is required toward one's parents: not unconditional and permanent bondage but preliminary obedience. In interpreting the testimony of the Bible, theology should begin with the tradition of the church. This will protect us against ourselves, against our own unconscious presuppositions, predilections, and provincialisms, and against a bad individualism. The individual theologian will depart from tradition only with great care since tradition represents the consensus of many individuals in many ages. But finally the theologian must be free to go on to criticize the tradition in the light of the theological norm.

The supremacy of Scripture over tradition does not mean that Scripture is the only theological authority. The Reformation principle of *sola scriptura* has sometimes been so interpreted, although the Reformers never meant it in this way. We cannot leapfrog over nineteen centuries and approach the

Bible *de novo* and directly. We can approach the Bible only in the light of the history of Western culture from the first century to the twentieth century and especially in the light of the cultural situation of the present. The church and its tradition imply the Bible as their foundation, and the Bible implies the church and its tradition as its fruit. They cannot be understood separately. But in this interconnection the Bible as interpreted by the church today has a theological authority above that of the church's tradition.

At this point there might well be a section with the traditional title of symbolics, the study and comparison of the various doctrinal statements which form the major part of the tradition of the church.[22] All that can be done here is a brief summary of the doctrinal authorities of the Episcopal Church.

Tradition in the Episcopal Church

First and prior to tradition is the Bible, as indicated in Articles VI, VIII, XX, XXII. Second, historically and in authority are the Apostles' and Nicene Creeds. (See Article VIII.) The American article omits the Athanasian Creed as the result of a churchmanship struggle in 1789. Thirdly, the ecumenical councils. Anglicanism has been somewhat ambiguous about the number accepted but it has never been less than four nor more than six. The Ten Articles of 1536 stated that the first four councils were of binding authority. One of the Homilies in the *Book of Homilies* (See Article XXV) refers to six councils as "received of all men." R. Hooker refers to only four.

The Articles of Religion were adopted and established by the General Convention of 1801 and are made a part of the Prayer Book under Article X of the Constitution. Although subscription to them was required of clergy in the Church of England until 1975, it was not thought necessary in the American church. The declaration required before ordination (Article VIII of the Constitution) was believed to be sufficient. The Articles express the mind of the Church of England on questions under dispute at the time of the Reformation and do not claim to be final or complete system of theology. *Doctrine in the Church of England* includes the following statement in regard to the Articles:

> Anglican formularies represent the doctrinal ecclesiastical and histori-
> cal position of Anglicanism in relation to the rest of Western Christen-
> dom in the sixteenth century, and the position of the Church of
> England in relation to other Christian bodies is still defined by the
> retention of those formularies. These formularies should not be held to
> prejudge questions which have arisen since their formulation or prob-

lems which have been modified by fresh knowledge or fresh conceptions. Nevertheless, if an Anglican theologian thinks a particular formulary not wholly adequate, he has a special obligation to preserve whatever truth that formulary was trying to secure, and to see to it that any statement he puts forward as more adequate does in fact secure this.[23]

It is often said that Anglicanism is not a confessional church and that the Articles of Religion are not a confession of faith in the sense of the Reformation confessions. In the seventeenth and eighteenth centuries the Lutheran Book of Concord and the Reformed Westminster Confession were often used as veritable textbooks for the resolution of theological issues, and they are still used in this way in wide areas of Protestantism. But the Articles of Religion were never looked upon in this way. They were considered as a guide rather than as a binding criterion of correct doctrine or the basis of doctrinal testing. They were intended as a guide for the avoidance of the aberrations of Roman Catholic doctrine on the one hand and Anabaptist doctrine on the other. This is indicated (quaintly) by Bishop Bramhall in his *Schism Guarded* of 1658.

> We do not suffer any man "to reject" the Thirty-Nine Articles of the Church of England "at his pleasure;" yet neither do we look upon them as essentials of saving faith or "legacies of Christ and of His Apostles;" but in a mean, as pious opinions fitted for the preservation of unity. Neither do we oblige any man to believe them, but only not to contradict them.[24]

This attitude toward the Articles provides an atmosphere of theological freedom in Anglicanism which is conducive to works such as those by Bishops Robinson and Pike. But to others it probably looks like theological sloppiness.[25]

The relations of the various elements in this view of theological authority can be diagrammed as follows:

Note on Reason

Sometimes reason is proposed as a theological authority beside that of the Bible and tradition, the implication being that some theological problems can be settled by reason alone. Reason in this connection is the means by which any claim to authority is accepted; it is not an alternative authority. As P. T. Forsyth puts it, "Reason is no authority; it is but the power of discerning authority." The only way an authority can be accepted as a criterion of true doctrine is by means of reason. If any acceptance of authority is entirely uncritical, it is not a case of acceptance of authority but of psychological compulsion. But sometimes reason is asserted as an alternative authority in a different sense, namely, in the sense that the human mind can arrive at objective conclusions on all philosophical questions, that unaided reason is a competent and impartial judge of truth and falsehood in all matters. But this is not reason but rationalism, a particular view of the human mind based on a particular philosophical world view.

Questions for Discussion

1. *The most important authority is that by which a person decides whether or not to become a Christian. Does not this authority transcend that of the Bible, tradition, Christian experience, or church consensus?*
2. *How would you go about deciding whether or not a particular theological assertion is true?*
3. *How does the average church member go about deciding theological issues? How is this related to the various views of authority outlined in this chapter?*
4. *What kind of experiences would you count for or against a theological statement about God, such as, God loves me? If experience can count for or against theological statements, is it not the basic authority in theology?*
5. *If theology is the analysis and description of the biblical consensus and its translation for the contemporary world, why should it be called normative? Is it not simply descriptive?*
6. *Has not the historical-critical approach to the Bible destroyed the Bible as the final theological authority?*
7. *The "supremacy of scripture" view of theological authority rules out the promise that the Holy Spirit will guide us into all truth (John 16:13). Therefore should not the Bible and tradition should have equal authority in theology?" Discuss.*
8. *"The Christian revelation is in the history itself. Therefore it is not in the apostolic testimony to Christ in the New Testament but in the concrete historical person of Jesus behind the New Testament picture. Thus historical research is the only way to determine the content of the revelation" (Pannenberg) Discuss.*
9. *How would the doctrines of the virgin birth, episcopal apostolic succession, and the*

trinity come out when tested by the various views of theological authority outlined in the chapter?

10. *What is the relation between "all things necessary to salvation" (Article VI) and the "true Christian faith" (p. 4) ? Is a distinction possible between essentials and non-essentials in Christian faith? What is the basis of this distinction? Can there be some elements of Christian faith which are true and valid and yet not "necessary to salvation?"*

11. *In a provocative passage Kierkegaard states: "If the . . . generation [contemporary with Jesus] had left nothing behind them . . . but these words: "We have believed that in such and such a year God appeared among us in the humble, figure of a servant, that he lived and taught in our community, and finally died," it would be more than enough. The contemporary generation would have done all that was necessary; for this little advertisement, this* nota bene *on a page of universal history, would be sufficient to afford an occasion for a successor, and the most voluminous account can in all eternity do nothing more" (*Philosophical Fragments, p. 87). *Is Kierkegaard correct? Why? If not, how would his observation have to be supplemented, changed, or replaced in order adequately to provide a theological authority?*

12. *"The Church accepted the Old Testament, wrote the New Testament, determined their limits, and interpreted their meaning in every age. Therefore, the authority of the Church is superior to that of the Bible." Discuss.*

13. *Is it still possible to be a heretic? If so, was Bishop Pike or Bishop Robinson a heretic? Why? If not, what does this mean for the task of theology?*

14. *Can we experience God directly and immediately or only indirectly and as mediated through the creation? How can we know we are experiencing God?*

15. *How can we determine what in "the consensus of the Bible" is testimony to revelation and what is simply part of ancient Near Eastern thought patterns and cosmology?*

16. *How is it possible for two people to debate the issue of theological authority who hold different views on this issue?*

4

Trinity

With this lecture we turn from preliminary considerations to the actual content of Christian faith, to what is affirmed in the Christian message. We will be attempting to carry out the various purposes of theology in accordance with the various principles developed in the first three chapters. As has been suggested, the order of topics is not necessary or decisive but expedient. We will be following the order of the traditional *loci* or topics of the Christian faith: God, creation, humanity, sin, Christology, and so forth.

The doctrine of God is entirely dependant upon what God is revealed to be, upon the divine self-disclosure attested in the Bible and interpreted in the tradition of the church. In the doctrine of God the most fundamental thing we have to say is that God is self-revealed as triune, as threefold, as Father, Son and Holy Spirit.

Bible

The doctrine of the trinity does not appear explicitly in the Bible. (Very few doctrines, if any, do.) Rather it is the immediate implication of the biblical testimony. The Bible contains the "seeds of the trinitarian understanding of God" (Moule), the "beginnings of a trinitarian theology" (Stauffer), from which the doctrine of the trinity was a "natural and necessary development" (Grant). The doctrine of the trinity is the result of the church's reflection upon the biblical testimony in the face of various distorted interpretations.

Does the Old Testament testify to the triunity of God? If it testifies to a God who could in no way be triune, and if the doctrine of the trinity is the immediate implication of the New Testament testimony, then Marcion was correct in affirming that the Old Testament testifies to a different God.

First of all, it is clear that the God attested in the Old Testament is one, a unity, and not a plurality. But secondly, it is also clear that the God of the Old Testament is not a simple mathematical unity. Sometimes it is claimed that Unitarianism, which sometimes asserts that God is a simple unity, is based on the Old Testament or is closer to Judaism than to Christianity. But this will not stand up, because the God of the Old Testament is not a simple unity but a complex, organic, or differentiated unity. All the anthropomorphisms of the Old Testament interpret the unity of Yahweh on the analogy of the unity of the human self. Furthermore, certain divine attributes or powers, such as Spirit, Word and Wisdom, are distinguished and tend to be personalized and hypostatized.[1] These terms refer to extensions of God's personal presence and powerful activity in relation to the world. They are not systematically related in the Old Testament, and they overlap in function. But they point to a differentiation in the Godhead which is similar to that referred to in the New Testament by the terms Father, Son and Spirit. The terms Word and Wisdom are applied to Christ, and Old Testament texts concerning the Spirit of God are applied to the Holy Spirit in the New Testament. In other words the New Testament authors understood the relation of the Son and the Spirit to the Father in roughly the same way as the Old Testament authors understood the relation of Word, Spirit, and Wisdom to Yahweh.[2]

This differentiation in the Godhead is simply the testimony of the Old Testament that God is a living God. "The dominant impression given by the Old Testament about God is the concreteness, definiteness, and energy of his being. . . . He is the *living* God."[3] And the main way in which this concreteness and energy and livingness are communicated in the Old Testament is by means of differentiation, the semi-personalized and semi-hypostatized attributes or powers of God. (Tillich has suggested that the understanding of a living reality requires a perception of its differentiation. There must be at least a differentiation of power and meaning, dynamics and form. If there is only power or dynamics without meaning or form, there is only chaos. If there is only form and structure without power or dynamics, there can be only static character without life or power of action.)

God is self-revealed in the New Testament as triune or threefold, as Father, Son and Holy Spirit. The God who is revealed in Christ by the Spirit is understood to be the same God who is revealed in the history of the old Israel. Furthermore the God attested in the New Testament is a unity. There is no evidence in the New Testament that the unity of God is questioned or in doubt. The divine unity is assumed and affirmed (1 Cor. 8:4f, Eph. 4:4f, Mk. 12:29). In other words the New Testament authors' understanding of Christ and the Spirit apparently does not challenge or raise the question of the unity of God but rather manifests the character of that unity.

There are several passages in the New Testament in which the three names are put together in a formula or in close proximity (2 Thess. 2:13f, Gal. 4:6, 1 Cor. 12:4f, 2 Cor. 13:14, Eph. 4:4f, 1 Pet. 1:2, Mt. 28:19, Acts 2:32f). These passages indicate the threefold character of the confession of God, which became the basis of the triadic form of the early rule of faith. This triadic confession indicates the structure of the Christian life in relation to God. It is an account of the pattern of the new life which the Christian has entered through faith and baptism, a new life which has a particular form in relation to God. It is a life from the Father, through the Son, and in the Spirit (see 1 Cor. 8:6). Thus the Christian prays to the Father, through the Son, and in the Spirit. This triadic confession, however, is not the doctrine of the trinity because it does not indicate anything about the relation of the three names.

Since we have spoken about God's activity of revelation in chapter 2, let us see how the relations of the three names are understood in the New Testament in regard to God's revelation. An investigation of the key passages indicates that the name Father designates the ultimate origin and content of the revelation, that the name Son designates the historical mediator of the revelation of the Father, and that the name Spirit designates the subjective mediator of the revelation of the Father through the Son, or the inner testimony by which the receiver of revelation perceives the revelation of the Father in the Son. Thus the function of the Son is to reveal the Father (Mt. ll:27, Jn. 1:18, 14:6f). And the function of the Spirit is to bear witness to the revelation of the Father in the Son (1 Cor. 2:l0f, Jn. 15:26).

Now what is the meaning of the three names? God is self-revealed as Father. (The idea of God as Father is not prominent in the Old Testament, although it is not absent. In the Old Testament it means creative power, providential care and redemption of Israel.) This does not mean simply that God is like a father but that especially God is the Father of the Son, the "Father of our Lord Jesus Christ," a phrase which occurs repeatedly in the New Testament. Thus God is "our Father" not simply as our creator but because through the Son we have been adopted as children of God by grace. Therefore the Fatherhood of God in this sense receives the content of its meaning from the significance of the Son.

God is revealed as Father through the Son, Jesus Christ. The Son is at the center of the stage in the New Testament, but the Son is there because the Father has "sent" him. And the Son's only mission is to act in complete obedience to the Father and thus to reveal the Father. The fundamental meaning of sonship throughout the Bible is obedience, and this meaning is fulfilled in the life and ministry of the "only" and "beloved" Son. Most of the New Testament testimony to the Son refers to what he does, to his function, namely, to announce and inaugurate the Kingdom, to accomplish liberation, reconciliation, salvation, and to reveal the Father. But on the basis of what the Son does the New Testament authors also testify to who he is, namely, the Lord, the Divine Son, the image of the invisible God, and so forth. The deity of the Son is affirmed in various ways in the New Testament, and these will be discussed in chapter 10. But the Jews who came to call Jesus Lord (the Old Testament title of Yahweh) were not affirming a second Lord. Jesus the Son of God is Lord with the same Lordship with which the Father is Lord.

It is through the Son that we have the Spirit who bears witness to the Son and thus to the Son's revelation of the Father, and who accomplishes in us the work of the Son which is the will of the Father. The Spirit is God's personal presence and activity in the world, from creation, through the history of Israel, especially in Jesus, and in the church as a foretaste of the fulfillment. The New Testament attests primarily the work of the Spirit in the life and ministry of Jesus and the gift of the Spirit from the Father and/ or the risen Lord to the church. The New Testament authors speak of the Spirit of God and the Spirit of Christ synonymously. And they speak of the activity of the risen Lord and of the Spirit in the same way, implying that the risen Lord acts through the Spirit. Again the lordship or deity of the Spirit is not a second lordship or deity but the same lordship and deity as that of the Father and the Son.

The biblical basis of the doctrine of the trinity is sometimes summarized in quite a different way. The early Christians had three types of experience; they were aware of three historical facts. As Jews they had known God as their heavenly Father; as disciples of Jesus they knew God as manifest in Jesus' life, ministry, death and resurrection; and as apostles they knew the gift of the divine Spirit in their hearts empowering them in their mission. Later Christians attempted to interpret the early Christians' testimony to these three types of experiences, and produced the doctrine of the trinity as the best formula for making sense of this testimony. The doctrine of the trinity is in fact the result of reflection on the New Testament testimony, but the New Testament will not bear out the association of these three types of experience with the distinctions of Father, Son and Holy Spirit. The church later rejected one form of this interpretation as Sabellianism.

First, the Jewish experience of God is not simply the experience of God the Father but of the God who was later understood to be triune. Furthermore the Jews knew God through the divine Word, Spirit, Wisdom, Power, Glory, and not simply as Father. Temple suggests that Yahweh is God the Son rather than God the Father. This raises other difficulties, but the point is that from the Christian point of view the God who is revealed to Israel is the triune God and not simply God the Father.

Secondly, the experience of those who knew Jesus was not simply the experience of God the Son. In the gospels (especially Luke) the whole life and ministry of Jesus is depicted as a manifestation of the power of the Spirit.His conception, baptism,beginning of his public ministry, and healings are marked by the activity of the Spirit. The text of his first sermon, so to speak, is Isa. 61:1, "The Spirit of the Lord is upon me." Futhermore, he speaks constantly of the Father and his kingdom, and he attributes his power, authority, teaching, and whole mission to the Father. He interprets Peter's confession as the work of the Father (Mt. 16:17; see Jn. 6:44, 65).

Finally, the Pentecost experience and the continuing experience of the presence of God in the church is not simply and solely the experience of the Spirit, except in the general sense in which all experinece of God is through the Spirit. As has been noted above, the distinction between the presence and activity of the risen Christ and the Spirit is not at all clear. Thus it is not possible to interpret the doctrine of the trinity as the adding up of the three types of experience mentioned above. The distinctions to which the names Father, Son, and Spirit refer are not types of experience but rather distinctions in the structure of each of these types of experience. We will return to this point in connection with the contemporary discussion of the doctrine of the trinity.

History and Tradition

Now we turn to the church's reflection on the New Testament tesimony to the triune God. The details of the development of the doctrine of the trinity will not be rehearsed in this chapter, because they are presented in many books.[4] The main points to be noted are the development of the Logos Christology in the second and third centuries, the rise of modalistic monarchianism (Sabellianism) in reaction to this, Tertullian's attack on the latter and his development of the classical western terminology, the rise of dynamic monarchianism (adoptionism) from philosophical and historical motives, the rise of Arianism and the council of Nicea, the condemnation of Macedonianism at the Council of Constantinople in 381, the clarification of the terminology by the Cappadocians, and St. Augustine's completion of the western development as symbolized in the Athanasian Creed.[5]

It is sometimes asserted that the development of Christological and trinitarian doctrine in the first few centuries of the history of the church was a fatal Hellenization and thus intellectualization of the gospel. This was the view of the Ritschlian school of theology as represented in the views of Harnack, for example. This view is widely challenged today in its basic

assumption that Hellenistic thought was intellectualistic and in his view
that the interpretation of the gospel in Hellenistic terms was a distortion.[6]
The point is that the interpretation of the gospel in Hellenistic terms was
a necessity if the church was to move out of a narrow Palestinian Jewish
milieu, since this is the only way the gospel could ever be understood,
affirmed, and communicated in the Hellenistic world. This is a permanent
problem confronting the mission of the church, and the danger is that any
interpretation of the gospel in any cultural setting may involve a distortion
of the gospel. But the risk must be assumed or the mission of the church
given up. Assessments of the success of the church of the first five centuries
in faithfully carrying out this task will vary, but it cannot be denied that it
devoted itself fully to the task of interpreting the biblical testimony with
the only tools it had at hand, namely, Hellenistic philosophy.

All that can be done in this chapter is to comment on various aspects of
the development of the doctrine of the trinity. First of all there was a great
deal of confusion over terminology in East and West. For example, *hypostasis* and *ousia* were considered to be synonyms by Origen and by the
Council of Nicea. Later the Nicene party, assuming one *ousia* and the
equivalence of *ousia* and *hypostasis*, condemned the Semi-Arians for the use
of three *hypostaseis* and accused them of tritheism. The Semi-Arians, taking
the terms the other way around as referring to the distinctions rather than
the unity of the godhead, accused the Nicenes of Sabellianism. It was the
contribution of the Cappadocian fathers to distinguish *ousia* and *hypostasis*,
and apply *ousia* to the unity and *hypostasis* to the distinctions. This usage
was confirmed at the Council of Constantinople in 381.

The final view of the East can be summarized very roughly as follows:
an *hypostasis* is somewhere between a substance and an attribute. Like an
attribute it presupposes a substance, and like a substance it has attributes.
If *hypostasis* meant substance, the result would be tritneism. If it meant
attribute, the result would be Sabellianism. *Ousia* means fundamental
reality, that which makes a thing what it is in distinction from something
else, that which exists in itself independently of anything else, that in which
attributes, qualities, and properties inhere. *Hypostasis* means mode of
being, the way in which a substance exists, the manner in which a reality
is presented. The relation of these terms to their Latin etymological and
theological equivalents can be diagrammed as follows:

The theological equivalents are indicated by the lines. The fact that the etymological equivalents are not the finally agreed upon theological equivalents was one of the main sources of confusion. The western affirmation of one *substantia* sounded like Sabellianism in the East. The affirmation of three *hypostaseis* sounded like tritheism in the West.

Augustine gave the classical formulation of the western tradition a strong emphasis on the divine unity. His fundamental principle was the famous trinitarian rule: the external acts of the trinity are indivisible. He also emphasized the equality of the *personae* and stated that the distinctions are grounded in their mutual relations in the godhead.

The major tension in the development of the doctrine of the trinity is that between the emphasis on the unity of the godhead and the emphasis on the distinctions in the godhead. This tension can be diagrammed as follows:

Emphasis on Unity		*Emphasis on Distinctions*
Modalistic Monarchianism (Sabellianism)		Logos Christology
	Nlcea	Dynamic Monarchiamism (adoptionism)
Augustine		
		Arianism
Athanasian Creed		
		Cappadocian Fathers

These differences in emphasis correspond roughly to the differences between East and West. (And we will see below that they also correspond to the positions in the contemporary debate over the doctrine of the trinity.) In the East the tendency was to look upon the Father as the whole of the godhead; the Father contains eternally within himself the Word and the Spirit, which are emitted in the divine economy of creation, revelation, and salvation. There is a resulting tendency to subordinate the Son and the Spirit to the Father and therefore a tendency to emphasize the distinctions and plurality in the Godhead. This is a manifestation of the influence of Neo-Platonism with its idea of a hierarchy of being between the one God and the world. This tendency to emphasize the distinctions is seen in the choice of *hypostasis* to indicate the distinctions, a word which originally meant substance and was considered to be synonymous with *ousia*. Thus Arianism is the typical eastern heresy.

In the West, on the other hand, the tendency was to emphasize the divine *monarchia* or unity and thus to minimize the distinctions and emphasize the equality of the *personae*. This tendency is seen in the choice of the term *persona* for the distinctions, a term which for Tertullian meant actor's mask or part, the presentation of an individual. Thus the emphases of *persona* and *hypostasis* lay in opposite directions. The East rejected the equivalent of *persona*, namely *prosopon*, because it carried with it the Sabellian implication of a passing aspect of God. The West rejected the equivalent of *hypostasis*, namely *substantia* as the term for the distinctions, because this sounded tritheistic. Thus Sabellianism is the typical western heresy.

This debate over the doctrine of the trinity may appear to be the height of theological hair-splitting and irrelevance, but it was in fact a debate over absolutely fundamental issues, a life and death struggle for the church. In the first place the church was concerned to affirm that God was really acting and being revealed in Christ and the Spirit. It was not just a second god or a created being subordinate to God. Arianism and the left wing of the Logos Christology endangered the reality of God's action in Christ and the Spirit and thus threatened the reality of Christian salvation with a relapse into pagan polytheism. So the church had to affirm the deity of Christ and the Spirit, their consubstantiality with the Father, using the terms one *ousia* and one *substantia*.

But secondly the church was aware of the danger of ignoring the distinctions between the Father, the Son and the Spirit. According to the New Testament testimony, Christ is not simply identical with God the Father, a substitute for God the Father. God did not change from the Father into the Son and then from the Son into the Spirit. God is eternally what God is. God was not born nor did God die. God is really acting in Christ and the Spirit but God the Father is not simply identical with Christ and the Spirit. So the church had to affirm, besides the consubstantiality of the Father, Son and Spirit, that they were distinct *hypostaseis* or *personae* in this one substance.

Besides the acceptance of the Apostles', Nicene and Athanasian creeds and the first four or six ecumenical councils, specific references to the doctrine of the trinity in what constitutes tradition for Anglicanism include Article I and various references in *The Book of Common Prayer*. In the Episcopal Church reference to the Athanasian Creed was omitted from Article Vlll, and there is no reference to the councils. Besides the frequent use of the *Gloria Patri* the American Prayer Book contains references to the trinity in the Catechism and in liturgical settings.[7] These will be discussed below.

In the nineteenth century the doctrine of the trinity was reduced radically in importance by two factors: the historical-critical study of the Bible and especially the elimination of the fourth gospel as a primitive historical source, and the influence of Schleiermacher who believed the doctrine to be an unnecessary and unwarranted addition to the Christian faith and who relegated it to an appendix in his work *The Christian Faith*. In our century as a result of the theological revival associated with the name of Karl Barth, there has been a renewed recognition of the necessity and importance of the doctrine which is the background of current debates.

Contemporary Debates and Reconstruction

One of the main modern debates on the doctrine of the trinity is that between Barth and his followers, especially Claude Welch in his book *In This Name*[7a], and certain Anglican theologians but principally Leonard Hodgson in his work *The Doctrine of the Trinity*.[8] It is primarily a debate over whether the modern concept of person is to be applied to the divine unity or the divine distinctions. It is really a revival of the debate between East and West, between the tendency to emphasize the unity of the godhead and the tendency to emphasize the distinctions.

Tertullian originated the use of the term *persona*, and while his meaning is ambiguous, it clearly was not equivalent to the modern concept of self-conscious personhood. This is indicated by the almost universal use of the psychological analogy for the trinity in the West following Augustine. This analogy suggests that the *personae* of the trinity are like memory, imagination, and will in a human person. In this analogy human personality is compared to the unity of God rather than to the distinctions in the godhead.

Since the time of Descartes and Locke when the essence of personality came to be seen as self-consciousness, theologians began to use the term "person" to refer to the divine unity rather than to the distinctions in the godhead. This is certainly in line with the anthropomorphisms of the Bible.

I believe that Barth and Welch have the better of the debate in the sense that their interpretation of the biblical testimony and the tradition of the church is more adequate than that of Hodgson and his colleagues. As D. Baillie suggests, if we regard the "persons" of the trinity as personalities in the modern sense of separate centers of consciousness, we imply that they are parts of God and limited by each other. And if, for example, it was only a part of God which was manifest in Christ, then there is no assurance as to what the other parts are like and how they are disposed toward us. So the church was concerned to affirm that the whole of the godhead was involved in each of the "persons."[9]

This debate raises one of the most difficult problems in the doctrine of the trinity, namely, that of the *inner-trinitarian relations*. It is clear from the biblical testimony that there is one kind of relation traditionally called the doctrine of original relations or processions, that is, that there is a certain order or pattern in the revelation of God. God the Father is the ground or presupposition of God the Son, and God the Father and God the Son are the ground or presupposition of God the Holy Spirit. God the Son is of or from God the Father, and God the Holy Spirit is of or from God the Father and God the Son. But the church interpreted this in such a way that there is no temporal priority or subordination, because God is wholly God in each "person." This order or pattern is the order of God's outgoing love; it is the basis for the New Testament testimony that God is love in God's very being.[10]

But the most difficult aspect of the problem of the inner-trinitarian relations is the question of communion or of personal relations between the divine "persons." It is obviously easier for Hodgson and his school to speak of this than it is for Barth and his followers, since the former affirm that the modern concept of person applies to the divine "persons." Brunner and Aulen, among others, will have none of this and insist that any discussion of the mutual relations of the "persons" in this sense is dangerous speculation. But there is one aspect of the New Testament testimony which raises this question in an unavoidable way. The New Testament speaks clearly of the mutual knowledge and love between the Father and the Son and implies it between Father, Son, and Spirit (1 Cor. 2:10f, Mk. 1:11, Mt. 11:27, Jn. 3:35, 5:20, 14:31, 15:9f, 16:13f, 17:24f).

The main emphasis of Hodgson and his followers, who are often referred to as the "social analogy school," is that the trinity is like a community of three human persons. Hodgson asserts that the relations between Father, Son and Spirit manifest in Jesus' earthly ministry are the same as the relations which obtain eternally between the divine "persons." This view of the trinity has been used by some English ethics scholars as one of the bases of social ethics. If persons are made in the image of God, then they are social in their very being.

Both Baillie and Welch argue, however, that this is a heretical Christology, namely, Apollinarianism, the view that God the Son took the place of the human mind or spirit in Jesus. But the New Testament testimony (confirmed at the Council of Chalcedon) is clearly that Jesus was fully human, a man who stood in a relation to God in which all people, through him, can stand. The church's decision was that Christ was fully human and fully divine at least in the sense that his deity and humanity do not limit each other, that no boundary could be drawn between them in Jesus' person. So the obvious fact that Jesus was a personality distinct from the personhood of God does not mean that God the Son is a personality distinct from God the Father.

Although this criticism of Hodgson seems valid, the problem of the inner-trinitarian relations remains the most difficult one for Barth and his school. All that can be said from their approach is that the relations between the divine "persons" are analogous to those within a human personality, for example, the relations manifest in the human pheon-omeon of self-transcendence or self-awareness, the fact that the human self can be both subject and object at the same time. Welch suggests that the finite personality is incomplete in the sense that it is dependent upon its relations with other persons, but that God as infinite or perfect personal-ity is self-sufficient and not dependent in this way because of the inner differentiation as Father, Son and Spirit. Welch, following Barth, bases this on the idea that God the Spitit is eternaly a communion between Father and Son, and that, the Spirit's work is to reproduce that communion between humanity and God. But here Barth and Welch seem to have gone beyond what they can justify on the basis of their approach.

If then the trinity is not a unity of three separate self-conscious persons, we must investigate further the adequacy of the main alternative view, which can be called *monarchianism*, the emphasis on the divine unity. This approach can take many different forms: (1) the divine "persons" are simply attributes, aspects, or qualities of God; (2) the divine "persons" are simply ways in which God is revealed or ways in which we experience God; (3) the divine "persons" are distinguished by function, type of activity, or are different ways in which God is related to the world (the "economic trinity"); and (4) the divine "persons" are modes of being of God, ways in which God is God in all of the divine activities.

(1) The difficulty with this view is that, if the divine "persons" are simply attributes, then there is no reason not to include a long list of other attributes, such as love, holiness, mercy, wrath, sovereignty, omnipresence, and so forth. D. M. Edwards actually makes the suggestion that mercy, providence and justice should be added to the trinity. Furthermore it is clear from the Bible that all attributes of God can be applied to each of the divine "persons," so that this is not the basis of the distinctions. Also, if the "persons" are simply attributes of God, they must inhere in something else, in the substance of God, to use the classical term, which would then be a fourth reality behind or beneath the "persons."

(2) If the trinity is *only* the way we experience or apprehend God's revelation or *only* the way God is revealed and does not refer to the essential reality of God, then we cannot say that God has really been revealed. This view calls into question the reality and veracity of revelation by separating God's revelation from the divine being or nature. If revelation is not the disclosure of the being of God, then God may well be quite different from what God is revealed to be in Christ, and revelation would better be called veiling or obscuring.

(3) This seems to be the view represented in the Litany, the Catechism, and the Prayer of Commendation in the Prayer Book. This approach

involves various difficulties. In the first place it is not the kind of distinction to which the Bible points, since each of the "persons" is involved in each of God's activities in the Bible. For example, God the Son is represented as the agent in creation, reconciliation and judgment, and seems to be as much involved in sanctification as the Spirit. Thus classical trinitarianism has always asserted the indivisibility of the external works of the trinity and affirmed the *perichoresis* or coinherence of each of the divine "persons" in each of the activities of God. Also such distinctions seem to refer primarily to God's relation to the world and not to God's essential being, which raises the problems mentioned in connection with (2) above. Furthermore in so far as these distinctions do refer to the essential being of God, they seem to be primarily attributes or qualities. For example, God is creative or sovereign, redemptive or loving, sanctifying or holy. This raises the difficulties mentioned in connection with (1) above. Finally, this approach may also lead to moral opposition between the "persons." For example, it may lead to a separation between God's creative and redemptive activity, or it may lead to an opposition between the Father as the righteous judge and the Son as the merciful redeemer, such as developed in Protestant scholasticism.

(4) The interpretation of the divine "persons" as modes of the being of God was first made by the Cappadocian Fathers. It has been used off and on since then, and is now affirmed by some contemporary Roman Catholic theologians and by Barth and Welch. This concept means that the Father, the Son and the Holy Spirit are ways in which God is God eternally and simultaneously. This is known as an essential or immanent trinity because these distinctions refer to God's essential being and not simply to God's relation to the world. Thus the divine "persons" are not attributes or ways in which God is revealed, or types of divine activity. They are the ways in which God is determined, or constituted, or differentiated as God. This approach could be called modalistic monarchianism, but it is not the heretical version in which the distinctions were apparently modes of God's relation to the world and were held successively.

So as against the economic interpretation of the trinity which distinguishes the "persons" by their function, the concept of modes of being points to distinctions in God's ways of being God which are manifest in the form, pattern, order, or structure of all of God's activities. It refers to a triad such as origin, objective mediator, and subjective mediator, or from whom, in whom, and through whom. The best analogy for this kind of distinction is the psychological analogy. For example, a person is a unity of thinking, willing and feeling. Each of these modes of being is involved in each of the person's activities. They constitute the structure, order, or pattern of all the person's activities. The limitation of this analogy is that these distinctions do not constitute the whole person but inhere in the person who can exist apart from them.

Thus the psychological analogy needs to be corrected by another analogy which is often used to interpret the doctrine of the trinity, namely, one person is at the same time spouse, parent, and citizen. He or she is this person in all these modes simultaneously. They are not parts of his or her being but modes of his or her total being. This analogy indicates that there is no successiveness in the divine "persons," that they are not parts of God, but that the whole of the godhead is involved in each of the "persons." It also indicates that each of the modes or distinctions is personal in the modern sense, not in their relations to each other, as in Hodgson's interpretation, but in the sense that they are modes of the whole godhead which is personal. The limitation of this analogy is that it is a form of the economic trinity. The distinctions are not essential or immanent. They are not exactly modes of a person's being which are involved in all of the person's activities, but rather distinctions in the person's external relations.

In summary we can say that the doctrine of the trinity is the immediate implication of the revelation of God attested in the Bible. It is the answer to the question, What is the nature of the God to whose revelation testimony is given in the Bible? It is the result of the analysis of this testimony. It is not a synthesis in the sense of an attempt to relate three different kinds of experience of God or to reconcile the New Testament testimony to the deity of Christ and the Holy Spirit with a received tradition of monotheism. The deity of the Son and the Spirit are not difficulties to be reconciled with a received monotheism but rather the explication of the nature of this monotheism.

The result of the analysis of the biblical testimony in the light of the tradition of the church is that the distinctions Father, Son and Spirit do not refer to persons in the modem sense or parts of God; each refers to the whole of the godhead. They do not refer to aspects, qualities, or attributes of God, because all of these apply equally to each of the "persons." They do not refer to functions or types of activity of God, because each of the "persons" is involved in each activity of God. They are not simply ways in which God is revealed or ways in which we experience God but rather essential or immanent distinctions in the godhead. The names Father, Son and Holy Spirit refer to modes of being of God, distinctions in the way in which God is God, distinctions in the form, pattern, order, or structure of all of God's activities. The rest of the topics in theology are elaborations of the meaning of these modes in relation to God's activity in creation and salvation. But finally we must say with Augustine that the doctrine of the trinity is affirmed "not that (the godhead) might (thereby) be completely spoken, but that it might not be left wholly unspoken."[11]

The Prayer Book and the Doctrine of Appropriations

The doctrine of the trinity implied in *The Book of Common Prayer* was criticized above as being a form of the economic trinity. Although the distinctions of Father, Son, and Spirit are not distinctions of function or type of activity, such as creation, redemption and sanctification, a connection can be made on the basis of a doctrine introduced by Augustine and elaborated by Aquinas and others and known as the doctrine of appropriations. This doctrine asserts that there is an analogy or an affinity between creation, redemption, and sanctification, on the one hand, and the Father, Son and Holy Spirit, on the other. Thus creation is "appropriated" to the Father, redemption to the Son, and sanctification to the Spirit, without denying that each of the "persons" is involved in each of these functions. For example, God the Father is God's mode of being in which God is the origin or ground of God's other modes of being. This relation between the Father and the other modes of being is analogous to the relation between God and the world in creation. Thus as a result of this analogy we can "appropriate" the function of creation to God the Father. Similar analogies are found for the other appropriations.[12] In this way a provisional justification can be given for the usage of the Prayer Book. It is interesting to note that the ascription of specific functions to the Father and the Spirit in the Litany was added only in the American edition of 1928. The Catechism, however, contained this implied economic doctrine of the trinity from its first edition in 1549.

This usage is occasionally also followed liturgically to avoid the exclusive male imagery of the "persons" of the trinity. This is acceptable theologically on the same basis as the Prayer Book usage. No particular words are essential to the doctrine of the trinity nor to any other doctrine. For example, the technical term *homoousion* in the creed of Nicaea, is not essential to christology in the sense that without this specific term one cannot have a valid or orthodox christology. But the decision about what words are appropriate for the liturgy involves other criteria besides the theological, namely, traditional, ecumenical, aesthetic, psychological, and so forth. That is, it may be decided on other grounds that the traditional language is essential in the liturgy, but not on theological grounds.

C. Richardson and Pike

Another debate on the trinity was initiated by Cyril C. Richardson in his book *The Doctrine of the Trinity*.[13] Richardson's main point is that the doctrine of the trinity is "an artificial construct." He agrees that we must make distinctions in the godhead, but he asserts that the terms Father, Son, and Holy Spirit are ambiguous, overlap, and do not point properly to the main distinctions or all the distinctions which need to be made. "There is no necessary threeness in the Godhead" (p. 149). In particular he states that the doctrine of the trinity is inadequate to deal with the fundamental religious paradox of God as at once absolute and related to the world, which is the main distinction to be made in the godhead.

Welch's response is that Richardson's idea of the main distinction in the godhead, the distinction of God as absolute and as related, is not of major importance in the Bible and was not the main issue in the development of the doctrine of the trinity. Absoluteness and relatedness are attributes of God which must be applied to each of the "persons" of the trinity, because they are attributes of God. Richardson's decision that this distinction is the most important one is made on grounds which fall outside the Bible. He seems to bring a doctrine of God to the revelation in Christ rather than basing his doctrine of God there. The real issue seems to be whether or not one is to take seriously the New Testament testimony to the reality and uniqueness of the revelation of God in Christ. When this testimony is taken seriously, a definite pattern of triunity appears which centers about the names Father, God and Spirit. This is a first rate theological debate involving exegesis, interpretation of the history of doctrine, and systematic reconstruction.

Bishop Pike's notorious views on the trinity were stated concisely in his book *A Time for Christian Candor*.[14] He is simply affirming the classical western doctrine of the trinity, although he does not seem to be aware of this. His essential point is that everything that is affirmed of the Son and of the Holy Spirit can be affirmed simply of God, and that these affirmations do not require the positing of separate or distinct entities or persons in the modern sense. This is simply one way of stating the classical trinitarian rule or the principle of coinherence.

What caused the most concern was his statement that "the Church's classical way of stating what is represented by the doctrine of the Trinity . . . is not essential to the Christian Faith" (p. 124). But this is hardly very radical since no particular way of stating any Christian doctrine is essential to the Christian faith. What may be essential to Christian faith is that to which a particular doctrine refers, and Bishop Pike affirms that the referent of the doctrine of the trinity is essential.

Moltmann

The most recent systematic treatment of the doctrine of the trinity is that of Jürgen Moltmann in his book *The Trinity and the Kingdom*.[15] He is critical of the two main trinitarian traditions in which God is understood as supreme substance and as absolute subject. In the latter he critcizes the modalist tradition from Augustine to Barth. He develops a view of the trinity based on the history of God in revelation which he calls a "social doctrine of the trinity." In affirming that the modern concept of person should be applied to ⌊the distinctions rather than to the unity of the godhead Moltman moves explicitly toward the Eastern view. (The feminist critique of male images for God will be taken up in the next chapter.)

Questions for Discussion

1. *"The doctrine of the trinity is a non-bibilical speculation, and therefore, according to the doctrine of the supremacy of Scripture it must be rejected." Discuss.*

2. *In the Bible the terms Father, Son, and Holy Spirit are ambiguous, overlap, and are used in different ways by different authors. On this kind of basis how can we claim that they are the distinctions in the godhead and that they are essential or immanent distinctions in the very being of God?*

3. *Why is not the biblical doctrine of the trinity (in so far as there is one) sufficient for the Christian faith and life? Why must it be interpreted in the terms of the fourth century or twentieth century metaphysics?*

4. *"The doctrine of the trinity may be one way of summarizing the early Christian experience, the ways in which we experience God, or the ways in which God reveals himself or is related to us, but one certainly cannot claim it to be asserting anything about the essential reality of God, for this is forever hidden from our finite minds in eternal mystery." Discuss.*

5. *"The Church's classical way of stating what is represented by the doctrine of the Trinity has in fact been a barrier with the well educated and the less educated alike. And it is not essential to the Christian Faith." (Pike) Discuss.*

6. *If Christ was God the Son, and if he prayed to God the Father, how can he be simply a "mode of being" of God?*

7. *In what respects could the doctrine of the trinity possibly be relevant to the Christian life? What is the significance of "relevance to the Christian life" for any particular doctrine?*

8. *Is the doctrine of the trinity a matter of knowledge of God (knowing God) or a matter of knowledge about God? Why?*

9. *Is not the doctrine of the trinity an excellent example of the weakness of the "supremacy of scripture" view of theological authority and an argument in favor of a "tradition" or "church" view of authority? Or is there a way nonetheless of defending the "supremacy of scripture" view of authority in relation to this doctrine without resorting to sophistry?*

10. *"The main trouble with the doctrine of the trinity is that it tends arbitrarily to force Christian thought about God into some sort of tri-partite mould. 'Unity in diversity and diversity in unity' would accomplish the goal of protecting a 'full,' and 'complex' concept of God without the unnecessary and unwarranted emphasis on the number 3." Discuss.*

11. *"The genius of the doctrine of the trinity is that it militates as much against polytheism as it does against vacuous monism. It stands within Christian tradition, therefore, as an essential synonym for the word 'God.' " Discuss.*

12. *"The doctrine of the trinity is the most fundamental thing we have to say about God in Christian theology." Do you agree or not? Why?*

13. *Is it necessary to believe the doctrine of the trinity in order to be a Christian?*

5

God

The doctrine of God has been at the center of theological debate in the second half of this century. Gilkey characterizes this debate as concerned with "the question of the reality of God and so of the possibility of meaningful language about him."[1]

The question of the doctrine of God has been raised in a number of ways in contemporary theology. Bultmann's interpretation of Christian faith has suggested that the reality of God is limited to the encounter with humanity, to the event of the proclamation of the Word, and that any confession of the reality of God outside this is an objectifying metaphysic untrue to Christian faith. H. Braun has carried this to the extreme and concluded that "God" is simply a term describing a determination of human existence, the whence of the encounter that liberates humanity, an aspect of humanity's self-understanding. He can state the New Testament message without using the term "God."[2]

Bishop Robinson, drawing on Bultmann, Bonhoeffer and especially Tillich in his book *Honest to God*, raised the question of the doctrine of God in a radical way, which will be discussed later. A. MacIntyre has concluded not only that Bishop Robinson is an atheist but also that contemporary Protestant theology is essentially atheistic.[3] Then there was the "death of God" theology, primarily an American phenomenon represented by T. Altizer, W. Hamilton, and P. Van Buren.[4] While Altizer's and Hamilton's views and their bases not very clear, Van Buren's were quite clear. He denied any meaning to the term "God" as a transcendent reality on the basis of a modified logical positivism.[5]

Process theologians influenced by the philosophy of A. N. Whitehead and C. Hartshorne have challenged the traditional doctrine of God as transcendent, omnipotent, immutable and impassible. They have proposed a new doctrine of God which stresses the divine immanence, the divine involvement in the world process, and the divine love as persuasive rather than coercive. Feminist and other liberation theologians have also criticized radically the traditional doctrine of God as patriarchal and oppressive. They have offered new approaches to the doctrine of God which emphasize feminine attributes and a divine relation to the world which involves a liberating partnership with humanity. These new approaches to the doctrine of God will be discussed further below.

Let us recall that the doctrine of God is entirely dependent upon what God is revealed to be, upon God's self-disclosure attested in the Bible. We have God, so to speak, only in divine revelation. It may be that on the basis of this revelation we may be able to perceive God's presence and activity throughout the creation and human experience, but this is secondary and dependent. To use the concept of contemporary existentialist philosophy, God is not *vorhanden,* simply at hand, at our disposal, like an object on the physical world. Rather we are at God's disposal, and we are given to know God only by grace in revelation, by God's meeting us through the testimony of Bible and church. This means that we do not have God in a way about which it is possible to be neutral and detached, but only in a way which determines our existence, only in faith.

Therefore theology oversteps its bounds if it attempts to consider God as a member of a class of divine supernatural beings from which various assertions follow on the basis of this class membership. But this does not mean that theological statements are limited to the ways in which God is "for us," to the ways in which God is related to us in revelation. For on the basis of the way in which God is for us, we are able to say something about God in the essential divine nature itself. That is, the way in which God is for us is based on the way in which God is in the divine self. Faithful testimony to God for us necessarily involves testimony to God in the divine nature itself. For the gospel is that *God* is for us in the way manifest in Christ. "God's outward action, towards his creatures, is anchored in his 'nature,' i.e., it is a manifestation of his own proper truth, it is his eternal will and not his passing fancy. . . . The identity between the revelation and the Revealer, between 'God for us' and 'God in himself,' is the nerve center of all confessing statements."[6]

We cannot discuss the history and meaning of each of the terms which has been applied to the nature and attributes of God. We can deal only with some of the main ones. Many of them overlap and can be subsumed under others. We have dealt with the nature of the unity of God under the doctrine of the trinity. The manner of God's immanence will be dealt with under the doctrine of providence. God's goodness can be subsumed under the divine love. God's righteousness and mercy will be dealt with under the doctrine of salvation.

The question of the divine nature and attributes is one of the main points at which the problem of the relation of theology and philosophy is raised. In this area there has always been a great deal of borrowing from the philosophical tradition. But on the other hand the theological tradition has always deeply influenced the philosophical tradition. Later Platonism and Aristotelianism were profoundly affected by Christian faith, and all of modern philosophy is dependent in varying degrees on Christian theology. As was suggested in connection with the doctrine of the trinity, the theological use of contemporary philosophy is a necessity in the mission of the church. The theologian should be completely free to use philosophical concepts and ideas. The criterion for judging this use will be only whether or not this use helps to clarify the meaning of the revelation of God attested in the Bible and thus to further the purposes of theology.

In the doctrine of the trinity we have already stated the most fundamental thing we have to say about the divine nature. What is said in this lecture will be dependent upon this. For example, we shall see that the being or nature of God as love is to be explicated in the light of the distinctions of Father, Son and Spirit.

A distinction can be seen in the Bible which was developed in the tradition of the church on the nature and attributes of God. (1) God is transcendent, holy, mysterious, absolute, infinite, self-existent, in complete independence of the creation. (2) God is creator, judge, redeemer, merciful, and related to the creation. Barth distinguishes these as the perfections of the divine freedom and the perfections of the divine loving. Other theologians have termed these the metaphysical and moral attributes of God, respectively. (1) is God in the divine self apart from any relation to the creation; (2) is God "for us," in relation to the creation. (At this point it is important to recall what was said about theological language on pp. 10-12.)

God as Spirit

In what way is God real? What kind of reality is God? These seem to be the most profound questions asked of Christian faith by the modern world. The modern world is so deeply influenced by the natural science approach to reality and by a naturalistic view of reality that it often cannot conceive of what Christians are talking about when they refer to God.

The fundamental answer of Christian faith to these questions is that God is spirit or spiritual reality. "God *is* spirit. This is the most embracing, direct, and unrestricted symbol for the divine life."[7] This is an analogy or symbol based on the spiritual character of human life. Spirit is that level or dimension of reality in the creation which takes up into itself all the other levels or dimensions of reality, such as matter and life. Tillich defines spirit as the unity of power and meaning which is manifest only on the human level. It does not stand in contrast to body, but includes body as its foundation. In the Bible spirit means the power of life and also the fulfillment of life and thus its goal or meaning. The level or dimension of spirit appears fully only in humanity, in freedom, self-transcendence, morality, rationality, creativity, selfhood or personhood. It should be noted, however, that the doctrine of God as spirit should not be confused with the doctrine of God the Holy Spirit. That God is spirit refers to all three "persons" of the trinity.

When the term spirit is applied analogically to God, it is these latter unique human functions which are emphasized. That is, God has no body. But this should not be understood to mean that God is the opposite of body or is antithetical to body or physical nature. On the contrary, God is the creator of the physical world, becomes incarnate in a human life, is manifest in the sacraments, and brings the whole creation to its fulfillment (the "resurrection of the body"). The Bible speaks of God's face, eyes, mouth, nose, ears, back, arm, hand, finger and feet. Biblical anthropomorphism understands God in the image of humanity, in so far as humanity is created in the image of God. Corresponding to man's flesh or body is God's glory. The visions of Ezekiel and others depict God's glory in terms of glowing fire, blinding light, or a burning stream. God's glory is understood to be the divine "garment." The fulfillment of this line of thought comes in the transfiguration of Jesus (which may be a reading back of a resurrection appearance) and in Paul's assertion that the glory of God is manifest in the face of Christ (2 Cor. 4:6). All this is simply to say that God as spirit comprehends and transcends the physical aspect of creation. God has no body, but the divine nature is not antithetical to body or physical nature.[8]

God as Living

An immediate implication of the above is that God is living, since spirit is the fulfillment of life. God is the living God in analogy to spiritual life or life on the human level. This is communicated in the Bible by a great variety of anthropomorphisms. God is depicted as deciding, planning, acting. Moreover God is affected by human response to the divine actions. God alters the divine activity in accordance with human actions. God withdraws and draws near. God even repents or changes the divine mind.

Spiritual life on the human level involves growth and fundamental change, but this aspect of life cannot be applied to God as living. God does not change and become something different; God is eternally the same. (See below.) But God's relation to the creation and especially to humanity changes. Various attempts have been made with the help of Hegelian or Whiteheadian philosophy to assert that God is becoming, growing, or involved in process. The theological issue involved here is that the Bible testifies to a God whose attitude of love toward humanity is unchanging, but who is affected by human responses to the divine action. These elements of unchangingness and change are often presented on the analogy of the love of a parent for a child. A decision on this question must be made on the basis of whether or not the theological explication illuminates fully both sides of the issue without sacrificing one to the other.

God as Personal

An immediate implication of the foregoing is that God is personal, since personhood or selfhood is involved in spiritual life or is identical with spiritual life looked at from one point of view. Nothing comes through more clearly in the Bible than the fact that God approaches humanity in a personal way in the divine words and acts. In revelation God confronts us as an "I." Brunner has pointed out that more than one thousand sentences of the Bible begin with the divine "I." The personal character of God is underlined by the ideas of the name and face of God. This personal approach of God to humanity culminates in the divine approach through the man Jesus (see pp. 29-31). But in this analogy elements of finiteness in human personhood such as birth and death cannot be applied to God. This raises the difficult problem of conceiving of non-finite or infinite personal reality. The only personal reality we know anything about directly is finite. Because of this difficulty some theologians have asserted that God is supra-personal. But others have responded that all concepts which are claimed to be supra-personal are in fact sub-personal or impersonal. "The personal way of speaking is unsurpassable for Christian talk of God. . . . There exists alongside the personal way of speaking only the impersonal and subpersonal way, but not a supra-personal one."[9]

The theological issue involved here is that God is self-revealed as personal, and yet God is not a finite object, limited by space and time, but rather non-finite or infinite. Thus any attempt to state the infinite personhood of God must not stress the infiniteness in such a way as to fall into sub-personal categories.

The concern to transcend the personal often derives from the presupposition that the more abstract a concept is, the more spiritual it is, and the more concrete or personal, the less spiritual. From the point of view of the Bible the opposite is the case, as we have seen above. The concrete, anthropomorphic, personal way of speaking about God is sometimes said to be primitive and naive, but it is the only way personal reality can be spoken about and it is therefore a necessity in our language about God.

If it is objected that the analogical application of the term personal to God is too anthropomorphic, it can be replied that the application of the term personal to humanity is too theomorphic. Only God is truly personal, truly free and responsible, whereas human beings are personal only by way of analogy to God's personhood. Our personhood is only a reflection or image of the divine personhood, and we come to realize our true personhood only through our relation to God.[10]

God as Lord

God is self-revealed as sovereign, free, independent and self-sufficient. The word in the Bible which unites all these meanings is "Lord." The phrases "I the Lord," and "I am the Lord" occur innumerable times in the Bible (see, for example, Ex. 20:2, Deut. 6:4, Isa. 43:11). It is used in the Bible as the proper name for Yahweh and for the risen Christ. On the human level lord means master, owner and ruler. Thus when applied to God it means that God is the absolute master of Israel and the church. God is revealed as the only one who can properly claim Israel's complete allegiance and loyalty.

God's lordship is not limited to Israel but includes all nations and their history and thus the whole world. Therefore God is the creator of the world. Moreover God has created freely and thus is not dependent upon the world. The essence of God's lordship is the divine freedom in relation to the world, and the fullness of the divine freedom is manifest in the divine freedom to be present in love and to forgive apart from the law. This God does through Christ, so Christ is called Lord. (See Ex. 33:19, Isa. 40:12f, 41:2f, 43:13, 45:7, 45:9f, Lk. 3:8, Rom. 3:21, 9:18f.)

Since God's lordship means the divine freedom in relation to the world, the divine self-sufficiency and independence of the world, many theologians, beginning with Anselm, have used the philosophical term *aseity* to express the fact that God stands *a se*, by or from the divine self, that God is self-derived. There is no matter or fate prior to God which conditions the divine freedom. It is in this sense that the term *absolute* is applied to God. But these philosophical terms stress the negative side of God's freedom, the divine freedom from all external conditions. The Bible, on the other hand, emphasizes the positive side of God's free lordship, namely, that God freely chooses to be with the creation in revelation and salvation.

Divine Hierarchy?

Feminist theologians have criticized the doctrine of God's lordship as patriarchal, hierarchical and oppressive. They have argued that the idea of divine lordship has always been used in Christian history to legitimate human patriarchy, hierarchy and oppression, and therefore that it can be seen as a projection of a male dominated society and culture. Feminist exegetes have argued that male images of God predominate in the Bible and that they need to be balanced and modified by attention to the female imagery of God which has usually been overlooked.[11] Feminist historians have argued that the doctrine of God as lord has caused male experience to be the norm of language, relationships and institutions and thus has perpetuated women's alienation from their true selves and denied them full humanity.

The main debate in feminist theology today is whether the Christian tradition can be reformed and its sexism overcome or whether it is irredeemably sexist and must be rejected. Rosemary Ruether represents the first point of view and Mary Daly the second.[12] Our task here is to inquire whether the doctrine of God as lord can be interpreted in such a way as to be a source not of oppression for women but of liberation and salvation.

If hierarchy is understood to be an order or rank based on power, authority, reality and value, then it is clear that in the Bible God as lord stands in a hierarchical relation to the world. As creator God has greater power and reality than the creature which is transitory (Ps. 103:14-17). As the only lord God has the authority to require complete loyalty and obedience over and above every other loyalty (Ex. 20:1-3, Deut. 6:4-5).

But God's hierarchical relation to the world is not one of domination, exploitation and oppression. Rather it is one of love, tenderness and longing for the salvation of the world which is fully and perfectly manifest in the love of Christ (Hos. 11:1-4, Jn. 3:16, Rom. 5:8, Eph. 2:4, 1 Jn. 4:7-10). In particular God's lordship and hierarchical relation to the world is manifest in the humility of Christ who took the form of a slave and humbled himself and was obedient unto death. And it is only for this reason that Christ is called lord (Phil. 2:5-11. See Mt. 11:29, 20:28, Mk. 10:45, 2 Cor. 8:9).

This kind of lordship and hierarchical relation to the world is not oppressive but liberating and is the judgment upon any and all oppressive hierarchical relations in the world. Any temporary functional human hierarchy in the world (parent-child, teacher-pupil, administrative or judicial) is to be for the sole purpose of loving service as modeled on the divine hierarchy. Thus oppressive human hierarchy is the result not of imitation of the divine hierarchy but of sin and can be redeemed only through the lordship of God in Christ.

God as Transcendent

One aspect of God's lordship is the divine transcendence. God is prior to, distinct from, and thus "beyond" the world. God is self-revealed as transcendent, and it is because God is transcendent that God must be revealed if the divine reality is to be known. The view of transcendence in the Bible combines both the ideas of distinctness and symbolic distance (see Isa 6:1 f, 40:22).

The problem of the transcendence of God is one of the most important questions in contemporary theology. The old spatial view of transcendence in the Ptolemaic view of the universe was fairly clear-cut. But Copernicus and Bruno ended all that for good, although before their time many Christian authors perceived the issue and prepared the way for the church's reception of the new cosmology. Copernicanism ended the possibility of interpreting God's transcendence in spatial terms, but it would seem that the church has never really come to terms with this. It is too easy to say that we no longer interpret the spatial symbols of transcendence literally but rather analogically. We have to specify what the symbols mean.

The liberal theologians did not really face this question because they emphasized the immanence of God and tended to water down the divine transcendence. But with the coming of Barth and his followers there was a renewed stress on the divine transcendence. Barth summarizes his early point of view as an emphasis on God as " 'wholly other' breaking in upon us 'perpendicularly from above,'" and on the " 'infinite qualitative distinction' between God and man.' "[13] But now the problem has arisen of the real meaning of this transcendence in the light of modern cosmology.

The problem of divine transcendence was also being raised in a new way by the followers of Bonhoeffer. Ronald Gregor Smith states, "The crucial problem for human life and thought is the problem of transcendence," and he calls for a "this-worldly transcendence."[14] It is the purpose of these theologians and also Tillich to criticize the neo-orthodox doctrine of transcendence, which Tillich calls supranaturalism, and to develop a new approach. Drawing on Tillich and Bonhoeffer, Bishop Robinson attempts to do just this in his book *Honest to God* (see below). He asserts, "The task is to validate the idea of transcendence for modern man."[15]

It is also the problem of divine transcendence which lies at the root of the challenge of analytical philosophy to theology. The linguistic analysts and logical empiricists claim not to be able to understand what transcendent reality or the transcendence of God can possibly mean. They can perhaps understand what a claim to religious experience might mean, but they cannot understand what it means to refer this experience to a transcendent cause. This is a sophisticated version of a widespread and pervasive naturalism, which is an aspect of the spirit of the age and which cannot conceive of transcendent reality.

The fundamental basis of the doctrine of the transcendence of God is the doctrine of creation (see chapter 6). God is revealed as transcendent because God is revealed as creator. God transcends the creation in the mode of the divine existence or reality. While the existence of the creation is dependent, contingent, temporal, and received from beyond itself, the existence or reality of God is independent, self-sufficient, eternal, and self-derived. As the scholastic theologians put it, the divine essence involves the divine existence. Furthermore, God transcends the creation in being distinct from it; God is not the essence of the creation. While the creation is dependent upon God, its essence is not identical with God but distinct. The creation has a limited measure of independence which has been given it by God. This latter point distinguishes the transcendence of God from monist views of the relation of God to the world.

Thus there is a fundamental duality in Christian faith between God and the world, a duality between creator and creature which cannot be transgressed. In almost every other religion and philosophy this distinction is either not made or is blurred so that there is some point of identity or a continuum between God and the world. Some aspect of the world, usually the human mind or spirit, is identified with the divine. But it is the uniqueness of the Christian view of divine transcendence that this distinction is never overcome. This radical doctrine of divine transcendence is the necessary presupposition for understanding the divine love as God's completely free decision to be with the creation.

If the doctrine of creation is the basis of the doctrine of transcendence, how is the latter to be understood, or what is the meaning of the old spatial imagery? The transcendence of God is best understood on the basis of what has been said above about God as spirit and as personal. That is, the best analogy for the transcendence of God is that of human personal self-transcendence. (This is the view of such diverse theologians as Bultmann, Farmer, R, Niebuhr, and Temple.) God transcends the creation in a way which is analogous to that in which persons or selves transcend their world, their environment, and also their bodies and their experience. "Man's inmost reality—his being a self or an 'I'—completely transcends not only the external world with which he is always inextricably involved, but also the inner world that is defined by his own subjective feelings and experiences."[16]

The self, person, or human spirit, lives in time and space, in nature and history, and yet transcends them. The self is not an object in time and space; it is not an object that can be discovered and examined by the scientist.[17] Hume denied to the self any empirical reality. The self is associated with a body, but it cannot be located in the brain. It is associated with a particular moment of time, but in remembering a past and foreseeing a future, it comprehends more than the moment and thus transcends the simple flux of time. The self seems to live in another dimension, and yet it is very much present in time and space.

Thus the transcendence of the self can be used as an analogy of the transcendence of God. As we have noted above, it is primarily on the analogy of a self or an "I" that God is understood in the Bible. Like the self God is not located in space and time, nature and history, and yet God is present in them.

Another analogy for the divine transcendence is that offered by Karl Heim, among others, namely, the analogy of dimensions or spaces. His suggestion is that God's relation to the world is analogous to that of a three-dimensional being to a two-dimensional world. God is not an object in our three-dimensional world and yet the divine presence impinges upon it at every point. We cannot conceive of the "space" in which God lives even as a two-dimensional being could not conceive of three-dimensional space. Heim elaborates this analogy in terms of the mathematical conception of multiple spaces.[18]

Honest to God

Bishop Robinson's main thesis in regard to the transcendence of God is as follows. When the Ptolemaic cosmology was overcome by the Copernican view, the spatial view of transcendence was interpreted by Christians in a symbolic sense. God was understood to be only metaphorically "up there." As this symbol gradually became less and less useful, there was substituted for it the concept of a God who is spiritually or metaphysically "out there." (There does not seem to be any essential difference, however, between the idea of a God "up there" understood symbolically and the idea of a God spiritually or metaphysically "out there." Robinson describes this as merely a "change in spatial metaphor," [p. 17]). Now, however, according to Robinson, this mental picture of a God "out there" is more of a stumbling block than an aid to faith, in fact "the greatest obstacle to an intelligent faith" (p. 43).

It is not clear whether his motive for seeking a new formulation is that the old one is no longer helpful or that it is simply untrue. He does state that "there is nothing intrinsically wrong with [the traditional view], any more than there was with the symbolism of a localized heaven" (p. 43, see p. 124). But the main thrust of the book seems to be that the idea of a God "out there" is wrong and untrue; he suggests that it is "a projection, an idol, that can and should be torn down" (p. 41, see p. 54).

While the transition from the God "up there" to the God "out there" was only a change in spatial metaphor, Robinson states that in the case of his approach "we are not dealing simply with a change of symbolism" (p. 46). It is not simply a change from a God "out there" to a God "down under."

But what it is a change to is not very clear, since he later states that "any alternative language—e.g. of depth—is bound to be equally symbolic" (p. 132).

His main theological assertion is that God is not a being, a person, or an entity at all, but the "infinite and inexhaustible depth and ground of all being" (p. 46). Robinson claims that this is not simply a change in symbolism, but it is clearly not the same symbolism, and he does not mean that he is going beyond symbolism to univocal statements. So he apparently means that he is attempting to transcend the traditional symbolism of God as a person. We have suggested above that this is impossible; that all concepts which claim to be supra-personal turn out to be subpersonal or impersonal. Robinson's effort seems to be an example of exactly this situation, for his formulations sound very similar to that of the absolute idealism in which the concept of personal God was denied.

Furthermore, the traditional symbolism of God as personal, when stated carefully, never implied that God is literally a finite person or entity. But the personal symbolism was essential for the reasons which have been discussed above. When the personal symbolism was "transcended," as in the case of the absolute idealism, the tendency was to undercut the personhood of God, the idea of God acting, the significance of personhood in humanity, and the doctrines of sin and creation. When we check Robinson at these key points, he seems always to fall back on the traditional personal symbolism in order to avoid the difficulties of impersonal concepts. For example, when he speaks about the doctrine of creation he has to assert that "it grounds all reality ultimately in personal freedom—in Love. . . . We are united to the source, sustainer and goal of our life in a relationship whose only analogy is that of *I* to *Thou*" (pp. 130f). It is difficult to see how he can make sense out of such personal freedom and personal relationships apart from personal symbolism. So at this crucial point for the doctrine of the divine transcendence Robinson seems to fall back on the traditional personal symbolism which he is claiming to transcend.

God as Holy

God is self-revealed as holy, as the holy one. In the Bible holiness is almost a synonym for deity; it is the essential deity or godness of God, so to speak, and is applied to other things only by derivation. Thus Tillich and Aulen hold that holiness is not a special attribute of God but that which qualifies all attributes or is the background of all the attributes. The first meaning of holy in the Bible is separate or distinct. God's holiness is, in the first instance, that which separates and distinguishes God from profanation by contact with anything else. Holiness is the unapproachable character of

God (see Ex. 19:21ff). Only God is essentially holy. Other things, persons, places, and acts may be called holy but only in a derived and secondary way, because they become the medium of God's revelation or action in the world.

This is the basis of the Christian denial of any essential cleavage between a sacred or holy sphere and a secular or profane sphere in the world. "Protestantism denies in principle the cleaveage between a sacred and a profane sphere. Since to it God alone is holy in himself and since no church, no doctrine, no saint, no institution, and no rite is holy in itself, every man and everything and every group is profane in itself and is sacred only in so far as it becomes a symbol of the divine holiness."[19]

Although the first element of holiness is one of separation and exclusion there is a second element which is outgoing and inclusive. In revealing the divine reality as holy, God offers us communion with the godhead, so that we too may become holy and that ultimately the whole creation will become holy or sanctified. In the vision of the Book of Revelation there will be no temple in the holy city, that is, no holy as distinguished from secular place, because the whole city will be sanctified by the presence of God (Rev. 21:22).

Thus God is the savior because God is holy (Hos. 11:9, Isa. 41:14, 43:3, 47:4). Because of the divine outgoing holiness, God makes Israel holy. God makes the church holy by the presence of the Holy Spirit. This is one way in which the Christian message can be stated: the *koinonia*, fellowship, or commonness of the Holy Spirit. That which belongs to God alone has become the common possession of all, the Holy Spirit who draws all people into communion with God.

There may be an early level of tradition in the Old Testament in which holiness has no moral connotations, but at an early stage it becomes identified with moral goodness, with love. God's holiness becomes the definition and determinant of what is morally good and right, what is demanded by God. Humanity is called to be absolutely determined by the holy will of God, to become holy as God is holy (Lev. 19:2, 1 Pet. 1:15f). The essence of all of Hebrew-Christian ethics is the nature of God received as a demand upon the life of humanity. Thus the highest moral calling of the Christian is imitation of the outgoing love of the holy God as it is manifest in Christ.

God as Love

God is self-revealed as love. God's love for humanity or Israel is not mentioned explicitly in the Old Testament before Hosea, but it is the clear implication of God's election, deliverance, covenant and providential care of Israel. It is described explicitly in Hosea on the analogy of parental and marital love (Hos. 2:19, 11:1, 14:4). God's love of Israel is not based on Israel's worthiness but upon the divine free decision (Deut. 7:7f).

God's self-revelation as loving comes to its fullness in the New Testament testimony, where the central message is that God's love is manifest in Christ (Rom. 5:8, Jn. 3:16, 1 Jn. 4:7ff). This testimony reaches its culmination in 1 Jn. 4:8, 16 in the assertion that "God is love." In context this is not the ascription of an abstract quality to God, but rather the definition of God in terms of the characteristic divine activity. Beyond this it means that all God's actions are the manifestations of the divine love.[20] God's love is the spontaneous, outgoing, total concern for the well-being of the creation and especially humanity which is manifest in the life, ministry, death, and resurrection of Christ and the gift of the Spirit. The order or pattern of the relations of Father, Son and Spirit constitute the basis of this outgoing love (p. 68).

Familiarity with the idea of God's love makes it easy to forget its uniqueness. God's revelation of the divine love for the world is "what no eye has seen, nor ear heard, nor the heart of man conceived," (1 Cor. 2:9) something absolutely new. Anders Nygren in his famous book *Agape and Eros* has contrasted the Christian and classical views of love and traced their history down through Luther. He makes the contrast rather too exclusive, and his work should be corrected somewhat by K. E. Kirk's *Vision of God*, (and vice versa).[21]

God's love as manifest in Christ is the final definition of the moral goodness which is demanded by God. It is the fundamental pattern for the Christian life in that Christians are called to imitate the love of God in Christ (Jn. 13:34).

God as Angry or Wrathful

God is self-revealed as capable of anger or wrath. Under the influence of the liberal theology it was common in the first quarter of this century to speak of the wrath of God as a primitive anthropomorphism which is found occasionally in the Old Testament but is replaced and superseded by the love of God in the New Testament. This was not only a distortion of the Bible but also a misunderstanding of the meaning of love and wrath. Throughout the Bible God's wrath or anger is the divine attitude toward sin. The Old Testament contains prophetic announcements of the wrath of God against the injustice and idolatry of Israel and the nations. This culminates in the coming "Day of the Lord" which will be a "Day of Wrath" or judgment upon sinners and sinful nations. The New Testament contains similar announcements of the wrath of God, both in the form of Jesus' condemnation of the Pharisees and in the form of apocalyptic announcements of the coming day of judgment.

All this testimony to the wrath of God, however, cannot be interpreted as being in contradiction to the love of God. In fact the wrath of God is simply the necessary correlate of the divine love. It is the way God's love appears when it meets sin. Luther called the wrath of God the strange work of divine love. Tillich asserts that it is "not the negation of love but rather the negation of the negation of love"[22] (see Amos 3:2). The wrath of God means that resistance to the love of God leads ultimately to self-destruction. God is long-suffering and shows forbearance but finally the divine love is not mocked (Gal. 6:7; see Heb. 10:30f, 12:29). To the sinner God's wrath often appears in the form of the divine law which condemns. This raises questions about the manifestation of the wrath of God in history and the final judgment which will be taken up in later chapters.

God as Eternal

God is self-revealed as eternal, as not limited by time. This is another aspect of God's transcendence (see above, pp. 85f). In the Bible this appears first as God's everlastingness. He is "before the mountains" and after them (Ps. 90:2ff). Cullmann believes that the Bible never gets beyond the idea that eternal means endless duration. But both in the Old Testament and the New Testament there are the beginnings of a qualitative distinction between time and God's eternity as a quality unique to God which is not simply everlastingness. It is the idea that God somehow comprehends or embraces all time, past, present and future.

The church soon had to come to terms with the Platonic idea of eternity as absolute timelessness. The danger here was that of making God's involvement in time into a problem rather than seeing it as the beginning point for the understanding of the relation of God and time. Augustine attempted to solve the problem by asserting that time is created by God (see p. 102). Thus God's eternity is the divine transcendence of time as the creator and lord of time. It is God's distinction from, freedom from, and sovereignty over the process of time. But this does not mean that God is unrelated to time, but rather it is the necessary basis for God's free involvement in time and human history. So God's eternity is neither absolute timelessness nor endless duration but rather the creator's transcendence of time which involves the divine power of embracing and being present in all periods of time.

The divine eternity also means that God is not a finite being which develops, changes, or becomes in time. As the medieval theologians put it, in God there is no distinction of potentiality and actuality; God is *actus purus,* pure actuality. This means that God is *immutable,* unchanging. But God's immutability cannot be interpreted to mean that God is not concerned with the creation, involved in time, and active in history. In the Bible God's unchangingness is the divine faithfulness, God's will to maintain the creation (Gen. 8:21), God's faithfulness to the covenant. What is unchanging is God's love, the divine will to save the creation and bring it to its fulfillment.

But this means that God is affected by the creation, by knowledge of it, by the divine concern and purpose for it, and especially by the freedom and sin of humanity. And this in turn means that God is not absolutely immutable. So any doctrine of the divine eternity must do justice to both God's unchanging will and purpose for the creation and God's involvement in its history. And the use of the philosophical concept of *actus purus* must be such as not to undercut the latter.

God as Immanent

God is self-revealed as immanent in the creation, as present in space and time, and as active in history. The purposive aspect of God's immanence will be considered in chapter 7 on providence. The mode of God's immanence by the Spirit has been outlined in chapter 4.

There is variety and development in the Bible in the understanding of how God is present. At first God is present only on Mt. Horeb or later in the Temple or in Heaven and is understood to come from there when God is present and active in other places. Later the divine presence is understood in the sense that it is impossible to be in any place where God is not, to escape God (see Ps. 139:7ff). Also there are various degrees or types of the presence of God all the way from the presence of the divine creative power which sustains the creation, through God's "coming" in word and act, in revelation, judgment and salvation, to the fullness of the divine presence in the end when humanity will see God "face to face." God varies the degree of the divine presence according to the divine will of love and purpose of salvation. Thus the Bible speaks of God as "coming" and "withdrawing." This depends in part upon Humanity, upon humanity's sin, repentance, and faith. In the case of sin God is said to hide the divine face, that is, to remove the divine gracious presence. This is God's judgment or wrath which is sometimes interpreted as the divine absence and sometimes as the destructive divine presence.

The Bible has various ways and concepts for describing the presence of God: the cloud, the ark, the temple, the glory, and the face of God. The fullness of this presence in history is in Jesus and by the Spirit (see 2 Cor. 4:6; also chapter 4).

In the theological tradition the tendency developed of interpreting im-manence or omnipresence as a logical implication of the philosophical con-cept of the absolute or the infinite. This implied that God's presence is constant and unvarying and that it is only our awareness of the divine presence which varies.[23] But this would seem to be primarily a mystical or philosophical rather than biblical idea.

God's transcendence is the theological presupposition of the divine im-manence. God's immanence is that of the God who is essentially transcen-dent, distinct from the creation as its creator and lord. God's immanence is therefore the freely chosen presence of the transcendent God and not some kind of necessary presence as would be the case if God were a world-soul. Furthermore, God is not immanent or present in such a way that the distinct reality and limited independence of the creature is undercut, which would be pantheism.

Other traditional attributes of God are closely related to the concept of immanence and draw out specific aspects or implications of this concept. The *omnipresence* of God means that there is no place from which God is absent, although God may vary the degree of the divine presence in any place. The *infinity* of God means both that God is not a finite object in space and time beside other objects and that no finite object or space or time can exclude the presence of God. Otherwise the existence of the finite would constitute a boundary of the infinite which would reduce the infinite to the finite. These are not biblical concepts, and their validity or usefulness depends upon whether or not they can be used fruitfully to draw out the implications of the biblical testimony to the nature of God.

Probably the best analogy for understanding and interpreting at least some aspects of the doctrine of God's immanence or presence is that of the presence of a human person. Persons are present to one another in varying degrees, from mere physical presence as on a subway to the full presence of personal communion (see pp. 20f). In the Christian life the meaning of the immanence or omnipresence of God is not only that we cannot escape God but also that there is no place in which we are of necessity lost from God.

God as Almighty

God is self-revealed as almighty, as able to carry out the divine will and fulfill the divine purposes. God's almightiness or omnipotence is one aspect of the divine lordship. (See pp. 82f. The way in which God's omnipotence is carried out is treated in chapter 7 among others.) In the Bible God's power is manifest in creation and in sustaining the creation, in judgment and deliverance of the people of God, and in the signs and wonders accompanying this. This is seen in Yahweh's title, *sabbaoth*, "God of hosts," which refers to the divine power in history. Another title, *el shaddai,* came to be translated "God Almighty" in the Septuagint, New Testament and English versions.

In the Bible the divine almightiness means that God has complete and sovereign power over the creation. Scholastic theology raised questions as to whether or not this meant that God could do what was logically impossible, and so forth, but the Bible is only concerned to affirm that God can do what God wills to do. Also God's omnipotence does not mean that all manifestations of power of any kind are directly that of God.There are creaturely powers, physical, biological and spiritual (both good and evil) which are provisionally independent of God. They are ultimately but not immediately dependent upon God. This applies especially to human freedom. In other words God wills in the divine love to give to the creation a relative independence in regard to power. Thus God is not the immediate and direct cause of all events in the creation including sin. (The possibility of God's being the immediate cause of some events will be discussed in chapter 7.)

The biblical testimony sees the clearest manifestation of God's omnipotence in salvation (Mt. 19:25f). This appears in God's power to use human sin in fulfilling the divine will to save (see Gen. 50:20, Acts 2:23f). Thus the perfection of God's almightiness is manifest in the weakness of the cross (2 Cor. 12:9f).[24]

God as Being

The Pre-Socratic philosophers invented the concept of being which is one of the most fundamental concepts of metaphysics or ontology. It can be defined as the a priori condition that there may be anything whatsoever. The early Greek authors of the church identified being with God. They were followed in this by Augustine and Aquinas. The Reformers and Pascal rejected this identification as speculation. It has always been maintained by Thomists and has been revived for Protestant theology in this century by Tillich and Macquarrie.

Barth, Brunner, R. Niebuhr, L. Dewart, and others have argued that the identification of God and being is Neo-Platonist speculative metaphysics and not the biblical revelation. They claim that it makes God into an impersonal abstraction. The process theologians have criticized this identification, because it implies that God is absolutely changeless and unrelated to the world. The theologians who assert the identity of God and being reply that the only alternative is to assert that God is *a* being beside others and thus finite and transcended by being itself.

All language we apply to God is analogical and not univocal. Thus the assertions that God is being itself and that God is *a* being are both analogical assertions. The biblical symbols point in the direction of interpreting God as *a* being. Even Tillich's equation of "being itself" with the "power of being" and the "ground of being" can be interpreted as pointing to the creative and sustaining activity of God understood as *a* being.

It would seem that it is easier to deal with the problems involved in calling God *a* being than with the problems involved in calling God being itself. But if we decide for this view, we must be careful to make it clear that God is not finite.[25]

Process Theology

Process theologians have been especially critical of the traditional doctrines of the lordship, transcendence, eternity, omnipotence and immutability of God. Employing the philosophies of Whitehead and Hartshorne they have developed a complex metaphysical doctrine of God in which these attributes are modified and often transformed. As against the lordship and transcendence of God the process theologians argue that God is completely correlated with and thus dependent upon the world. As against the eternity and immutability of God they argue that God, at least in the concrete or consequent divine nature as distinct from the abstract or primordial nature, is completely temporal, relative and constantly developing. As against the omnipotence of God they argue that God's power is entirely persuasive through the offering of an initial aim to each emergent event or actual occasion which may accept this initial aim in varying degrees.

Process theology has developed rich resources for explicating various aspects of the doctrine of God, and especially the activity of God in the world (see Chapter 7).[26] Its major limitation at this stage seems to be its inability to interpret the doctrines of divine transcendence and creation in a way which is coherent with the Bible. William Temple made use of many of the ideas of Whitehead in the development of his dialectical realism in the Gifford Lectures, but he finally had to part with Whitehead over the issue of divine transcendence.[27]

Questions for Discussion

1. *How would you go about deciding whether or not God exists or is real? Is your method one belonging to theology or philosophy? Why?*
2. *What kind of reality is God? How the divine reality like and unlike other kinds of reality?*
3. *Prayer is entering into a personal relation with God, talking with God. But we can*

have a personal relation only with another person. So if prayer is possible, God must be a person. But if God were a person, God would be a finite object in time and space, and thus limited, conditioned and dependent. But then God would not be God. Therefore God is not a person. So how is prayer possible?

4. *"Christians talk about the existence of reality of God. Now the only valid way to ascertain what is real is the way of science. But science has found no evidence of God. So how can Christians say that God is real?" Discuss.*

5. *"Talk about transcendent reality (God) makes absolutely no sense to modern, secular, empirical humanity. Furthermore, Christian faith can be interpreted successfully without any reference to such a 'God.'(Hare, Miles, Braithwaite, Van Buren). So let's have a modern interpretation of Christian faith without God." Discuss.*

6. *Has the doctrine of God always been interpreted in the terms of the contemporary philosophy? Why? Is that necessary today? If not, why not?*

7. *Does the statement "God is love" say more than the statements "God loves" or "God is loving?" If so, what? If not, why should "love" be given as an attribute of God?*

8. *What does it mean to say that God is being itself? Is this theological assertion about God valid or invalid? Why?*

9. *What is God's relation to time? Is God temporal in any sense?*

10. *How is God present or immanent in the world without being observable by scientific method?*

11. *Is God male, female, neuter, or trans-sexual? Why?*

12. *"If God is infinite, there is nothing which limits God, because this would make God finite. But the creature is not God and thus limits God. Therefore God is not infinite but finite." Discuss.*

13. *"The hierarchical view of God's relation to this world is a projection of hierarchical relations in the world and serves to legitimate them." Discuss.*

14. *How can God be personal and also infinite and omnipresent?*

6

Creation

The doctrine of creation is fundamental for everything that follows in Christian theology. It is the basic assertion about the relation of God to the world, and about humanity and the world, namely, that they are creatures. It is the theological presupposition of the Christian affirmations about the incarnation, salvation and eschatology. It is also, incidentally, the basis of the unique Western attitude toward the world which is at the foundation of modern science, technology, and secularism.

We know that God is creator only through revelation, the special revelation attested in the Bible, and not by reason by science. The arguments of natural theology which claim to demonstrate that God is creator conclude with the doctrine of creation only if they are guided by Christian faith. When they are not, they usually end up with deism or pantheism or emanationism. The approximations to the doctrine of creation in non-Christian religions and philosophies can be understood on the basis of the doctrine of general revelation.

Bible

God's lordship includes God's being creator. That is, because God is Lord, if there is anything distinct from God, then God must be its absolute origin and it must be absolutely dependent upon. Thus it was after God was revealed to Israel as the universal Lord of history and nations and nature, that God came to be known clearly and explicitly as creator, as the absolute origin and sustainer of the world. In the Bible the idea of creation is tied in closely with the covenant; it is the beginning of the unfolding of the divine purpose manifest in the covenant.

The main reference to creation before the prophets is the story in Gen. 2:4bff. Here God forms the world out of a primeval chaos. It is the transformation of ancient Near-Eastern mythologies in such a way that the lordship of God appears. The full and clear testimony to God as creator comes in Second Isaiah and in the documents dependent upon it. Here in many passages the absolute sovereignty of God and the dependence of the creature are attested. This is put in narrative form in the P account in Gen. 1 and 2. In this story and in the other later accounts God creates through the divine Word which is God's act or command which accomplishes the divine will (Ps. 33:6, 9). In the Wisdom literature the instrument or agent through whom God creates is the divine Wisdom (Prov. 8:27, 29 f; Wisdom 7:22, 9:1, 9).

This understanding of creation is assumed by Jesus and the New Testament authors. But the later authors go on to interpret creation christologically. On the basis of the Old Testament testimony to the word and Wisdom of God as the divine instrument in creation, these authors identify Christ as the agent in creation (1 Cor. 8:6, Col. 1:16, Heb. 1:2, Jn. 1:3; see pp. 70). The fundamental meaning of this is that in Christ is manifest the meaning of God's plan or purpose which began to unfold in the act of creation (Eph. 1:9f, Col. 1:16). History from beginning to end is under the sovereign purpose of God as revealed in Christ. Salvation is the fulfillment of creation and not an escape trom the creation. In Christ humanity meets the one who is the essential meaning and structure of its created nature. The basic message of the New Testament is that the redeemer is the creator. Gilkey describes this as "the most fundamental affirmation of the Old and New Testaments," "the heart of the theological battles of the early church," "the dominant concern of the whole Christological controversy of the fifth century." "The identity of God the Creator and God the Redeemer, of the almighty power of existence with the love of Christ, is the theological axis of the Gospel of good news."[1]

Creatio ex Nihilo

The doctrine of creation is that the universe of space, time, energy, matter, life, and humanity is absolutely and solely dependent upon the free and sovereign will of God. Creation is an act of the divine freedom. It is not necessary for God to create in the sense of something external to God determining the divine action. God wills or chooses to create on the analogy of the free historical decision of a person.

The freedom of the divine creativity has traditionally been expressed in the doctrine of *creatio ex nihilo*, creation out of nothing. Although this is the implication of the sovereign lordship of God in the developed doctrine of creation in the Old Testament. (See Isa. 45:7.) It is stated explicitly only in the intertestamental period (2 Macc. 7:28) and in the New Testament (Rom. 4:17, Heb. 11:3).

This doctrine was formulated by the church to distinguish the Christian view of creation from other interpretations which endangered the fundamental meaning of the Christian view. It was formulated primarily against the *dualist* view which was very common in the Hellenistic world. Dualism asserts that there are two primary, equal, and eternal principles or realities, namely, the principle of structure or meaning usually called the forms or ideas, and the passive material principle which receives its form from the other principle. Here creation is understood on the analogy of human creation or fashioning out of some given material.

Christians realized that this view contradicted two of their basic beliefs about the relation of God to the world. First, it contradicted the biblical testimony to God as sovereign lord of all reality by asserting that God is only one of two primary and fundamental principles of reality, both of which are self-sufficient and eternal. Thus in a dualistic view God is always finite and limited by the other principle and therefore not sovereign lord. Tertullian wrote, "(God) could not have been the Lord of a substance which was co-equal with himself."[2]

Secondly, a dualism in which one principle is divine and the other is not always tends to become a moral dualism in which all good comes from the divine principle and all evil from the other principle. Thus in later Hellenistic thought the material principle came to be understood as the source of all evil. Furthermore, such evil is necessary, inevitable, eternal and irredeemable. This leads to a passive attitude toward it and to a meaningless or pessimistic view of history, such as we find in Celsus.[3] So for these two reasons the early Christians formulated the doctrine of creation in distinction from dualism by asserting creation out of nothing. By this they denied that there was any primary, eternal principle beside God out of which God created the world.

But in denying dualism the church was also asserting something positive. First, God is the sole source of all existence or reality; every aspect of reality is dependent upon God. Secondly, nothing is essentially or intrinsically evil. Nothing in the material, dynamic, or structural aspects of reality is evil. Therefore, everything is essentially good, although it may be existentially disrupted and evil. Thus everything which is evil is redeemable. Thirdly, creation is not like human creation but is a completely unique act of absolute origination, in which there is no presupposed material, in which finite reality comes into being "out of nothing."

But the doctrine of creation out of nothing was also formulated against the *monist* or *pantheist* view of creation. Monism asserts that the creation is made not out of pre-existent matter nor out of nothing but out of God. Here creation is understood as generation on the analogy of reproduction in animals, or as water from a fountain or the emission of light from a candle. Again this view of creation contradicted certain basic Christian convictions about God and the world. First, it implied that humanity is essentially divine or contained a divine principle. Thus a person cannot really be a sinner but only perhaps ignorant of the good and the true because of involvement in lower levels of being. Secondly, this view tends toward the idea that all finite existence is illusory and evil. This tendency follows from the idea in monism that the reality and value of individual finite things consists in the degree to which they are united with or identical with God. What is not God is neither good nor real. But the more things are considered in their finitude and individuality, the more they are distinct from God who is one and infinite. Thus finite things tend to be considered to be essentially fallen from perfection into evil and unreality, and salvation comes to be understood in terms of the loss of individuality and finitude.

Because of these tendencies the church asserted against monism the doctrine of creation not out of God but out of nothing. *"Non de deo, sed ex nihilo"* (Augustine). This again involved certain positive affirmations. First, creatures are not essentially evil or illusory in their finite individuality. Rather they are solidly real and essentially good as creatures to whom God has freely given a limited independence of existence. In humanity this relative independence includes freedom over against God, which however is ultimately dependent upon God for its reality. Secondly, finite individuality is not essentially evil and therefore can be redeemed from sin, and its salvation does not involve the loss of its individuality.

It follows, therefore, that creation is not like the generation or emanation which we know of in this world but again is an absolutely unique act for which there is no very good analogy. Recently an attempt has been made to interpret the act of creation on the analogy of suicide. All persons have their own unique worlds which are constituted by their own perceptions and feeling response to their environment. When a person dies this particular world disappears into absolute nothingness. When this person's death occurs as the result of a free act in suicide, we have the free and absolute negation of a world. This is an analogy of the free absolute origination in God's creation of the world.[4]

Although there is no very good analogy to explain the "how" of creation, there is a good analogy for the "why" of creation. This is the analogy of human freedom, deliberation, purpose and action. Knowledge of the freedom and purpose of a human action gives it meaning; we understand why it was done. Thus God's creation of the world is like a free human purposeful action. And God's purpose in creation is simply the divine will to express the divine love and goodness by giving reality to the creation. Calvin states, "There was no other cause why He should make all things, neither can He be moved by any other reason to conserve them, than for his only goodness."[5]

Creation and Science

The doctrine of creation is not a scientific theory of how the world came into being. It is not a description of an "event" which took place 4,000 years ago or twenty billion years ago. The confusion arises because both theology and science seem to be talking about the "origin" of the universe. The point is that the word "origin" is ambiguous. It can mean the natural conditions or causes which preceded a particular event or situation, or it can mean the ultimate source of an event or of the whole context of all events. When scientists talk about the origin of the universe they are referring to the earliest state of affairs they can describe in the history of the universe, such as the vast closely packed mass of neutrons in the "big bang" theory. They are attempting to describe the earliest set of conditions in the space-time-energy system of the universe as we know it. But when theologians speak of the origin of the universe, they are talking about its ultimate origin, namely, about the question as to why there ever was a mass of neutrons or the whole space-time-energy system in the first place. They are speaking to the question of why there is a universe at all and not simply nothing.

Scientific theories are not concerned with the question of what "preceded" the space-time-energy system of the universe. They are not concerned with the question of ultimate origin, the question of that upon which the whole universe is dependent. This is not the kind or order or level of question which science is concerned to ask or which it could ever answer by its methods. But this is exactly the question with which theology is concerned and which it intends to answer in the doctrine of creation. And its answer is that the universe is not self-existent, that it does not exist of itself without any reason or purpose, but that it exists because God wills that it should exist, and that therefore everything in the universe including the whole space-time-energy system itself is dependent upon God.

It has sometimes been suggested that the "big bang" theory of the origin of the universe supports the Christian doctrine of creation, whereas the "steady state" theory, that the universe has always existed in the form we know it today, undercuts or disproves it. The reason given is that the "big bang" theory implies that the universe had a beginning in time while the "steady state" theory does not.[6] But the Christian doctrine of creation does not necessarily mean that the universe had a beginning in time or a finite number of years ago (see below). And the "big bang" theory is now often interpreted to mean that the universe goes through successive cycles of explosion, expansion and contraction.

But the fundamental point is that proper scientific statements or theories cannot conflict with or support proper theological statements and vice versa, because they are of a different order or on different levels (see pp. 6f).

Creation and Time

This raises the question of the relation of creation to time. Did the creation of the universe occur at a particular time in the past, or did it occur at the beginning of time, or is the universe infinite in time? The traditional theological answer to this question since Augustine has been that time was created with the world so that creation did not begin in time but at the beginning of time. This means that the universe had a beginning a finite number of years ago.

But as a result of the revolution in the understanding of God's revelation which took place at the hands of the historical critical study of the Bible, it became clear that theology does not include scientific or cosmological assertions. Now the idea of a beginning of the universe in time seems to be a scientific statement, or at least the description of the first moment of time would be a scientific task. So contemporary theologians are divided over the question of whether or not the doctrine of creation necessarily involves the assertion that the universe had a beginning in or with time a finite number of years ago. William Temple states:

> It is not of direct importance to Religion to assert a date for the act of creation, or even to assert that it is an act having any date at all; it may be a never-beginning and never-ending activity.[7]

Gilkey agrees:

> Theology could not include such a concept [of an absolute beginning of process]. The first moment of time, if there was such a moment, is a cosmological fact about the natural world. Therefore, only if revelation and religious truth inform us of cosmology, of the size, form, and age of the universe, could Christians possess this sort of knowledge through the means of their faith.[8]

He points out that Aquinas, for example, could assert that theology can inform us about this, only because he affirmed a propositional revelation.

On the other hand Barth, Brunner, and apparently Tillich and Kaufman assert that the doctrine of creation does involve the absolute beginning of time in creation a finite length of time ago. They argue that anything else would involve a universe coeternal with God. But the denial of creation a finite length of time ago would seem to mean that the universe is unlimited or infinite in time. This is something quite different from being eternal, which means transcending and comprehending time. It may be, however, that the beginning of the universe in time is the best symbol for asserting that it is ultimately dependent upon God.

Continuing Creation

If creation were understood to be only an event of the past, this would approach *deism*. This is the view that God created the world in the beginning but that God does not have to sustain it, guide it, or intervene in it. God is the cosmic watchmaker who made the watch and wound it up, and now it runs independently. As against deism traditional theology has always affirmed God's continuing creation of the world, the divine preservation of the world or sustaining creativity (Tillich).

The doctrine of creation does not mean simply that God originated the world but that the world in every moment is absolutely dependent upon God for its existence, that God in every moment preserves or sustains the world in being. This is what it means to be a creature, to be a contingent or dependent being.

The traditional view before Darwin was that God created all the forms of life including humanity at the very beginning and that they have remained fixed since then. With the demonstration of the validity of the theory of evolution it became clear that the above assertion was an (incorrect) scientific rather than theological one. Then the evolution of the forms of life was interpreted as the result of the providential plan and guidance of God, an aspect of the divine continuing creation. (The "how" of providence will be taken up in the next lecture.) The current debate on creationism is an example of the failure to understand this point. The creationists who argue that the world came into being in its present form are simply biblical literalists who are trying to promote their views as better science than evolutionary theory. Therefore creationism has the form of an (erroneous) scientific statement and is thus not a theological statement at all.

In what sense then are individual persons creations of God and not simply the result of the biological reproduction of their parents? The traditional view is that each individual soul is created out of nothing by God and implanted in the body at conception (*creationism*). This doctrine was formulated in opposition to *traducianism*, the view that the soul is not newly created in each person but is generated by the union of the parents (see chapter 9). The testimony of the Bible seems to be that the individual person is both the product of the parents and the new creation of God at the same time without any distinction implying that the body comes from the parents and the soul from God. (See Gen. 17:6, 21:1f, 25:21, 30:22f, Ps. 139:13-16.) But many problems remain. What does it mean to say that a particular event is at the same time a biological process and also an act of God? Is the emergence of a unique self to be attributed more to the divine activity than to a psychobiological process? One aspect of these questions will be taken up in the next chapter.

Goodness of Creation

Another element of the doctrine of creation which was mentioned in connection with the denial of dualism is that the creation is good, that finite existence is essentially good, even if existentially evil (Gen. 1:31, 1 Tim. 4:4). Now goodness is usually ascribed to the will, to intentions, or to acts. What does it mean when applied to the creation? In the Bible the goodness of creation refers to the fact that it is the result of the loving will of God, to its reliable order and harmony, to the fact that it reflects God's glory, and that it is to be rejoiced in. The goodness of creation also means that human existence has meaning and is not simply a meaningless accident, that evil is not essential, necessary, inevitable, or irredeemable, but rather a disruption, an intruder, which can be overcome or redeemed. Finally, the goodness of creation means that the created order is intelligible and thus can be known and understood and used by humanity.

Note on Existentialist Theology

Contemporary existentialist theology has a particular approach to the doctrine of creation which has a strong hold on one element of the biblical testimony but seems to ignore others. Its main thesis is that the doctrine of creation is not primarily about the origin of the world or humanity but rather the expression of a particular interpretation of human existence. This interpretation is that human being is entirely contingent, constantly threatened by nothingness, and completely subject to a power which lies beyond it, that is, God. It stresses the transcendence of humanity in relation to the world and asserts that humanity is not a part of the world process, that our existence is not derived from the cosmos, and that we are not at home in the world.[9]

This approach to the doctrine of creation is an explication of the biblical testimony that God is Lord and that humanity is dependent upon God for its being. But it seems to ignore the biblical testimony that the world is also dependent upon God, and that humanity is embedded in nature, made from the "dust of the ground," and essentially a living body. Thus existentialist theology belongs to the Platonic-Augustinian tradition of theology which has been primarily concerned with humanity rather than with the world and has been uneasy about human involvement in the physical world.[10]

The Modern World

Many contemporary theologians and historians are pointing out that the Christian doctrine of creation is one of the main sources of the typical modern Western attitude toward the physical world as exemplified particularly in modern science. They argue that as against classical, Hellenistic and medieval attitudes toward nature the Christian attitude as manifest in the doctrine of creation (as well as incarnation and salvation) is positive and affirmative and sees nature as neither illusory nor evil nor divine but as creature. The impact of this attitude upon Western culture appears in the modern sense of being at home in the world, in the naturalism of Renaissance art, and in the rise of modern science.

In particular many historians of science are beginning to see that one of the main reasons for the rise of modern science was the impact of the Christian doctrine of creation upon the tradition of Greek science which reigned in the Middle Ages. This impact took two forms. First of all, the doctrine of creation secularized the world. The pagan and Hellenistic attitude toward nature had tended to see it either as quasidivine or as inhabited by and under the control of divine or demonic powers. As against this the doctrine of creation asserted that the whole world is simply creature and under the ultimate sovereignty of God the creator. This opened the way for people to exercise their dominion over the creation to which they are called in the Christian dispensation. It opened the way for the investigation and transformation of nature in modern science and technology.

Secondly, the doctrine of creation implies that the details of the structure and processes of nature can be known only by observation, by an empirical approach rather than by a deductive approach alone. If the world is a creature, the product of God's free act, then its actual structure is contingent upon the divine will and cannot be known by deduction from first principles but only by observation. By contrast the tradition of Greek science followed a generally deductive approach. Starting from general principles one should be able to infer how all the details of the world are ordered. But the key to modern science is the combination of the deductive and inductive approaches, the mathematical and the empirical methods. Thus the historians argue that modern science was able to arise only through the impact of the doctrine of creation upon the tradition of Greek science.[11]

Ecology

Lynn White has argued in a well-known essay that Christianity bears "a huge burden of guilt" for the global ecological crisis, because it has taught that humanity is to have dominion over the rest of the creation, that the only purpose of the creation is to serve the purposes of humanity, and that "it is God's will that man exploit nature for his proper ends." [12]

I would argue that the fault lies not in Christian faith but in human sin and its distortion of Christian faith. The testimony of the Bible is that humanity is called to be God's gardener and obedient agent in caring for the creation to promote the well-being of the creation and of humanity under God (Gen. 2:15, Lev. 25:1-5, Deut. 22:6, 25:4). "Dominion" in Genesis 1:26, 28 means this rather than greedy exploitation and despoiling of the creation. The rest of the creation fulfills the divine purpose of manifesting and praising God and mutual service (plants for animals, Gen. 1:30) as well as the service of humanity, which is thus not its only purpose.

We have noted above that it was Christian faith which made possible the rise of modern science and technology. But the arrogant exploitation of the creation by humanity through technology is not the purpose of the creator but rather the prideful pretension of sinful humanity which rebels against the divine command and attempts to make itself "like God" (Gen. 3:5). Humanity can be satisfied and fulfilled only in communion with and obedience to God, but in its sinful bindness humanity attempts to satisfy this infinite desire for God in the finite creation resulting in a world voracity or conscupiscence which is never satisfied.

Another response to the ecological crisis has been to turn away from the biblical secularization of nature and to return to a pagan romantic pantheism in which the creation is resacralized and even divinized. It is argued that this will restore the mystery, wonder and terror of nature and thus overcome the exploitation of it. Needless to say, this way is not open to the biblical Christian tradition. Christian faith sees the beauty, richness, mystery and dignity of the creation in its creatureliness and not in its being divine or quasi-divine.

Questions for Discussion

1. *Both Christian faith and modern science have theories of the origin of the universe, and these theories are contradictory. So how can a modern person believe in creation?*

2. *Why did God create the world? If it was out of need for an object of the divine love, then God is not perfect. If it was a purely an arbitrary act or the result of whim, then the existence of the creation would be irrational and have no meaning.*

3. *What is the relation of the following phrases in the Nicene Creed: "maker of heaven and earth," and "through whom all things were made?"*

4. Is the idea of creation as an event a finite number of years ago essential to the doctrine of creation or is it not essential? Why?

5. "The doctrine of creation means that my existence is absolutely dependent upon the will of God. It says nothing about the origin of the universe." (paraphrase of Bultmann). Discuss.

6. What are the implications of the doctrine of creation for the Christian life?

7. "There is evil within the created order. God is the source of the created order. Therefore either God is good but not omnipotent or God is omnipotent but not good." Discuss.

8. What are the ethical implications of the doctrine of creation? What does it mean to say that creation is good?

9. Bertrand Russell: "That Man is the product of causes which had no prevision of the end they were achieving; that his origin, his growth, his hopes and fears, his loves and his beliefs, are but the outcome of accidental collections of atoms; that no fire, no heroism, no intensity of thought and feeling, can preserve an individual life beyond the grave; that all the labours of the ages, all the devotion, all the inspiration, all the noonday brightness of human genius, are destined to extinction in the vast death of the solar system, and that the whole temple of Man's achievement must inevitably be buried beneath the debris of a universe in ruins— all these things, if not quite beyond dispute, are yet so nearly certain, that no philosophy which rejects them can hope to stand." On the basis of the Christian doctrine of creation, what would your response be to Mr. Russell?

10. What are the implications of the doctrine of creation for the relation of humanity to nature? Do they offer any insights on the problems of ecology which would not be perceived by an agnostic ecologist?

11. Does Christianity bear "a huge burden of guilt" for the global ecological crisis?

7

Providence

The aspect of the doctrine of creation referred to as God's sustaining or preserving of the world leads directly to the doctrine of providence. The divine preservation is often considered the first aspect of the doctrine of providence. The doctrine of providence is sometimes interpreted broadly to include all aspects of God's relation to the world, such as election, predestination, salvation, history and eschatology, all of which will be considered in later chapters. This chapter will deal with the doctrine in the narrower sense of the general aspects of God's present relation to the world.

The doctrine of providence is unique in being at the same time one of the simplest and also one of the most obscure elements of Christian faith. Its central assertion is one of the most primary affirmations of faith, and yet so many complex problems surround it that it turns out to be one of the most difficult to understand. The difficulties derive from the fact that it is the doctrine which asserts most comprehensively God's present relation to the world. D. Baillie suggests that we fall into paradox whenever we introduce God as the ultimate source of anything in our experience.[1]

Put most simply the doctrine of providence asserts that God is self-revealed as the one who is in control of the world and the course of history and who wills to bring the creation, and especially each human person, to its fulfillment. Thus the doctrine of providence is a combination of the lordship and the love of God. God is revealed as lord of the creation and of history, and also as loving the creation and willing its fulfillment. Because God is Lord, God can carry out the divine will of love in history.

Specific words for providence are not important in the Bible, but the idea of God's providence, both in the sense of God's controlling and guiding of history toward its fulfillment and in the sense of the divine concern and care for the individual, are affirmed throughout the Bible. (For the latter point, see, for example, Ps. 23, Mt. 6:25-34, 10:29, Rom. 8:28-39.) These two aspects of the doctrine can be called historical and indvidual providence. The traditional concepts of general and special providence refer to a somewhat different distinction, namely, God goodness as manifest in the orderly processes of nature and God's special care for individuals which may involve miracles.

The doctrine of providence has been an issue off and on in the history of Christian thought especially in connection with the question of how God acts on the human will. The Thomists and the Calvinists emphasized the direct action of God on the will, and the Molinists and Arminians stressed the freedom of the will in relation to the divine influence. This issue will be discussed below. There is nothing explicit about the doctrine of providence in the creeds or the Anglican formularies, but there are several references to providence (preservation, governance, guidance, blessings) in the prayers of *The Book of Common Prayer*.[2]

The doctrine of providence was central in the liberal theology of the last century. But with the exception of Barth[3] it is notable mainly by its absence from contemporary theology. Gilkey argues that the reasons for this are the breakdown of liberal theology, the contemporary sense of the meaninglessness of history, the existentialist tendency to limit the lordship of God to the inner self, the modern emphasis on human freedom and the autonomy of nature, and the resulting tendency to limit theology to the articulation of the inward relation to God. Gilkey sees the doctrine of providence as one of the major tasks before contemporary theology.[4]

Human Freedom

The doctrine of providence bristles with difficulties, and the analysis of them will help to clarify the meaning of the doctrine itself. The first difficulty can be stated as follows: How is God's lordship and control of history and events compatible with human freedom and responsibility? This was known traditionally as the problem of the divine *concursus* or concurrence, that is, the way in which God's will and action are related to the actions of the creatures. The spectrum of answers to this question runs from the Calvinists who identified the activities of the creatures with the actions of God, through the Thomists who asserted that God's actions concur with those of the creatures, to the Arminians who affirmed that God's action assists or directly influences but does not determine the human will.

Under the doctrine of creation it has been suggested that God is self-limited to provide a provisional independence for the creation, which in humanity takes the form of freedom. In the chapters on humanity and sin it will be asserted that God does not infringe upon human freedom in any way, and that God does not will our sin but can overrule it and use it in the fulfillment of the divine purposes (see Gen. 50:20, Acts. 2:23). But if human freedom is not infringed, how is God lordship in fact exerted and carried out in the realm of human decision? One difficulty in the traditional debates was that the model used was often a mechanical one. The influence of grace and the human will were interpreted on the analogy of physical forces. When this is the case, the problem is insoluble; it is either grace or freedom or a mixture which determines an act. When the model or analogy is that a human personal relations, however, the difficulties can be overcome. The influence of a great and good person upon another person can be exerted in such a way that the freedom of the latter is not overridde but rather enhanced. Thus there is no necessary contradiction between the influence of grace and human freedom. This problem will be analyzed further in the chapter on the doctrine of sin.

Evil

How are God's lordship and love compatible with the existence of evil? In relation to the existence of evil the doctrine of providence asserts that no situation or event can finally frustrate the fulfillment of God's purpose for the individual or for history. The problem of evil or theodicy is not how this is possible but how the very existence of evil can be reconciled with the goodness and omnipotence, the love and lordship of God. This is a problem of apologetics rather than systematic theology, and although apologetics is an omnipresent element in theology, it is separated off for reasons of expediency.

An apologetic approach to the problem of evil can begin with the assertion that Christian faith has a practical answer to the problem of evil and seeks a theoretical answer. The practical answer is that in and through the suffering caused by the various forms of evil, persons can be drawn into that deeper fellowship with God which constitutes their fulfillment. The theoretical problem is best approached by an analysis of the various forms of evil: error, ugliness, animal suffering, moderate and dysteleological human suffering, accident, natural catastrophe, disease and sin. Many of these forms of evil do not in fact constitute theoretical problems for Christian faith. Natural evil is usually found to be the most difficult problem area, and there have been various attempts to deal with it in contemporary theology.[5]

In the last two decades, however, theological attention has focused on the holocaust as a major problem for Jewish and Christian theology.[6] Since the holocaust was at least in part the result of Christian anti-Semitism, Christian theologians have been reticent to try to interpret it. The fundamental question is whether the doctrine of sin is adequate to interpret the holocaust or whether this monstrous evil requires a reinterpretation of other elements of Christian faith.[7]

The 'How' of Providence

How is God's providence actually carried out? How is the divine lordship over history and the life of the individual actually exerted? Does God intervene miraculously in the order of nature and the human psyche in such a way as to cause a discontinuity from the point of view of natural or psychological science? Or is God's lordship carried out mysteriously and inscrutably, in such a way that there is no discontinuity or irregularity from the point of view of science? This is the question of the "how" rather than the "what" of providence, but the way in which the "how" is understood will undoubtedly affect the nature of the "what."

The difficulty of this question is underlined by a point made by Rogel L. Shinn.[8] Much of what happens in history is apparently the result of blind necessity or blind chance, concepts which may seem to be logical opposites but whose practical significance is about the same. A sudden change in the weather, the chance movement of a leader, quirks of personalities, for example, can have decisive effects on the course of history. If God does not determine or affect such matters of detail, it is difficult to see how God can be understood to be in control of great affairs.

The issue of how God acts in history has been raised sharply by Gilkey and Dilley in the essays referred to on page 19, note 1. Gilkey raises the following question, in the light of the fact that the cosmology of the Bible has been superseded by that of modern science, is it still possible to understand the actions of God as involving interruptions in or departures from the natural-psychological order which would in principle be discernible by the scientist? Gilkey answers that it is not. D. Baillie, Bultmann, Farmer and Tillich would agree. Barth, Brunner and Temple would disagree.

Now what kind of a question is this? Is it a scientific or a theological question? It is not a question with which modern science is in fact concerned, and it does not seem to be decided one way or the other by modern cosmology. But Gilkey seems to think that it is a scientific question. He asserts that modern theologians assume the "causal continuum of space-time experience. . . . Since they participate in the modern world of science both intellectually and existentially, they can scarcely do anything else" (p.

195b). This implies that the other view would be obscurantism and a rejection of modern science. But there are many theologians who understand and accept modern science and who at the same time deny the absolute necessity of acceptance of the uninterruptable causal continuum.

Is this then a theological question? Most of the above-mentioned theologians treat it as such. They offer theological reasons for views which agree or disagree with that of Gilkey. Tillich, for example, asserts that any idea of a supernatural interference in natural processes would be demonic and would amount to a religious dualism involving the destruction of the structure of being by the ground of being.[9] Barth, on the other hand, claims that the lordship of God involves the divine freedom in relation to the laws of nature and the possibility of God's intervention in natural processes.10 Thus Gilkey's view would seem to be the result of a theological decision (for which he does not give the reasons) rather than as the necessary result of openness to modern science.

There are five main views of how God acts providentially in the world: the primary-secondary cause theory, the uniform action view, the two perspectives and languages approach, the personal action analogy, and the process view.[11] The primary-secondary cause theory was formulated by Thomas Aquinas[12] and was followed by Calvin, Protestant orthodoxy, and modern neo-Thomism.[13] It holds that God is the primary cause of all activity in the world, but that God usually acts through secondary causes. God as primary cause and finite secondary causes are both understood to be fully active in all events on the analogy of artisans and their tools. Sometimes God acts apart from secondary causes in miracles. This view involves the assertion of the two causes achieving the same result which is criticized by Dilley.

When miracles are deleted from this theory it becomes the view of liberal theology in which God acts in and through all finite causes in nature and history. This view is exemplified by Bultmann who holds that God's action in the world is not an intervention in the finite causal nexus but takes place "within" worldly events and is visible only to the eye of faith. This does not involve a general identity of divine and worldly action, as in pantheism, but rather a paradoxical identity which is believed in the moment of existential decision. "This is the paradox of faith, that faith 'nevertheless' understands as God's action here and now an event which is completely intelligible in the natural or historical connection of events."[14]

In Bultmann's view, however, it is not clear whether God is in fact acting in such a way that the world is different from what it would be apart from God's action or whether it is only that faith sees the world *as if* God were acting. If the former, then presumably the results of God's action would be visible to anyone. If the latter, then God is not really acting.

Another version of the liberal view is that God's action in the world is purposive but uniform rather than special or particular. The appearance of particular divine activity is given by the variety of human response to the uniform divine purposive action.[15] It is not clear in this view how purposive activity can be uniform, and it is significant that all Pike's analogies for this view are impersonal in character.

In the two perspectives and languages approach faith in God's providential activity and the scientific view of the world are understood to be simply two ways of looking at the natural historical process. They are expressed in two different languages, that of scientific description and that of faith assertions about the purpose and activity of God. Thi view is expressed in the quotation from Bultmann above. John J. Compton offers the analogy of the movement of one's arm which can be seen either as a purposive human action or as a causal series of biological events. "What happens is that the evolution of things is seen or read, in religious life—as my arm's movement is read in individual life—as a part of an action, as an expression of divine purpose, in addition to its being viewed as a naturalistic process."[16] This is not in fact a theory of how God acts in the world but rather a theory about the relation of religious talk about God's action to scientific talk about the world process. Furthermore, it sees these two kinds of talk as two unrelated "language games."

The personal action analogy holds that God's activity in the world is like that of human activity in the world in that it involves an intention to fulfill a purpose and effects changes in the world which are interventions in the finite causal nexus. This seems to be the view of God's activity held by the biblical authors.[17] The main difficulties with this analogy are that it does not explain God's relation to ordinary events or those in which God is not acting and that there is nothing in God corresponding to the body in human agency.[18]

The process theologians see God as active in all events as one efficient cause among many others. According to the process view God acts in the world by infiuence or persuasion. By being prehended or experienced God offers to each emergent event or actual occasion an initial aim which the event may accept in varying degrees.[19]

William Temple's view of God's providential activity in the world is a combination of the personal action analogy and the process approach. He asserts that "the action and reaction of all parts of the world are determined at every moment by the wisdom of God."[20] Thus God's providence operates through his personal response to the varying situations of the world. Where the situation is uniform, as in nature, the divine response is uniform, as in the so-called laws of nature. Where human freedom is involved, the situation may be such as to require a divine response which will vary from the normal in the light of God's constant purpose of salvation. The personal nature of God is exhibited not by rigid uniformity of response but by constancy of purpose expressed through a response which may vary from the normal when the situation so requires.

> Our contention is that an element in every actual cause, and indeed the determinant element, is the active purpose of God fulfilling itself with that perfect constancy which calls for an infinite graduation of adjustments in the process. Where any adjustment is so considerable as to attract notice it is called a miracle; but it is not a specimen of a special class, it is an illustration of the general character of the World-Process.[21]

Thus Temple's response to Gilkey's demand for a specification of ontological difference would be that there is no ontological difference, since all events are equally the action of God. This is a solution to Gilkey's problem but not on his terms.

Pollard

William G. Pollard outlines a view of the "how" of providence which is similar to the process view.[22] As against the view represented by Bultmann, Pollard offers an explanation of the way in which God acts to affect the course of events so that in crucial situations it is different from what it might have been otherwise. As against the view represented by Temple, he affirms that the action of God in providence takes place without the modification of the laws of nature.

Pollard's theory is based on his suggestion that all levels of scientific investigation are statistical in character and that scientific predictions or laws can be stated only in terms of probability. He affirms with Bohr and against Einstein that the principle of indeterminacy refers to an actual random character in subatomic processes and not simply to our lack of knowledge. He points out further that this statistical-probability approach applies not only to physics as in quantum mechanics, but also to biology especially in genetics, to all research and prediction in the social sciences, and finally to human history in the form of chance and accident.

His main point is that at any particular time or situation in history there are various possible ways in which the course of events may proceed, on the analogy of probability theory in quantum mechanics. Thus what looks like chance or accident plays a very large role in the course of history. But the way in which the course of events actually proceeds is determined by God's providential guidance of the event. So the "how" of providence is that God picks the divine way, so to speak, among the possibilities which are presented to God in history. The main difficulty with Pollard's approach is that it depends upon Bohr's view that indeterminacy applies to reality and not simply to our lack of knowledge and upon the view that statistical behavior above the subatomic level is not simply attributable to a similar lack of knowledge.

The Visibility of Providence

Can providence be seen in history either by the historian or by the eye of faith? Is there historical evidence of God's providential rule of history and the lives of individuals? The prophets and apostles claimed to see God's providential activity in the ups and downs of Israel's history, in its deliverances and defeats and hardenings (see Rom. 9-11). Theologians have seen evidence of providence in the expansion of the church, in the failure and chastisement of the church, and in the rise and fall of empires.

Butterfield finds evidence of providence in the deeper processes of history which create good out of evil. Reinhold Niebuhr sees manifestations of providence in the life of nations. There is an element of judgment which limits the power of evil; the worse the tyranny, the shorter it lasts. And there are possibilities of renewal for a society which perceives its sin and begins to amend through social change. On the other hand, Löwith rejects the idea that there is any historical evidence of providence. To ask that providence be evident in the course of history is like asking with Satan that the Son of God tempt God by throwing himself off the pinnacle of the temple. The cross is the only answer to the request for evidence of providence.

Christian faith in God's providence affirms God's sovereignty over history and individual lives and God's power to fulfill the divine purpose of love. But we walk by faith and not by sight. Neither God's sovereignty nor God's love lie openly on the surface of history. They may be perceived by the eye of faith, but even then not as a clearly perceptible pattern. As Tillich puts it, faith in providence is faith "in spite of." Or as Helmut Thielicke puts it, "History has in it too much sense for us to be able to regard it as a gigantic playground of the forces of blind chance. History has in it too much nonsense for us to be able to deduce from it a purposeful providence that guides it."[23]

Miracle

The doctrine of providence obviously has opened up the problem of miracles. The two aspects of this problem are the interpretation of the miracles of the Bible, and the question of the occurrence of miracles today, for example, in connection with God's providential guidance of history or in answer to prayer.

The New Testament miracles can be divided into the healing miracles and the nature miracles, that is, the miracles involving the human body and mind, and the miracles involving non-human nature. The fundamental meaning of the New Testament miracles is their significance as sign-events (Tillich), powerful wonders which point to the Messiah. They are events which are unusual and astonishing, but they do not necessarily involve departure from the laws of nature. In any case the latter point is a question which could have been formulated in only a very rudimentary way, if at all, in the first century. The theological views on this problem fall on the same spectrum as those on the doctrine of providence, wrth Bultmann and Tillich on the left and Temple on the right.

A modern miracle may be interpreted as an unusual event which is interpreted by the eye of faith to be a result of God's action in a way which is more special than the divine action in other events. This may be such a thing as the weather at the evacuation at Dunkirk, a positive answer to prayer, or an unexpected recovery from a critical illness. Under such a definition a miracle may or may not involve a departure from natural law, a discontinuity in the natural-historical-psychological continuum. That is, the action of God may be interpreted according to Bultmann, Tillich, Farmer, or Pollard, on the one hand, or according to Barth, Brunner or Temple on the other.

In any case most theologians would not deny the possibility in principle of divine action which involved the interruption of natural or psychological processes. Tillich and Bultmann seem to be the only theologians who give theological reasons for denying this.[24] Tillich's argument is not very convincing. For example, Temple's approach would not seem to make God's varying response demonic or destructive of the structure of being. Furthermore, Tillich seems to move in this direction in his analysis of the concept of ecstasy. He states that all revelation involves an objective and a subjective aspect which he calls miracle and ecstasy and which are analogous. "Ecstasy is the miracle of the mind and . . . miracle is the ecstasy of reality."[25] He states that in ecstasy, although the rational structure of the mind is not destroyed, the mind transcends its ordinary situation, and reason goes beyond its subject-object structure, which is thereby "put out of action."[26] Now if miracle is the ecstasy of reality, it might be expected that in miracle, although the rational structure of reality is not destroyed, reality would transcend its ordinary situation and go beyond its usual structure which would be put out of action. This would seem to be about the same as Temple's view: a variation in the structure of reality as an expression of the constancy of the divine purpose.

Tillich's view of the structure of reality seems quite rigid and thus more like the eighteenth century mechanistic view of nature than the modern more open and flexible understanding exemplified in the statistical-probability approach analyzed by Pollard. This means simply that an eighteenth century concept of the laws of nature is no longer relevant to the problem of miracle. A miracle need not be interpreted necessarily as an event in which the structure and processes or nature are set aside.

Questions for Discussion

1. *Are all events equally providential, that is, guided and controlled by God for the fulfillment of the divine purpose? Or are some events more providential than others, for example, the weather at the deliverance at the Red Sea, or at the evacuation at Dunkirk? If the former, does this mean that natural catastrophes have a purpose? If the latter, does not this amount to deism, the view that God is unrelated to the world except in special events?*

2. *Does providence mean that God controls all events for the good of each individual or that no events can frustrate the divine purpose of bringing all persons to their fulfillment?*

3. *How is God's providence compatible with the existence of natural and moral evil?*

4. *If God is to control and guide the great affairs of history, God must of necessity control and guide the matters of detail, since the former so often depend on the latter. But this would mean that all forms of evil, both natural and moral, are the result of God's will. Does this not undercut both human freedom and divine goodness?*

5. *Is God's lordship over history carried out by modifying the natural historical-psychological continuum or not? If not, how in fact is it carried out?*

6. *In the prayers for the sick, for rain, for fair weather, etc., in The Book of Common Prayer (pp. 458, 826, 831) are we asking for miracles in the sense of interruptions of the laws of nature?*

7. *Can you specify any events of recent history, individual, national, or international, in which you perceive the providence of God? If so, on what grounds? If not, what is the significance of that?*

8. *In talking with a person who has been bereaved through war, an automobile accident, plane crash, or disease, what use would you make, if any, of the doctrine of providence?*

9. *It may be that a few of us make use of the language of miracle or of God's providence in reference to any contemporary happenings. If you agree, then what bearing does this have on the doctrine of the providence of God? If you do not agree, then illustrate and explicate a rationale for the use of this language.*

10. *What kind of situation or events might count against the reality of God's providence? If there are none, how is God's providence different from an absence of God's providence?*

11. *Does God do anything specific or particular or only things in general?*

8

Humanity

In one sense the doctrine of humanity has always been the implicit center of Christian faith, not only because it is human beings who "have" Christian faith and who reflect on its meaning in theology, but also because Christian faith focuses on the man Jesus who is the Christ. Thus the doctrine of God begins with Jesus who is the "image of the invisible God" (Col. 1:15) and is elaborated by the application of elements of human experience analogically to God (anthropomorphism). Furthermore, it is human beings who receive the revelation of God, understand themselves as creatures and as sinners who have been redeemed by God.

Although the doctrine of humanity has been the subject of explicit debate off and on during the history of Christian thought, it has been the subject of theological discussion especially in the last century. The discoveries of Darwin and Freud caused a revolution in the understanding of humanity which the church is still assimilating. The doctrine of humanity was at the heart of the liberal theology of the last century under the influence of Schleiermacher's concentration on the Christian religious consciousness. Thus it is not surprising that the Barthian theology began in a struggle over the doctrine of humanity, over the possibility of human knowledge of God and the nature of human estrangement from God. The famous debate between Barth and Brunner in the 1930s centered about the concepts of the *imago dei* and the point of contact in humanity for revelation.[1]

In contemporary theology the influence of Bultmann has again made the doctrine of humanity central through his use of existentialist philosophy. He understands the mythological statements of the New Testament as assertions about human existence which can best be interpreted by means of the philosophy of Heidegger. It is now being argued that process philosophy is more adequate to this task than existentialist philosophy.[2] The followers of Bonhoeffer have joined issue with the followers of Bultmann over the question of the understanding of modern humanity. The former have asserted that the existentialist understanding of humanity corresponds to a religious stage which has now been superseded. Humanity has come of age and is able to deal with all its problems, including anxiety and guilt, apart from God.[3] This has led to a renewed emphasis upon the dignity of humanity.[4]

Using Heidegger in a somewhat different way the transcendental Thomists led by Karl Rahner have developed a unique approach to the doctrine of humanity. Beginning with an analysis of human knowledge they argue that all conscious activity involves both self-knowledge and also an openness to all of realty, to being as such. This means that the human knower is involved with an infinite horizon in an awareness which is called transcendental experience. It is transcendental in the sense of belonging to human self-transcendence, in the sense of going beyond any and all possible objects of knowledge, and in the sense of being the precondition of all conscious activity, moral and aesthetic as well as intellectual. This transcendental experience is always oriented toward the infinite horizon and is an unthematic or unreflective awareness of the holy mystery, the absolute and the incomprehensible, which is God. It is this transcendental experience which constitutes humanity, as subject, person and spirit. This is a particular form of the fairly common modern theological idea that humanity is constituted by it's relation to God.[5]

Finally, feminist theologians have argued that throughout Christian history the understanding of humanity has been seen from the point of view of male experience, interests and concerns, and has thus neglected half the human race. Human nature has been understood from the perspective of male stereotypes of what is natural, virtuous and sinful, and therefore has been seriously distorted.[6]

Today in a time of rapid social change there is intense interest in what it means to be human or humane. So the doctrine of humanity addresses a question which is of potentially greater interest than any other in theology. The Christian doctrine of humanity is in competition with many other views of humanity, Freudian, Marxist, mystical and naturalistic. In debate with these views the Christian doctrine of humanity can be presented as a Christian humanism. As such it is based on a double distinction (not separation) between God and the world, and between humanity and the rest of creation. The first distinguishes Christian faith from Greek and idealistic humanism and from some Eastern philosophies, such as Vedanta, in which some element of humanity, usually mind or spirit, is identified with the divine. The second distinguishes Christian faith from all naturalistic humanisms from Feuerbach to Dewey and Skinner which see humanity as simply a part of nature.[7]

The foregoing indicates that it is in the doctrine of humanity that the question of the relation of theology to philosophy and science is raised most sharply. A constructive philosophy can ignore the question of the nature of God but not that of the nature of humanity. The theological followers of both Bultmann and Whitehead assert that theology must make use of a philosophical doctrine of humanity worked out independently of Christian faith, but the followers of Barth would deny this. New developments in biology, psychology, and sociology often lead to claims to definitive interpretations of humanity which are on the same level as philosophy and theology.[8] This raises in a radical way the question of the relation between the scientific and the theological understanding of humanity.[9]

The doctrine of humanity has three parts: humanity as created in the image of God, as sinner, and as redeemed. The doctrine of humanity (like all other doctrines) is based on God's revelation. It might be objected that we may need revelation to know God but that humanity is a phenomenon which can be investigated. However, theology deals with the nature of humanity in relation to the question of its ultimate origin, meaning, and destiny, that is, in relation to God, and not just its phenomenal structure as organic and psychic being. This is why it is the revelation of God and not the human sciences which are decisive for the doctrine of humanity. It is only when God is revealed as lord, creator and savior that we know that we are creatures, sinners, and redeemed. Apart from God's revelation attested in the Bible we usually understand ourselves as essentially identified with nature (naturalism) or with the divine (idealism) or as an unstable mixture of the natural and the divine (Platonism). Apart from revelation we may be aware that we are embedded in nature, but we may interpret this as a fall, an unfortunate accident, or an illusion. But in revelation we know it as our creaturehood. Apart from revelation we may experience the fact that all is not well with us, that we are unfulfilled, but in revelation we know this as sin.

Bible

The first and most fundamental thing which the Bible says about human beings is that they are creatures, part of God's creation, and thus dependent upon God for their being and continued existence. As we have seen in chapter 6, creation *ex nihilo* means, as against dualist and monist views of origin, that human existence is neither essentially evil, nor illusory, nor essentially divine, but rather essentially good and real. Yet it is still creature, that is, dependent and contingent. Thus human existence is not a chemical accident, "a fortuitous concourse of atoms," but has meaning because it is the result of the will and purpose of the creator. Many Eastern and classical views of human life see its vulnerability, its organic basis, and its historical involvement as threats to its meaningfulness. But the doctrine of creation provides the basis for the affirmation that human creaturely life in all its finiteness, individuality, and temporality is meaningful and good.[10]

The testimony of the Bible is quite clear that human beings a *finite* and limited, that they are born and die, that their life involves pain and suffering (Gen. 2:7, 3:19, Isa. 40:6, Job 14:1, Ps. 49:12, 103:14, 144:4, Jas. 4:13). But this is not deplored in such a way that human fulfillment is understood to be an escape from this. Rather this situation of human life is seen as the will of the loving creator and thus good (Gen. 1:31). This is true of even the most decisive aspect of human finitude, namely, *death* (Gen. 25:8). It is sometimes argued that in the Bible humanity is naturally immortal and that physical death is the punishment for sin. But there is no suggestion in the Genesis 3 story that mortality is the punishment for sin.[11] This idea appears clearly only in the Apocrypha and Pseudepigrapha (Wisd. 2:23f, 2 Esdr. 3:7 etc.). Paul affirms this view in Romans 5:12 (although Dodd interprets this passage as a reference to spiritual death rather than physical death). In any case it is clear that physical death becomes a symbol of the divine judgment on sin (Rom. 6:23, 1 Cor. 15:56). Although Paul argues that death is the result of sin, he does not argue that humanity is naturally immortal. So the consensus of the Bible is that physical death is an aspect of the divine ordering of creaturely life, and that it becomes terrible through sin.[12]

The biblical view of the constitution of humanity, the *biblical psychology*, as it is called, is extremely complex, and any systematization of it is highly artificial. But a threefold pattern emerges: body, soul or life (*nephesh, psyche*) and spirit (*ruach, pneuma*). The latter two elements refer generally to the vital principle and to personhood and capacity for relationship to God. The overlapping of these terms indicates that humanity is conceived of as a vital unity composed of various interdependent elements. (See the biblical theologies for the details.) In any case there is no divine element and no essentially evil element in humanity. We are totally creature and thus essentially good. "Good" here means the result of the purposive and loving will of the creator and thus possessing meaning. Any evil in humanity is a disruption or estrangement, existential rather than essential, and thus redeemable.

The question can be raised at this point as to whether the biblical psychology as outlined above is the result of revelation or the result simply of empirical observation and similar to the primitive and general Near Eastern view of humanity. That some of it falls within the range of empirical observation is indicated by the fact that it is very close to the view of humanity in modern psychology.[13] But it is unique in relation to Hellenistic and Eastern views of humanity, and the presuppositions of modern psychology have been influenced by the biblical tradition through Western philosophy and theology.

The last element in the bibical psychology, namely, spirit, is what distinguishes humanity from the rest of creation. Our special dignity in the creation is also indicated by the statement that we are created in the *image of God* (Gen. 1:26, 5:1, 9:6, Wisd. 2:23, Ecclus. 17:3). These are the only uses of this phrase in the Old Testament, but the idea for which it stands is quite common, namely, our preeminence in the creation (see Ps. 8:5f). This idea appears in Adam's naming of the animals, the dominion given to humanity over the other creatures, and in the fact that it is primarily with humanity that God enters into covenant. "Image of God" refers to some kind of correspondence between God and humanity, probably to human freedom, capacity to plan, decide, and act, that is, to all those aspects of human personhood which are applied analogically to God.

The concept of the image of God plays a much larger part in the New Testament, because it is now affirmed that Jesus Christ is the image of God (Col. 1:15, 2 Cor. 4:4). This means not only that Jesus is the revelation of God, but also that Jesus is true humanity, humanity as it was created to be. Thus Christian salvation is understood as humanity being conformed to Christ, humanity being restored to its true being (Eph. 4:24, Col. 3:10, Rom 8:29, 1 Cor. 15:49, 2 Cor. 3:18, 1 Jn. 3:2). Since a child is understood to be in the image of its parent (Gen. 5:3), a closely connected concept of salvation is that of adoption as children by grace (Rom. 8:14f, Eph. 1:5, Gal. 3:26, Jn. 1:12). The Christian moral imperative is often expressed in the language of imitation of God or being children of God (Mt. 5:44f, 48, Eph. 5:1, 1 Jn. 3:2, 1 Pet. 1:16). Thus the original human likeness to God is fundamental to the New Testament message.

One aspect of human uniqueness, of being in the image of God, is human *freedom*, the capacity to choose between obedience and disobedience, good and evil (Deut. 30:15f). This is the immediate implication of human responsibility under the demand of God, under the covenant. Human freedom is to be exercised in carrying out the dominion over the earth as God's stewards and under God's law. Freedom is put in question by rebellion and sin, and it is reconstituted by God's salvation. These questions will be discussed in the chapters on sin and salvation.

Various aspects of the doctrine of humanity as creature have been discussed in the history of Christian thought.[14] There are no specific references to the doctrine of humanity as creature in the creeds or Anglican formularies, except for the reference to original righteousness in Article IX.[15]

Image of God

One aspect of the doctrine of humanity as creature which has received recurring attention in the history of Christian thought is that of the image of God. Irenaeus was apparently the first theologian to distinguish the meaning of "image" and "likeness" in Genesis 1:26. He defined the image as the natural endowment of reason and freedom, and the likeness as a supernatural endowment by the Spirit. This distinction was taken up by later theologians who defined the likeness (*similitudo*) as the supernatural gift of sanctifying grace which gives righteousness, immortality, and integrity. According to this later development the likeness is lost in the fall but the image is not. Thus, since rationality and freedom are still intact, a rational natural theology and ethics are possible. The reformers argued that this distinction was bad exegesis and that the image of God was lost or seriously corrupted in the fall.[16]

Because of the emphasis in recent theology on the doctrines of revelation and sin, the doctrine of the image of God has been an important subject of debate. Tillich defines the image of God in humanity as that which distinguishes us from the other creatures, namely, our rational structure, with reason defined as the structure of freedom.

Man is the image of God because in him the ontological elements are complete and united on a creaturely basis, just as they are complete and united in God as the creative ground. Man is the image of God because his *logos* is analogous to the divine *logos*, so that the divine *logos* can appear as man without destroying the humanity of man.[17]

Barth interprets the image of God as human life in confrontation with the fellow human being and especially the relationship of man and woman, which is an analogy of the confrontation in the godhead.

As the original form not only of man's confrontation with God but also of all intercourse between man and man, [the sex differentiation and relationship] is the true *humanum* and therefore the true creaturely image of God.[18]

Brunner's view of the image of God is similar to that of Barth but without the reference to bisexuality. In humanity God wills creatures who freely respond to the divine love, and this means selves or persons. The image of God is our free responsibility before God. This is what Brunner calls the formal or Old Testament image. But in order that our response be truly free, there is the possibility of our not fulfilling our responsibility before God. So the material image of God is the perfect response to God which is manifest in Jesus Christ, who is thus the true image of God. As created in the image of God we are responsible to God and are called to respond in perfect trust and obedience to the love of God in imitation of Christ and through Christ. In responding to this call we are a "new creation" in the image of God (2 Cor. 5:17, Gal. 6:15). Thus the image of God is not a substance but a relation. "It is the distinctive quality of human existence that its 'structure' is a 'relation'; responsible existence, responsive actuality." [19] (The further elaboration of the content of the image of God will come in the doctrine of the person of Christ.)

Feminist historians have pointed out that historical Christian authors have sometimes stated or implied that only men are created in the image of God and not women. Besides denying women their humanity this has distorted the meaning of the image of God in humanity in the direction of male stereotypes, such as rationality, and domination.[20]

Freedom

Recent developments in biology, psychology and cybernetics have raised again for theologians the problem of the nature of human freedom. These developments have underscored the theological view that human freedom is limited, conditioned, relative and dependent. First of all human beings are creatures of God. Our being and therefore our freedom are dependent upon and derive from the freedom of God in creation. Secondly, we are finite, bounded by space and time. We are bodily and therefore must eat, sleep and die. We may err in our sense perceptions and our judgments. Our judgments and actions are affected by our bodily, emotional, and unconscious states, as well as our social and cultural situation. So human freedom, the capacity for self-determination, is only a vague reflection of the absolute freedom of the creator.

Because we human beings are creatures, the fulfillment of our being is not indeterminate as in Sartre's existentialism. Because we are creatures, we human beings and our freedom can be fulfilled only in relation to our creator, in a relation of trust, love and obedience. Thus we human beings live in and with responsibility, especially in moral and religious decisions. The marginal cases of mental retardation, brain damage and brain washing only underscore the normal situation of human freedom and responsibility. The nature of the loss of freedom in sin will be discussed in the next chapter. The fulfillment of human freedom will be discussed in chapter 11.

Humanity as Social and Political

Philosophers since Plato and Aristotle and theologians since Augustine have known that we human beings are essentially social and political beings, that we are created in large part by the social, economic and political structures in which we live. Therefore our life, its problematic character, and its fulfillment must always be understood in this social context. Biblical faith was born in the political liberation of the exodus, refined in the struggles of the prophets with the monarchy, culminated in the confrontation of the messiah with the rulers of his day, and strains forward in hope to a fulfillment modeled on a perfect realm of justice and peace. The reign of God has always been seen as the basis of Christian resistance to tyranny and the Christian critique of all ideologies. The criticism of the influence on human thought and practice of the forms of economic and social life by Marx, Durkheim and Weber is a continuation of the prophetic critique of all human blindness, pretension and self-serving provincialism.

This tradition of social thought and criticism has been renewed and developed in the latter half of this century by the political theologians (Moltmann, Metz and Soelle) and the Latin American liberation theologians (Gutiérrez, Segundo and Sobrino). They have criticized the private and individualistic character of much of modern theology, especially existentialist theology, and have underscored the inescapable social matrix of human life and the economic and political context in which theology is done. They have pointed out that in the modern period Christian theology including its view of humanity has been almost exclusively white, male, affluent, upper-middle class, university-based, first world in character and thus dominated by the ideology of this elite. This has had the predictable results of ignoring the experience of the people of color, women, the poor and oppressed, the so-called uneducated, and the third world generally and thus distorting the resulting doctrine of humanity. The political and liberation theologians have taught us that the Christian doctrine of humanity must treat the social, economic and political context as essential to human life and its interpretation in Christian faith.[21]

Original Righteousness

Another aspect of the doctrine of humanity as creature, which can serve as a transition to the doctrine of humanity as sinner, is the doctrine of the primitive state, *justitia originalis*, original justice or righteousness (see Article II). On the basis of a literal or allegorical interpretation of the Garden of Eden story theologians beginning with Athanasius developed a doctrine of the original state of humanity in paradise before the fall. This was elaborated by the Cappadocians and the early Latin theologians and reached its classical form with Augustine. According to Augustine Adam was in a state of justification, illumination, beatitude and immortality. He was immune to physical ills and had supreme intellectual gifts. He was able to avoid sin and had the gift of perseverance.

As an historical assertion about a historical situation, this doctrine has to be denied. But the theological purpose of the doctrine is to distinguish between human existence as created by God and the existence of sinful humanity, between creation and sin. This doctrine also bears witness to the fact that as sinners we are aware of the fact that we are not what we are supposed to be. A bad conscience or a sense of conflict between what we are and what we ought to be is the testimony to a mythical original righteousness.

A creative reinterpretation of the doctrine of original righteousness has been given by Reinhold Niebuhr in his Gifford Lectures. His thesis is that this doctrine refers to our awareness of a contradiction between what we are essentially and what we are existentially, between what we are called and destined to be and what we in fact are. The content of original righteousness is Jesus' Summary of the Law: perfect harmony with God, with the self, and with the neighbor (see Mk. 10:17ff).

The sense that an obedience which is less than love is not normative even though it is universal, is the *justitis originalis*. It is the sense that there ought not be a sense of ought; it is the "thou shalt" which suggests that there are no "thou shalts" in perfection.

Questions for Discussion

1. *What does it mean to say, "God created me?" What is the relation of this to the statement, "My parents produced me," "I am the product of my age, culture, race and class?"*
2. *We do not need revelation to tell us that we are finite, embedded in nature, different from other animals in our self-consciousness, self-transcendence, and freedom, have a history, make moral decisions, live in personal and social relationships, become anxious and neurotic, ask the question of the meaning of our life, and must live by some meaning. So cannot most of the doctrine of humanity be based on biology, psychology, and sociology?*
3. *If cultures change and if culture determines the character of human life, does not human nature change in history? If so, how can we affirm a view of humanity which was elaborated 2,000 years ago in a quite different culture?*
4. *Science and theology both speak about human the nature of humanity. What is the relation between their statements about humanity?*
5. *"Christian faith is an affirmation about human existence and what happens to it in the preaching and hearing of the kerygma. Therefore theology must make use of an analysis of human existence developed by philosophy" (Paraphrase of*

Bultmann). Discuss.

6. *Is physical death part of the doctrine of humanity as creature or part of the doctrine of humanity as sinner? That is, is physical death an aspect of God's will for us in his ordering of human life or is it the result of sin and thus against God's will?*

7. *One goal of psychology is to give a complete causal picture of human acts in terms of impulses, drives, needs and feelings. How can such a picture be reconciled with the theological affirmation of human freedom?*

8. *On what grounds does Christian faith look upon human beings differently from dolphins and apes?*

9. *If we are created in the image of God, if Jesus Christ is the image of God, and if fulfillment is to be conformed to him, how do we decide what aspects of the New Testament picture of Christ are culture-bound and what aspects are normative?*

10. *Is a person annihilated at death? If not, what remains? Is it immoral? If so, what is it that is raised from the dead?*

11. *What is the proper relation of humanity to nature?*

12. *Does the rest of the creation exist for our benefit or does it have rights of its own?*

13. *What is the relation of body and soul?*

9

Sin

The doctrine of sin is in a way the negative presupposition of the whole of Christian faith and theology. Apart from human estrangement from God there would have been no need of revelation, the history of salvation, church, or theology. Sometimes the economy of salvation has been presented in such a way that revelation, incarnation, and so forth, were part of God's plan even apart from sin to raise humanity from innocence to fulfillment.[1] But the reality of sin has cast the economy of salvation in the form of a solution to the problem of sin. This is not meant to imply that there was any historical period without sin, but simply that the doctrine of sin is logically the negative presupposition of the Christian dispensation.

In reaction to the traditional orthodox doctrines of the fall and original sin the liberal theology of the last century played down the doctrine of sin. The tendency was to interpret sin in terms of ignorance, finitude, the hangover of animal inheritance, and the result of bad social conditions. The neo-orthodoxy of the second quarter of this century involved a heavy reemphasis on the doctrine of sin in terms of what may be called the sins of strength: pride and rebellion. Tillich and Bultmann have reinterpreted sin in the terms of existentialist philosophy: estrangement and inauthentic existence. The secular theology of the followers of Bonhoeffer has again tended to play down the doctrine of sin. Where it is mentioned it is interpreted in terms of what may be called the sins of weakness: immaturity, sloth, inertia and indifference.[2]

As has been suggested in chapter 8 the doctrine of sin is based on revelation. We know that we are sinners only through the revelation culminating in Christ. We may be aware of moral failure, meaninglessness, frustration, neurosis and lack of fulfillment, but we cannot understand this as sin or the result of sin apart from revelation. Sin is known as sin only from the point of view of salvation from sin. (The only references to sin in the creeds are to the forgiveness of sins.)

Bible

"The breach of the covenant is the kernel of sin" (Pedersen). In the Old Testament sin is essentially that which is contrary to the norm, which is the will of God. It is erring, straying, deviating, transgressing, resisting, repudiating, rebelling, in relation to the divine will. Thus sin also constitutes apostasy, being unfaithful, idolatry. Although it may be external and unconscious in relation to the cult, in its most serious form it is a matter of the center of personhood, the "heart" (Jer. 4:14, 7:24, Ps. 51:6, 10).

The Genesis 3 story makes no use of technical terms for sin but simply tells a story to explain how sin began, what it is, and how it works out. The central theme of the story is that sin is disobedience to the divine command, the desire to overstep the status of a creature and to become like God. But it includes other elements involved in the situation of the sinner: the sense that freedom has been limited, doubt about God's goodness, desire for what is to be gained by disobedience, concern to involve others in responsibility, shame over disobedience. The "knowledge of good and evil" probably refers to the knowledge of the good and evil destinies of humanity which is the prerogative of the divine wisdom alone.[3]

Jesus assumes the prophetic understanding of sin as disobedience and rebellion. Sin is any failure to be worthy children of God by being perfect in love as God is. Jesus does not speculate on the origin and nature of sin but simply indicates its actuality in his teaching and parables. He underlines the prophetic idea that sin is a matter of the heart, of the inner attitude and intention (Mk. 7:21). But his message is that sin and its results are overcome by the presence of the kingdom.

For Paul "sin is man's wanting to dispose of his existence, to raise claims for himself, to be like God" (Bultmann). Sin is also understood to be a quasi-personified alien power which takes over humanity (Rom. 5:21, 6:17, 23). The sphere in which sin reigns is the "flesh," which is the whole person as a weak, finite, historical being. The comprehensive term for the results of sin is death, spiritual death (Rom. 6:23, 7:9). The law arouses sin, gives the occasion for and knowledge of sin, and shows up sin for what it is (Rom. 3:20, 5:20, 7:5, 7, 13).

The *universality* of sin is either stated explicitly or assumed throughout the Bible (Gen. 6:5, 8:21, Ps. 14:2). In Jesus' teaching this universality is implicit (Mt. 7:11, 12:34, Mk. 8:38, etc.), but in Paul it is quite explicit (Rom. 3:9, 22). This leads to the question of the *origin* of sin for which there is no clear theory in the Bible but rather many suggestions. Although the Genesis 3 story records the first act of disobedience and purports to tell how sin began, it does not say that this is the cause of all subsequent sin, and it is not so understood until the intertestamental period. In the later Old Testament period the idea developed that Satan was the source of sin (1 Chr. 21:1). In Wisdom 2:24 Satan or the devil is identified with the serpent of Genesis 3. In the New Testament Satan tempts Jesus and Christians and is known as the ruler of this world. But in all this material Satan suggests and tempts but does not cause sin. Later Judaism used the Genesis 3 and 6 stories as explanations of the origin of sin (2 Esdras 3:21, 7:46f).

Paul has two theories of the origin of sin which do not seem to be related. The first is based on the later Jewish reflection on the fall of Adam (Rom. 5:12, 19). He here makes use of the Old Testament idea of tribal solidarity in which the sin of one member brings a curse on the whole tribe. His other theory is elaborated in Romans 1:18-32. Although humanity can know God through the divine revelation in the creation, they suppress the truth, refuse to honor and acknowledge God, and worship the creature rather than the creator. Although this is not strictly a theory of origins, it explains how sin arises without reference to Adam.

There is some suggestion in the Bible of *a fall of nature*, namely, either that human sin has affected nature or simply that the sub-human creation is not what it was created to be (Gen. 3:16ff, Rom. 8:20f). Other passages indicate that nature will be transformed in the fulfillment (Isa. 11:6f, 35:1f, 2 Pet. 2:13, Rev. 21:1), but this does not necessarily mean that there has been a fall of nature. It depends upon whether the fulfillment is a restoration or a transformation into something entirely new. Later Judaism developed the theory that fallen angels or demons were the source of evils in nature, such as disease, as well as the sin of humanity. This is reflected in New Testament demonology.

Tradition [4]

The traditional Western theory of the fall and original sin was developed as the result of the Pelagian-Augustinian debate. In general it can be said that Augustine won out in the debate but that his extreme views were moderated or tacitly dropped. At the Second Council of Orange in 529 Pelagianism and Semi-Pelagianism were explicitly condemned and it was affirmed that as a result of Adam's transgression sin and death have been passed on to all his descendants, and that human free will has been so corrupted and weakened that a person cannot believe in, love, or obey God apart from God's grace. The medieval theologians and the Reformers stood generally in the Augustinian tradition, and the views and debates of the latter can be seen reflected in the Anglican formularies.

The Anglican Articles of Religion represent a moderate version of the Augustinian views on sin of the continental Reformers. Most of the statements on sin are directed at the Pelagian views of the Anabaptists of the sixteenth century. (For instance, the parenthesis in Article IX originally included the words "which also the Anabaptists do nowadays renew.") The main articles dealing with the doctrine of sin are IX, X, XIII, XV, XVI.

Article IX is a straightforward statement of the classical doctrine of original sin and assumes a literal interpretation of Genesis 3 with Adam understood as the ancestor of all humanity. The word for "corruption" is *depravatio*, depravity, and is thus related to the Reformers' doctrine of the total depravity of humanity. This is often interpreted to mean that humanity is totally corrupt whereas the intention of the Reformers was to assert that the whole person was corrupt, that is, that there was no aspect of human nature, such as reason or freedom, which was not distorted by sin. The article implies that original sin is inherited, that all people bear original guilt (Art. II) and that unbaptized infants are thus condemned. These points and the problems arising from literalism will have to be criticized in reconstructing the doctrine.

Article X is not really on "free will" but rather on the nature of the bondage of sin. The second sentence should not be interpreted as a statement about the good works of non-Christians but only as the Christians' confession that their good works are the result of grace. Article XIII deals with the former question and amounts to a criticism of one aspect of the medieval doctrine of merit, namely that works done before justification merit the grace of congruity, that is, that grace which is given as a matter of fitness. It might be argued that no good works are done apart from grace and that all good works "have the nature of sin" to some extent. In any case the article should be interpreted as a denial that works "deserve" (*merentur*) anything. Articles XV and XVI amount to another assertion of the universality of sin and a denial of the Anabaptist doctrine of the unpardonability of "deadly" (*mortale*) sin after baptism. Besides the Articles *The Book of Common Prayer* contains a great deal of general and pastoral teaching about sin in the penitential orders, confessions, catechism and collects.

Reconstruction

Now what is wrong with the traditional doctrine of the fall and original sin? First of all we must reject its historical literalism with a historical Adam in a state of original righteousness followed by a historical fall. The fall story must be understood as a myth and interpreted accordingly.[5]

Secondly, we must reject its *traducianism*, the theory of the physical inheritance of a corrupt soul from Adam. This takes the idea of sin out of the area of personal responsibility and puts it in the sphere of biology. In stressing the universality and inevitability of sin Augustine seemed to say that it is a natural necessity, but if it were, there could be no responsibility. We cannot inherit sinfulness or moral evil or a defect of the will. It is the very nature of the will (understood as the capacity of the self to direct itself) that it determines itself and cannot be entirely determined by external factors and still remain will as defined. What we do inherit is a temperament or tendencies which will determine the nature of our temptations. Socially speaking we inherit a sinful situation in the sense that we are born into a world in which the people and institutions are distorted by sin. And since persons develop only through interaction with their environment, they will be deeply affected by it. But this is not original sin in the traditional sense.

Thirdly, we must reject any idea of *original guilt* such that "every person born into this world . . . deserveth God's wrath and damnation" (Article IX). Guilt will be defined below as the personal and objective consequences of actual sin and thus involving responsibility. This rules out the idea of inherited guilt.

What is valid in the traditional doctrine? First of all, the traditional doctrine of the fall based on Genesis 3 correctly interprets and clarifies our deep awareness that we are not as we should be, that our existence is in contradiction to our essence, that our relation to God, neighbor, self and nature is disrupted. The traditional doctrine interprets this as the result of disobedience to and estrangement from God.

Secondly, the traditional doctrine avoids the errors of *Pelagianism*. That is, it explains the origin of sinful acts in a way which is truer to the biblical view than does Pelagianism. It avoids the error that we are perfectly free to avoid sin and that all we need to do is simply to decide to avoid it. Human life and activity are not atomic in the way Pelagius apparently believed them to be. Each sinful act is not a completely discrete, conscious, deliberate, and perverse act of defiance and rebellion against God. A sinful act comes at least in part out of a bondage, a weakness. Original sin is the source of actual sin; sin as a state is the source of sins as acts (Mt. 7:18).

Some contemporary theologians suggest that depth psychology tends to support Augustine as against Pelagius and thus neo-orthodoxy as against liberalism in regard to the nature of sin. They suggest that Augustine's view makes more sense of the moral and psychological facts. that as against Pelagius there is less freedom in the actual sins and more responsibility for the bias toward evil. Human action is largely determined by habit, impulse, and inner conflict, and each act is not a completely free act. For example, David E. Roberts writes:

> At certain points there is a remarkable parallel between the Pauline-Augustinian conception of original sin and the psycho-analytic conception of neurosis. Freud more than once called attention to the parallel. In

both instances man finds himself in a condition of inner conflict, and filled with hatred, envy and mistrust toward his neighbors. In both instances it is the basic condition that is enslaving; particular "sins" or "symptoms" are peripheral effects deriving from this central cause, and particular "good deeds" make little dent upon the basic condition.... It is almost impossible to disentangle the respects in which a man has fallen into sin (or neurosis) by necessity or through his own "fault." In both instances the central problem cannot be solved merely by an effort of will; insofar as it ever gets solved at all, the solution comes about through a change in the "will" itself.[6]

Roberts clearly implies that psychoanalytic studies support the Pauline-Augustinian view against the Pelagian view.[7] But it has been suggested in chapter 1 that proper scientific conclusions can neither support nor undercut proper theological statements. However, psychology can give concrete content and specification to the psychic or emotional side of the reality to which the theological statement is referring. Thus to say that the Augustinian view makes more sense of the moral and psychological facts is not a systematic theological statement but an apologetic statement, that is, an assertion about the illuminative and interpretive power of the Augustinian theological view.

Thirdly, the traditional doctrine of original sin is the most adequate interpretation of the biblical testimony to the universality of sin individually and historically. The revelation of God in Christ makes it clear that from a time before we were conscious or aware of it, we have been estranged and alienated from God, neighbor, self, and nature. Original sin refers to the fact that apparently previous to any responsible choice or decision we are involved in pride and sloth. So the traditional doctrine of original sin as reformulated is not an attempt to answer the question of the origin of sin but an attempt to state in symbolic terms that human life as we know it is a spoiled thing, not as it was created to be, and that we are responsible for this.

This leads directly to the most difficult theological problem in the doctrine of humanity as sinner, namely, how to reconcile the apparent universality and inevitability of sin with human *responsibility*. The Pelagian answer is quite simple: sin is not necessarily universal or inevitable but only empirically so. There is no person who is not a sinner, and since sin is avoidable, all sinners are responsible. Thus we have universality and responsibility but no inevitability. Pelagius' disciple Celestius said: "We must ask whether sin comes from necessity or from choice. If from necessity, then it is not sin; if from choice, then it can be avoided." But this does not take account of the biblical testimony that sin is not only universal but also somehow inevitable, the fatal or tragic element, what Paul calls "bondage" or "slavery" from which we are delivered only by the power of God.

There is another group of answers to this problem which go to the opposite extreme from Pelagianism. F.R. Tennant asserts that sin is essentially sensuality, an evolutionary survival from our animal origins, the fact that animal instincts have not yet been controlled by reason. There are many difficulties with this theory. First, animals are not sinful. They have a will to survive but not a will to power. Secondly, sin is not simply emotional or instinctual but spiritual. It is pride which derives not from the impulses but from the will. Even the so-called sensual sins or sins of the flesh originate not from the body but from the spirit. The desires may be an occasion or a temptation but not the cause of sin. Thirdly, if we are caused to sin by the natural fact of our animal inheritance, then we are certainly not responsible. In general we can never specify a cause for sin without explaining it away. This is simply the result of the fact that, since sin is a matter of the will or the direction of the self, it cannot be caused by anything other than the will or self without ceasing to be sin. This point applies to several other modern theories of the origin of sin, for example, that it is the result of our finitude, or our evil environment. All these theories relieve us of responsibility. Finally, Tennant's view implies a negative dualistic view of the body and its desires, which is denied in the Bible.

If the Pelagian and determinist answers are inadequate, how can we relate the universality of sin to responsibility for it? The biblical testimony to our responsibility, our being "without excuse," takes the form of the bad conscience which follows the sinful action, the sense that in spite of all extenuating circumstances, we are responsible. Here we confront a central paradox of the biblical witness and Christian experience: Christians testify to the element of fateful necessity, bondage, inevitability in their sin, and also to their own responsibility. Reinhold Niebuhr puts it this way: Sin is a defect of the will; therefore it is not completely deliberate. But since the will presupposes freedom, we are responsible for it.[8] Pascal writes, "Certainly nothing offends us more rudely than this doctrine [original sin]; and yet, without this mystery, the most incomprehensible of all, we are incomprehensible to ourselves."[9] Tillich suggests that there are two elements of the doctrine of sin which must be affirmed together, a fatal and inevitable element and a free and responsible element, a moral and a tragical element.[10] Roberts has stated the paradox clearly:

> It is at this point that the paradox of determinism-and-responsibility arises for theological thinking. If man is caught, not merely by external circumstances beyond his control, but by internal bondage to a predisposition to evil, then how can he take responsibility for the latter? The Christian doctrine asserts that man becomes caught in bondage to his own nature, not because the nature he has received from God is evil, but because man makes it evil himself. As we have seen, the most influential

contemporary statements of the doctrine do not contemplate a chronology wherein man started, historically, as good, and then became evil through his own act. They conceive of every human being as finding himself in a setting, from birth to death, wherein he is continually violating his own good nature, not merely because he is ignorant of what he ought to do, or because social and physical influences prevent him from doing what he ought, but because he *will* not do it. Yet he is so enslaved to this evil will that he cannot unfetter himself by an act of will; for every act of will issues from a center that is already wrongly disposed. If one asks how, temporally speaking, he got into the position where his will was thus rebelliously fixed, most writers on the problem agree that there is no answer. They agree that every particular refusal to follow the good presupposes a will which is already set in such refusal. As Kierkegaard put it: "Sin presupposes itself." Yet these same writers insist that continuation in bondage to sin is carried forward responsibly, not ignorantly or automatically.[11]

In reformulating the doctrine of sin several points need to be made clear. Sin is primarily a religious and theological term and not a moral term. Sin is not primarily breaking the moral law but rather breaking the relationship with God. It is not primarily immorality but rather rebellion and estrangement. Thus sin is not the opposite of virtue or goodness but rather of faith (see Rom. 14:23). Sin is spiritual and not carnal, a matter of the spirit or self and its pretensions rather than the body and its impulses. Sin is a state or condition rather than an act although it issues in acts. Sin is neither essential to human nature nor a simple deliberate decision. The first takes away responsibility and the second belies the reality of human bondage and weakness.

There are three main ways in which the doctrine of sin can be interpreted today. *Self-centeredness:*

When we open our eyes as babies we see the world stretching out around us; we are in the middle of it; all proportions and perspectives in what we see are determined by the relation—distance, height, and so forth—of the various visible objects to ourselves. This will remain true of our bodily vision as long as we live. I am the centre of the world I see; where the horizon is depends on where I stand. Now just the same thing is true at first of our mental and spiritual vision. Some things hurt us; we hope they will not happen again; we call them bad. Some things please us; we hope they will happen again; we call them good. Our standard of value is the way things affect ourselves. So each of us takes his place in the centre of his own world. But I am not the centre of the world, or the standard of reference as between good and bad; I am not, and God is. In other words, from the beginning I put myself in God's place. This is my original sin. I was doing it before I could speak, and everyone else has been doing it from early infancy. I am not "guilty" on this account because I could not help it. But I am in a state, from birth, in which I shall bring disaster on myself and everyone affected by my conduct unless I can escape from it.[12]

This is a spatial metaphor and its danger is that it tends to make finitude the cause of sin and thus remove responsibility.[13] Also Tillich suggests that the use of the term self-centeredness for sin is dangerous in that it suggests that the essential being of a person as a fully centered self is essentially evil.

Pride and Rebellion: We are God's creatures and completely dependent upon God. The only reason for our existence and the only purpose in our lives is to live in trust and obedience to God. But we don't like being dependent and subservient; we want to run our own lives. In our pride we rebel against God's sovereignty and proudly pretend to be like God with responsibility to no one but ourselves. Since this will usually involve allegiance and loyalty to some other ultimate, sin can be defined as idolatry or the opposite of faith.

Breaking of Communion: We are created to live in perfect communion and fellowship with God and with our neighbors. But we find that prior to any act of conscious choice we are out of communion with God, alienated and estranged from God. This estrangement is deepened by conscious acts. Furthermore our relations with our neighbors are disrupted and distorted by our acts and attitudes. Sin is the state of estrangement from God and neighbor. It is therefore the opposite of love. "The only intrinsic evil is lack of love."[14]

It follows from this that the *results of sin* can be summarized as a fourfold disharmony between humanity and God, self, neighbor and nature. The disharmony or estrangement from God is the fundamental one and the basis of the rest. The inner disharmony appears in the Genesis 3 story as shame and the bad conscience. It is described by Paul as an inner warfare between the law of the mind and the law of sin (Rom. 7:19). Augustine asserted that when the soul revolts against God, the passions revolt against the soul, and the person becomes a mass of conflicting desires (see Rom. 1). This is what psychiatry describes as the disintegration of the personality. Disharmony with the neighbor has been mentioned above. When persons assert their independence of God and seeks their own will, they come into conflict and competition with their neighbors who are also seeking their own wills (see Rom. 1:29f). Finally humanity comes into a state of disharmony with nature. This appears in Genesis 3 as the curse of the ground and the pain and toil of life. Human dominion over nature turns into tyranny, despoiling and exploitation in the bad sense. As Augustine put it, our infinite desire for God is turned toward the creature and becomes inordinate and insatiable (concupiscence) since it cannot be satisfied by the creature. Our estrangement from nature can be seen in the contrast between St. Francis' "Canticle of the Creatures" (Hymn 307) and Bertrand Russells' essay "A Free Man's Worship."

One aspect of the results of sin is man's *bondage* to sin. This is Augustine's *non posse non peccare* and Luther's *servum arbitrium.* This was overstated by the Augustinians and the Reformers in their debates with the Pelagians and the humanists. Our bondage in sin, our bondage of the will or unfreedom consists in the fact that we have lost our freedom to realize our divine destiny, to live in perfect trust and love toward God and neighbor. It does not mean that we have lost our capacity for creating civilization and culture, the state, the economic order, the family, the sciences, education, and the arts. Sin infects all aspects of our cultural creativity. We cannot create a truly humane culture, but we can create a culture. The effect of sin on our cultural creations lies on a spectrum and becomes more evident as we proceed from the most abstract, for example, mathematics, to the most concrete and personal, for example, family and religion.[15]

Our bondage in sin does not mean that we have lost completely our *moral freedom.* We still have what the Reformers called civil righteousness, the capacity to obey the laws of the state, to avoid murder, and so forth. But we do not have the freedom for that perfect goodness which is love for our neighbors as it is defined by Christ. Thus we can be virtuous or vicious sinners. As sinners we can avoid every wrong action which can be defined legally, as Paul did before his conversion (Phil. 3:6). To say that all people are sinners is not to deny the difference between good people and bad people. The New Testament authors assume the possibility and actuality of doing good apart from Christian faith. But this type of moral freedom refers primarily to outward acts and not to inner disposition. Where the sinner, even the virtuous sinner, is not free, is in the inner disposition, in the "heart." Our bondage is that we cannot make this into perfect love. The more closely one looks at the inner disposition, the less possible it is to distinguish between virtuous and vicious sinners, and the more it is clear that all people are sinners. Sinners are capable of avoiding every particular sinful act, but they are not capable of not being sinners. Thus the bondage of sin does not mean absolute unfreedom, but only the lack of freedom to cease being a sinner.

The distinction between the virtuous and vicious sinner leads directly to the problem of *guilt.* In the Bible guilt is the consequence of sin, the responsibility of sinners for their actions. It is interpreted as a burden or an obstacle standing between God and the sinner which is removed through the expiatory sacrifices of the cult and finally of Jesus. The objective side of guilt is the responsibility for the concrete consequences of sin and the resulting disruption of the relation with God. Niebuhr suggests that the Bible teaches the equality of sin and the inequality of guilt. The prophets and Jesus singled out the rich, the powerful, and also the wise and righteous for special condemnation not because they were greater sinners but because their guilt was greater, that is, their responsibility for the greater consequences of their sin.

The subjective side of guilt is the feeling of guilt, remorse, the bad conscience. Normal guilt feeling is not psychologically harmful but rather one of our best insights into reality. If we feel no guilt after hurting another person, no responsibility for a failure in love, then we are in psychological as well as theological trouble. In the extreme case this is a manifestation of a psychopathic personality. Abnormal or exaggerated guilt feeling and repressed or unconscious guilt are of course neurotic.

The analysis of the types of sin belongs to the discipline of moral theology. Niebuhr has an illuminating analysis of sin as pride, injustice, and sensuality.[16]

Feminist Theology

The main criticism by feminist theologians of the doctrine of sin in contemporary theology is that while it claims to refer to universal human experience, it in fact reflects primarily men's experience and not women's. The result is that it is largely irrelevant to women and also to parts of men's experience which have tended to be ignored. In particular it is argued that the doctrine of sin as pride, rebellion, and selfassertion and the corresponding commendation of the virtues of humility, submissiveness, self-abnegation and sacrificial love are exactly the opposite of what is relevant and appropriate to women's experience. Typical women's sins are interpreted as virtues and are thus reinforced, and typical women's virtues are turned into sins and are thus suppressed.

In an important essay originally published in 1960 Valerie Saiving states,

> The temptations of woman *as woman* are not the same as the temptations of man *as man*, and the specifically feminine forms of sin ... have a quality which can never be encompassed by such terms as "pride" and "will-to-power." They are better suggested by such items as triviality, distractibility and diffuseness; lack of an organizing center or focus; dependence on others for one's own self-definition; tolerance at the expense of standards of excellence; inability to respect the boundaries of privacy; sentimentality, gossipy sociability and mistrust of reason—in short, underdevelopment or negation of the self.[17]

Inspired by Saiving's essay Judith Plaskow has carried out a systematic critique of the doctrines of sin and grace in the theologies of Reinhold Niebuhr and Paul Tillich from the point of view of women's experience and has come to the same conclusion. She summarizes the feminist consensus on this point as follows:

"Women's sin," it is implied again and again, is not self-centeredness but what have historically been considered the Christian virtues. Self-sacrifice, obedience, etc., while perhaps necessary counterweights to the behavioral excesses of a stereotypically male culture, have been preached to and taken to heart by women, for whom they are already a way of life. Practiced in excess, they undermine the self's relationship to itself and ultimately to God.[18]

Any future reformulation of the doctrine of sin will have to take into account the experience of women as well as of other groups (colored, poor, third world) whose experience has also been largely ignored. The fundamental question raised by the feminist theologians here is whether the Bible and the Christian tradition can supply the foundation for doing this or whether they must be transcended, as Mary Daly, for example, argues.

Questions for Discussion

1. *In what sense and in what way if any is a newborn infant or one-year-old child involved in sin?*
2. *"We must ask whether sin comes from necessity or from choice. If from necessity, then it is not sin; if from choice, then it can be avoided,"(Celestius). Discuss.*
3. *Does the inevitability of sin and our responsibility for it constitute a logical contradiction (and thus nonsense), a paradox, a mystery, a myth, or what?*
4. *In what ways and to what extent are we free and not free? Is this a theological or a psychological question or both?*
5. *Original sin is the source of actual sin; sin as a state is the source of sin as acts. Does the inevitability of sin and our responsibility for it apply to the state or the act or both?*
6. *What does the theological doctrine of sin add to the psychological interpretation of human personality, acts, freedom, lack of freedom, hostility, self-assertion, and so forth?*
7. *What is the relation of the theological and the psychological interpretation of guilt?*
8. *Does the doctrine of sin apply to the non-Christian or the Christian or both? If both, does it apply to them in the same way or different ways?*
9. *How is it the doctrine of humanity as sinner related to the assertion that humanity has "come of age"? (Bonhoeffer)*
10. *If we cannot be conscious of ourselves as sinners until we have been saved from sin,*

how then can we be thought of as responsible for our condition as sinners?

11. What is the implication of theories of human inheritance of animal instincts of aggression (Lorenz, Ardrey) for the doctrine of sin?
12. What is the relation of neurosis to sin?
13. What is the origin of sin?

10

Christ

Christology or the doctrine of Christ is not simply one topic or part of systematic theology but the basis of the whole. "Dogmatics must actually be Christology and only Christology" (Barth). "If we have not a sound Christology, we cannot have a sound theology either" (Baillie). The doctrine of Christ is not an added difficulty for the doctrine of God but the only way in which it can be expressed. Christology is not a matter of attempting to reconcile the incarnation with a doctrine of God which we have already, for example, from the Old Testament or from philosophy, but it is the basis of our doctrine of God. And the same is true for all the other doctrines as well. Oscar Cullmann points out that the oldest confessions are expressed exclusively in christological terms. They were expanded into the threefold form from the christological part and not from the theological part (see 2 Cor. 13:14). "Early Christian theology is in reality almost exclusively Christology. In so far as it concentrated its whole theological interest for several centuries on Christological discussions, the early Catholic Church remained close enough to the early Church." [1]

Brunner claims that the work of Christ should be treated before the person of Christ, because we know who Christ is, through what Christ does. He quotes Melanchthon's famous dictum: "This is to know Christ, to know his benefits." Forsyth states, "The canon for the Incarnation . . . is soteriological. It is the work of Christ that gives us the key to the nature of Christ."[2] In the New Testament and the primitive church the knowledge of Christ moves from the work to the person. The earliest christological titles indicated Christ's work or function rather than Christ's being or nature. "When it is asked in the New Testament 'Who is Christ?' the question never means exclusively, or even primarily, 'What is his nature?', but first of all, 'What is his function?'"[3]

But in systematic theology it can be argued that we should follow the logical order of treating the subject or the agent of salvation before the act itself, that is, treat Christology in the order of being rather than in the order of knowing.

In any case we cannot separate the person and work of Christ; they are a unity. "The being of Christ is his work, and his work is his being."[4] "Christ is what he does and does what he is "(Brunner). We cannot conceive of Jesus being the Christ without being the savior, nor can we conceive of his being the savior without being the Christ.

Bible

To deal with the biblical basis of the doctrine of the person of Christ really amounts to dealing with the whole Bible, since most of it is related in one way or another to this question. So we shall have to be very selective and refer to the various biblical theologies and wordbooks for the details.

One of the main elements of the Old Testament revelation is hope for the final fulfillment of God's covenant promise in a new age of blessedness. Occasionally this fulfillment is seen as taking place through a human agent, an ideal ruler in the Davidic line or a heavenly figure. In the intertestamental period this hope becomes more apocalyptic, and God is sometimes seen as acting directly to inaugurate the kingdom. The other main element of the Old Testament revelation which forms the basis of New Testament Christology is that of differentiation in the godhead (see p. 60). Certain divine attributes or powers, such as Word, Wisdom and Glory, are distinguished and tend to be personalized or hypostatized in the Old Testament and Apocrypha. New Testament Christology is based on a combination of these traditions of messianic hope and hypostatic differentiation.

Although the problem of Christology has always been at the center of New Testament studies, it is especially so today as the result of the work of Bultmann. This can be seen in the continuing debate over demythologizing, the discussion about hermeneutics, and the so-called new quest for the historical Jesus. The literature is vast and the situation is quite fluid.[5] The elements of the historical and theological problems involved in New Testament Christology can be sketched in the following way: [6]

1. The Real Jesus (as he really was as distinct from historical knowledge of him)
   a. His empirical historical reality and activity
   b. His theological status and activity
2. Historical Records about Jesus (New Testament)
   a. Historical evidence of 1a
   b. Historical testimony to 1b
3. The Historical Jesus (results of attempt to determine 1a by means of historical critical analysis of 2)

4. New Testament Christology (description of 2b in its diversity and unity through historical critical analysis)
5. Christology (attempt by systematic theology to state 1b by means of interpretation of 4 in the light of tradition so that it can be understood today)

Christian faith assumes that 1 is a unity, that 1b is grounded in and manifest in 1a. This is confirmed by the present historical critical consensus that there is very little, if any, of 2a which is not also 2b. The motive of the old quest for the historical Jesus was to get behind the church orthodoxy to the real teaching and personality of Jesus. But the result of historical critical study and especially of form criticism demonstrated that the Jesus of the old quest was a theological projection and that little, if anything, could be known of 1a. Bultmann concluded: "I do indeed think that we can now know almost nothing concerning the life and personality of Jesus, since the early Christian sources show no interest in either."[7] The basis of the new quest is that the Christian kerygma is in fact about the concrete historical figure of Jesus, that the kerygma is stated by means of elements from the life and ministry of Jesus, and that the gospels convey a general impression about the person of Jesus which is independent of any particular passages, for example, his humble submission to God, his sense of authority, and his confronting people with a decision.

It is important to note that 4 is the work of historical critical study rather than systematic theology. New Testament scholars have been rather reticent to discuss the unity or consensus of the New Testament on Christology, thus implying either that there is none or that it is not their task. But they are not at all reticent in warning systematic theologians that it is not the latter's business.

Christology poses in its sharpest form the problem of the relation of systematic theology to the historical critical study of the Bible. Do the conclusions of systematic theology in the area of Christology fluctuate in dependence on whether historical criticism is radical or conservative? Or is systematic theology independent of such fluctuations? Can historical research lead to skepticism about the validity and veracity of the New Testament records and testimony? Can it lead to the conclusion that the New Testament picture of Jesus is unreliable and misleading? Can the results of historical research contradict the affirmations of Christian faith?[8]

On these questions the views of Brunner and Tillich represent two of the main options. Brunner's view is that once we affirm an incarnation of God in history, we enter the realm of historical research with the possibility of radical conflict between faith and historical criticism.

Not only the historical existence of a man called Jesus, but the credibility of the story of Jesus in its main features, and of the Gospel picture of the person of Jesus, of His teaching, working, suffering, and dying, belong to the essence of the Christian faith. Christian faith cannot arise, nor can it exist, without a historical picture of Jesus, or without a knowledge of the fact that this picture corresponds with reality, that He was "this kind of person," and that He lived in such and such a way, and behaved in a particular manner.[9]

So the question of the possibility of radical conflict between faith and criticism can be answered only by the concrete results of historical criticism. Brunner believes that the results of historical criticism to date have confirmed the essentials of the New Testament picture of Christ.

Tillich's view is that Christian faith is independent of the results of historical criticism. "Historical research can neither give nor take away the foundation of the Christian faith."[10] He specifically rejects Brunner's view; faith cannot rest on the unsure ground that historical research has not yet undercut Christian faith. That the man Jesus really existed is essential to Christian faith, but the methodological skepticism of historical research does not (cannot?) deny this factual element. Faith cannot guarantee the validity of the New Testament picture of Jesus. What it can guarantee is the appearance of the reality which has created it, namely, the appearance of the New Being in a concrete personal life. What we have in the New Testament is a picture of Jesus as the Christ, and Christian faith guarantees that this is an adequate picture of the personal life in which the New Being has appeared. Or, to put it the other way around, it is the New Testament picture of Christ which has mediated Christian faith in every age. It is impossible to get behind the New Testament picture of Christ and find a historical Jesus which is independent of the New Testament picture.

The views of Brunner and Tillich which have been outlined refer more to the relation of historical research to faith than to the work of systematic theology. They would agree generally on the nature of the contribution which historical research on the Bible has made to the work of theology, namely, in making available the biblical testimony on its own terms. The fundamental principle of the relation must be a complete openness to the method and results of historical critical study. Such openness is an immediate implication of the doctrine of salvation by grace.[11]

There are two main christological problems in regard to the New Testament. What did Jesus believe and teach about his own person and his relation to God? What did the New Testament authors affirm about the person of Christ? Since there is very little, if any, of 2a which is not also 2b, it may not be possible to determine the answer to the first question. But since the purpose of 2b was served by preserving some of 2a, it may be possible tentatively to determine Jesus' understanding of his person. The results of historical research seem to be that Jesus was aware at the end of his ministry that he stood in an intimate and unique relation to God and that his mission was closely associated with the coming of the kingdom. Bultmann believes that this question cannot be answered and that it is of secondary importance. Cullmann, on the other hand, believes that it can be answered and that it is of utmost importance. "The early Church believed in Christ's messiahship only because it believed that Jesus believed himself to be the Messiah. In this respect Bultmann's faith in Christ is fundamentally different from that of the early Church." [12] It is conceivable that God was accomplishing the divine will through Jesus without Jesus' knowledge or consciousness of this, but this is not the way God deals with people according to the Bible. God may act through Cyrus without his knowledge, but God acts through the prophets, for example, only by means of their conscious and responsible freedom.

What do the New Testament authors affirm about the person of Christ and his relation to God? Is there an earliest tradition which did not understand Jesus christologically or theologically but rather as simply a teacher, for example? As has been suggested above, the consensus of New Testament scholarship up until the beginning of the "new quest" was that there is very little, if any, 2a which is not also 2b, or that all of 2a is used for the purpose of 2b. Now, however, the "new questers" have asserted that, although this is true, it is now possible by means of form criticism to separate 2a from 2b. Thus we now have a second avenue to the historical Jesus which is independent of the kerygma (Bornkamm, Robinson). This raises the question of the relation between the historical Jesus and the kerygma.[13]

The New Testament material on the person of Christ can be analyzed under the titles ascribed to Jesus (Cullmann, Hahn, Dunn), under the various New Testament authors (V. Taylor), or historically by stages (Bultmann, Fuller). Cullman discusses the titles which refer to Jesus' earthly work, future work, present work, and pre-existence. Fuller distinguishes Jesus' self-understanding, the Christology of the earliest church, of the Hellenistic Jewish mission, and of the Hellenistic gentile mission. It is important in investigating New Testament Christology to treat not only the titles, such as Messiah, Son of God, Son of Man, Word and Lord, but also the implicit Christology of the teaching of Jesus and his actions, such as his healings and attitude toward the poor. Besides the passages asserting or implying the real humanity and pre-existence of Christ there is a group of passages which affirm the highest christology without using any of the traditional titles (2 Cor. 4:4, Col. 1:15, 19, 2:9, Phil. 2:6, Heb. 1:3).

Tradition [14]

What is the significance of the orthodox Christology as we find it in the Chalcedonian definition and the Athanasian Creed? Here the church is attempting to express its understanding of the Bible and the Christian message in the language of the day. The one God who is revealed in the law and the prophets is finally and fully revealed in Jesus Christ for humanity's salvation. In order to make this affirmation as clear possible and to protect it from distortion, the church rejected all attempts to qualify it. Lest it be suggested that in Christ we see something less than God, the church affirmed that the Son is of one substance with the Father. Lest it be thought that God's action in Christ might not be effective for all of human being and for all people, they affirmed that Christ was fully human, a complete human being. Lest God's action in Christ be thought to be temporary or partial, the church affirmed a full and perfect unity of the divine and human in Christ. And lest it be thought that there was anything accidental or contingent or simply dependent upon human initiative in Christ, the church affirmed that the actual reality of Christ (*hypostasis*) was perfectly united with that of God the Son.

Thus orthodox Christology does not attempt to explain the substance of Christology, that is, how the two natures are united in one person. It attempts to indicate where the mystery lies, so to speak, and to defend the mystery against the attempts to dissolve it into a neat formula which would distort it. Orthodox Christology gives the only possible answers to the questions posed by the various heresies. Is Christ just an inspired man like the prophets? (Adoptionism) No, Christ is of one substance with the Father. Is Christ God masquerading as a human being? (Apollinarianism, Monophysitism, Monothelitism) No, Christ is fully human, true humanity. Is Christ linked to the Word of God in a perfect moral union? (Nestorianism) No, Christ is one person. Is Christ an intermediary being, semi-divine and semi-human? (Arianism) No, Christ is truly God and truly human.

Thus the Chalcedonian definition does not make much sense in itself unless it is seen as the church's answer to the various distortions of Christian faith which arose in the first five centuries. "The truth is that this great formula derives part of its value from the clearness with which it refused to explain.... It is content to reaffirm the fact. But that is all that an authoritative formula ought to do."[15] We must reject the liberal interpretation of Chalcedon deriving from Ritschl and Harnack that the use of Greek philosophy resulted in an intellectualization and thus a distortion of Christian faith (see p. 63f). The church had to use the most precise conceptual tools available to it in order to interpret the gospel in such a way as to avoid the distortions which threatened it. And these tools were the concepts of contemporary Middle Platonism.

Cullman states, "In the light of the New Testament witness, all mere speculation about (Christ's) nature is an absurdity. Functional Christology is the only kind which exists." [16] Thus he sees a basic shift of emphasis in the early church from a functional to an ontological Christology which he seems to deplore. Fuller argues, however, that beginning with the gentile mission the New Testament testimony includes ontic (as well as functional) statements about Christ which raise ontological problems about Christ's relation to the Father and about the unity and humanity of Christ's person (see Phil. 2:6f, Jn. 1:1f).[17] In any case ontological problems are unavoidable if any attempt is made to talk about reality. Although some "biblical" theologians apparently define ontology as "bad, static, unhistorical, impersonal, or Greek" ontology, ontology should be used as a neutral term to describe the effort to talk consistently about the nature of reality. The conciliar theologians may be faulted for the character of their ontology but not for their attempt to deal with the ontological problems raised by the biblical testimony. The results of their labors have made it possible for modern philosophers and theologians to develop dynamic personal historical ontologies.

Most contemporary theologians would agree, however, that although the use of Hellenistic philosophy was a necessity, it was not very adequate to the task of Christology. It should be noted, however, that if later terminology is considered more adequate, this is the result of the transformation of our concepts of person, nature, and substance through the influence of Christian faith, including the Chalcedonian formula itself.

Most criticism has been concentrated on the term "nature" in the Chalcedonian definition. "One and the same Christ, Son, Lord, only begotten, made known in two natures (*en duo phusesin*)." Tillich points out that the concept of nature is derived from Greek religion and the philosophy dependent upon it. Here nature is the all-embracing concept, including humanity, the cosmos, and the gods. When this concept is applied to humanity, it is ambiguous. It may mean our essential created nature, our existential sinful nature, or the combination of these. Furthermore, since the Christian God transcends the reality comprehended in the Greek concept of nature, it is quite inadequate when applied to God.

W. R. Matthews, Casserley, and others assert that the chief defect in the Hellenistic philosophy used by the council was the absence of an adequate concept of personhood. This is crucial because the Christian faith is that the personal God has acted in a human personal life. Thus subpersonal concepts, such as nature, substance, and *hypostasis* will be inadequate to the precise formulation of the gospel. Matthews has suggested, for example, that the difficulties of the Chalcedonian definition came out clearly in the Monothelite controversy. Either answer to the problem of the will in Christ seems to land in error. If you affirm one will, namely, that of the Word, you deny the fullness and reality of the human nature in Christ. If you affirm two wills (declared orthodox at the Third Council of Constantinople in 681), you undercut the unity of Christ's person. The difficulty was that will had been distinguished from (human) nature, whereas in modern thought they are very closely associated if not identified. Paul of Samosata had attempted to state the relation of Christ and the Word in terms of will, which he distinguished from nature, and which he properly considered to be more appropriate to human personhood than nature. But his view was condemned because it seemed to involve a too external and tenuous relation between Christ and the Word. Thus because a Christology in terms of will had been ruled out, the only other group of terms available was that of nature and substance, which we have seen to be essentially inadequate to divine and human personhood.

H. W. Montefiore has indicated an even more fundamental problem in the Chalcedonian definition. The formula asserts of Christ, "the same perfect in Godhead and the same perfect in manhood, truly God and truly man. . . ." The implication is that apart from Christ we know what perfect godhead and perfect humanity are, and that on the basis of the New Testament testimony we are affirming that Jesus possessed both. But in fact the Christian faith is that it is precisely in Christ and nowhere else that we see what perfect godhead and perfect humanity are. Now Middle Platonist philosophy involved a doctrine of God as impassible, completely transcendent and immutable. Thus on these terms it is extremely difficult to understand how God and humanity could be united in one person. But the fundamental thing we know from Christ is that God can be perfectly united with humanity. This is where we begin in speaking about God and humanity. The problem is not how a union of God and humanity in one person is possible, but given the union manifest in Christ what perfect godhead and humanity are. "The theory or doctrine of the Person of Christ will not be found by merely stating His nature and works in terms of God and Man, but will involve restating God and Man in terms of the revelation given in Him."[18] Although the available terminology was not very adequate to such restatement, it was slowly transformed by its Christian theological usage. And today this area of philosophical terminology is deeply influenced by Christian concepts.[19]

The Christology of the Articles of Religion and *The Book of Common Prayer* adheres closely to the western orthodox tradition. Article II, the main one on the person of Christ, is based on the Augsburg Confession and was drawn up to oppose various christological heresies propounded by the Anabaptists.

Articles III, IV, VII, and XV deal with the descent into Hell, the resurrection, and ascension, the Old Testament testimony to Christ, and Christ's sinlessness. In the Prayer Book see the Christmas Collects and Prefaces, the Catechism, and the Historical Documents.[20]

Reconstruction

In attempting to reformulate the doctrine of the person of Christ we shall concentrate on the central problem of the "two natures" since it is posed by the New Testament testimony and has always been at the center of attention in the tradition. We shall investigate two tendencies in contemporary Christology which hold some promise for creative reinterpretation of the person of Christ.

The first tendency might be called the christology of the new liberalism since it has roots in Nestorianism and Schleiermacher. It is represented in varying degrees in the work of D. Baillie, Pittenger, Tillich, and the followers of Bonhoeffer. Its fundamental assertion is that essential or true humanity is identical with godhead or with the divinity of Christ. A corollary of at least some formulations of this approach is that the difference between Jesus and other people is a matter of degree. We shall illustrate this tendency by reference to Tillich's approach.

Tillich's basic statement is as follows:

> It is essential man who represents not only man to God but God to man; for essential man, by his very nature, represents God. He represents the original image of God embodied in man, but he does so under the conditions of estrangement between God and man. . . . One could also speak of essential God-manhood in order to indicate the divine presence in essential manhood.[21]

Tillich finds the background of this concept of essential or eternal God-manhood in the myths of the "original man," and the "man from above" in Persian religion. In the New Testament this takes the form of Paul's doctrine of the second or last Adam, the spiritual man, and the man from heaven (I Cor. 15:45ff). Tillich also interprets the New Testament titles Son of Man and Son of God in this sense.[22] He relates his approach to the traditional one in the following way:

> The assertion that Jesus as the Christ is the personal unity of a divine and a human nature must be replaced by the assertion that in Jesus as the Christ the eternal unity of God and man has become historical reality.

In his being, the New Being is real, and the New Being is the re-established unity between God and man.We replace the inadequate concept "divine nature" by the concepts "eternal God-man-unity" or "Eternal God-Manhood."[23]

The two main criticisms which can be made of this approach to Christology are that essential humanity cannot be identified with deity and that it implies that the difference between Jesus and other people is a matter of degree rather than kind. Temple puts it bluntly:

> If the question means, "Is Perfect Man *eo ipso* God?" the answer is, "No." Nothing that happens to a creature could possibly turn him into his own Creator. At that point the gulf between God and Man is plainly impass-able.[24]

Since Tillich's concept of eternal God-manhood is rather obscure, it is not clear in how far these criticisms apply to him. The difficulties of a "degree" Christology will be discussed below.[25]

The other tendency in contemporary Christology which shows some promise is one which is concerned to move away from the Middle Platonist categories of substance and nature to personal-historical, dynamic or functional categories. The fundamental thesis of this tendency is that the function or activity of Jesus is identical with the function or activity of God. This approach is represented by such theologians as W. R. Matthews, H. W. Montefiore, and J. Hick. We have noted Cullmann's assertion that the only Christology in the New Testament is a functional Christology. And Temple can state,

> The functions which [Christ] discharges are functions of God. Now functions, that is actions and reactions, are all we know. If Jesus Christ performs the acts of God, then Jesus Christ is God in the only sense in which any name can justifiably be attributed to any object.[26]

Matthews begins his approach by pointing out that in the light of modern philosophy and science it is possible to regard the changing world as "a complex of moving patterns," and persons as "moving patterns of behavior events." Thus we must think of the will of God as "a perfectly coherent moving pattern of acts of will, and a pattern which is not yet completed."[27] Then Matthews proposes his basic thesis:

> I contend that there is no contradiction or absurdity in holding that the moving pattern of the will of God could be also the moving pattern of the behavior events which constitute the temporal and historical aspects of a human life. The scale on which the pattern is manifested makes no essential difference. A personal life of which it could be said that it is of

the same pattern as the temporal will of God would be the supreme revelation of God: it would be God manifest 'in the flesh.' The pattern of the Father's will, on this hypothesis, is the essential reality of the temporal personality of the Son. It is his life; without it, or departing from it, he would cease to be himself. And the pattern, like the temporal will of God, is a moving pattern—the work is not yet completed.[28]

Montefiore expands on Matthews' thesis and points out that the concept of a moving pattern of activity is in accord with the biblical revelation. God is revealed in divine acts in history, and the pattern of God's activity is the same in the life and ministry of Jesus as it is in the Old Testament. As G.W.H. Lampe has put it, a genuine biblical typology "seeks to discover and make explicit the real correspondence historical events which have been brought about by the recurring rhythm of the divine activity."[29] Montefiore argues that the same pattern of activity is involved in creation, the election of Israel, the covenant and law, judgment and deliverance in the history of Israel, *and* in the life and ministry, death and resurrection of Jesus. This pattern is an outgoing love which is not coercive but leaves the beloved free.[30]

Hick has elaborated on Matthews' approach.[31] His basic christological thesis is that the *agape* manifest in the life and ministry of Jesus is identical with the divine *agape*, where *agape* is understood as an activity rather than a substance. This means that the attitudes, volitions, and acts which were expressed in Jesus' dealings with people are identical with the attitudes, volitions, and acts of God toward these same people, and that these are the manifestations of the eternal and universal *agape* of God. Thus Jesus' attitude and relation to those he healed, taught, summoned, and condemned are identical with God's attitude and relation to these people. So from the New Testament picture of Jesus' attitudes and actions toward a random assortment of individuals in the first century, we perceive the eternal pattern of God's attitude and activity. Then the Nicene and Chalcedonian *homoousios* can be interpreted to mean that Jesus' *agape* toward the people he met is not *like* God's *agape* toward them (that would be the Semi-Arian *homoiousios*) nor a reflection or imitation of the divine *agape* but identical with it.

Jesus' *agape* is God's *agape*. This "is" is not the "is" of definition or class membership but the "is" of identity. There are, however, two kinds of identity, qualitative and numerical. The above statement might mean that Jesus' *agape* is qualitatively identical with God's *agape*. This would be like saying that the love of Mrs. A for her children is qualitatively identical with the love of Mrs. B for her children. It would be meaningless to say that the love of Mrs. A and Mrs. B for their children are numerically identical since these two acts of loving are necessarily numerically distinct. Thus it might be argued that Jesus' *agape* is qualitatively identical with God's *agape*.

Hick suggests that the difficulty with this view is that it does not allow for the uniqueness of Christ to which testimony is given in the New Testament and in the church's tradition. The qualitative identity of Jesus' *agape* with God's *agape* is something which is in principle capable of occurring in other people or in all people or at least in other people in varying degrees. Then the difference between Jesus and other people would seem to be essentially a difference of degree rather than of kind. We noted above that this was a possible corollary of the Christology mentioned above. This seems to be the view of D. Baillie, and Pittenger.[32] But this falls short of the understanding of the uniqueness of Christ summed up in the phrases of the Nicene Creed: "the only Son of God, eternally begotten of the Father, . . . begotten, not made, of one being with the Father." In this sense Christ is unique: the only Son. We may become children of God but only in a secondary or derived sense by adoption. Hick also argues that a "degree" Christology always involves some form of Adoptionism. "The Degree Christology holds that Jesus Christ is unique in fact but not in principle, whilst the classical Christology holds that he is unique in fact and in principle, and unique in fact because unique in principle."[33]

This leads Hick to the consideration of the possibility of the numerical identity between Jesus' *agape* and God's *agape*. We have seen that it is not logically possible to assert a numerical identity of the love of two finite persons, because finite persons exclude one another. But it is not necessarily logically impossible to affirm that the *agape* of the finite Jesus is numerically identical with the *agape* of the infinite God. The reason is that the infinite is not excluded by the finite but must include the finite, otherwise the existence of the finite would constitute a boundary which would reduce the infinite to finitude. Thus the infinite and the finite can overlap or interpenetrate. So it is logically possible to say of the finite *agape* of Jesus that it is numerically identical with the infinite *agape* of God. The finite *agape* of Jesus is not coterminous with the infinite *agape* of God, that is, it is not identical with the whole of the infinite *agape* of God, but it is wholly the infinite *agape* of God. The finite *agape* of Jesus is, so to speak, a temporal cross-section of the infinite *agape* of God. The divine activity in the life of Jesus was wholly divine but not the whole of the divine activity in relation to the creation.

Hick then proceeds to specify the nature of this suggested numerical identity more closely. There are three types of numerical identity: self-identity (A=A), identity through time (A at t_1=A at t_2), and identity by continuity or inclusion. It is the latter type we have in mind when we assert the numerical identity between the *agape* of Jesus and God. In this case it is a continuity of activity rather than a continuity of entity.[34] This is quite close to the analogy of the incarnation which was used most widely in the patristic period, namely, the analogy of the sun and light from the sun, especially when light is understood as in the modern wave theory as a continuous moving pattern of activity of the sun. Thus the activity of sunlight on the earth is numerically identical in the sense of continuity with the radiating activity of the sun. So when we say that Jesus' *agape* is numerically identical with God's *agape* we mean that there is an identity of pattern or structure and a direct causal connection between them.

Hick's approach is an attempt to explain what we mean by *homoousios*, to clarify the meaning of the doctrine of the two natures of Christ. It is not an attempt to explain how this can happen. He believes that this will always remain a mystery.[35]

Van Buren

One of the most valuable parts of Paul Van Buren's *The Secular Meaning of the Gospel* is his interpretation of the intention of the theologians of the "right" who are influenced by biblical theology, especially the section entitled "A Christology of 'Call' and 'Response'."[36] He begins with the title Son of God and quotes Cullmann to the effect that this title involves the idea of election to participation in divine work through the execution of a particular commission, and the idea of strict obedience to the God who elects. Thus "Jesus as 'Son of God' meant Jesus as the obedient bearer of a specific election or commission."[37] According to the biblical picture God has a plan for the world which began to unfold in creation, was continued in the calling of Israel, and came to its climax in the election of Jesus. Jesus is the man elected by God as the full expression of the divine will and purpose and plan for the world (see Eph. 1). God's plan and his decision to carry it out express the very heart of God and not a casual, accidental, or incidental whim. Furthermore, it is eternal; we know nothing of a God who does not have this plan and has not made a decision to carry it out.

Then in the fullness of time God's plan was made flesh. It became a plan enacted in human history. What God had planned for humanity from the beginning, what God had in mind for humanity, what God had to say to humanity, became flesh and was to be seen and heard in the man Jesus. Thus he is the Word of God incarnate. In Jesus an intention became an action, a plan was enacted. Jesus is a real human being. He is completely and willingly involved in history and all the relationships of human life. But he is unique because he bears a particular calling and election from God, to which he responds in perfect obedience.

This interpretation of New Testament Christology, according to Van Buren, fulfills the intentions of the early church as expressed in the councils. The fact that Jesus is the embodiment of God's plan, the expression of the divine will, meets the problem posed by Arianism. The New Testament will not allow us to say of God's plan and decision that there was a time when it was not or that it is a manifestation of anything less than the will of God. The assertion of Jesus' full humanity meets the problems posed by Apollinarianism and Monophysitism, not by affirming that Jesus possessed all the parts of humanity but by asserting that he was completely involved in human life and all its relationships. The picture of Jesus as the enactment of God's plan meets the problem raised by Nestorianism. Jesus' life and ministry are so fully a manifestation of obedience to a divine election that we cannot speak or conceive of a Jesus who might have existed independently of God's plan, purpose and election. Jesus is *anhypostatos* or better *enhypostatos*; he has his actual historical existence only in the fulfillment of God's plan and election. It is clear that Van Buren's approach includes some of the emphases of both of the tendencies discussed above.

Van Buren's interpretation puts the problem of "degree" Christology in a new light. It is God's plan that through Jesus all people should come to share his relationship to God, namely, to become faithful and obedient to God's calling and will. So in this sense the difference between Jesus and other people is a matter of degree. But the fundamental difference is in their calling or election. Jesus is called to be the Messiah, the Word of God for all people, the beginning of the new Israel, whereas we are called to be members of the new Israel through him. We are called to be adopted children of God, adopted brothers and sisters of the "only-begotten Son."

Recent Christology

In the past decade there has been more theological attention to Christology than to any other doctrine in most Christian traditions: Roman Catholic (van Beeck, Bouyer, Kasper, Küng, Rahner, Richard, Schillbeeckx, Schoonenberg), Latin American liberation (Boff, Miranda, Nolan, Sobrino), Protestant (Driver, Frei, Moltmann, Ogden, Teselle), feminist (Daly, Ruether), black liberation (Cone), process (Cobb, Griffin, Suchocki), and Anglican (Moule, Pittenger, Robinson, and the volumes edited by Sykes and Slayton, Hick, Green, and Goulder). There have also been studies of particular issues in Christology, such as the relation of Christ to other religions and cultures (Cobb, Cupitt, Davis, Pannikar, Rahner, Richard, Rupp) and in particular to Judaism (Borowitz, Ruether, Van Buren).

Furthermore, most of this recent literature on Christology has pursued the themes which have been outlined above. It has been focused on the historical figure of Jesus as this is available through historical critical study. It has emphasized the full humanity of Jesus. It has stressed Jesus' prophetic teaching on and relation to the kingdom of God. It has tended to be functional rather than substantial in its approach. In other words recent Christology has been developed "from below," that is, from the historical humanity and experience of the man Jesus as distinguished from being developed "from above," that is, from the eternal Word, the divine Logos, God the Son, the divinity of Christ.[38]

Karl Rahner distinguishes these two approaches as the two basic types of Christology and describes them as the ascending and descending types or the saving history and metaphysical types. Although both are necessary in the church, Rahner commends the former for its credibility and significance for the present situation,[39] and he elaborates it in his *Foundations of Christian Faith* [40] one-fourth of which is devoted to Christology. Hans Küng goes even farther in this direction in his book *On Being a Christian*.[41] He is very critical of the Chalcedonian tradition and asserts that Christology must begin with the human life and ministry of Jesus as the disciples did. The earthly Jesus as made available to us by historical critical study is the final norm of Christian faith and life.

Edward Schillebeeckx pursues the same approach in a somewhat different way in his two massive studies of Christology.[42] Again the starting point is the human Jesus known through historical critical study, but the focus is on experience as the medium of God's revelation: Jesus' Abba-experience, the disciples' experience of Jesus, the disciples' Easter experience, and our Easter experience mediated by the church. Thus Christian faith is faith in Jesus of Nazareth, the eschatological prophet, but this first-order assertion of faith needs to be explicated in second-order affirmations, such as those of Nicea and Chalcedon, which need to be worked out anew in every generation.

Jon Sobrino follows Rahner in his distinction of Christologies of ascent and descent, and he argues for the necessity of the former in his liberationist Christology. We must begin with the historical Jesus, but adequate knowledge of Jesus comes only through following Jesus in his identification with the oppressed and his confrontation of the oppressors. Then we can see that the divinity of Jesus consists in his surrender and obedience to God.[43]

Rosemary Radford Ruether is most sympathetic with Latin American liberation theology, but her Christology is more radical. The necessary starting point is the historical figure of Jesus, but we must approach him with certain concerns in mind: political commitment in the light of poverty and oppression, anti-Semitism, justice for women, and human survival in the face of environmental abuse. This leads to a Christology of Jesus as the messianic prophet, a political figure who proclaims a this-worldly and non-eschatological kingdom of justice and peace.

Ruether raises the question of whether Christology can be liberated from the structures of patriarchy or whether it is unredeemable as good news for women. She is sympathetic with women who conclude that the maleness of Christ is so fundamental to Christianity that women cannot see themselves as liberated through him.[44] She is critical of androgynous Christologies and concludes that a prophetic iconoclastic liberationist Christology is the only possible one for women.[45]

Another version of liberationist Christology is offered by James H. Cone. He asserts that the title of Jesus as Black Messiah is "the only meaningful Christological statement in our time." "Blackness" is defined as participation in being oppressed and in liberation from oppression.[46] It is because Jesus was a Jew, identified with his people in their oppression, and especially with the outcast, in order to liberate them, that he is properly described as black.[47]

Process theology, which has offered important new insights on many topics of theology, has recently addressed itself to Christology. John B. Cobb Jr., borrowing an idea from art history, defines "Christ" as the image of a process of creative transformation of our imagination and life orientation. He argues that this process is produced by the universal presence of the transcendent Logos, interpreted in Whiteheadian terms. Since the Logos was distinctively embodied in Jesus, Jesus is properly called the Christ.[48] Beginning from the other end David R. Griffin uses the mind-body analogy as interpreted by process philosophy to explain how Christ can be understood to be God's special action. Jesus is the special action of God in the sense that God's purpose or initial aim for his life reflected God's overall purpose in the highest degree and Jesus' response actualized God's purpose for his life also in the highest degree.[49]

In recent years Anglican thought on Christology has been preoccupied with the debate surrounding the book entitled *The Myth of God Incarnate*.[50] In this volume seven authors (five of whom are Anglican) argue that a major adjustment is required in Christian theology comparable to those which resulted from the theory of evolution and from the historical critical study of the Bible. This is that the conception of Jesus as God incarnate, the Second Person of the Holy Trinity living a human life, is "a mythological or poetic way of expressing his significance for us" rather than a literal truth (p. ix). In his introductory essay Maurice Wiles questions whether incarnation is an essential concept in Christian faith and also whether it is an intelligible concept. The two following groups of essays on the New Testament and the tradition generally support Wiles' critical view. The ensuing debate has not produced much in the way of constructive Christology, but it has clarified many logical, historical and theological questions.[51]

The Virgin Birth

This doctrine is more accurately and properly called the virginal conception, since the concept of the virgin birth is sometimes in Roman Catholic theology related to the perpetual virginity of Mary. The basis of the doctrine is found in the birth stories in Matthew and Luke. It is not mentioned in any other part of the New Testament. Although other New Testament authors speak of the birth of Jesus (Gal. 4:4, Rom. 1:3), and of the incarnation of the Son of God (Rom. 8:3, 2 Cor. 8:9, Phil. 2:17, Jn. 1:14), none of them speaks of Jesus' virginal conception, including those who must have known the gospels of Matthew and Luke. It is also clear that the virginal conception formed no part of the earliest Christian preaching. The consensus of non-fundamentalist non-Roman Catholic historical scholarship is that the birth stories of Matthew and Luke are legendary material deriving from a Palestinian Jewish milieu.

The virginal conception of Jesus was not mentioned by any of the apostolic fathers except Ignatius. Among the second century apologists it is mentioned only by Justin and Aristides. From about 150 A.D. on it was affirmed by most Christian authors, both orthodox and heretical. It was included in some forms of the rule of faith in the second and third centuries as a defense against gnosticism, docetism, and adoptionism. But it was not included in the Creed of Nicea (325). Beginning in the nineteenth century the doctrine of the virginal conception was subjected to historical criticism by the new historical critical approach to the Bible, and to theological criticism by the new liberal theology beginning with Schleiermacher.

The main theological issue in regard to the doctrine of the virginal conception of Jesus is whether or not this doctrine is an essential element in Christian faith, that is, an essential element in the doctrine of the person of Christ. Conservative Roman Catholic and Protestant theologians affirm that it is essential, while liberal Roman Catholics (Küng, Schillebeeckx) and Protestants deny that it is essential. Most Anglican theologians deny that it is essential, but there are some exceptions.

Among twentieth century Protestant theologians the doctrine of the virginal conception is either ignored, rejected, described as legendary and mythological (Bultmann and Tillich), or affirmed as an occasionally helpful pious symbol. Pannenberg and Brunner, however, declare that it stands in contradiction to the doctrine of the incarnation in the sense of the assuming of human nature by the preexistent Son of God.[52] Although the two concepts were later harmonized by interpreting the virginal conception as the way in which the eternal Son assumed human nature, the original meaning of the virginal conception was the explanation of the way in which the Son of God came into being. Brunner also sees the doctrine of the virginal conception as threatening the true humanity of Jesus and as having a strongly docetic trait and a negative valuation of sex.

Unique in neo-orthodox theology is Karl Barth's defense of the doctrine of the virginal conception.[53] Barth is aware that the virginal conception is only "thinly and dubiously" attested in the Bible. But he asserts that "the decision as to the necessity of the dogma" cannot be made on the basis of literary analysis of the New Testament passages but only on the basis of whether or not there is "a certain inward, essential rightness and importance" of the doctrine in relation to the person of Christ. Barth concludes that the miracle of the virginal conception points validly to the mystery of the person of Christ, namely, the union in him of true deity and true humanity. In this sense it is parallel to the story of the empty tomb in relation to the resurrection of Christ. The sign and the thing signified must be distinguished but cannot easily be separated. The doctrine of the virginal conception points to the fact that human nature of itself possesses no capacity for becoming the human nature of Christ. Human nature is involved in the incarnation not as willing, achieving, creative, and sovereign, but only as receptive. Barth's conclusion is that we must acknowledge the "necessity" of the doctrine of the virginal conception.

The doctrine of the virginal conception involves the assertion of a historical fact, namely, that Mary conceived Jesus without male assistance. Barth seems to argue for the doctrine and thus for the historical fact on the basis of the essential coherence of the doctrine with other doctrines. This may be a valid procedure in physics but it is not valid in theology, because the systematic character and the relation to observable fact is not the same in theology and physics.

If the birth narratives in Matthew and Luke are legendary, there is no historical evidence for the historical fact of the virginal conception, and it must be held to be historically highly improbable. Therefore the only significance the doctrine can have is a symbolic one, which, however, is fundamental to the doctrine of the person of Christ. It is significant because in the new beginning which God made in Jesus Christ for the salvation of humanity the initiative was entirely that of God and not of humanity. The historical reality and existence of Jesus is not based on the action of humanity but is entirely dependent upon the action of God. (This is the real meaning of the doctrine of *anhypostasia* or *enhypostasia*.) But this action of God was carried out in connection with the free submission, receptivity and obedience of humanity as symbolized in Mary.

Questions for Discussion

1. *If Christology is the basis of all theology, why is the Old Testament in the canon?*
2. *Jesus prayed to God. Was this God the Son praying to God the Father, or a man praying to the triune God, or what?*
3. *"It is not two 'natures' which have to be related; but two 'histories'. There is the*

history of our human existence with its fate, its freedom, and its course of events. In this history stands the real person, Jesus of Nazareth, who is just as truly 'historical' as any other. There is also the history of God's creative and redemptive dealing with men which has come to its climax in the history of Jesus. It is these two histories which we have to relate to each other" (Williams). In what ways is this approach a help or a hindrance to the problem of Christology?

4. *If Jesus was "one Person," and if this person is God the Son, then his humanity must be impersonal (anhypostatos) and thus he was not true humanity. What is the source of this apparent contradiction and how can it be overcome?*

5. *Is the difference between Jesus and other people a matter of degree or kind? If degree, how is he unique? If kind, how is he human?*

6. *"In the early church the main christological problem was to preserve the full humanity of Christ, whereas in the present day the main christological problem is the establishment of his divinity." How would you interpret the divinity of Christ today? Why would you take this approach?*

7. *Do the New Testament and church tradition assert that Jesus was sinless? If so, which is preferable, to say that Jesus could not sin or that he did not sin? Why?*

8. *Temptation presupposes sin (Niebuhr). Jesus was tempted. Then in what sense can we say that he is sinless?*

9. *What aspects of traditional Christology must be demythologized? Why?*

10. *Does the historical critical approach to the Bible affect or determine the doctrine of the person of Christ? If so, in what way? If not, why not?*

11. *What historical assertions are necessarily involved in Christian faith? That Jesus lived? That he believed himself to be the Messiah? That he was raised from the dead? Others? Is Christian faith therefore dependent on the results of historical research?*

12. *How would you interpret the meaning of the Chalcedonian formula so that it can be understood today?*

13. *"Any statement about Christ today that fails to consider his blackness as the decisive factor about his Person is a denial of the New Testament message" (J. H. Cone). Discuss.*

14. *Is the virginal conception of Jesus a historical fact? Is it an essential element in Christian faith? How do you decide?*

15. *Does Jesus Christ save us because he is the Son of God, or is he the Son of God because he saves us?*

16. *Is the incarnation a myth?*

11

Salvation

With the doctrine of salvation or the atonement or the work of Christ, we come to the "center of all Christian knowledge," to the "heart of the Church's dogmatics" (Barth), to "the heart of every Christian theology" (Tillich). As center, this topic is integrally related to all the other topics of Christian theology. In particular salvation is the beginning of the fulfillment of creation and the manifestation of the nature of the final consummation. Thus the doctrines of creation, salvation and eschatology are mutually implied in each other. Creation, salvation and consummation are not independent acts of God but rather moments in God's one great action in relation to the world. "Creation, reconciliation, and consummation are not separate acts but only distinguishable aspects of one awe-inspiring movement of God—his love or letting be, whereby he confers, sustains, and perfects the being of his creatures."[1]

Our task here is essentially to inquire as to the nature and meaning of the Christian gospel, the message of the good news about God's love manifest in Christ for our salvation. Our task is to determine how the gospel can best be stated and presented to people today and related to their situation. According to our criteria of theological judgments this will involve a determination of how the gospel is stated in the Bible. In this connection we would have to investigate the question of whether there is a consensus in the New Testament on this or whether we will have to choose among different interpretations. The same applies to the various ways in which the gospel has been interpreted in the tradition of the church. This cannot all be done in this chapter but various aspects of these questions will be treated.

The doctrine of salvation can be focussed narrowly on the significance of the death of Christ, somewhat more widely in the concept of the work of Christ, or most broadly in the idea of God's plan and will to bring the creation to its fulfillment, as suggested in the quotation from Macquarrie. In the latter sense it includes many other theological concepts which have often been treated separately, namely, election, predestination, grace, regeneration, justification and sanctification. Some of these concepts will be discussed in later chapters. But it is important to recognize that they constitute an organic whole and represent facets or elements of such a unity. In addition, it should be noted that the question of the appropriation of salvation involves the doctrines of the church, sacraments, preaching and worship, which will be dealt with in later chapters.

The present situation in the doctrine of salvation is rather confused. Barth has reinterpreted the essentially Pauline and Reformation themes of judgment and substitution as has Pannenberg. Bultmann has used the existentialist analysis to interpret salvation as the transition from inauthentic to authentic existence effected by the kerygma of the cross. Tillich has added to existentialist analysis the ontological concepts of healing and participation in the New Being. The secular theologians (Robinson, Cox) have offered a variety of interpretations of salvation including personal, psychological and political analogies. The radical theologians (Hamilton, Altizer, Van Buren) have either ignored the problem or have concentrated on the image of liberation from bondage. The most important recent contribution to the doctrine of salvation has come from the black, feminist and Latin American liberation theologians, and their work will be discussed later.

V. A. Harvey suggests that there are two basic perspectives . Christian history on the doctrine of salvation. One is characteristic of Roman Catholicism and Eastern Orthodoxy, and the other is characteristic of Protestantism. In the first, salvation is understood as the participation of humanity in the divine life, sometimes called in patristic theology the deification of humanity. The means is primarily the sacraments, and the theological language is primarily that of being, substance and nature. The focus of theological emphasis is the incarnation of Christ. In the second perspective salvation is understood as the restoration of a broken personal relationship, communion and fellowship with God through the forgiveness of sin. The means is primarily the preaching of the word of divine favor and forgiveness. The theological language is that of personal existence, and the focus of theological emphasis is the atonement of Christ.

Herbert W. Richardson has outlined a third perspective on the doctrine of salvation which is similar to the Catholic-Orthodox one but which was developed in American Protestantism. According to this interpretation the key question is not *cur deus homo?*, Why did God become human?, but *cur creatio?*, Why did God create the world? The answer given is that the goal of creation is the sanctification of the world by the Holy Spirit of God, symbolized in the sabbath. Since the divine holiness is incommunicable, God must personally enter the world in Christ. Thus the incarnation is not contingent upon or a consequence of sin but rather is part of God's plan in creation.

Redemption from sin is therefore subordinate to sanctification.[2] This is an important perspective which is often overlooked in Protestant theology today because of the dominance of neo-orthodox theology.

What is the problem which confronts us in interpreting the doctrine of salvation? On the one hand we have the record of the biblical story, the testimony to the history of salvation, culminating in Christ, his life, ministry, death, resurrection, and exaltation, and the coming of the Spirit. On the other hand, we have the record and testimony of human participation in salvation in the Bible and the history of the church and also our own experience of Christian salvation. The problem of the doctrine of salvation is how the one is related to the other. In particular how are the events culminating in Christ related to Christian salvation? How are these events the cause of salvation?

We shall approach these questions by first asking what form the answers might take. There seem to be three possible forms:

(1) *Metaphors.* For example, the events culminating in Christ are related to or are the cause of Christian salvation:

- (a) as Old Testament sacrifice is related to Old Testament salvation (Hebrews);
- (b) as acquittal in a court of law is related to civil righteousness and freedom (Paul);
- (c) as warfare leading to military victory is related to the liberation, safety, and security of a nation (Christus Victor theme);
- (d) as the suffering involved in forgiveness between persons is related to their reconciliation (Paul);
- (e) as the ransoming or manumission of slaves is related to their freedom (Paul);
- (f) as the coming of a king into one house in a city is related to the safety and security of the whole city (Athanasius);
- (g) as the payment of a satisfaction is related to the discharging of an offense against a person's honor in private law (Anselm);
- (h) as the suffering of a punishment under criminal law is related to the discharging of the debt for a criminal offense (Reformers);
- (i) as the relaxing of a positive law by a ruler accompanied by a public punishment as a deterrent example is related to the liberation of the guilty under the law and the promotion of the common good (Grotius).

In these metaphors for Christian salvation there is no necessary assertion that the metaphor describes what is actually going on between God and humanity. The essential form of the metaphor is: salvation is *like* x. Some of the authors of the above metaphors may have thought they were not simply metaphors but rather theories.

(2) *Theories:* Each theory of Christian salvation claims to explain in as exact and precise terms as possible what is really happening between God and humanity in the work of Christ rather than just comparing it to something else. For example, the Christian events are related Christian salvation in the following way:

  (a) The passion and death of Christ are an expiatory sacrifice which does away with sin and guilt as obstacles between God and humanity and thus restores humanity to communion with God (V. Taylor). The point here is that the sacrifice of Christ is not simply like Old Testament sacrifice but that it is the fulfillment and end of Old Testament sacrifice. The problem here is that the Bible supplies no explanation of the modus operandi or mechanism of sacrifice, and so modern interpreters are hard put to offer any explanation of what is actually going on.

  (b) In the Christian events the evil powers of the world which hold humanity in bondage have actually been overthrown or undercut, so that humanity is freed for fellowship with and obedience to God (Aulen). Here the evil powers may be understood as real spiritual beings or demythologized into symbolic representations of destructive individual and social structures. In any case they have actually been destroyed or their power broken by Christ. Again the actual modus operandi is not clear.

  (c) Since the relation between God and humanity is essentially the same as that between human beings and since forgiveness and reconciliation between people is effected only by suffering love, the passion of Christ is in fact the suffering love of God in action which accomplishes God's forgiveness of humanity and its reconciliation.

  (d) The union of deity and humanity in the one person of Christ has brought about in principle a transformation of the whole of humanity in the image of Christ. This theory is based on a Platonic or medieval realist view of reality.

  (e) The three legal metaphors of Anselm, Calvin and Grotius can be interpreted as theories in the sense that they actually describe what is going on between God and humanity in Christian salvation.

  (f) The Christian events effect Christian salvation because they are the revelation of God's love which overcomes ignorance and wrong ideas about God, and they move humanity to repentance and faith (Abelard and liberal Protestant theology).

(3) *Theological Analogies:* This third possibility in regard to the form of the doctrine of salvation falls somewhere between the first and the second. A

theological analogy is like a metaphor in that it involves the assumption that all theological terms are symbolic or analogical in character rather than univocal. However, it goes beyond a metaphor in attempting to interpret and explain the exact meaning of its assertions as clearly and precisely as possible. Thus a theological analogy attempts to be as precise as a theory without assuming the possibility of a univocal description of the mechanism of Christian salvation.

It is not clear to what extent the biblical and ecclesiastical authors were aware of the above distinctions and whether they would describe their interpretations as metaphors, theories, or analogies. For the purposes of theology, however, it is clear that metaphors are not precise enough and that theories are ruled out in the nature of the case.[3] Therefore the form of the doctrine of salvation must be a theological analogy.

Now what is the basis of the possibility of metaphors and analogies of Christian salvation? Their possibility implies that God's act of salvation in Christ has something in common with events in human experience and thus can be compared with them. Don S. Browning argues on the basis of monotheism and the unity of the world that psychotherapy and other healing processes are possible only because they participate in God's healing activity itself. This is why they can be analogies of salvation.

> Every limited and preliminary healing-producing activity is fundamentally grounded in, participates in, and finally, is derivative of God's ultimate healing activity. Insofar as it is grounded in God's ultimate healing activity, it must show some proportionality to the structure and form of the ultimate source of all healing.[4]

This is one way to state the basis of the possibility of theological analogies of salvation. It suggests that every analogy of salvation is actually a manifestation of this salvation. Many complex questions arise at this point. Is this thesis true of all of the metaphors of salvation which have been mentioned above? Since all these human experiences existed before Christ, what is their relation to Christ? What is the relation of God to the proximate agents in these experiences? Could some of these be fruitful metaphors of salvation without actually being manifestations of it?

The construction of a theological analogy for the doctrine of salvation involves the following steps; the selection of an analogy, its justification, and its precise interpretation and explanation. What criteria are involved in selecting an analogy? The first criterion is faithfulness to the testimony to Christ in the Bible in the light of the church's tradition. The second criterion is the capacity of an analogy to communicate the doctrine of salvation to the modern mind. This means that the doctrine must be stated in terminology and with concepts which are understood today. There may obviously be a tension between these two criteria. The dangers involved in overemphasis on one or the other are archaistic irrelevance and modernistic dissolution. These two criteria are admirably represented in contemporary theology by Barth and Tillich.[5]

Tillich believes that a theological doctrine must be the answer to a question implied in the "situation," which he defines as "the totality of man's creative self-interpretation in a special period."[6] Thus each main section of Tillich's theory begins with an existential analysis to determine the question implied in the situation. The danger is, of course, that the theological answer will be constructed out of the question rather than out of the biblical testimony. It is quite clear that human longing for salvation or the interpretation of what it is we want to be saved from and to varies from age to age.[7]

Thus one way to study the doctrine of salvation is to investigate in the Bible and the history of Christian thought the different interpretations of what one is saved from and what one is saved to. Then the question of the doctrine of salvation can be posed as the question of what we need to be saved from and saved to today. That from which we need to be saved is usually formulated under the doctrine of sin.

This leads to another question about the selection of an analogy. Must the analogy be taken from the Bible or can it be taken from other areas of experience? The doctrine of the "supremacy of Scripture" (chapter 3) would seem to indicate that the analogy must be taken from the Bible. But these alternatives do not turn out to be mutually exclusive because the choice of analogies both within and outside the Bible comes down to the same general possibilities. The fundamental reason for this is that the basic structure of human life and experience today is not essentially different from what it was in the first century. The New Testament authors drew metaphors to interpret Christian salvation from various areas of human experience, and the same general areas are still open to us today. This situation has been admirably described by F. W. Dillistone:

> Our fundamental claim is that there are four great areas of the imagination from which words and metaphors may be drawn. These areas cover the whole of human existence and it is probable that every man has at least some experience within each. The precise structure of these areas will differ from generation to generation and from people to people, but not entirely so. Always, we believe, it will be possible to discover some common pattern, some comparable elements, and therefore a meaningful exposition derived from any one of these fields will contain something of universal relevance. These areas we shall now briefly describe.
>
> The first corresponds to the struggle of life, that struggle in which all

mankind is, in some form, engaged; the struggle with the elements, the struggle with the earth, the struggle with pestilence and disease, the struggle with other members of society, the struggle with demonic powers. The second corresponds to the ordering of the life of the community: the establishment of law, the administration of justice, cooperation and collaboration for the common good, the maintenance of harmony and peace. The third corresponds to the creative activity of men: the construction of useful and beautiful objects, the development of the arts, the advancement of science, the upbuilding of all that is included within the general term 'culture' within the life of mankind. The fourth and last corresponds to the life of the family; the provision of a centre of shelter and protection, the nurture of the young, the warmth of mutual love, the experience of the most intimate personal relationship. Within these four areas—the field of conflict, the life of the community, the development of culture, the intimacy of the home—the whole of human existence is encompassed.[8]

Dillistone describes his theological method as that of making "imaginative comparisons between dramatic events such as might happen upon the human plane and the supreme dramatic event which took place, as we believe, within the economy of God."[9] In a more recent book on this subject, Dillistone describes his method as the establishment of a vital connection between the historical event and the transcendent effect. This is accomplished by the development of "a theory, an imaginative pattern of comparison which somehow links the record of the death and resurrection of Christ with the wider experiences of mankind."[10] In this volume his analysis of human experience is somewhat different and results in four main areas: persons in relation to their universe, to their total society, to their kin group, and to themselves. But his general method remains the same.

For the interpretation of the doctrine of salvation in this chapter I have chosen the analogy of family life or human personal relations. Kaufman states that the best analogy for the interpretation of salvation is interpersonal relations.[11] Browning's use of psychotherapy as an analogy of salvation is simply a special form of the analogy of personal relations. The justification of this choice is as follows: First this analogy is fundamental and pervasive in the Bible. The basic biblical metaphor for the relations of God and humanity is the realm of human personal relations. This will be analyzed in more detail below. Secondly, this area of human experience is probably the most universal of all the areas, and thus interpretations of salvation based on this area will be the most universally understandable. To be sure the structure of family life varies greatly in different cultures and has been subject to radical change and some disintegration in advanced industrial civilizations, but the basic structure of familial relations, husband-wife, parent-child, involves some con-

tinuity and universality. Furthermore, the negative aspects of human existence and experience, or theologically the manifestations of sin, that from
which one needs to be saved, appear as clearly in the realm of family life or
personal relations as in any other area. The use of personal analogies is one
of the most significant developments in systematic theology in this century.[12]

It is important, however, to note some reservations and limitations of the
analogy of family life or personal relations. Although the experience of this
area of human life may be universal, today it is generally limited to private life
and thus its analogical use in theology tends to limit the understanding of
salvation to personal life. Furthermore, family life is on the passive and
receiving end of society today and is determined largely by decisions in the
public realm. Therefore, this particular analogy needs to be supplemented
and complemented by analogies taken from the sphere of public life, such as
politics (Cox, Moltmann), and from our relation to the universe (de Chardin).

The next step in the justification of this analogy for the doctrine of salvation
is to demonstrate its basic in the Bible. In brief, the fundamental biblical
metaphor for the relation of God and humanity is that of human personal
relations and in particular the life of the family. This is the source of most of
the anthropomorphic language about God in the Bible. God loves Israel, is
angry with Israel, jealous over Israel, patient and long suffering with Israel;
God is the husband of Israel. The metaphors of the faithful and unfaithful
wife and children and of the relation of father and son run through the whole
Bible. "The New Testament has a character all of its own amidst the other
writings of the ancient world. Its form is determined by personal problems
and personal encounters to an extent to which there is no obvious parallel
elsewhere." [13]

In particular the analogy of the family is fundamental in the Old Testament. The covenant with Abraham and his descendants is the context of the
whole Old Testament. Thus Israel is understood to be God's chosen family or
son (Ex. 4:22). The great danger for Israel was that it would be unfaithful to
the covenant as a rebellious son or an unfaithful wife. God's judgment on this
rebellion and the patience of the divine forgiving love are proclaimed by
Amos and Hosea (Amos 3:2, Hosea 11:1-9). Thus salvation is interpreted in
terms of the restored family (Isa. 43:5f).

The family theme is continued in the New Testament and is summed up in
Jesus' saying about his mother and brothers (Mk. 3:34f). Thus the church,
the new Israel, is the new family of God built up around the Son of God.
Central to this theme throughout the New Testament is the image of God as
the Father of the Son and thus of the family whom God loves, judges, forgives
and cares for. Within the family metaphor the Old Testament themes

concerning the disruption of family life in disobedience, rebellion, and unfaithfulness are also continued in the New Testament. The metaphors of salvation as the gathering of the family and as the reconciliation of the disrupted family are elaborated throughout the New Testament.

At the heart of the metaphor of the family in the New Testament is the relationship of the Father to the Son. This title of Jesus appears at the crucial turning points of the gospel story. Sonship means faithful trust and loving obedience, and it receives its most thorough development in the fourth gospel. Here Jesus' knowledge, power, words and authority as Son are from the Father with whom he stands in the closest filial communion. On the Father's side there is love for and confidence in the Son (Jn. 3:35).

According to Paul salvation involves becoming children of God through association with the Son of God. By the grace of God we become adopted children of God and thus brothers and sisters or joint heirs with the Son. Thus the new family of God is created by the grace of adoption (Gal. 4:5f). The basis of this is the love of the Son of God which Paul analyzes in terms of forgiveness and reconciliation, terms taken from the realm of intimate personal relations which are seen most clearly in family life. Thus it is clear that the theological analogy of family life and personal relations is fundamental in the understanding of salvation in the Bible.

The next step in the construction of this theological analogy for the doctrine of salvation is the more exact specification and interpretation of the analogy. Within the life of the family the relationship of husband and wife, brother and sister, or parent and child could be chosen for detailed analysis and interpretation of the doctrine of salvation. I have selected that of parent and child because of its prominence in the Bible and its usefulness in explicating Christian salvation. In the relationship of the parent to the child there are two fundamental aspects, self-giving and authority. The parent is called to give himself or herself unsparingly to provide food, shelter, protection, guidance, encouragement and love for the sake of the child. This relationship also involves an element of structure or requirement. This should be flexible and open but also directed toward some goal, standard, or ideal which is the fulfillment of the child. The corresponding attitudes on the part of the child are gratitude and faithful obedience.

The relationship between parent and child can be broken or disrupted by ingratitude, by the child's despising or being indifferent to the self-giving of the parent, or by disobedience, by the child's claiming complete independence before coming of age and rejecting all requirements laid upon by the parent. The result is the disruption of all the aspects of the life of the child.

How is this situation overcome? How is the disrupted relation between the parent and the child restored? The parent's concern is not to exact a penalty but rather to achieve reconciliation, the restoration of the relationships described above. The necessary means to this end is a change of attitude on the part of the child. But this goal must be pursued with great care and patience in order to avoid reconciliation on the lower level of compulsory subservience. The kind of parental love which longs for reconciliation and which may be met with rebuff is a costly love, a suffering love, which bears the hurt of the broken relationship and the continued hurt of the rejection of love. It is also a love which attains its end by sympathy, compassion, and identification with the plight of the child. The parent must take the initiative and go out to meet the child where the child is, to meet the child with love. D. Baillie describes this in terms of the love of a friend but it is equally applicable to the love of a parent for a child.

> We may, I think, find at least a faint analogy of this in the love of a true friend who receives a grave wrong but who generously forgives. If I play my friend false behind his back in a weak moment, basely betraying his confidence, and he discovers it, will he pass over it lightly, without any painful explanation and restoration? If he is a shallow soul, and not a very true friend, he may treat the matter in that light way, for the sake of comfortable relations, because he does not care very deeply for me. But he cannot do that if he is a good man and a true friend who loves me deeply. It is not that he will be slow to forgive me; but his forgiveness will not be a good-natured indulgence. It will come out of an inexorable fire of love which I shall shrink from facing. I shall be far more afraid to meet him and look him in the face than I should be if he were a shallow friend. So great a thing is his forgiveness.
>
> But if these things are true, it is also true that in the whole great process of forgiveness it is my friend that has the hardest part to play. It is he that bears the brunt. He suffers more than I. Not because he is the person that has been wronged; nay, it is the shame of what I have done that weighs most on him. He bears my shame as if it were his own, because of his great love for me. He bears more of the agony than I, because he is a better man and loves more deeply. And it is out of this noble anguish that his forgiveness comes. All that is what lies behind it.
>
> How much more deeply all these things must be true of God, both in His judgment of our sins and in His 'atonement' for them![14]

This leads to the following statement of our theological analogy: the Christian events are related to or the cause of Christian salvation as the suffering love of a parent is related to or the cause of the reconciliation between the parent and the child.

Now let us summarize the main points being made by the analogy. Reconciliation between the parent and the child is based on the parent's love for the child. It is established by the parent's initiative. It is costly and involves suffering. It is accomplished in specific acts of confrontation, repentance, and reconciliation. The parent's love must be accepted by the child. The child must trust the parent, become aware of responsibility for their estrangement, and be open to the parent's love. Then reconciliation between the parent and the child is the basis of the fulfillment of the life of the child.

Thus the meaning of the analogy is that reconciliation between God and humanity is based on God's love for humanity. It is established by God's initiative manifest in the history of Israel culminating in Christ. It is costly and involves suffering which is prefigured in the Old Testament and manifest in the passion of Christ. It is accomplished in specific acts, namely, in the events of the biblical history culminating in Christ. God's love must be accepted by us. We must trust Cod (faith), become aware of our responsibility for our estrangement (repentance), and open ourselves to God's love. Then our reconciliation with God is the basis of our fulfillment.

In any theological analogy it is important to note its limitations, namely, those aspects which are not applicable to the relation between God and humanity. In the first place in any estrangement between a parent and a child the parent is usually in part to blame because of pride, self-assertion, and possessiveness. Furthermore, the parent's love for the child is never perfect and may not be able to achieve reconciliation. Therefore, often reconciliation may take place as a result of the initiative of the child. Finally, the right relation between parent and child becomes less important for the fulfillment of the child as the latter grows older. None of these aspects of the analogy can be applied to the reconciliation between humanity and God.

Let us now see how this interpretation of salvation or the atonement is related to some of the issues which have been raised in the history of this doctrine. The death of Christ as often been interpreted as an expiatory sacrifice which removes sin and guilt as obstacles between God and humanity and thus restores humanity to communion with God. In the personal analogy the sacrificial idea can be seen as one way of interpreting the costliness of the suffering love of God in Christ. Jesus' death is an expiation only in the sense that it is God's suffering love which can overcome the results of sin and restore the sinner to fellowship with God.

The same applies to Anselm's concept of the death of Christ as a satisfaction for the offense against God's honor caused by sin. When Anselm says that God cannot forgive without the payment of a satisfaction, the personal analogy would interpret this to mean that forgiveness and reconciliation are not achieved by an easy overlooking of sin but only through the costly suffering love of God in Christ.

The Reformers asserted that the death of Jesus was the vicarious endurance of the penalty due on our sin, a penal substitution. It is clear that sin was the cause of Jesus' suffering and death and that his death was a judicial execution and in that sense a penalty. But it is not clear that there is any connection between Jesus' suffering and the "penalty" due on the sin of his contemporaries or of us. The "penalty" on sin is the suffering of the sinner resulting from estrangement from God. In a broader sense this "penalty" also includes the suffering inflicted by the sinner. Jesus' suffering included the latter but not the former, although there are some passages in the New Testament which can be interpreted in this way (2 Cor. 5:14f, 21).[15] From the point of view of the personal analogy all that can be said about this substitutionary idea is that it points to the fact that in the divine compassion for us God in Christ shares our lot completely and identifies with us in our suffering.

The statement of a theological analogy for salvation still leaves open the question of how we participate in this salvation. This is taken up in the last four chapters. But this in turn raises the question of how this salvation is effective for us, how events in the past can be the basis of our salvation in the present. This is the problem of the relation between the objective and the subjective aspects of salvation.

In many passages of the New Testament (Rom. 5:18, 1 Cor. 15:21f, 2 Cor. 5:19, Heb. 9:12, 10:12, 1 Pet. 3:18) and in many theories of the atonement (sacrificial, Christus victor, satisfaction, penal substitution) it is affirmed that in the events culminating in the death and resurrection of Christ something objective is accomplished by God in regard to human salvation which is not dependent upon human awareness, acceptance, or participation. In all these versions of the doctrine of salvation, however, although salvation has been objectively accomplished, it must be subjectively appropriated in order to be effective in a person's life.

Karl Barth offers an analogy for the relation of the objective and subjective aspects of salvation. A monarch of a nation signs a decree which makes all exiles citizens again. Then the monarch sends out heralds to inform the exiles of their new status. Some of the exiles cannot be found; some do not believe the heralds; and some believe and return to their homeland to take up their citizenship. All were made citizens *de jure* when the monarch signed the decree, but only those who believed and returned became citizens *de facto*.

Bultmann claims to avoid the objective aspect in his theory that the Christian events do not involve some objective transaction but rather simply open up the possibility of salvation. This possibility becomes actual when the kerygma of the cross is preached and accepted. But the creation of this possibility in the cross of Christ would seem to be the same kind of objective accomplishment as in the other theories.

All these theories seem to be based on a Platonic idealism or medieval realism in which transactions in a transcendent realm are eternally valid for all people, dead, living, and yet to be born. Kaufman claims to avoid such ideas in his historical approach. He argues that what is objectively accomplished in the Christian events is the creation of the Christian community. This was not in some eternal realm but concretely in history. The possibility of salvation which was opened to all people was a historical possibility, namely, that they might come into contact with the Christian community, be moved to join it, and thus participate in Christian salvation. So a present salvation is dependent upon events of the past not because they constituted some eternal transaction but rather because they were the cause of the historical movement which has produced the experience of salvation in the present.[16] However, even in this historical view there is a residue of objective universality in the Christian events. God was acting in them to create the Christian community and continues to act on the basis of them in the expansion of the church. Therefore something of universal significance occurred in them. It would seem that this historical view is the interpretation of the objective aspect of the doctrine of salvation which is most suited to the personal analogy of salvation.

The doctrine of salvation which reduced the objective element to a minimum is the moral influence theory of Abelard and the liberal Protestant theology. There the only objective accomplishment in the Christian events is the manifestation of God's love and the overcoming of human selfishness and ignorance through the life and teaching of Jesus.

Liberation Theology

One of the major contributions of the various forms of liberation theology is to the doctrine of salvation. According to the liberation theologians salvation is essentially and fundamentally liberation from oppression. This is usually interpreted to include all kinds of oppression, but the greatest emphasis is always placed on social, economic and political oppression.

The liberation theologians base their doctrine of salvation mainly on the story of the Exodus in which God liberates the Israelite slaves from bondage in Egypt. They also refer to Isaiah in 61:1-2 in which the servant or the eschatological prophet of second Isaiah is anointed by the Spirit to proclaim liberty to the captives. But special emphasis is placed on Luke 4:18-21 in which Jesus takes the Isaiah passage as the text for his first sermon in the synagogue at Nazareth and proclaims that the calling of God to "set at liberty those who are oppressed" is fulfilled in him.

The liberation theologians argue that this fundamental theme of salvation as liberation was spiritualized in the later New Testament and especially in the tradition of the church. The purpose of this spiritualization was to conceal the radical and revolutionary meaning of Christian salvation and thus to preserve the social, economic and political status quo. The church came to have a large stake in the status quo especially after its recognition in the fourth century, and it used this spiritualized version of Christian faith as an ideology to preserve the power and status of the ruling classes who dominated the church. In this situation the oppressed found the Christian gospel incredible, because it was so deeply implicated in the structures of the unjust system which was oppressing them.

Therefore, according to the liberation theologians, the traditional interpretation of Christian faith and salvation must be de-ideologized and given a political interpretation which draws out the social and political implications of the Gospel. This has been made possible in our time by reading the Bible from the point of view of the oppressed and also with the help of critical social theory derived from Marx.

The main problems in the doctrine of salvation in liberation theology are whether liberation is to be interpreted as primarily from social, economic and political oppression, and if so, how God is understood to achieve this. In the Bible salvation is understood to be the gift of well-being in the most comprehensive sense: physical, psychological, social, economic, political and spiritual. But the spiritual aspect or the relation to God is seen to be fundamental and the basis of all the rest.[17] Furthermore salvation in history is understood to be fragmentary and partial in all its aspects, and the fullness of salvation will come only at the consummation of history in the completed reign of God.

Liberation theologians often contest this interpretation and argue that spiritual salvation in the sense of divine forgiveness, reconciliation, and communion with God is entirely subsidiary. I take this to be an exaggeration in order to correct the balance in the traditional doctrine of salvation which has often been interpreted to be only spiritual. James H. Cone, the foremost black liberation theologian, however, understands this in the way I have suggested. "Fellowship with God is the beginning and end of human liberation. . . . This vertical dimension of faith is the essential response to the gospel and is thus the heart of liberation's meaning from the human side. . . . This vertical sense of personal relationship with the God of Jesus is logically prior to the other components of human liberation. . . . It is from the knowledge of this vertical divine-human relationship that the struggle of liberation in history is based."[18]

Some aspects of salvation are more directly the work of God than others. On the one hand, God's forgiveness of sin, for example, although proclaimed by the prophet or the apostle, is a direct gift of God on the condition of repentance and faith. On the other hand, the repeal of unjust laws and the redistribution of income, for example, although as aspects of the fullness of salvation they may be inspired by God, are accomplished mainly by human political activity. Thus the spiritual aspect of salvation involving the restoration of communion with God received through faith is the beginning and the foundation of the totality of salvation, whereas the social, economic and political aspects of salvation belong to faith working through love, to the task rather than the foundation of the Christian life. Schubert M. Ogden in presenting what he calls "a christology of liberation" makes this point in somewhat different terms.

"I have insisted, with all the classic expressions of the christology of witness in Scripture and tradition, that the freedom we have in Christ can cever be simply identified with secular freedom or with our political responsibility for achieving it. On the other hand, I have also insisted that the two kinds of freedom are as inseperable as they are distinct, in that our political reponsibility for achieving secular freedom follows necessarily from the freedom that is ours in Christ."[19]

Questions for Discussion

1. *If Christian faith involves a gospel of salvation, how can this best be stated, interpreted, and understood today? How do you go about deciding this?*
2. *What is the best way of stating the significance of the life, ministry, death and resurrection of Jesus Christ for Christian salvation? Give your reasons.*
3. *In Christian salvation what are we saved from and what are we saved to? How do you decide this?*
4. *What is the difference between salvation in the Old Testament and in the New Testament?*
5. *Does the Christian understanding of salvation necessarily involve the idea of expiation or atonement? Why or why not?*
6. *How is Christian salvation related to and distinguish from mental health or psychological maturity?*
7. *What is the empirical or experiential manifestation of Christian salvation? How is it different from the empirical or experiential absence of salvation?*
8. *Is Christian salvation best described as an objective reality, an objective possibility, a subjective reality, or a subjective possibility? Why?*
9. *Is Christian salvation a yes-or-no proposition, that is, are people either saved or not saved? Or are there other categories or possibilities, for example, partly saved? How do you know?*
10. *Are the various interpretations of Christian salvation mutually exclusive or complementary? Why?*

11. *"My father is a good man. He always does what he believes to be right. He goes out of his way to help people. He is always kind and generous to those closest to him. He is actively concerned about justice for minority groups and the poor. But he does not believe in God or Christ or salvation. I guess you could call him a humanist. Is he saved?" Discuss how you would respond to this question and why.*

12. *Are all interpretations of Christian salvation metaphors or analogies rather than exact (univocal) descriptions of what is going on between God and humanity in Christ?*

13. *Does the Christus Victor theory of salvation require demythologization? If so, what is the result? If not, why not?*

14. *Is it possible to hold that the passion of Christ is in some way his suffering of a debt we owe or a punishment we deserve?*

15. *How can a present salvation be dependent upon events of the past?*

16. *Do theories of the objective and universal character of the work of Christ require a Platonic or medieval realism in order to be valid?*

17. *Is salvation essential participation in the divine life or restoration of a broken personal relationship with God? Are these two approaches mutually exclusive? If so, which would you choose? If not, how are they related?*

18. *Is salvation the restoration of an original state or the gift of a new status? Why?*

19. *To what extent is understanding necessary to salvation? Is it possible to be saved without understanding salvation or without knowing it at all?*

20. *At what point is a person saved? When the person is baptized as an infant? At the "age of reason"?*

21. *In the light of John 14:6, Acts 4:12 and similar passages, is there any possibility of salvation for members of other religions and world views?*

22. *What is the relation between Christian salvation and liberation from social, economic and political oppression?*

23. *How does God liberate the oppressed? (Lk. 4:18.)*

12

Justification

The doctrine of justification by faith, or more correctly, the doctrine of justification by grace through faith, was described by the later Reformers as the *articulus stantis et cadentis ecclesiae*, the article (of faith) on which the church stands or falls. Brunner describes it as "the true center and climax of the Christian message." Tillich states that it is "the universal principle of Protestant theology" and "the principle which permeates every single assertion of the theological system."

Bible

A fundamental theme of the Old Testament is that God is righteous and will judge Israel and the nations. But it becomes clear, especially in the Second Isaiah, that in the divine righteousness God will also vindicate, deliver and save Israel. God is "a righteous God and a savior" (Isa. 45:21; see 45:8, 50:7-9, 51:4-8). This theme is elaborated in Jesus' parable of the Pharisee and the Publican (Lk. 18:9-14), and especially by Paul in Galatians and Romans. According to Paul the gospel is that in Christ the righteousness of God is manifest in such a way that the sinner is accounted righteous or justified before God, not by works of the law but by grace apprehended through faith. People are justified because God in Christ by the Spirit takes them into union with Christ and his righteousness. Because they are in Christ they appear before God as righteous (2 Cor. 5:21, Phil. 3:8f).

Tradition

The idea of justification is alluded to often in theological writings down through the medieval period but usually without being understood in the sharp sense in which Paul had stated it and not as the central theme of the gospel of salvation. In Aquinas, for example, justification is treated in a question on the effects of grace at the end of the long treatise on law. He affirms that justification is by faith, but he defines faith as informed by love and as a gift of grace infused into the soul which leads to good works and which thus makes a person actually righteous before God.

The doctrine of justification received its classical theological formulation by Luther. For him it was fundamental. "If the article of justification be once lost, then is all true Christian doctrine lost." Luther's main religious concern was how he could become worthy to receive the grace of God, how he could acquire the holiness on the basis of which he would be able to stand before God. It was in order to seek certainty in this matter that he became an Augustinian monk. The accepted view at the time was that if one confessed one's sins and received the sacraments, one would become acceptable to God. But Luther's scrupulosity led him to worry about whether he had really confessed all his sins. He could not be sure that he had achieved a total contrition, even with the help of divine grace. This led him to greater exertions and finally to despair. During the years 1513-1519 Luther, whether gradually or suddenly is not clear, achieved a fundamentally new understanding of the Christian faith which resolved his religious problem and challenged the basis of the medieval understanding of Christianity.

The fundamental point was a recovery of the central theme of the Bible and especially of St. Paul in regard to the righteousness of God. The medieval church generally understood the righteousness of God to be the demanding justice of God. This was connected with the fact that the Latin translation of the biblical words for righteousness was *justitia* which meant justice in the sense of the equitable administration of reward and punishment according to law. Luther's discovery was that in the Bible, the righteousness of God is essentially the mercy of God.

At first Luther believed that the righteousness of God as mercy transforms a person so that the person is in fact made righteous. This is accomplished by God's grace alone and not by any human action, merit, or good works. This was the view shared by some Augustinian theologians of Luther's time. But later Luther came to affirm not that the grace of God's righteousness makes a person actually righteous, but that God's righteousness is shown in treating a person as righteous no matter what the person's actual state of life. Acceptability or righteousness before God is imputed or ascribed to a person by grace alone so that actual righteousness of life and a person's activity in good works are irrelevant to justification.

Luther's fundamental teaching here is that the righteousness of God is seen most clearly in the divine grace in Christ by which we are a accounted righteous or justified before God. Faith is the apprehension or reception of this grace. This rules out all attempts to justify or make oneself righteous before God by means of sacraments or good works. Justification can be received only as a gift and this receiving is faith. It is essentially trust in God's righteousness or mercy shown forth in Christ.

Thus our fundamental sin is our attempt to justify ourselves in God's eyes. Good works are of no account in one's relation to God, only faith. But in the life of faith good works follow from faith as good fruit from a good tree. Where there are no works, there is no faith. Apart from faith the temptation is always to look at our works as a way of self-justification. Because of God's accounting us righteous, we are totally saints. Because of our actual life, we are totally sinners. Thus we are *simul justus et peccator*, at the same time righteous and sinners.

Luther's teaching on justification was one of the main points of contention with the Catholics. Their position was clarified and solidified in the sixth session of the Council of Trent which ended in 1547. In the 16 chapters and 33 anathematizing canons of this session Luther's doctrine of justification is flatly contradicted. There is a complex preparation for justification which includes the acceptance of prevenient grace, belief in the teaching of the church, hope in the divine mercy, love of God, hatred of sin, and purpose to be baptized and begin a new life. Then comes justification itself which is not merely the remission of sins but includes sanctification or the infusion of hope and love. Thus justification is by faith but faith informed by love, and justification is increased by good works. The point is that while God freely forgives penitent sinners, God does not and cannot accept them and enter into fellowship with them in their sinful state. First they must be made holy and righteous by the infusion of love. The mere imputation of righteousness is anathematized.[1] These have continued to be the main points of debate between Protestants and Catholics down to the present day, although Küng argues that there is no fundamental difference between Catholic teaching and that of Karl Barth.

Luther's teaching passed into the Reformation confessions and thus into the Anglican Articles. Many phrases of Article XI, "On the Justification of Man," are taken from the Lutheran Confessions of Augsburg and Würtemberg, but the Article avoids the extreme statements which grew out of the polemics with Rome. (The "Homily of Justification" referred to in the Article is really the "Homily of the Salvation of all Mankind" in the first *Book of Homilies*.) Article XII, "Of Good Works," is simply an elaboration of Luther's teaching which avoids the overestimation of good works in Catholic teaching and their under-estimation in some extremes of Lutheran teaching. Article XIII, "Of Works before Justification," was included to condemn the scholastic theory of congruous merit that good works merited grace. It also follows Luther's teaching in "The Freedom of a Christian." The meaning is that apart from trust in God, we are always tempted to look upon our good works with pride as our way of justifying ourselves before God and humanity. If it is taken to mean that there are no selfless good works apart from explicit faith in Christ, then it is contrary to the teaching of the Bible.

The general acceptance and special emphasis on the doctrine of justification in early Anglicanism is indicated by the "Homily of Salvation" (1547) attributed to Cranmer and by Hooker's "Discourse of Justification" (1585). Hooker analyzes the disagreements with Roman Catholic teaching and asserts that the main error of Rome is the notion that a person is justified by the infusion of grace which produces an inherent righteousness and that this grace of justification can be increased subsequently by the merit of good works.[2]

The centrality of the doctrine of justification was generally agreed on in Anglicanism down through the seventeenth century. But since then some Anglican theologians have argued for the Tridentine interpretation and against the Lutheran. Some feared that the Lutheran doctrine would lead to antinomianism, to a neglect of duty and good works Bishop Jeremy Taylor in 1663 warned against the excluding of good works from the justification of the sinner and asserted that obedience and love as well as faith were the conditions of salvation. Newman thought that the Lutheran doctrine of justification was grounded in subjective reality of God's presence through Christ in the believer which is mediated by the sacraments. In *Tract 90* he argued that the Thirty-Nine Articles could and should be interpreted according to traditional Catholic teaching. In 1944 Dom Gregory Dix argued that the doctrine of justification by faith was wrong because it implied that what saves is the believer's consciousness of feeling confidence in Christ. In his *Principles of Christian Theology* John Macquarrie asserts that the doctrine of justification is archaic, has been vastly exaggerated, is neither indispensable nor specially illuminating, and is confusing and misleading.[3] It is clear, however, from the analysis above that the classical doctrine of justification avoided the errors which have been mentioned. It involved an objective work of God, moral commitment or good works, and growth in grace or sanctification. Its main concern was to avoid a view of salvation in which it is offered as a reward for human effort and achievement, either moral or religious.

Reconstruction

In one sense the doctrine of justification is but one metaphor among many for Christian salvation. It is a metaphor drawn from the law court. The prisoner is brought before the judge and pleads guilty but is acquitted of the charge and thus is accounted righteous. But in another sense the doctrine points to and underscores the most fundamental theme of the doctrine of salvation and of the gospel, namely, that salvation is really by grace and free, that we cannot and do not have to merit, deserve, or be worthy of it, and that God really loves us as we are. In this sense it is the article on which the church stands or falls, as the Reformers said.

It is important to note the scope of this theme. We are accounted righteous by grace apprehended through faith. This means that we are not justified by our works in any sense, neither by works of the law, that is, moral good works, nor by intellectual good works, that is, by believing a lot of doctrines handed to us by the church or by believing incredible historical assertions, nor by religious good works, that is, by public worship and sacraments and other pious acts. Tillich makes this point in relation to the intellectual sphere:

> The principle of justification through faith refers not only to the religious-ethical but also to the religious-intellectual life. Not only he who is in sin but also he who is in doubt is justified through faith. The situation of doubt, even of doubt about God, need not separate us from God. . . . You cannot reach God by the work of right thinking or by a sacrifice of the intellect or by a submission to strange authorities, such as the doctrines of the church and the Bible. You cannot, and you are not even asked to try it. Neither works of piety nor works of morality nor works of the intellect establish unity with God. They follow from this unity, but they do not make it. They even prevent it if you try to reach it through them.[4]

Gerhard Ebeling makes a similar point when he asserts that "the critical historical method has essentially a deep inner connection with the Reformer's doctrine of justification."

> The *sola fide* of the Reformation doctrine of justification . . . destroys all secretly docetic views of revelation which evade the historicalness of revelation by making it a history *sui generis*, a sacred area from which the critical historical method must be anxiously debarred. . . . As everywhere in Reformation theology, so also here in regard to the relation to history, the assent to lack of guarantees is merely the reverse side of the certainty of salvation *sola fide*.[5]

What he means is that if we know we are justified by grace and not by any kind of works, then we are freed to face honestly any and all difficulties involved in faith, such as the challenge and threat of historical critical study of the Bible.

Bultmann makes the same point in a somewhat different way:

> Our radical attempt to demythologize the New Testament is in fact a perfect parallel to St. Paul's and Luther's doctrine of justification by faith

alone apart from works of the Law. Or rather, it carries this doctrine to its logical conclusion in the field of epistemology. Like the doctrine of justification it destroys every false security and every false demand for it on the part of man, whether he seeks it in his good works or in his ascertainable knowledge. The man who wishes to believe in God as his God must realize that he has nothing in his hand on which to base his faith. He is suspended in mid-air, and cannot demand a proof of the Word which addresses him. For the ground and object of faith are identical. Security can be found only by abandoning all security, by being ready, as Luther put it, to plunge into the inner darkness.[6]

An even broader cultural result of the doctrine of justification was its effect of turning human energy away from religious works to secular cultural and economic activity. In opposition to the medieval view Luther stated (in his "Address to the German Nobility") "The sphere of faith's works is worldly society and its orders." Wilhelm Dilthey said of this statement, "With this sentence there enters into history one of the greatest organizing thoughts a man has ever had."

The doctrine of justification expresses the fundamental theme of the gospel which is the answer to the universal need and striving for acceptance, recognition esteem and respect. The paradox of human experience here is that the more we strive for this kind of recognition, the less do we attain it. This is true in the realm of our relations with other people and in our relation to God. This has been the experience of Paul, Luther, and innumerable others. The gospel is that in Christ this ultimate recognition and acceptance which we long for is given to us freely, by grace, that in Christ God has accepted us into fellowship though we are unacceptable. Or, in the words of the doctrine, God had treated us as righteous even though we are not righteous. Faith is trust in this good news, the acceptance that we are accepted.[7]

Therefore, as Tillich points out, justification is first an objective event and then a subjective reception of this.

Justification in the objective sense is the eternal act of God by which he accepts as not estranged those who are indeed estranged from him by guilt and the act by which he takes them into the unity with him which is manifest in the New Being in Christ.[8]

The subjective side is the acceptance of this. "He must accept that he is accepted, he must accept acceptance. . . . It means that one is drawn into the power of the New Being in Christ, which makes faith possible." [9] But faith is not the cause of God's justifying act. "Not faith but grace is the cause of justification because God alone is the cause. Faith is the receiving act, and this act itself is a gift of grace." The principle of justification is "the Protestant principle that, in relation to God, God alone can act and that no human claim, especially no religious claim, nor intellectual or moral or devotional 'work,' can reunite us with him." [10]

The result of all this is that the question of salvation is put behind us. We don't need to worry about that anymore. We can forget about the problem of our salvation because it has been accomplished for us. Our only concern now is in thanksgiving to God to love our neighbors, to imitate God in accepting those who are unacceptable. As Alexander Miller has put it, "It is the very recognition that salvation is *sola gratia, sola fide* which lifts the Christian man out of his preoccupation with salvation (which can neither be manipulated for himself or for others) and frees him for disinterested service."[11]

Questions for Discussion

1. *Is the doctrine of justification by faith that doctrine on which the church stands or falls? Why or why not?*
2. *Does justification mean primarily being accounted as righteous or being made righteous? Why?*
3. *How are faith, works, and salvation related? How do you decide?*
4. *What are the implications of the doctrine of justification by faith for Christian ethics?*
5. *Luther asserted that merit, works and holiness of life play absolutely no part in a person's acceptability before God. Do you think that this accords with the teaching of the New Testament as a whole or its main theme?*
6. *"If faith is a human act, then it is a work. Therefore, if we are justified by faith, we are justified by works. So the whole debate is a misunderstanding." What do you think? Why?*
7. *Is faith in any sense a work, a human act by which we are justified before God?*

13

Election and Predestination

Election and predestination deal with a particular group of issues within the doctrine of salvation which have often been at the center of attention in Christian history. Today they are often considered to have a rather archaic ring and to be of only historical interest. Thus Tillich and Bultmann, for example, say very little about them. On the other hand Brunner can assert, "Election constitutes the center of the Old and New Testaments." And Barth can say, "The doctrine of election is the sum of the Gospel" and write 500 pages about it. So our first task is to see how the ideas behind these doctrines arose in the Bible and then how they became important in Christian history.

Bible

The fundamental theme of these doctrines is the conviction of the biblical authors that God has chosen Israel to be God's own people and to be the agent or instrument in the fulfillment of the divine purposes for humanity. This receives its earliest statement by the J author in the story of the call of Abraham (Gen. 12:1-3). It is assumed and asserted in various ways throughout the history of Israel (Amos 3:2), but it receives explicit expression by the Deuteronomist. The classic text is Deuteronomy 7:6-11. Here the basis of God's choosing of Israel is not Israel's kinship to God or its deserving but simply God's love. The act of choosing is manifest in the historical and legendary events associated with the covenant tradition. Reference in Deuteronomy and later authors is always made to the covenants with the patriarchs, especially with Abraham, culminating in the Mosaic covenant at the Exodus.

The idea of being chosen is often mixed up with nationalistic pride. Being chosen sometimes means election to special favor and protection. But already in the eighth century prophets this nationalistic pride is criticized (Amos 3:2). In the covenant tradition God's favor is always associated with the divine demand for faithfulness and obedience.

The idea of election reaches its culmination in the Old Testament in the Second Isaiah. Here there occurs the close association between being chosen and being the servant of God, the clear assertion that Israel is chosen and called primarily to serve as God's instrument in the fulfilling of the divine purposes for all humanity (Isa. 42:5-9, 49:5-6).

At the center of the New Testament is the affirmation, both explicit and implicit, that Jesus is the chosen one, implying that the election of the old Israel is fulfilled in his election (Lk. 9:35, 23:35, 1 Pet. 2:4-6). Jesus is the one chosen by God to fulfill the divine purposes for humanity, and the purpose of Jesus' election is stated in Old Testament terms. He is a light to lighten the gentiles and the light of the world (Lk. 2:32, Jn. 8:12).

The foundation of the church in the election of God is indicated by the fact that Jesus, the chosen one of God, chooses the twelve apostles (Lk. 6:12, Jn. 15:16). The election of Paul is indicated in the introduction of most of his letters by such terms as "called," and "set apart by God." (See Acts 9:15.) Thus election now includes the church, whose members are often called the elect or chosen ones *(eklektoi)*. Old Testament terminology is used in 1 Peter 2:9 where election is associated with mission as in the J author and the Second Isaiah. The Old Testament emphasis on election as dependent upon the divine initiative rather than upon human worthiness is repeated in 1 Corinthians 1:26-31 (see Mt. 22:10).

As in the Old Testament, election is contingent upon faithfulness. There is the possibility of rejection for unfaithfulness and the closely related distinction between those who are called and those who are chosen (Mt. 22:1-14). This is probably a reference to the concrete historical distinction between those who heard the message of Jesus or the church and those who actually followed Jesus or joined the church.

The fact that the church was believed to be the chosen of God raised a serious problem for the early Christians in regard to the status of the Jews before God. Paul struggles with this in Romans 9-11. His problem is that he cannot reject the Old Testament testimony to God's election of Israel with its promises. But since the majority of the Jews have rejected Jesus in whom God's promises have been fulfilled, their status is ambiguous. Paul's solution is stated in Romans 11:25-36. The problem with which Paul is struggling is the theological issue at the root of the question of the relation of Christianity and Judaism today, namely, the place of the Jews in the economy of salvation. Although traditional theology has assumed that the Jews are excluded from salvation, many contemporary theologians both Protestant and Catholic affirm that they fall within the plan of salvation.[1]

Throughout the New Testament the purpose of election is primarily to fulfill God's purposes for humanity, but it is assumed and implied that it includes salvation, the fullest theological statement of the idea of election appears in the first chapter of Ephesians (vv. 3-14). Here *proorizein* is translated "destined" in the RSV,"predestinated" in the KJV, and "foreordained" in the ASV. Election is part of God's great plan of salvation which precedes the creation. It is understood primarily as election to salvation but secondarily as election for the purpose of "living to the praise of his glory." This is one of the main sources for the later development of the idea of election into the concept of predestination.

Two passages in the letter to the Romans have been the classical bases of later developments in the doctrines of election and predestination. In Romans 8:28-30 there is a progression from foreknowledge, to predestination, to calling, to justification, to glorification. It is quite clear that the words for foreknowledge and predestination mean divine determination to Paul. The rabbis of the first century clearly taught this, but at the same time they also affirmed human freedom and responsibility. Paul does the same without much concern for the problems posed thereby. The paradox is moderated somewhat by the fact that Paul may be referring to the church as a whole rather than to particular individuals.

In any case this is the testimony of twice-born Christian experience. People who have been redeemed through Christ by way of conversion often express and interpret their experience in terms of predestination. They proclaim that this is God's doing from beginning to end, that it is not a whim or sudden arbitrary decision on God's part but rather part of the divine plan from the beginning. Paul did not erect this into a speculative theological doctrine, but some of his later interpreters did and thus drew some conclusions which Paul himself would probably have denied.

The most difficult passage is Romans 9:14-24. C. H. Dodd throws up his hands and describes this as "the weakest point in the whole epistle." He calls it "a mechanical determinism [which] annihilates morality." But it is important to note that this is an ad hominem argument directed at the Pharisaic rabbis of the day who would have accepted the deterministic references to God's hardening of the heart. Also Paul is here speaking primarily of nations and not individuals. Furthermore, the text and the syntax are obscure, and Dodd suggests that "when Paul becomes obscure, it usually means that he is embarrassed by the position he has taken up."[2] In any case Paul's final position in Romans 11 :25f is that God hardened Israel's heart so that the gentiles would be saved, and then Israel itself would be converted and saved.

Tradition

The doctrines of election and predestination were subordinate themes in the theologians of the church before Augustine. The primary reason for this was that the church was in conflict with gnosticism and other forms of determinism and fatalism and tended to stress human freedom and responsibility rather than the divine determination of human life and salvation. But when we consider that Augustine was converted with the Letter to the Romans in his hands, we can understand why the doctrines of election and predestination received such sharp formulations by him. These formulations were the center of controversy for generations and influenced Calvinism and orthodox Protestantism down to the eighteenth century.

Augustine's theological argument on these doctrines is developed quite logically. All people are lost in sin as a result of the fall of Adam. Humanity is a *massa damnata*, and all deserve damnation. People are saved by grace alone, and God's grace for faith and salvation is irresistible. God determines from all eternity to whom will be given divine grace for salvation. The number of the elect is strictly limited to the number which is required to replace the fallen angels. Thus Augustine is able to speak of certain people as being predestined to eternal salvation and others as being predestined to eternal damnation. "These we also mystically call the two cities, or the two communities of men, of which the one is predestined to reign eternally with God, and the other to suffer eternal punishment with the devil."[3] This is the famous doctrine of double predestination which was condemned at the Second Council of Orange in 529. Augustine's view is moderated somewhat when we consider that according to him all people deserve damnation, that it is only by God's grace that any are saved, and that he occasionally distinguishes between God's predestination to salvation and God's foreknowledge only of reprobation. Aquinas followed Augustine's teaching but described reprobation in terms of divine "permission" rather than of a positive decree in order to preserve the guilt of the lost.[4]

Both Luther and Calvin affirmed a generally Augustinian doctrine of election and predestination. But Luther in some of his later works suggested that the doctrine of double predestination was speculative and not biblical and turned away from it. Calvin's is the classic systematic statement of double predestination.

> Predestination we call the eternal decree of God, by which he has determined in himself, what he would have to become of every individual of mankind. For they are not all created with a similar destiny; but eternal life is foreordained for some, and eternal damnation for others. Every man, therefore, being created for one or the other of these ends, is, we

say, predestined either to life or to death.[5]

This deserves Calvin's description of it as the *decretum horrible*, but it should be noted that in Calvin's thought it is presented in order to promote gratitude, humility and hope. And it does not allow anyone to know or designate who is elect and who is reprobate. Calvin's view has been called supralapsarian in that God's decree is eternal, determined before (*supra*) the creation and fall (*lapsus*) of mankind. The somewhat more moderate version is called infralapsarian since God's determination of the saved and the lost comes after (*infra*) the fall.

The Calvinist doctrines of election and predestination were attacked by the Arminians and reaffirmed at the Synod of Dort in 1618 and in the Westminster Confession of 1646.[6] These doctrines are treated in Anglican Article XVII which was originally written in 1553. It was carefully drawn up to follow the language of the Bible, especially Romans 8 and 9 and Ephesians 1, to avoid the doctrine of double predestination, and to avoid certain Anabaptist ideas.

Brunner argues that the doctrine of double predestination is not in the Bible and that passages which seem to suggest it refer to the double possibility of the end of history rather than to God's determination of this. People are always responsible for their decision about the gospel of Christ. Augustine, Calvin and other teachers of double predestination were led astray through misinterpretation of the Bible and succumbed to the temptation to speculate.

Barth has offered a radical reformulation of the doctrines of election and predestination which is the most extensive since the seventeenth century. He rejects the doctrine of double predestination. His basic thesis is that Jesus Christ is both the electing God and the elected human. But Christ is also the rejected one who takes upon himself God's rejection of the sinner. Therefore for all people there is only election. There is no eternal decree of God for humanity apart from Jesus Christ. Therefore, all are elected in Christ. This seems to imply a universalism of election but Barth denies this.

Reconstruction

There has been a fateful ambiguity in the meaning of election from the beginning. Does election mean being chosen by God for salvation or does it mean chosen by God as the divine instrument in achieving salvation for all people? Does election refer to the means by which God brings about a more general or perhaps universal end or does election refer to that end itself, that is, salvation? We noted this ambiguity in the Bible. Sometimes Israel or the church is chosen simply for the blessing of salvation and sometimes to bring God's blessing to all the nations. But it seems to be the consensus of the biblical authors that election is for the purpose of fulfilling God's plan of salvation for all people. This comes out most clearly in the servant passages of the Second Isaiah and in the New Testament passages on the vocation of Jesus. Along with this election to fulfill God's purposes goes the gift of salvation itself, but the latter is subordinate to the former.

In the history of the church, however, this relationship became reversed and almost all attention was concentrated on election to salvation. So the first thing that needs to be done in reinterpreting this doctrine is to reverse this tendency. Thus election means being chosen primarily for special responsibility rather than primarily for special favor. Election means being chosen as an instrument for the fulfillment of God's purposes for all people. It means being chosen for mission and service. It also means being chosen for salvation since this is necessary for the primary meaning of election. Thus the church is the means or instrument in the fulfillment of God's purposes but it also represents (fragmentarily) the end or goal of these purposes which is salvation.

In relation to the traditional doctrine the following points have to be made. God wills to save all people, to bring them to their fulfillment in relation to God and to their fellows (1 Tim. 2:4). God does not will to save only certain persons and to reject others. The doctrine of double predestination turns God into a monster who does not deserve our worship and obedience. It also undercuts human freedom and responsibility and makes the mission of the church pointless.

This, however, does not prejudge the question as to whether all people will in fact accept God's offer and be saved. The consensus of the biblical authors seems to be that some or many will reject salvation. This is a problem in eschatology. In any case the doctrine of election cannot be interpreted in such a way as to undercut human freedom and responsibility. We are free to accept or reject the gospel. Often the orthodox doctrines of election and predestination were interpreted in such a way that a person was the mere passive object of the workings of divine grace (Article XVII gives this impression). But this involves a sub-personal model for the relation of God and human beings and issues unavoidably in a determinism. Only a personal model can avoid this and preserve human freedom and responsibility while maintaining the divine initiative.

Thus Christian salvation is open to all people, and the election of the church is primarily for the purpose of giving testimony to this. Salvation apart from Christian testimony, that is, apart from response to the gospel of Christ and membership in the church, is a separate issue.[7] Article XVIII appears to give a negative answer to this issue, but it was not addressed to this question but rather to the question of those who would achieve salvation through joining a religious order and to certain views of the Anabaptists.

Another important element in the traditional doctrine is that salvation is not an arbitrary or capricious act on the part of God but derives from the eternal divine will. It is not simply a modification of God's relation to the creation but rather derives from God's very being. Salvation is the manifestation of God's love which is not an accidental aspect of God but rather is of God's very nature. This is the meaning of references to God's election "before the foundation of the world" (Eph 1:4, etc.). But the doctrine of election also makes it clear that salvation is a manifestation of God's freedom. Otherwise it could not be a manifestation of the divine love. Most of all it emphasizes the priority of the divine initiative. We can choose God only because God has first chosen us.

This reinterpretation of the doctrines of election and predestination has avoided one of the traditional problems associated with these doctrines, namely, the relation of God's foreknowledge to human freedom and responsibility. The traditional doctrine asserted that before the foundation of the world God had chosen certain individuals for salvation apart from any consideration of future faith, merit, works, conduct, or deserving. But a more moderate version of the doctrine held that God's election was based on his foreknowledge of the individual's faith and righteousness of life. This raised the problem of whether God's foreknowledge undercuts human freedom and responsibility. Our reinterpretation has avoided this issue by not basing election upon God's foreknowledge. God's will and plan is to elect all people to salvation. Some may accept and others reject this offer. Whether or not God foreknows this is a separate issue usually treated in the doctrine of God's omniscience. In that connection it can be argued that God's omniscience means that God knows what is knowable, that is, God knows the actual as actual, the necessary as necessary, the indeterminate as indeterminate, and the possible as possible.

Questions for Discussion

1. *Does God will to save all humanity? Will God succeed? How do you know?*
2. *Does election refer primarily to mission or to salvation, that is, to the means by which God brings about a more general or perhaps universal end or to that end itself? Defend your answer.*
3. *What is the issue between supralapsarianism and infralapsarianism? Is it of any significance for Christian faith? If so, how would you decide between these views?*
4. *What is your interpretation of the original meaning of the author in one of the following passages: Romans 8:28-30; Romans 9:14-24; Ephesians 1:1-14? How*

would you interpret the meaning of this passage for today?

5. *Does God have foreknowledge of who is to be saved? If so, is this reconcilable with human freedom and responsibilty? Does foreknowledge mean foreordination?*

6. *Is grace primarily God's favor or his influence or his indwelling power? Is it irresistible?*

7. *Is God's grace offered to all people? If so, how? If not, why not?*

14

Holy Spirit and Sanctification

The doctrine of the Holy Spirit was treated in connection with the doctrine of the trinity in chapter 4. In this chapter we shall expand on this and discuss the doctrine of sanctification which is appropriated to the Holy Spirit.

In chapter 11 on salvation and atonement we considered the general character of salvation and its basis in the Christian events. In chapter 12 on justification we considered salvation as based on God's grace and not on human merit or works. Chapter 13 on election emphasized God's freedom and initiative in salvation. In this chapter we consider salvation as a process in human life and history.

Sometimes the whole doctrine of salvation has been treated under the doctrine of sanctification, as has been the tendency in Pietism, Methodism, and other spiritualist and pentecostal movements. Herbert Richardson has recently offered a new interpretation of this view (see p. 164f). But we will follow the traditional approach in treating sanctification as one aspect of the doctrine of salvation.

Bible

In the Old Testament the Spirit of God as the personal presence and power of God is understood to cooperate in the work of creation (Gen. 1:2, Ps. 33:4, Job 33:4), to guide rulers (1 Sam. 16:13), and especially the messianic king (Isa. 11:2, 42:1), to inspire the prophets (Isa. 61:1, Ezek. 11:5), to be manifest in a widespread manner in the messianic age (Joel 2:28f), and to sanctify Israel (Isa. 59:21, Ps. 51:10f, Ezek. 11:19f, 37:1-14).

Thus sanctification means making holy or being made holy. Holiness is the distinctive characteristic of God in the Bible. It involves the element of separateness and exclusion and the element of outgoingness and inclusion. The holy God wills to make the people of God and the creation holy, to sanctify them, to make them like God (see pp. 87f).

In the New Testament the Holy Spirit is seen as the manifestation of the power and presence of God at Jesus' conception (Lk. 1:35) and baptism (Mk. 1:10f), at the beginning of his public ministry (Lk. 4:1, 14-21), and in his works of healing (Lk. 11:20). After the resurrection the Holy Spirit is given to the community of the church (Acts 2) and guides and empowers its mission (Acts 4:31, 6:3, 11:24). These themes are elaborated by Paul in his teaching that the Spirit is the way the risen Christ is present in the church and its members. Christ dwells in the individual Christian and in the community through the Spirit to assist in their prayers (Rom. 8:26f), and to produce the fruit of the Spirit (Gal. 5:22, 1 Cor. 12), and especially love (1 Cor. 13), which are the foretaste and guarantee of the age to come (Rom. 8:23, 2 Cor. 1:22, 5:5). Thus the Christian life is a life "in Christ" and in the "body of Christ" through the Spirit of Christ (1 Cor. 12:12f). In the Johannine literature the function of the Holy Spirit as counselor, who is sent from the Father by the Son (Jn. 14:16, 26, 15:26, 16:7), is to bear witness to Christ (Jn. 15:26) and to confirm Christ's teaching (Jn. 14:26).

In the New Testament it is clear that the basis of God's activity of sanctification is the Christian events culminating in the death and resurrection of Christ, who is known as the holy one (Mk. 1:24, Jn. 6:69, Acts 3:14) and the one who sanctifies (Heb. 2:11, Eph. 5:25). This means that sanctification is something which has already been accomplished for Christians, because they have received the Holy Spirit and are called holy ones or saints (1 Cor. 6:11, 1 Pet. 1:2, Acts 26:18). However, sanctification is also something which is yet to be fulfilled for Christians in a way which involves their responsible participation (Rom. 6:19, 2 Cor. 7:1, Heb. 12:14, 1 Pet. 1:15). Sometimes both of these ideas are combined in the same passage, as in 1 Corinthians 1:2. But, in general, the full achievement of sanctification is still the work of God and is finally accomplished only at the parousia (I Thess. 3:12f, 5:23f). Thus sanctification is both a gift and a goal, and there is not simply progress *toward* sanctification but rather progress *in* sanctification. This is another aspect of the combination of indicative and imperative in the New Testament: you are sanctified, therefore manifest it and grow in it. So sanctification can be understood as a status conferred by the gift of the presence of God, but a status which requires exemplification and exercise. Growth in sanctification involves both a purification from sin and an increase in the fruit of the Spirit: love, joy, peace, etc. (Gal. 5:22). And the goal is the sharing of the holiness of Christ, (Heb. 12:10) and being changed into the likeness of Christ by the Spirit (2 Cor. 3:18).

Tradition

The creed of the Council of Nicea simply affirmed belief in the Holy Spirit, but the question of the relation of the Spirit to the godhead became an important issue after the council. The developments in the doctrine of the Holy Spirit include Athanasius' argument for the full deity of the Spirit, the elaboration of this by the Cappadocians who taught that the Spirit proceeds out of the Father through the Son, the affirmation of the consubstantiality of the Spirit at the Council of Constantinople in 381, and Augustine's teaching on the Spirit as the bond of union between the Father and the Son and on the double procession of the Spirit from the Father and the Son (*filioque*). This latter doctrine became official in the West in the sixth century and contributed to the split with the Eastern church in the eleventh century.[1]

The *filioque* issue represents the difference in approach to the doctrine of the trinity in East and West (see pp. 65f), and it has been a subject of debate off and on since the sixth century. Various unsuccessful attempts have been made in Anglicanism to remove the *filioque* from the Nicene Creed, the most recent being in connection with the 1979 American Prayer Book. But today it is more of a symbolic and political issue than a substantive one between East and West. It is interesting to note, however, that Karl Barth argues for the *filioque* on exegetical and theological grounds. For example, he asserts that the Eastern view opens up the possibility of an unmediated human relation to the Father apart from the Son.[2]

Sanctification did not become a theological issue until the latter period of the Reformation when a fundamental difference of emphasis appeared between Protestant and Catholic formulations. As we noted in the debate over the meaning of justification, the Reformers and their followers tended to interpret justification as the imputing of righteousness to the sinner while the Catholics asserted that the gift of faith makes the person actually righteous (see p. 181). Thus the Reformers and their followers tended to distinguish justification and sanctification in order to preserve their main emphasis that justification is by grace and not by the merit of the believer. The Catholics on the other hand tended to emphasize the unity of justification and sanctification by insisting that the gift of the grace of faith makes the believer actually righteous and holy and thus acceptable to God. Both Catholics and Protestants agreed, however, that after this beginning sanctification is a continuing process in the life of the faithful brought about by grace, that is, by the influence of the Holy Spirit, mediated by the word and the sacraments. According to Catholic teaching from Augustine on, sanctifying grace is given to the soul initially at baptism and remits original sin. It is increased through the sacraments and good works. It can be lost by mortal sin and restored by the sacrament of penance. There is no explicit teaching on sanctification in the Anglican formularies.

In Calvinism and Catholicism sanctification is seen as proceeding on a slowly upward-turning line. Faith and love are progressively actualized. The power and influence of the Holy Spirit in the individual are supposed to increase steadily. Perfection is approached but never attained. In Lutheranism, because of the emphasis on the paradoxical understanding of the Christian person as at the same time justified and sinner, the development of sanctification is usually seen as an up and down affair with no unambiguous progress.

The Pietist movement of the eighteenth century, exemplified in the Methodists, asserted the possibility of complete sanctification in this life. They argued that the New Testament calls for perfection in the Christian life and promises it by the power of the Holy Spirit. They emphasized the direct, personal, inward communion with Christ by the Spirit leading to the complete sanctification of life. Wesley defined Christian perfection or complete sanctification as "pure love reigning in the heart and life," and his teaching on this point is often considered the unique contribution of Methodism to Christian thought.

In recent decades the charismatic movement and the pentecostal or holiness churches, which emphasize the baptism of the Holy Spirit and the gift of speaking in tongues, have grown in strength and influence. This has led to new attention to the work of the Holy Spirit and the doctrine of sanctification.[3]

These varying views of sanctification produced different images of the ideal goal of sanctification. In Catholicism it became the saints, who manifested the theological virtues, denied themselves ascetically, and manifested their power in miracles. The Reformers and their followers rejected the ideal of the saint because of their view that all Christians were at the same time righteous and sinners and because of their rejection of dualistic asceticism and the cult of saints. Somewhat different pictures of the goal of sanctification were developed in Calvinism, Lutheranism and Pietism. Both Catholicism and Protestant Orthodoxy developed an idea of the goal of sanctification in terms of mystical union with God. This idea was continued in Pietism but was denied by liberal (Ritschlian) Protestantism. This issue has produced a debate in twentieth century theology over whether the goal of sanctification should be understood on a mystical model (union with God) or on a personal model (communion with God). The same debate emerges in eschatology as the issue between the beatific vision and the Kingdom of God as models of the final fulfillment (see chapter 16).

Reconstruction

Sanctification is the process of being made holy like God in Christ by the presence of God the Holy Spirit working in us. It is both gift and task, as

suggested above. It is the work of the triune God and is associated with God
the Holy Spirit only by appropriation (see pp. 72f). God the Holy Spirit is the
mode of being of God in which God is the subjective mediator of all the divine
actions. Sanctification is a subjective process in the sense that it takes place
within the person. Since there is an analogy between the two, sanctification
can be appropriated to God the Holy Spirit.

Sanctification and justification are different aspects of God's one act of
salvation. As Tillich and Kaufman point out, to separate them as independent
acts of God is misleading. If God's act of justification were independent of any
human consequences or effects, we could not even know about it. If we know
of it, it must have certain effects in us already, that is, the beginning of
sanctification. This is why Tillich states that the first element in the doctrine
of salvation is participation in the New Being which he calls regeneration.
This is followed by the acceptance of the New Being or the experience of the
New Being as paradox (justification), and the transformation by the New
Being or the experience of the New Being as process (sanctification).[4]

Jesus is the only fully sanctified person in human history, so we perceive
what sanctification means by looking at him. He is the holy one and also the
one who sanctifies. This is symbolized by the Holy Spirit coming upon him at
his baptism (or his conception) and remaining on him (Jn. 1:32), and by the
picture of his whole life and ministry being inspired and guided by the Holy
Spirit, especially in Luke. Baillie interprets the incarnation of God in Jesus to
mean the fullness of grace of sanctification in him.[5]

The fullness of sanctification in Jesus means the presence of the fullness of
God's love in him, the greatest of the gifts of the Holy Spirit (1 Cor. 13, see
pp. 153f). Other aspects of the fullness of sanctification in Jesus are his faith
or trust and his hope for the fulfillment. All of these constitute the goal of
sanctification in the Christian life. Tillich elaborates the meaning of sanctification in terms of increasing awareness, freedom, relatedness and self-
transcendence.[6]

Sanctification involves concrete change in human life and not simply an
"imputed" righteousness or holiness. This means actual forgiveness and
reconciliation among people, actual service of the neighbor, actual manifestation of the fruit of the Spirit: love, joy and peace (Gal. 5:22).

What is actually going on in sanctification? How does God the Holy Spirit
affect human beings? We cannot describe it univocally but only analogically
(see pp. 1 lf). Because God is personal, the analogy of the mutual influence
between persons is better than that of the influence of a psychedelic drug, for
example. The influence of God the Holy Spirit upon us in sanctification is like
the influence of another person upon us, especially a person who loves us. But
God the Holy Spirit influences us more internally and more deeply than

another person (see Ps. 139:1-4, Rom. 8:26f, Rev. 2:23). H. W. Richardson describes it in the following way:

> His indwelling is a form of presence which is closer and more "unitive" than even the most perfect communion among created beings. . . . Creatures cannot indwell one another. Rather, the perfect form of unity among creatures is the moral communion of friendship. When Jesus Christ sends the Holy Spirit to dwell in us, however, He makes God present to us in a way which exceeds even the most perfect moral communion. In our union with the Holy Spirit, we are joined to Him even more closely than we are joined to ourselves (since even "self-conscious-ness" is a form of created presence). Hence Scripture tells us that the Spirit knows us not only better than even our closest friends know us, but even better than we know ourselves. For when we do not know our true desires, the Holy Spirit interprets them to God for us.[7]

The influence of God the Holy Spirit is therefore not limited to the mind or intellect and the conscience or will. Following the analogy of the mutual influence between persons, the influence of God the Holy Spirit involves the whole person including the emotions and the unconscious.[8]

Failure to realize this leads to the twin dangers of intellectualism and moralism in the doctrine of sanctification. The traditional Protestant empha-sis on the preaching of the word and the teaching of correct doctrine tended to limit faith to the response of the intellect and to interpret sanctification as growth in intellectual knowledge of God. But faith is the response of the whole person to God, and sanctification involves the influence of God the Holy Spirit on the will, the emotions, and the unconscious as well as the intellect.

Also the influence of God the Holy Spirit is not limited to enabling a person to fulfill the requirements of the moral law. Paul claims that he had fulfilled the "righteousness under the law" before his conversion (Phil. 3:6). What he needed was deliverance from the bondage of the law. Sanctification is the gift of love which transcends the moralistic interpretation of the law.

Such analogies as breathing and pouring (inspiration and infusion) for the activity of God the Holy Spirit in sanctification are valuable because they tend to undercut the dangers of intellectualism and moralism. These physical analogies also point to the influence of God the Holy Spirit upon the unconscious and the body, but they need to be balanced by the personal analogy.

Sanctification, as well as the other aspects of the Christian life, is not simply or primarily an individual affair but occurs in the community of the church, in the fellowship of the Holy Spirit. As against some forms of Protestant and

Catholic individualism the life of the church precedes the Christian life of the individual. Paul in 1 Corinthians 12 asserts that God the Holy Spirit works in the lives of individuals because they are members of the church and not vice versa.

This leads to the critical question as to whether sanctification is limited to members of the church or applies to others or to all people. The Augustinian-Calvinist tradition limited salvation to the elect (see chapter 13). Other more liberal traditions (Clement of Alexandria, Schleiermacher) saw God working in the lives of all people leading them toward their salvation. Karl Barth, following the distinction in the New Testament between the indicative and imperative mentioned above, argues that all people are sanctified *de jure* but only the members of the church have been sanctified and attest it *de facto*.[9] Kaufman seems to limit sanctification to the church but asserts that God wills it for all people.

This question is not dealt with directly in the Bible or in the tradition (with the exceptions noted above) but only by implication. Today a consensus seems to be emerging which affirms that God the Holy Spirit is present to and influences all people moving them toward the fullness of sanctification which Christians see in Christ. This is seen, for example, in the piety of other religions, the moral growth of the individual, the commitment of the humanist to justice, the scientist's devotion to truth, and the artist's dedication to beauty. But this sanctification is known for what it really is and can come to its full flowering only in Christian faith.[10]

Tillich and Browning see all processes of healing on all levels of reality, from psychotherapy to movements for justice and peace as manifestations of the presence of the New Being and thus of sanctification (see p. 167). This theme has been expanded by some theologians to include the psychological development of the individual person and also the evolution and growth of all forms of life. Any such doctrine, however, must preserve the relative independence of the creature.

These ideas take us beyond the doctrine of sanctification into issues which are usually treated in the doctrine of providence.[11] Here, however, the emphasis is on God's guidance of natural events rather than his transformation of nature. This latter point is taken up in the discussion of eschatology in chapter 16.

Questions for Discussion

1. *Is sanctification one aspect or the fundamental theme of Christian salvation? Why?*
2. *In what sense is sanctification something which has been accomplished for*

Christians, and in what sense is it something which Christians have to accomplish? How are these two senses related?

3. If sanctification is essentially the attainment of holiness, does it cut one off from the secular world?

4. If sanctification is primarily a divine gift, how is it related to human freedom?

5. What was at stake in the "filioque" controversy? Is it an important issue today? Why?

6. Does sanctification come before (Trent), with (Tillich) or after (Luther) justification? Why?

7. Does sanctification involve progress in the Christian life? Why?

8. Is Christian perfection (complete sanctification) possible? Why?

9. What is the relation between sanctification and increasing psychological maturity? Are they identical, mutually exclusive, overlapping, or what?

10. Is sanctification best characterized as increasing awareness, freedom, relatedness and self-transcendence (Tillich) or as increasing faith, hope and love? Why?

11. Does sanctification involve only persons or does it also involve institutions, nature, things, places, times, events and processes? Why?

12. Is the goal of sanctification primarily sainthood or servanthood? Why?

13. What model or analogy is most useful for understanding the relation and influence of the divine Spirit upon the human spirit?

14. How would you go about determining whether or not a particular phenomenon such as speaking with tongues or some other alleged manifestation of the Spirit is in fact the work of the Holy Spirit?

15. How is Christian sanctification related to analogous realities and processes in other religions?

16. Is sanctification empirically visible or can it be perceived only by the "eye" of faith? Why?

17. Who is being sanctified? The baptized? All people? Why?

15

History

History as a topic in theology or the theological doctrine of history is an extraordinarily complex subject which involves many other doctrines. One of the reasons for this is that the idea and problem of history are fundamental and pervasive in the Bible and in Christian tradition but they usually have been left implicit. The material which is now considered under the doctrine of history was formerly treated under several other doctrines: providence as God's guidance of the course of history, humanity as historical being, the church as the agent of God's purposes in history, and eschatology as the goal and end of history. It was not until the last century that theologians began to include a topic entitled "history" alongside other doctrines. This was largely the result of the rise of modern historical consciousness, historical critical research, and the philosophy of history. It was not until 1955 that a church, the Reformed Church of the Netherlands, produced a confessional statement with a section on the doctrine of history.

But there is little doubt that the problem of history has been at the center of theological attention during this century, largely as a result of the great historical crises of the first half of the century. John McIntyre asserted in 1957 that the problem of history has been the dominant theme of Western theology since World War II. The most current forms of the concern with the question of history derive from the work of Bultmann, Pannenberg and Moltmann.[1] Among systematic theologians, however, it is only Tillich who has devoted a major section of his theology explicitly to this doctrine. Kaufman's concern with the problem pervades his *Systematic Theology*.

Our purpose in this lecture is to clarify the questions to which the doctrine of history is addressed and to evaluate the ways in which these questions have been resolved in recent theology. Because the doctrine of history is so closely tied up with eschatology, this latter topic will be treated in this chapter as well as in the next.

The first step is to perceive that the term "history" is highly ambiguous, especially in theology. It can refer to any of the following:

(1) the actual course of events, past, present and future, as distinct from our knowledge of them;

(2) the study which attempts to determine and reconstruct the course of events in the past through the investigation of documents, monuments and reminiscences;

(3) the results of such study;

(4) the course of events seen theologically as the arena in which God is present and active in self-revelation and to save humanity;

(5) the whole of reality. (Pannenberg: "History is reality in its totality.")

The result of this ambiguity is that when theologians make solemn and resounding statements about history, it is often impossible to know what they mean. For example, we may hear it asserted that "Christianity is an historical religion," that "history is the fundamental category of Christian thinking," or that "history is the most comprehensive horizon of Christian theology" (Pannenberg) but we may have no idea of what is meant. Thus Kaufman asserts "The present work has been composed in the conviction that many of the problems, both of contemporary theology and of the Christian witness to the contemporary world, are rooted in a great fogginess about the theological conceptions of history [and] historical knowledge, ..."[2]

The focus of the theological doctrine of history is the interpretation of the meaning and significance of human history from the foundation of the church to the end of history, the meaning of history between the times of the coming of Christ and the second coming of Christ, the meaning of the history in which the church is involved. But this focus has as its context the Christian understanding of the whole of history from beginning to end, from creation to fulfillment. Thus in this larger sense the doctrine of history includes the doctrines of creation, the fall, the election of Israel, the incarnation, the founding and mission of the church, and eschatology. Sometimes the whole of Christian theology has been presented as a doctrine of history in this sense. In the first paragraph of chapter 1 I suggested this kind of approach. Pannenberg makes this point in the following way:

> History is the most comprehensive horizon of Christian theology. All theological questions and answers are meaningful only within the framework of the history which God has with humanity and through humanity with his whole creation—the history moving toward a future still hidden from the world but already revealed in Jesus Christ.[3]

Bible

Israel was the first nation that lived in the faith that the whole of the history of the world from beginning to end had a meaning and a purpose and that

Israel itself had a crucial function to perform in this history. Their under-standing of the origin of this history was stated in the myths of creation. Their understanding of human history was informed by the myths of the first man and woman, of their disobedience, of the flood, and of the covenant of God with all humanity through Noah. Their understanding of their own history was informed by the legends of the patriarchs and especially the call of Abraham, Isaac and Jacob. This became focussed in the traditions about their deliverance from bondage in Egypt, the Mosaic covenant, the wilderness wandering, the conquest of Canaan, and the establishment of the monarchy.

As it came to fullest expression in the post-exilic prophets, Israel's under-standing of its history was that God had called Israel into being for a universal mission, to be a light to the nations, so that all humanity might come to know its true creator and Lord, who is the origin, meaning and goal of the history of the world. Israel lived in the faith that God was the Lord of history in the sense that God guided the course of history toward its goal in the fulfillment of the divine purposes. So Israel saw the events of its history as events in which God is present and active to reveal the divine will and purpose, to judge those who go against the divine will, and to bless those who are faithful and obedient to the divine will. The destruction of the kingdoms and the exile are seen as God's judgment upon the faithlessness and disobedience of Israel. But the hope remained that God would redeem them. Even the actions of the other nations fall under God's sway and judgment, and God can use their arrogance to promote the divine purposes (Amos 9:7, 8; Isa. 10:5-19, Jer. 25:8, 9; Isa. 45:1-7).

Throughout the Old Testament there is a central strand of hope that God will fulfill the divine purposes through Israel, that Israel will be redeemed and all the nations will flock to Israel and her God. This hope becomes intensified in the post-exilic prophets and takes a variety of forms, the first of which is the restoration of the Davidic monarchy in a time of peace and plenty. Then as the historical situation gets worse under the Persians and Greeks, this hope is transformed into apocalyptic in which God will act directly to defeat Israel's enemies and transform the world into the divine kingdom. Sometimes this is depicted as occurring through the agency of an individual, earthly or heavenly, the messianic king or the Son of Man.

The central message of the New Testament authors is that the hope and expectation of the prophets of Israel have been fulfilled in Jesus, that God's kingdom on earth has been inaugurated in Jesus' obedience and resurrec-tion, and that God has acted decisively in Jesus to transform Israel again into a missionary body to be the light of the world. The early Christians pro-claimed Jesus as the manifestation of the meaning of history, the end of history in the sense of *telos* or goal, and also as the manifestation of the beginning of the end of history in the sense of *finis* or finish. Thus Jesus and the earliest New Testament authors probably expected the early arrival of the final consummation of history in the fullness of God's reign.

The delay of the final consummation, the *parousia*, apparently constituted a crisis of faith for the early church which was resolved in different ways by Paul, the author of Luke-Acts, and the Johannine author. Paul foresaw an extension of the time of the church for the purpose of its mission before the final end. The author of Luke-Acts perceived that the church was to have a history like that of Israel which was indefinite in length, a continuation of the history of God with the people of God. So this author was probably the first Christian writer to see the theological problem of the doctrine of history, namely, the meaning and significance of history under God in the time of the church.

Previous writers had seen two stages in salvation history, that of Israel and that of Jesus. They had assumed that the resurrection of Jesus and the coming of the Spirit of God upon the disciples were, in fact, the beginning of the final consummation. But the author of Luke-Acts, facing the crisis of the delay of the *parousia* and probably building upon some suggestions in Paul, saw that the history of God with the people of God had not ended but rather had entered upon a new stage, the age of the church. So in Luke-Acts the church emerges on the stage of world history. This author alone among the synoptists dates the beginning of Jesus' ministry in relation to imperial history. For the author of Luke-Acts history has not stopped. The Christian life is not merely a waiting for the end. Time and history still have meaning. God has a purpose in this time and it is the Spirit-guided mission of the church.[4]

According to Bultmann the Johannine author has completely demythologized the apocalyptic eschatology of the earlier tradition so that the contrast between the present age and the age to come has been transformed into a contrast between the temporal and the eternal. The final consummation has arrived in Jesus' resurrection and glorification, history has been concluded, and all that remains is for individuals to respond to the Christian message. In particular, judgment and eternal life are present realities for the faithful.

Tradition

In general the early church followed the lead of the author of Luke-Acts and perceived that the prophetic hope had been divided in two: first, the final disclosure of the meaning and goal of history in Jesus which was the beginning of the final stage, and second, the final consummation itself. The meaning of the history between the times was understood to consist primarily in the mission of the church under the guidance of the Spirit.[5]

One fundamental issue in the history of the Christian doctrine of history is that which arose between what may be called the relatively static ecclesiastical view (Augustine and Aquinas) and the dynamic transformationist view (Joachim and the Reformation sects). Speaking *very* generally, for Augustine and Aquinas the meaning of the course of history between the times is simply the conflict and interweaving of the earthly and heavenly cities, the slow progress of the Christian mission. The decisive event has occurred in the coming of Christ and the establishment of the church. The age of the church is identified with the millennial reign of Christ, and the final judgment and consummation will come in a relatively distant future.

But in the strange writings of Joachim of Floris (ob. 1202) certain elements in the biblical view of history which had been an undercurrent in Christian thought burst out again. Joachim saw three ages in history. The first, from Adam to Christ, was the age of the law, of the married, and of God the Father. The second, from Christ to 1260, was the age of a mixture of law and gospel, of the clergy, and of God the Son. The third age, which was to begin in 1260, was to be the age of love and liberty, of the monks, and of God the Holy Spirit.

The unique element in Joachim's thought was the expectation that a new age was about to break into history before the final consummation. The old institutions would be superseded and a radically new order would appear. Joachim's ideas have been the source of almost all modern dynamic progressive revolutionary philosophies of history, including those of Lessing, Comte, Hegel and Marx.[6] Similar views were expressed by some of the left wing sects of the Reformation and the seventeenth century. The more optimistic or "fighting" sects foresaw the near approach of a radical transformation of society before the final consummation. A contemporary version of this doctrine of history has appeared in the theology of hope (see below).

Another fundamental issue which arose after the first century in regard to the theological interpretation of history was that posed by the recognition and establishment of the church in the Roman Empire. At this point the question of the church's responsibility for the state, for justice, and for culture in general emerged alongside that of the church's mission. This in turn raised the question of the theological significance in this history of the rise of civilizations and cultures, the rise and fall of states and empires, the emergence of modern science and technology, the rise of liberal democracy, and the struggle for justice, equality and freedom. This question was answered in a positive way in the last century by the liberal Protestant doctrine of history whose key concept was that of progress. According to this view history is a steady upward ascent of humanity with the help and guidance of God toward the achievement in history of the kingdom of God. History is the story of the growth of the kingdom of God through the progressive moral and spiritual development of humanity. The key figures here are Kant, Hegel, Ritschl, Harnack and Troeltsch in Europe, and McGiffert, Brown, Rauschenbusch, and the social gospel movement in the USA.[7]

The downfall of the liberal Protestant theology of history was brought about by history itself in the form of World War I which uncovered the arrogant and destructive militarism and imperialism which lay just beneath the surface of the Western nations. There was also the critical influence of the more pessimistic philosophies of history of Schopenhauer, Nietzsche, and Spengler. Within the theological world, however, the critical development was the rediscovery by J. Weiss and A. Schweitzer of the radically apocalyptic outlook of Jesus and the early Christians.

Weiss' *The Preaching of Jesus Concerning the Kingdom of God* (1892) and Schweitzer's *The Quest of the Historical Jesus* (1906) demonstrated that the kingdom of God in Jesus' preaching was not a new social-political order which people could build on earth in partnership with God, but rather it was a reality breaking in from above as a great crisis and transformation accomplished by God alone. These critical influences achieved the destruction of the liberal Protestant doctrine of history and produced an extensive debate about the theological meaning of history which has continued down to the present. A variety of positions or schools have emerged from this debate.[8]

1. *Consistent Eschatology*—This is a continuation of the views of Weiss and Schweitzer by M. Werner and F. Buri. They hold that since Jesus' teaching is thoroughly apocalyptic, it has been nullified by the ongoing character of history. Therefore we must seek the meaning of history elsewhere. For Schweitzer this became the ethical mysticism of his reverence for life. For Buri it became the existentialism of K. Jaspers.

2. *Realized Eschatology*—This term was coined by C. H. Dodd in his book *The Parables of the Kingdom* (1936). His view is that the final consummation has occurred in the coming of Christ. In Jesus' death and resurrection the reign of God has fully arrived and there is no further consummation in the future. The result of this view is that history since Christ is essentially epilogue, the slow expansion of the reign of God in the world. This is close to the Johannine view. In his later writings Dodd conceded that there were futuristic elements in Christian faith and that there was some significance in the missionary history of the church for the fulfillment of the reign of God.

3. *Heilsgeschichte or Salvation History*—The general meaning of this term is the same as the interpretation given to the biblical history above. *Heilsgeschichte* is the history in which God is present and active to reveal the divine will and to save humanity, the history beginning mythically in the creation and ending mythically in the return of Christ, the judgment, and the consummation. In this sense *Heilsgeschichte* has been the continuing theme of theology

and the theology of history. It received special elaboration by Irenaeus, Augustine, the Reformers, and certain schools of the last two centuries. The main representative of this view today is Oscar Cullmann who sees history as a straight line running from creation to consummation with the coming of Christ as its midpoint. He attempts to hold the tension between the present and future elements in Jesus' teachings about the kingdom and in the doctrine of salvation. He uses the metaphor of the distinction between D-day and VE-day to illustrate that in Jesus' coming the decisive event has occurred but that final victory is still in the future.[9]

According to Cullmann the whole of world history is included in salvation history. Specifically this means that creation comprehends the beginning of world history. Then there is a concentration of salvation history in the election of Israel and culminating in Christ. Then from this midpoint there is a progressive expansion of salvation history again so that at the end or consummation it again comprehends world history. Thus the theological doctrine of the history between the times centers upon the mission of the church as the bearer of salvation history under the lordship of Christ and the guidance of the Spirit. Cullmann's view represents the consensus of the neo-orthodox doctrine of history.

4. *Dialectical Theology*—This view is similar to the last one but differs from it in a particular emphasis of the earlier dialectical theology of Barth and Brunner. This emphasis is the dialectical view of the relation between time and eternity, between the world and God. These theologians were not primarily interested in the end or goal of history. They interpreted the "last things" of traditional eschatology to refer to the ultimate concerns of the present moment. This connection is indicated by the fact that the German adjective *letzt* means both last and most significant or ultimate. They asserted that each generation is equidistant from the "last things," equidistant from eternity. So eschatology is concerned primarily not with the end of history but rather with the eternal meaning of each moment in history. Judgment, resurrection, and eternal life are primarily present realities rather than events or states which lie in the future. God or eternity is supra-temporal and therefore always contemporary. The final or ultimate reality does not await us primarily at the end of history but rather is breaking in constantly from above, judging and saving in the present moment. Thus the name dialectical: God is saying yes and no to every moment of history. God is negating and affirming every present of human life.

The dialectical view of history is a half-way house between the Platonic idea that eternity is timelessness and Cullmann's salvation history interpretation that eternity is endless duration. The theology of history which is implied by this dialectical approach gives eternal meaning to the present moment but tends to ignore the question of the meaning of the course of history. It often presents a comparatively pessimistic view of the course of history in contrast to the optimistic view which is criticized.

5. *Existentialist Theology*—This is an extreme version of the dialectical view which was developed primarily by Bultmann. In the dialectical interpretation a subordinate place was left for eschatology in the sense of last things at the end of history in the future. Thus the course of history had some meaning at least in the sense that it was moving toward a fulfillment and consummation in the future. But in Bultmann's thought all future reference in eschatology is dropped completely, and history in the sense of world history and the course of public events is declared to be void of meaning.

Bultmann sees the term "eschatological" as characterizing human existence under God, and especially as describing the moment of ultimately significant decision in regard to the gospel or obedience to God. The eschaton does not lie in the future of humanity's history but rather in the immediate future of my existence which impinges upon every present moment. Thus Bultmann speaks not of a historical or temporal future but of an existential future which he calls the futurity of existence. The proclamation of forgiveness in the kerygma of the cross, the momentary opportunity to decide about this, the decision itself, and the authentic existence resulting from a positive answer are all described by Bultmann as eschatological.

Bultmann's understanding of the meaning of eschatology is the result of his program of demythologizing and existential interpretation of the futuristic eschatology of the New Testament which he claims was already begun in the Fourth Gospel. The *Heilsgeschichte* and futuristic elements in the New Testament literature must be radically demythologized according to Bultmann. In one sense Bultmann's view of eschatology is similar to the realized eschatology of Dodd. But the fundamental difference is that for Dodd the eschaton is realized in the coming of Christ, whereas for Bultmann it is realized in the preaching of the kerygma in the present.

The result of Bultmann's approach for the doctrine of history is quite negative. It is summed up in his statement, "History is swallowed up in eschatology," in his special meaning of the latter term. He means that salvation history has come to its end in Christ, end in the sense of both goal and finish. As Christ is the end of the law, so also is Christ the end of history. Thus history is no longer salvation history but simply profane or secular history. In the coming of Christ the history of the Jewish nation and the history of the world lose their interest, because in Christ the true historicity of the individual person is disclosed.

By historicity Bultmann means that human being is historical being, that human existence is determined in every moment by the decisions made by the individual. So the decisive history is not the history of the world, or of Israel, of other peoples but rather the history in which individuals experience themselves and determine their existence. In the encounter with Christ in the preaching of the church the world and its history come to an end, and the believer is freed from the world and its history by becoming a new creature.

Thus Bultmann can say that the church is not a historical phenomenon but rather an eschatological community. It has no real history, for it represents the coming of the eschaton in the sense defined above. But according to Bultmann the church soon lost this eschatological understanding and came to see itself as an institution with a history as in Luke-Acts. Bultmann concludes his Gifford Lectures as follows:

> Man who complains: 'I cannot see meaning in history, and therefore my life, interwoven in history, is meaningless,' is to be admonished: do not look around yourself into universal history, you must look into your own personal history. Always in your present lies the meaning in history, and you cannot see it as a spectator, but only in your responsible decisions. In every moment slumbers the possibility of being the eschatological moment. You must awaken it.[10]

6. *Pannenberg's Theology of History*—Since 1959 a new theology of history has begun to emerge which is centered in the work of W. Pannenberg. He believes that the concrete course of events investigated by historical research is being avoided by theologians. The existentialist theologians have retreated from concrete history into the inner life of the individual. The *Heilsgeschichte* theologians have retreated to a sacred history which tends to be conceived as a supra-history which historical research cannot examine.

Pannenberg asserts that history is reality in its totality or that all of reality is historical, involved in a universal history. History arises because God makes promises and fulfills these promises; it is the tension between promise and fulfillment that makes history. Since the revelation of God is identical with historical events, the historical process itself is the bearer of meaning. The unity and meaning of history is grounded in the God who transcends history. God's freedom is the source of contingency in history; God's faithfulness is the source of continuity. Since it is only the whole of history in its unity and totality which reveals God, the meaning of world history will be perceivable only at the end of history. But Jesus' resurrection is the proleptic anticipation of the end of history, and so faith in the resurrection is the key for understanding history before the end. Since Jesus' resurrection can be demonstrated by historical research, faith rests on historically proven fact. Although the end of history has been manifest in the resurrection of Jesus, history is still incomplete and moves toward an open future We cannot make the resurrection into a key for calculating the course of history, because it is present to us in such a mysterious way.

7. *Theology of Hope*—The most recent important development in continental theology on the doctrine of history began with the publication in 1965 of Jürgen Moltmann's *Theology of Hope.* Although his doctrine of history is quite close to that of Pannenberg, his main concern is with eschatology.

> From first to last, and not merely in the epilogue, Christianity is eschatology, is hope, forward looking and forward moving, and therefore also revolutionizing and transforming the present. The eschatological is not one element *of* Christianity, but it is the medium of Christian faith as such, the key in which everything is set, the glow that suffuses everything here in the dawn of an expected new day. For Christian faith lives from the raising of the crucified Christ, and strains after the promises of the universal future of Christ. . . . Hence eschatology cannot really be only a part of Christian doctrine. Rather the eschatological outlook is characteristic of all Christian proclamation, of every Christian existence and of the whole Church. There is therefore only one real problem in Christian theology, which its own object forces upon it and which it in turn forces on mankind and on human thought: the problem of the future.[11]

The doctrine of history which results from this approach is that history is that reality which is instituted by and constituted by the promise given by God in the crucifixion and resurrection of Christ. The appropriate human response to this promise is hope, hope in the future realization and fulfillment of the promise. The response of hope involves three elements: the mission of the church to all nations, the hunger for righteousness in the world and the struggle for public obedience to God, and love for the true life of the whole imperilled and impaired creation. These constitute the meaning of history for Moltmann. In one passage they are all subsumed under the mission of the church: "The Christian mission . . . aims at reconciliation with God, . . . but also at the realization of the eschatological *hope of justice,* and *humanizing* of man, the *socializing* of humanity, *peace* for all creation." [12]

Christian hope expects that which is radically new in history and looks for the transformation and fulfillment of history in the end. God's promise keeps history open to the future. Moltmann continually emphasizes the fact that the promise stands in contradiction to the present state of the world and mankind, and he seems to understand the end of history in the quite traditional terms of second coming, general resurrection, final judgment and transformation of the world.

Reconstruction

The fundamental affirmations on which a doctrine of history must be based are that God is the Lord of history, that the course of history is ultimately under God's control, and that God wills to bring the whole creation including human history to its fulfillment. In chapter 7 on Providence, I suggested that this was a combination of the lordship and love of God. God is self-revealed as Lord of the creation and also as loving the creation and willing its fulfillment. Because God is Lord, God can carry out the divine will of love for the creation. This means that history in the largest sense of the history of the cosmos from creation to fulfillment is the story of God's fulfilling the loving divine will for the creation.

The doctrine of history in the narrower sense as history between the times of the coming of Christ and his return, the time of the church, has its meaning within this larger context. It is a stage in the fulfillment of God's purposes for his creation. In what way does this stage, the period of the church, contribute to or move history toward the final fulfillment? The traditional answer to this question has always been the mission of the church. Bishop Lesslie Newbigin has given a clear statement of this view:

> Thus the meaning and purpose of this present time between Christ's coming and His coming again is that in it the Church is to prosecute its apostolic mission of witness to the world. . . . It is for this that the end is held back. The end has been revealed once for all; it must now be made known to all that all may believe. . . . That is the meaning of the time still given to us. It is the time for bringing all men and all nations to the obedience of faith. It is for no other purpose that the end is delayed.[13]

This seems to be the view of the New Testament authors (Mt. 24:14, Acts 1:6). But this limitation of the task of the church to its evangelical mission needs to be expanded to include other responsibilities in service to the world. This can be done by interpreting the meaning of the mission of the church to include service to those in need, the struggle for justice and liberty, and the humanizing of life in society. Or it can be done by subsuming the missionary imperative under the love commandment. Then the love of neighbor will include testimony to God in Christ as well as service of those in need, the struggle for justice, and so forth.

This leads to the question of the significance of the accomplishments of the church in its mission of testimony and service. Their significance is challenged by the fact that, since they are historical accomplishments, they can be swept away by the tides of history, by the fact that in each new generation the task of testimony and service must be performed anew, and by the fact that the percentage of world population which can be called Christian (about 33 percent) is steadily decreasing.

The question of the significance of the accomplishments of the church in its mission of testimony and service comes down to this: What is their relation to God's final fulfillment of the divine purposes for the creation? Is the completion of the church's mission a necessary condition for the final fulfillment apart from which God will not accomplish the divine purposes? Do they contribute directly to the fulfillment even though they are swept away by history? That is, can God use these accomplishments in the achieving of the divine purposes even though they may be lost in history? Or is God's fulfillment of history accomplished partially or fully apart from human accomplishments? If the latter, what is their significance? It is upon the answers to questions such as these that the meaning of our present history depends.

The testimony of the Bible, the Christian tradition, and contemporary theology on these questions is obscure, to say the least. If there is any glimmer of a consensus, it is that the meager accomplishments of the church in testimony and service are somehow remembered by God, saved eternally, and used by God in the achieving of the divine purposes. Apart from such a view it is hard to see how these accomplishments could have any meaning at all except in the sense of acts of obedience. Tillich puts it this way:

> The ever present end of history elevates the positive content of history into eternity. . . . Therefore nothing which has been created in history is lost. . . . Eternal Life, then, includes the positive content of history, liberated from its negative distortions and fulfilled in its potentialities. . . . Life in the whole of creation and in a special way in human history contributes in every moment of time to the Kingdom of God and its eternal life. What happens in time and space, in the smallest particle of matter as well as in the greatest personality, is significant for the eternal life. And since eternal life is participation in the divine life, every finite happening is significant for God.[14]

This is similar to the view of the process theologians that since God prehends or experiences every completed actual occasion or event, it is preserved in God's consequent nature.[15] This view of the significance of human accomplishments for God's fulfillment of the divine purposes obviously includes those of the adherents of other religions and of no religion at all, as well as of Christians. Also there is an increasing number of theologians, mostly Roman Catholic, who are asserting that the other religions can be ways of salvation for their adherents and implying that the actions of these other religionists bear the same relation to God's fulfillment of history as do the actions of Christians.[16]

Another problem is the significance for the fulfillment of God's purposes of human creativity and activity in so-called higher culture, the arts and sciences, which are not necessarily included under the heading of the service of human need and the search for justice and liberty. What is the church's responsibility in relation to these aspects of culture? H. Richard Niebuhr in his book *Christ and Culture*[17] elaborated a spectrum of views on this question ranging from the identification of a Christian's calling with his cultural responsibility to the exclusion of any responsibility for culture from the Christian's task. Among contemporary theologians Tillich has been most concerned with the problem in his various writings on the theology of culture. His main thesis is that Christian faith should inform or act as the substance of culture and thus produce what he calls a theonomous culture. This is a culture which is completely oriented toward God, a culture whose freely chosen principles are identical with God's will for human culture. This is quite similar to the middle position described by Niebuhr as the conversionist view in which the Christian is called to follow Christ as the transformer of culture in the tradition of Augustine, Calvin and F. D. Maurice.

A final question: Does the Christian doctrine of history enable us to interpret theologically the significance of particular events, developments, trends, or movements? There is a spectrum of theological views on this question which I outlined on page 116. Theologians of the past have engaged in much more theological interpretation of particular events than contemporary theologians. This was especially the case in regard to the persecution and recognition of the church, the downfall of the empire, the rise of monasticism, the Reformation, and the expansion of the church and western culture in the last century.

Contemporary theologians have seen the hand of God in the various liberation movements and in such developments as secularization, urbanization and the rise of technology. But they are sharply divided over the significance of these latter developments. On the one hand the neo-orthodox and existentialist theologians have tended to see these developments and their results in society as manifestations of human sin and divine judgment. Some have described the Western history from the Renaissance as the second fall of humanity and the vain repetition of the Gentiles. But on the other hand the secular theologians such as Bonhoeffer, Cox and van Leeuwen, have seen these developments as the cooperation of God and humanity in the coming of age of humanity, in human fulfillment and salvation.

Questions for Discussion

1. What does it mean to say that God is the lord of history? If it means that God is in control of the course of history, how does God exercise this control? Is it by modification of natural or psychic processes? If not, how can God's control be distinguished from lack of control?

2. *Does the meaning of the history in which we are involved consist essentially in the mission of the church? If so, how would you define this mission? What then is the significance of the struggle for liberty, justice and equality, and for scientific, technological and cultural advance? If not, how would you state the meaning of history?*

3. *Is there progress in history? If so, what is the nature of it and what is its connection with reign of God or the goal of history? If not, what is the significance of the course of history?*

4. *What is the significance of human achievements in history in the light of the fact that they can also be destroyed in history: for example, in regard to the mission of the church, the struggle for justice, scientific and cultural advance, and so forth?*

5. *If the Christian faith holds that the end of history is the fulfillment of God's purposes for the whole creation, does this not empty the course of history of any meaning since the end is already decided?*

6. *What is the relationship of (a) human accomplishment to (b) God's accomplishment of the goal of history? Is (b) independent of (a), dependent upon (a), or is (a) complementary to (b)?*

7. *What is the nature of the Christian responsibility in history for the advance of so-called higher culture, that is, science and art? What is its connection with the goal of history?*

8. *Describe and interpret an event during your lifetime whose meaning and significance is illuminated by the Christian doctrine of history.*

9. *Is God's lordship of history visible to all, only to faith, or not at all? Defend your answer.*

10. *Should we expect a radically new age in history or simply a continuation of the present age? Why?*

11. *What is the meaning of history?*

12. *What is the place of the history of the cosmos in the Christian doctrine of history?*

16

Eschatology

Eschatology or the doctrine of last things deals with the end of humanity, history, and the cosmos in the sense of both goal and finish. In the last chapter we introduced this topic, summarized its treatment in the Bible, and outlined the debates on it in modern theology.

Tradition

During the early Christian centuries eschatological teaching amounted largely to the exposition of the biblical themes of the *parousia*, the general resurrection, the last judgment, heaven and hell. A unique feature of early eschatological teaching was the widespread affirmation of millenialism, the idea that at the *parousia* Christ will reign on earth with the saints for a thousand years before the final fulfillment (see Rev. 20:4f). After the third century, however, this idea faded and it emerged only occasionally in later periods. One of the causes of its fading was the influence of Middle Platonism with its teaching on the immortality of the soul and its concern for the journey of the soul to heaven, as exemplified in the Alexandrian theology.

Origen's views are rather unique and produced a complex debate on eschatology. His doctrine of the resurrection of the body affirmed the identity of the resurrection body with the earthly body but denied its fleshly character. At death there is a provisional separation of souls and an intermediate state which is probationary. Origen spiritualizes the second coming and denies a literal millenium. Similarly he spiritualizes the sufferings of the damned and asserts that the punishments of hell must have an end. This is part of his famous doctrine of *apocatastasis* or universal restoration in which he affirms that the conclusion of cosmic history will be identical with its beginning. All things will be brought into subjection to God; rational creatures will freely submit through persuasion and instruction. Even the Devil will participate in the final restoration. This view was later condemned.

After the recognition of the church Eusebius and Augustine tended to identify the millennial reign of Christ with the church. In general, the delay of the *parousia*, the influence of Middle Platonism, and the recognition of the church led to the relaxation of the eschatological tension of the early generations and the relegation of the last things to an indefinite future. From Augustine on the theologians of the church did little more than organize and elaborate on the main themes of scriptural teaching. Attention was more and more focussed on individual eschatology, the fate of the individual soul at death.

A new sense of the imminence of the end appeared at the Reformation. The Reformers believed that they lived in the last days. The signs of the end were appearing: the Pope was seen as the Anti-Christ, and the mission of the church was believed to be complete. The Anabaptists renewed a form of the millenialist teaching.

But the rise of Protestant orthodoxy in the later sixteenth and seventeenth centuries was accompanied again by a relaxing of eschatological tension, the relegation of the end to an indefinite future, and a renewed concentration on individual eschatology.

The result of these developments is that the outlines of eschatological teaching in Catholic and Protestant orthodoxy are roughly the same. At death the immortal soul is separated from the body, undergoes what is known as particular judgment, and proceeds to hell or a state of waiting until the end. Some affirmed that the martyrs and saints went directly to heaven. The punishment of hell includes the negative *poena damni* or the forfeiture of the divine presence and the *poena sensus* involving the inner torture of despair and anguish and the external torment of demons and fire.

Catholic theology included the intermediate state of purgatory for baptized souls who had died without repentance for venial sins or who had not suffered the punishment for sins whose guilt had been forgiven. This is not a state of probation or a second chance but is only for those who are destined to be saved but who cannot enter heaven directly. Protestants rejected the doctrine of purgatory because they believed that it was without scriptural foundation, that punishment after forgiveness was untrue to the gospel, and that it implied that the sacrifice of Christ for sins was not fully sufficient.

The end of history is to be marked by the return of Christ in power and glory visible to all. This is followed by the resurrection of the bodies of the dead and their reunion with their souls. Then comes the final judgment at which the eternal fate of all persons is determined. Presumably it is simply a confirmation of the particular judgment made upon each soul at its death. Then the saved enjoy heaven and the damned suffer in hell. It was sometimes taught in the doctrine of annihilationism that condemned souls do not suffer eternally but are destroyed.

Roman Catholic theology also added the doctrine of limbo with its two divisions: the *limbus infantium* for the souls of unbaptized infants who do not suffer the pains of hell but are excluded from the beatific vision, and the *limbus patrum* where the saints of the old covenant repose. It is to be noted that the doctrine of *apocatastasis* or universal salvation is denied.

Because both Protestant and Catholic orthodoxy concentrated upon the destiny of the soul, little attention was given to the destiny of the physical universe. It was simply asserted that it was transformed or renewed. Some Lutheran theologians, however, taught that it was to be annihilated .

This is the traditional scheme of eschatology which was generally accepted down to the eighteenth century. It is the view taught and implied in the Anglican formularies. The only explicit references in the Articles are to the "return [of Christ] to judge all men at the last day" (IV), "everlasting felicity" (XVII), and a condemnation of the "Romish doctrine of purgatory" (XXII).

The rise of Pietism in the eighteenth century saw a renewal of millennial hope for the establishment of the reign of God in history. But the Enlightenment and the emergence of idealist philosophy tended to water down eschatology to the ideas of the immortality of the soul and historical progress toward an ideal society which was interpreted as the kingdom of God. These became the themes of the liberal theology of the last century which were criticized by the dialectical or neo-orthodox theology of this century. Chapter 15 includes an outline of seven views of eschatology which have emerged out of this critique.

Reconstruction

The eschatological affirmations of Christian faith are not primarily assertions about states of affairs in the future but rather assertions about God, namely, that God is the God of history, the Lord of the beginning and the end of the world. Conversely, affirmations about God are affirmations about the end of history. The reason for this is that since God is carrying out the divine purposes in history, the ultimate purpose and thus character of God will be expressed in the final state of history. "What is ultimately real will be ultimately realized. . . . The essential . . . . [is] what holds true at the end of time. . . . The ultimate truth about God is necessarily the final event in history." [1]

Furthermore, all eschatological assertions refer to the present as well as to the future, in two senses. First, they are based on present knowledge and experience. Because of our present relation to God in Christ, we know what the future will ultimately be. Secondly, the last things which these assertions point to are present realities. We know judgment, resurrection and eternal life fragmentarily in the present, because we participate in Christ who is the end or goal of history.

As we have seen, theological assertions mean that we see all things in relation to God. Eschatological assertions mean that we see all things in relation to God who is the end or goal (as well as the beginning) of all things. More specifically in eschatological assertions we see all things in the light of Christ, who is the end or goal of all things, the last as well as the first, the last Adam (Rev. 1:17, 1 Cor. 15:45).

The fundamental issue in eschatology today is that between the existentialist interpretation which excludes all future reference in eschatology except in the sense of the immediate future of the individual, and the neo-orthodox reinterpretation of the biblical and traditional view which includes a reference to the future of human history and the universe as well as the individual. We have noted in chapter 15 that Bultmann demythologizes and eliminates all future reference in eschatology except in the existentialist sense mentioned above. Neo-orthodox theology from Barth to Moltmann and Pannenberg has tried to take the biblical and traditional eschatology seriously but not literally. It has attempted to interpret it symbolically in such a way that the reference to the future fulfillment of history and the cosmos is maintained.

Any such future reference has to come to terms with the scientific picture of the future of life, the planet, and the universe. This can be outlined as follows: The radiant life of the sun will begin to come to an end in about five billion years. At that time the radiation from the sun will first increase and the sun will expand until it swallows the planets out as far as Mars or Jupiter. Then it will collapse and pass through several stages until it becomes a radiationless black dwarf. Thus if life on earth is not snuffed out by atomic holocaust or ecological disaster, it will come to an end when the temperature of the earth reaches the boiling point. If people escape to the outer planets and if they escape death there from the increased radiation from the sun, they will die either from the cold or the lack of energy soon after radiation from the sun ceases.

The universe has been going through fifteen billion years of expansion deriving from a primal explosion. This may be followed by a period of contraction and another explosion. But these cycles of expansion and contraction cannot go on forever. Assuming that the universe is a closed system, that is, that it cannot gain or lose any energy, it cannot escape the second law of thermodynamics in regard to entropy. Entropy is the degree of dispersion or disorder or inconvertibility of energy. The second law states that the entropy of a closed system may increase or remain constant but it cannot decrease. This means that the final state of the universe will be what has been called "heat death" or the state in which all temperatures are equalized and there is no more conversion of energy. De Chardin has attempted to avoid or overcome the second law by means of a concept of "radial energy," but this is not acceptable to modern science.

The advantage of the existentialist theology is that it has no problem with this scientific picture since it has nothing to say about the future which has any connection with this. Neo-orthodox and traditional theology, however, must come to terms with this picture, since it has to deal with the future of world history and the cosmos. In affirming the fulfillment of history and the cosmos, it seems to have to contradict the scientific world picture. For example Macquarrie asserts, "If it were shown that the universe is indeed headed for an all-enveloping death, then this might seem to constitute a state of affairs so wasteful and negative that it might be held to falsify Christian faith and abolish Christian hope."[2] Neo-orthodox theologians often fail to face up to the fact that the only alternative to Bultmann's position is a view which must involve the assertion that human history and the universe will come to some kind of end a finite length of time in the future.

This raises the question of the relation between temporal and moral urgency. Both existentialist and neo-orthodox eschatology affirm that the distinctive attitude of Christian hope is that which has been described above as the sense of eschatological tension, namely, the sense of expectancy and moral urgency and decisiveness. Robinson describes it as follows:

> The fashion of this world looks different when seen from the End. The neutrality goes out of it. It is as though the beam of a searchlight has been turned upon it, immeasurably deepening the contrast between light and shade. The flatness is taken from living. A new edge and tone is given to it. The common round becomes charged with fresh moment and decisiveness.[3]

In the early church, at the Reformation, and in the period of Pietism this sense of tension was based upon the belief in the temporal imminence of the end. It can also be caused by momentous personal, national, or world situations, such as impending death, war or national crisis, or the danger of imminent nuclear holocaust or ecological disaster. But these latter causes come down to the same thing: the imminent expectation of the end. Existentialist eschatology denies such imminence completely, and neo-orthodox eschatology is generally agnostic about it. Both are uneasy when the sense of eschatological tension is based only on the sense of temporal urgency, because they believe that the eschatological character of the gospel and the Christian life is independent of the temporal factor. When it is confused with the temporal factor, it is subject to misunderstanding in terms of a literalistic view of the biblical apocalyptic.

That the eschatological character of the Christian life is independent of any temporal urgency is indicated by the fact that the church survived the delay of the *parousia*.[4] Robinson describes this situation as follows:

> To be brought home effectively to men's consciences such moral urgency has necessarily, perhaps, to be *expressed* as temporal urgency, decisiveness of *kairos* translated into immediacy of *chronos*. . . . A matter is not really made morally more urgent by the fact that one has only a short while in which to make up one's mind about it. Such urgency is derived from the intrinsic nature of the situation and cannot be increased or decreased by time, any more than it can be by space. . . . The note of temporal imminence, struck so constantly in the New Testament, is only an external way of expressing the essential element in Christian eschatology, which is that of moral urgency. . . . The moral urgency is expressed in the temporal, not derived from it.[5]

Thus, a valid eschatology will have to combine the sense of moral urgency which has been clarified by Bultmann and a reference to the future fulfillment which cannot be eliminated from the testimony of Bible and tradition. This future reference cannot be reduced to the existential future but must include the world-historical future and indeed the cosmic future. Apart from such future reference history can have no direction, purpose, or meaning, as Bultmann frankly admits. Therefore the basic task of eschatology is to interpret the various aspects or symbols of this future reference. In this connection it is important to recall that all theological assertions are symbolic or analogical in character and not univocal or literal.

The fundamental assertion of eschatology is that the God who is creator and Lord and who has revealed the divine purposes for creation fully in Jesus will in fact fulfill these purposes and that this fulfillment will be the end of history in the sense of goal and finish. This is the basic meaning of the doctrine of the *parousia* or the second coming of Christ. By affirming the return of Christ in the creed we are asserting that the purposes of God revealed in Christ will be fulfilled. Another way of stating this is to say that the main symbol for the end of history and the fulfillment of God's purposes is the reign of God. Now Jesus was the one in whom God's reign first became fully actual. Therefore the symbol of the return of Christ in power and glory means the fulfillment of the reign of God.

The symbol of the second coming of Christ also includes the idea that this is for the purpose of the judgment of the world. This is an elaboration of the theme that in the end God's purposes will in fact be fulfilled and that all of human activity and history will be assessed in the light of these purposes as manifest in Christ, that is, in the light of the actual possibilities of human life and not of some super-human ideal. The ambiguities of the conflicts between good and evil in history will be overcome, and the love of God manifest in Christ will be victorious over sin and the powers of evil.

The symbol of the resurrection of the body involves a variety of theological meanings. In the first place, the hope of eternal life rests entirely on the nature of God and not on the nature of humanity. No aspect of human being is immortal; humanity is entirely subject to death (see p. 122). Thus any victory over death is entirely God's doing. This symbol also means that as the whole person dies, so also the whole person participates in the fulfillment and not simply the rational or spiritual part of the person.

Since the body is the necessary basis of interpersonal communication and thus of communal life and historical life, the symbol of the resurrection of the body means that human social and historical life will be brought to its fulfillment. The Christian hope is thus neither an escape from the body nor from communal and political life, but rather the fulfillment of these. Here the symbol of the resurrection of the body merges with that of the reign of God. Finally, since it is impossible to separate the body from the rest of the natural world, this symbol also points to the fulfillment of the whole cosmos. This is the import of the biblical references to the new earth, the desert blooming as the rose, the wolf dwelling with the lamb, and so forth (see Isa. 11:6f, 65:17, Rev. 21:1f, Rom. 8:19f).

In Middle Platonist thought that which makes a person human is participation in the universal reason or spirit, and what makes a person an individual is the body. Thus early Christian thought affirmed the resurrection of the body in order to affirm that individuality was good and was to be fulfilled by God. In biblical thought, however, the reverse obtains. The principle of individuality is a person's relation to God. The body represents a person's solidarity with nature, with the human community, and with the cosmos. So the doctrine of the resurrection of the body means the replacement of the solidarity in sin and death of the first Adam with the solidarity in love and eternal life of the last Adam. This is why the resurrection of the body is placed at the *parousia* and not at the individual's death. The individual is redeemed not *out* of all these relationships of solidarity but only in and with them. There is, however, a sense in which according to Paul a Christian participates now in the resurrection of the body. Although the general resurrection will occur only at the end, the church already participates in the end, that is, in Christ by the Spirit. "The resurrection of the body begins, not at death, but at baptism."[6]

According to the Bible and the tradition all people participate in the resurrection, because the resurrection does not depend upon any essential human capacity or virtue or worthiness but only upon the unconditional love of God. Thus there is no place in Christian eschatology for "conditional immortality," the doctrine that eternal life is a divine reward conditional upon the worthiness of the life on earth. (This was condemned at the Fifth Lateran Council in 1513.)

This leads to the issue of universalism versus eternal condemnation or annihilationism, the question of whether or not all people are finally brought to their fulfillment. The New Testament is ambiguous on this issue, (Cp. Rom. 5:18, 1 Cor. 15:22-28, Eph. 1:9 with Mt. 25:31ff, Rev. 20:10) and the tradition with a few exceptions, such as Origen, affirms eternal condemnation. The traditional view took the form of double predestination in Augustine and Calvin. Brunner argues that the issue remains open until the end.

Aquinas asserts that God's purposes can be fulfilled even though some are condemned. God's love wills that all should be saved, but, because the divine love is just and holy, some may be condemned. But this amounts to a failure of God's love and a failure in the fulfillment of God's purposes for the creation.

So this issue comes down to a decision as to whether we are to give more weight to human freedom to turn away from God's love or to the power of God's love to win all people freely to God. Any victory of God which violates human freedom is not a victory of love but of coercion. But it is possible to conceive a love which is so powerful that ultimately no one will be able to resist free and grateful surrender. This, in fact, seems to be what the New Testament testimony is pointing to.

How can this be reconciled with the other side of the New Testament testimony, namely, the possibility of eternal condemnation? Robinson's solution is that the two aspects of the New Testament testimony point to what may be called the objective and the subjective sides of Christian faith.

> The two myths represent . . . the two sides of the truth which is in Jesus. The one says: "Christ is all in all, and always will be." The other says: "Christ has to be chosen, and always must be." Though both are the truth, one is the truth as it is for God and as it is for faith the further side of decision; the other is the truth as it must be to the subject facing decision.[7]

The main symbols for the final consummation are eternal life and the reign of God. These point to individual and communal fulfillment, respectively, and their fundamental theme is communion with God, with our fellows, and with the rest of creation. They are essentially projections of the present experience and understanding of salvation understood as a fragmentary foretaste of the fulfillment. Another symbol is the beatific vision, the unhindered and immediate vision of God which is held to be the final destiny of the redeemed in traditional theology. Although this idea has some basis in the Bible (Mt. 5:8), under the influence of Greek philosophy it was interpreted in an individualistic and intellectualistic way which does not do justice to the other symbols of the fulfillment.[8]

These symbols point to the fulfillment of creaturehood, individuality, community, physical embodiment, temporality, and not to the denial or transcending of these aspects of human and cosmic history. Beyond this, however, these symbols are not very specific but rather evocative and poetic. Paul's description of the final state is that God will be "all in all," or "everything to everyone" (1 Cor. 15:28). On the specific details of the fulfillment the Christian must remain agnostic.

Finally, a word on what has been called individual eschatology. The ground of individual Christian hope remains focussed in the resurrection of Christ which Paul interprets to mean that the power of death has been overcome, that the first fruits of the final harvest have appeared, and that the beginning of the end has occurred. Paul also interprets the resurrection of Christ to be the seal on the promise that God has drawn us into such a real and intimate relationship in Christ that nothing can disrupt it, not even death (Rom. 8:31-39).

Doctrines of the intermediate state arose to explain what happened to the individual between physical death and the general resurrection. The Catholic tradition affirmed the doctrine of purgatory which has been described above. Article XXII denies the "Romish doctrine of purgatory" but may be interpreted not to rule out other doctrines of purgatory. If it is affirmed that all die imperfect and that the fulfillment involves the perfection of all persons, then the alternatives would seem to be a sudden transformation or a process of moral growth involving purgation from sin. The prayers for the dead in *The Book of Common Prayer* imply the latter view.[9] But here again the theologian must probably remain agnostic.

The Resurrection of Christ

I have stated that the basis of Christian hope is the resurrection of Christ. Paul and others described Christ as the first fruits or first born from the dead or the first to rise from the dead (Col. 1:18, 1 Cor. 15:20, 23; Acts 26:23; Rev. 1:5). The resurrection of Christ is the beginning of the end, the first fruits which assure the fullness of the harvest to come. These authors thus implied that the resurrection of all people was to be like the resurrection of Christ.

Therefore the content of Christian hope is related to the nature of the resurrection of Christ.

Was the resurrection of Christ an objective historical event or was it a subjective event in the minds of the disciples? Barth and his followers, including Pannenberg and Moltmann, affirm the former.[10] Bultmann and his followers affirm the latter.[11] According to the New Testament authors the resurrection of Christ was an objective event but of an unusual kind. Although it was not simply an event in the minds of the disciples, yet it was not publicly observable. Christ appeared only to chosen witnesses (Acts 10:40f).

The testimony to the resurrection of Christ is of two types: accounts of appearances of Christ and accounts of the empty tomb. The accounts of the appearances are not of a ghostly apparition nor of a physical body but of what St. Paul called a spiritual or glorified body (see 1 Cor. 15:43f, Phil. 3:21). "All the appearances, in fact, depict the same phenomenon, of a body identical yet changed, transcending the limitations of the flesh yet capable of manifesting itself within the order of the flesh."[12]

The empty tomb is not mentioned in the earliest level of testimony, but it may be implied there (see 1 Cor. 15:4, Acts 2:31, 13:29f). However, it is an integral part of each of the earliest gospel accounts. Robinson argues that since it would have been inconceivable for a Jew to think of resurrection except in bodily terms, the earliest proclamation of the resurrection of Christ must have implied an empty tomb.

It can be argued that if the tomb were not empty, the resurrection of Christ did not involve his physical body. This would mean that the eschatological fulfillment does not include the physical body and the physical world and thus amounts to an escape from them. Or the argument can be put the other way around. Since on other grounds we know that the eschatological fulfillment does include the physical world, and since the resurrection of Christ is an authentic foretaste of the fulfillment, it must have involved his physical body, and the tomb must have been empty. But this is to argue for a potentially observable historical fact on the basis of theological consistency. As we saw in the case of the virginal conception, this may be possible in physics but not in theology. This kind of argument is better understood as an indication of the consistency of theology with the New Testament testimony.

It should be noted, however, that the affirmation of the empty tomb is an assertion of the transformation of the atoms of Jesus' body and their disappearance from the space-time-energy system, or in traditional terms a miracle. On the other hand it might be argued, as Tillich and others do, that although the final fulfillment includes the physical world, the resurrection of Christ did not, perhaps because it occurred before the end and was not a foretaste in that sense.[13]

Questions for Discussion

1. *Jesus and the early Christians expected the eschaton in the first century. They were wrong. What is the significance of this fact for Christian eschatology?*

2. *According to some parts of the New Testament the final judgment will be on the basis of our works (Mt. 25:31ff, 2 Cor. 5:10, Rev. 20:12f). How can this be reconciled with the teaching of Paul and the church in regard to justification by grace through faith?*

3. *Is the reign of God, interpreted as the goal of history and fulfillment of God's purposes, to be achieved in history or only " beyond" history? Why?*

4. *Does Christian eschatology involve the affirmation that the end or transformation of history and the cosmos will occur a finite number of years in the future? Why? If not, can history have any meaning?*

5. *How would you decide between eternal condemnation, annihilationism and universalism.*

6. *If all human life were to be destroyed in an atomic holocaust, as in Neville Shute's novel* On The Beach, *what would be the relation of this event to the eschaton of Christian theology?*

7. *How is the Christian eschatology related to the predictions of scientists about the future of the earth, the solar system, and the universe?*

8. *Which is the better image or symbol for eternal life, "beatific vision" or "communion of the saints?" Why?*

9. *An older person asks you, "What is going to happen to me when I die?" What would you answer? Why?*

10. *Does Christian eschatology logically lead to ethical passivity or ethical activity? Why?*

11. *What, if anything, does the doctrine of the resurrection of the body imply about the atoms constituting the body at death? Why?*

12. *"Most of the books of the Old Testament were written at a time when the Hebrew people had no belief in an afterlife for the individual" (G. B. Caird). What is the significance of this for Christian eschatology?*

13. *What would be the significance for Christian eschatology if physical research were to prove or disprove survival after death? Why?*

14. *Does Christian hope involve a temporal urgency or only a moral urgency? Why?*

15. *If the doctrine of creation does not necessarily the assertion that the universe had a beginning in time a finite number of years in the past (pp. 102f), then does this mean that eschatology does not necessarily involve the assertion that the universe will have an absolute end or transformation a finite number of years in the future?*

16. *Is the idea of reincarnation in conflict with the Christian view of humanity?*

17

Church

With the doctrine of the church we begin those topics dealing with participation in salvation, the human response to the redemptive action of God which has been treated in chapters 11-16. Some theologians treat all the remaining four topics under the doctrine of the church, because it comprehends everything that needs to be said about the human response to and participation in salvation.

Existentially the doctrine of the church comes first of all, for that is where we are and where we find ourselves as we begin to do theology. In this sense it is the presupposition of everything else in theology. Thus Schleiermacher begins his systematic theology with this thesis: "Since Dogmatics is a theological discipline, and thus pertains solely to the Christian Church, we can only explain what it is when we have become clear as to the conception of the Christian Church." [1]

The doctrine of the church is central to the curriculum of theological education, since it is the fulcrum or transition between the biblical, historical, systematic studies and the practical disciplines. The various disciplines of practical theology deal with the various aspects of the practice of the church and its members. The basis of these disciplines is the doctrine of the church, that is, the interpretation of the nature and purpose of the church, what the church and its members are called to be and to do. [2]

Bible

In the New Testament the church emerges as the historical result of the series of events culminating in the death and resurrection of Christ and the coming of the Spirit. Historically the events produced the community. But the members of the community claimed that it was God acting in these events who created the community, that they had been chosen out of Israel by God as witnesses of the resurrection and recipients of the divine Spirit.

The New Testament authors interpret the church in a great variety of ways. Paul Minear claims to have isolated almost one hundred different images for the church in the New Testament. But the main approaches can be summarized under four headings.[3]

The congregation of the faithful. Jesus' first preaching was a call to repentance and faith, belief in the good news of the nearness of the reign of God. Many of the accounts of Jesus' healings as signs of the presence of the reign of God conclude with his announcement, "Your faith has saved (or healed) you." The disciples were those who believed in Jesus and followed him. The author of John wrote his gospel in order "that you may believe that Jesus is the Christ, the Son of God, and that believing you may have life in his name" (20:31; see Acts 2:44, Rom 10:9f).

This emphasis on faith as the basis of the Christian life in the church is elaborated by Paul in his teaching about law and justification. Salvation is by grace received through faith and not by any works of the law. According to this approach the church is constituted by faith in Jesus Christ. This is the classical Protestant emphasis and is reflected in Article XIX which begins, "The visible Church of Christ is a congregation of faithful men . . . ," and in the thanksgiving in the Eucharist where the church is defined as "the blessed company of all faithful people."

The body of Christ. Jesus did not leave behind a creed or a code of ethics or a set of cultic instructions but rather a community of people whom he had called and taught and with whom he had shared his life and Spirit. Jesus' purpose in calling together this community was that its members would represent him in preaching and healing. The description of the church as the body of Christ appears only in Paul's letters and Ephesians, and it is his only image of the church, with the possible exception of the olive tree in Romans 11. He uses this phrase also to refer to Jesus' physical body, his resurrection body, and his sacramental body. Paul's assertion that the church is the body of Christ cannot mean the identity of the church with one of these other meanings but is rather an analogical or metaphorical use of the phrase. (Some theologians, such as Pittenger, Kirk and Johnston, have asserted that Paul's statement is "more than a metaphor," but the only thing more than a metaphor is an identity.)

The basis for Paul's metaphor is his understanding of the Christian life as life "in Christ," as a participation in the life, death and resurrection of Christ through the Spirit of Christ. The main points that Paul is making about the church in his use of the body metaphor are as follows: First, Christians are united with Christ and with each other by the Spirit of Christ or the Holy Spirit. Thus the church is the body of Christ because it is the community in which the Spirit of Christ dwells.

Secondly, Christians receive various gifts of the Spirit for different functions in the community. These are given for the benefit and well-being of the whole community. So the church is the body of Christ in that the Spirit of Christ gives gifts to the members so that they may function in the way that various parts of the human body function in relation to the whole body (1 Cor. 12). Thirdly, and following from this, the life and well-being of the community depends upon the service and function of all the members, and it suffers if any of the members is separated from the community, on the analogy of a human body. Thus the church is the body of Christ in that each of the functions made possible by the Spirit of Christ is necessary for its well-being.

Fourthly, Christians become members of the church by sacramental incorporation, by baptism into the death and resurrection of Christ, and by participation in the body and blood of Christ in the eucharist. Thus the church is the body of Christ in that membership in it is gained and sustained by sacraments understood by reference to various meanings of the body of Christ. Fifthly, the church is the body of Christ in that through the Spirit Christ is the ruling, inspiring, sustaining and uniting power in the church. This comes out most clearly in the modification of the body metaphor in which Christ is the head of the body which is the church.

Thus it becomes clear that Paul's metaphor of the church as the body of Christ serves primarily to explain the nature of the unity of the church. Although Paul does not draw them out explicitly, there are other implications of his body metaphor, namely, that the purpose of the church is to continue Christ's work in the world, and that the church is essentially a concrete, visible, organic reality with continuity in history. The body of Christ theme can be called the classical catholic emphasis in the doctrine of the church.

The fellowship of the Spirit. This approach is obviously closely connected with the body metaphor, and in one sense it is more basic, for it is the presence and working of the Holy Spirit which makes the church the body of Christ. It also underlies the idea of the church as the congregation of the faithful, since faith is a gift of the Holy Spirit (1 Cor. 12:3).

According to the New Testament authors when the risen Lord gave the apostolic commission to the church and empowered it to carry out this mission, the essential act was the gift of the Holy Spirit. The beginning of the church's mission to the Gentiles was determined by the fact that they received the Holy Spirit even as the Jewish Christians had. Possession of the Spirit is the decisive mark of being a Christian (Rom. 8:9, 1 Jn. 4:13). It is the presence of God the Holy Spirit which makes the church what it is: the place where the new birth takes place, the place where the first fruits of the age to come are manifest, the community which is led into all truth and in which testimony is given to Christ. This is why in the Apostles' and Nicene creeds belief in the church is associated with belief in God the Holy Spirit.

Newbigin points out that the founding of the church by the gift of the Holy Spirit is often forgotten in the Protestant-Catholic ecumenical discussion, because it brings into the picture a revolutionary freedom which is viewed somewhat uneasily by those concerned with proper form, order and continuity. The point is that according to the New Testament, Christ is the free and sovereign Lord over the church, and he exercises this freedom and sovereignty by the presence and working of the Holy Spirit (see Jn. 3:8). Jürgen Moltmann has stressed this aspect of the doctrine of the church in his recent book *The Church in the Power of the Spirit.* [4]

The community of hope. In the New Testament the church is depicted as the eschatological community, the fellowship of the end-time, in which the powers of the age to come are already at work, and which looks forward eagerly to the return of Christ and the fulfillment. Therefore, the church is not fully what it is essentially. It must be understood in the light of what it is called to be, in the light of the goal toward which it presses in hope (see 1 Jn. 3:2, Rom. 8:23f).

Furthermore, the church in history lives under the sign of the cross. The power of God is present in the church, but it is manifest only to the eye of faith. It is a power which is hidden, which is made perfect in weakness, and which takes the form of a servant. The life of the church is only a foretaste, an earnest, a guarantee of the fulfillment which is to come. The image of the church as the bride of Christ must be seen as an eschatological image. The church is now betrothed to Christ, but the actual wedding and marriage feast takes place only at the end. (We will return to some other aspects of the New Testament understanding of the church below.)

Tradition

It has sometimes been asserted that the doctrine of the church has been strangely neglected in Christian history.[5] But these statements are somewhat exaggerated, because the doctrine of the church has quite often been at the center of attention in the history of the church.

In the early period debate centered on the authority and limits of the church in reaction to Gnosticism and to schismatics, such as the Montanists, the Novatianists, and the Donatists. In response to the Gnostics, Irenaeus stressed the possession by the Catholic Church of the rule of faith, the apostolic writings, the succession of bishops in the apostolic sees, and the primacy of the bishop of Rome.

The Montanists defined the principle of the true church as the presence of the Spirit, as against all the things emphasized by Irenaeus. In reaction to this and to the rigorist orthodoxy of the Novatianists, Cyprian asserted the actual unity of the church on the basis of the bishops. For him the criterion of membership in the church is not faith or morals but rather submission to the bishop. There are no sacraments or salvation outside the Catholic Church.

The development in the West was completed by Augustine who wrote on this issue in response to the Donatists. They held the rigorist view that the church is a society of actual saints and that the validity of the sacraments depends upon the worthiness of the minister. Augustine affirmed that the church is the mystical body of Christ whose principle of unity is that it is a fellowship of love. As against the Donatists, however, he asserted that the church is a mixed community comprising both good and bad people. But he also made a distinction between the essential church consisting of those who genuinely belong to Christ and the outward or empirical church. This was refined in his doctrine of predestination with the result that the only true members of the invisible church are the elect whose number is fixed.

The Reformers attacked the doctrine and authority of the Catholic Church, and using Augustine's distinction between the visible and invisible church they defined the church in terms of election, faith, the word, and the sacraments. It is significant, however, that Article XIX drops any reference to election and the invisible church and defines the church in terms of faith, the word, and the sacraments. The Anabaptists took up the rigorist sectarian view of the church and defined it as consisting only of those who are truly regenerate.

We can see that there have been two main emphases in the history of the doctrine of the church which have appeared in reaction to each other. The first is the tendency to define the church in a legal way in terms of outward and visible factors such as subscription to a creed or submission to a bishop. The second is the tendency to define the church in inward, invisible, or spiritual terms such as faith, election, regeneration, purity of life, and the presence of the Spirit. We will return to this issue later.

Contemporary Issues and Reconstruction

Since the publication of Wedel's book in 1945 the doctrine of the church has been at the center of attention in theology. The main reason for this is the ecumenical movement which came to its first major fruition in the first assembly of the World Council of Churches in 1948. However, the main impetus for the ecumenical movement came from the mission fields of the church, especially in Asia and Africa, but also in the universities of the West under the auspices of the Student Christian Movement. Where the missionary concern was alive, the division of the church became an unbearable burden. The ecumenical movement forced the churches to face the question of their own self-understanding, the question of the nature of the church and its unity in the face of its divisions.

Williams points out that the discussion of the nature of the church in recent decades has gone through three periods. The first he describes as the period of high-church rediscovery. This involved the search for a common doctrine of the church in the Bible and the traditions lying behind the divisions. The second period was marked by the suspicion that the first period was too inward-looking, too church-centered. The result was the conviction that "mission" must be added to the traditional marks of the church in the creed (one, holy, catholic, apostolic). The idea was that church unity could not be based simply on continuities such as the sacraments and church order, but that unity would be a gift resulting from obedience to the mission of the church.

The third period has been a more radical following out of the theme of the second period. It could be called the church-world period. Here the consensus is that the doctrine of the church must move out of the center of attention if we are to get clear on the true nature of the church. The doctrine of the church can be approached indirectly through direct attention to its responsibility for the world. The church does not exist as an end in itself for its own sake but for the sake of the world, that the world may come to know its origin, meaning, and goal in God. The church exists to be the instrument of God in the divine mission to the world and thus as the servant of the world. The church is that part of the world where God's love, lordship, and purpose of salvation are recognized, responded to, and celebrated. Thus the mission of the church is not to be understood in terms of the world being drawn into the church but in terms of the world attaining its own true fulfillment through the testimony and service of the church. This was summarized in the slogan, "The church does not have a mission; it is mission."

Another aspect of this transition in the understanding of the church is the growing realization of the radically different relation of the church to Western culture today. The traditional doctrines of the church assumed the Christendom model of this relation. In this model the typical situation was the established national church which dominated and sought to christianize all areas of life and culture. The church represented the universal Christian world-view and value system which informed and unified society and culture. The growing realization that the Christendom situation has largely disappeared has informed much of the recent discussion of the doctrine of the church.

This realization has also brought to the fore certain themes in the Bible which were not discussed above but which are connected with the understanding of the church as the community of hope. These themes are derived originally from Old Testament ideas such as people of God, exodus, exile and dispersion. Throughout the New Testament the church is described as the people of God, with the use of Old Testament passages (Rom. 9:24-26, 2 Cor. 6:16, Heb. 8:10-12, Rev. 21:3), and also directly (Acts 15:14, 1 Pet. 2:9-10, Tit. 2:14, Rev. 18:4). Hans Küng asserts, "The idea of the people of God is the oldest and most fundamental concept underlying the self-interpretation of the ekklesia. Images such as those of the body of Christ, the temple and so on, are secondary by comparison."[6]

This theme is focussed in the ideas of exodus and exile. They are drawn from the story of Israel's being called out of the bondage and security of Egypt to follow the Lord into wilderness wandering, without worldly security, and living only by faith in the promise that God is leading them toward the promised land. The imagery of exile and dispersion is very similar (see James 1:1, 1 Pet. 1:1, 17, 2:11). The clearest statement of this theme is in Hebrews 11. Here the emphasis is on walking by faith and not by sight, going out in answer to a call and not knowing where it will lead, sojourning in the land of promise, living in tents, being strangers and exiles in the earth, pressing on only in the light of the promise of God, and looking to Jesus as the pioneer. This idea is confirmed in the picture of the homelessness of Jesus (Lk. 9:58) and in his instructions to his disciples to travel light (Lk. 9:3).[7]

After the recognition and establishment of the church this image of the church as the pilgrim people of God in exodus and exile fell into the background, and it has come into prominence again only since the breakdown of Christendom. The point is that the situation of the church today is much more like that of the first century than that of the thirteenth or sixteenth centuries.[8] An additional reason for the importance of this approach to the doctrine of the church is that Western culture as a whole, is undergoing rapid change and is described by Williams as an exodus culture.[9] It can be argued that it is the historical impact of Christian faith which has transformed the relatively static culture of the medieval period into the rapidly changing exodus situation of today.

In the light of these developments there is a growing consensus in regard to the understanding of the mission of the church. The church is called to be the place where God's purpose for the world becomes visible in history as a sign to the world of its own destiny. Thus the church is called to struggle in history against the powers and structures that stand in the way of God's purpose for the world. This presupposes that God is already at work in the world in self-disclosure, leading people to strive for justice, liberty, equality, and the humanizing of society and culture. The church is called to perceive where God is at work, to take visible shape and form in these places, and to call others to the struggle. [10]

This approach means that the church cannot cling to institutional forms inherited from the age of Christendom but must be prepared to assume forms required by the rapidly changing shapes of need and hope in the world. This also means that the church must pay attention to those who study and interpret the new social, economic, and political structures and processes in the modern world and the ways in which they help or hinder in human fulfillment. In addition it means that we have to see the inherited residential parish structure as ministering primarily to the private and family life of people today rather than to their public life in the economic and political sphere. And it is important to note that today private and family life is on the passive and receiving end of society and is determined largely by decisions in the public realm.[11] At this point, however, we come to the expedient dividing line between systematic and practical theology.

Summarizing many of these themes in the doctrine of the church Avery Dulles proposes five models of the church which represent valid and essential aspects of the doctrine of the church and which are complementary: institution, community, sacrament, herald and servant. Each model can be used as the primary one for integrating the values of the others, except the institutional one.

> The institutional model makes it clear that the Church must be a structured community and that it must remain the kind of community Christ instituted. . . . The community model makes it evident that the Church must be united to God by grace, and that in the strength of that grace its members must be lovingly united to one another. The sacramental model brings home the idea that the Church must in its visible aspects—especially in its community prayer and worship—be a sign of the continuing vitality of the grace of Christ and of hope for the redemption that he promises. The kerygmatic model accentuates the necessity for the Church to continue to herald the gospel and to move men to put their faith in Jesus as Lord and Savior. The diaconal model points up the urgency of making the Church contribute to the transformation of the secular life of man, and of impregnating human society as a whole with the values of the Kingdom of God.[12]

Behind this general consensus in contemporary theology on the nature and mission of the church there are some debates which indicate the main issues in the doctrine of the church today. In analyzing these debates I will try to indicate how we might move toward a reconstruction of the doctrine of the church.

One of these debates is about whether the church is essentially an event between God and humanity or a body continuous in history, whether its reality is essentially vertical or horizontal, whether the church is essentially an eschatological community or a sacramental institution The first is obviously the traditional Protestant emphasis and the second the traditional Catholic emphasis. Most theologians would agree that these emphases are complementary and must be held together. The debate is over which emphasis is primary.

In the vertical emphasis the church is renewed if not created anew in every moment of the preaching and hearing of the word, and the stress is on the relation of God and humanity in the present. In the horizontal emphasis the church's life is based on the given continuities of sacrament and church order reaching back to the foundation of the church by Christ and the apostles, and the stress is on the working of God in and through these continuities.

For Bultmann the church exists only in the event of the preaching, hearing, and obedience to the kerygma. He states that the church is constituted by the kerygma and is real only as an event.[13] Brunner stresses another aspect of this approach: "The New Testament *Ecclesia*, the fellowship of Jesus Christ, is a pure communion of persons and has nothing of the character of an institution about it."[14] This is based on his personalist-existentialist distinction of the I-Thou realm and the It realm, the church belonging to the former and institutions to the latter. The most he is able to say on the other side is that, although the church is not an institution or organization, it has institutions and needs organizations.

There have been a great many examples of the horizontal emphasis in Christian history from Augustine's doctrine of the mystical body, down to the encyclical *Mystici Corporis* of 1943, and the Anglican authors Gore, Hebert, Mascall, Pittenger and Thornton. Pittenger states:

> The Christian community belongs more to the order of vertebrates than to that of invertebrates, that is to say, it requires some persisting skeletal structure which shall guarantee persistence of type and identity of being. . . . Such a historic guarantee is provided for the tradition by the historic ministry of the Church.[15]

How can these two approaches be held together? On the one hand the continuity of the church in history can be maintained only by continuous openness to the event-presence of God in word and sacrament, or else the continuity will go astray or die. On the other hand, apart from some continuity the event-presence of God in word and sacrament cannot be effected. There must be a remembrance of Christ informed by Scripture which is preserved and handed down through tradition or else the presence of God cannot be mediated.

The event character of the church can be understood as manifest in moments of special individual and communal awareness of the presence of God which renew and reform the life of the individual and the community. However, the individual and communal Christian life must continue and be maintained between these moments of special awareness, and this requires structures of institutional order and continuity.

Since the event character of the church is not empirically visible while the continuous character of the church is, this debate leads directly the another about whether the church or the true church is a visible or an invisible reality. This debate is not over the issue of whether or not faith, hope, and love are visible in the life of the church, or the issue of whether or not the church is properly an article of faith, as in the creeds. All would agree that they are not simply visible and that the church is an article of faith in the sense that this visible group of people is called by God to be an instrument in fulfillment of the divine purposes for the creation.

The subject of the debate over the terms "visible" and "invisible" is whether the church of which the New Testament authors and the creeds speak is to be identified with a certain group of people who are distinguished by such outward signs as baptism, affirmation of a creed, and participation in the eucharist, or with a certain group of people who are or will be saved and who are not known by any outward sign but are known only to God.

We have noted that it was Augustine who gave clear formulation of this distinction for the Western tradition. He held that the true church consisted of the elect, some of whom were inside and some of whom were outside the visible church. Luther and Calvin followed Augustine in this distinction.[16] We have noted that Article XIX departs from the other Reformation confessions in defining the church as only visible.

The consensus of contemporary theology is that the definition of the true church as invisible is erroneous. The church of which the New Testament authors speak and which is affirmed in the creeds is a visible community, a society of specific human beings, and not an invisible group of the elect known only to God. (This, of course, is to leave aside the question of the members of the church who have died, in traditional terms, the church triumphant.) This conclusion is derived from the fact that Israel was always understood as a visible community. The same applies to the church, even as Jesus was a particular human being. Thus a doctrine of the true church as invisible is analogous to docetism in Christology. Newbigin concludes, "This actual visible community, a company of men and women with ascertainable names and addresses, is the Church of God."[17] It may well be that some members of the church are not or will not be saved and that some non-members are or will be, but that simply means that being saved is not identical with being a member of the church.

The visibility of the church means that it can be the object of study by the various human sciences, including social psychology, sociology, anthropology, economics, political science and history (see pp. 6f). This means that the church is a human community which can be compared to other human communities. It has a variety of structures and procedures. It is a political community involving various decision-making processes. It is also a community of language, interpretation, memory and understanding like many other human communities. James M. Gustafson states; "Precisely the natural community, political community, the community of language, interpretation and understanding, the community of belief and action, is the Church, God's people."[18] He claims that the approach to the church through social theory has been ignored, and that when the church has been interpreted only in doctrinal terms, much oversimplification, confusion and distortion has resulted. He calls this "doctrinal reductionism."

This means that derogatory references to the "institutional church" in contrast to some other church are misleading. The same applies to theological assertions that the church is not an institution but a community (Bultmann and Brunner). This does not mean that the church does not have an inner, invisible, spiritual life, but that it cannot have this in a vacuum without or apart from an outward institutional life, even as a Christian cannot have an inner spiritual life apart from an outward bodily life.

The theologian is asserting about this particular visible human community that it is also the object of faith affirmed in the creeds. What is the relation between these two kinds of statements about the church, namely, the sociological and the theological? The human sciences deal with the church in so far as it is a visible, observable, and occasionally measurable reality. Theology deals with this same church in relation to God (see pp. 6f). Thus Moltmann states that as in Christology there is an ecclesiology "from above" beginning with the church as an object of faith as in the creeds, and an ecclesiology "from below" beginning with the observable institution.[19]

The visible character of the church leads directly to the question of its limits, the question of the criterion by which it is determined whether or not a particular person is a member of the church. This question is raised by the existence of such groups as the Unitarians, the Quakers, the Jehovah's Witnesses, the Mormons, the Christian Scientists, and so forth.[20] It is also raised by such anomalies as persons who were baptized in infancy but never participated in the life of the church or vice versa. It involves the question of whether or not it is possible to be a Christian without being a member of the church.

In the New Testament the conditions of membership in the church were fairly clear: baptism in the name of Jesus, confession of faith in Jesus as Lord, and participation in the eucharist. In the second and third centuries there was added to this the affirmation of the rule of faith and being in communion with a bishop in an apostolic see. With the rise of the primacy of the Roman see there was also added the condition that the bishop in question must be in communion with the bishop of Rome. We have noted the debates about the limits of the church which were precipitated by the Montanists, the Novatian-ists, and the Donatists, and the different views about the validity of the sacraments of the schismatics. At the East-West split the Eastern church obviously denied that communion with the bishop of Rome was a condition of membership in the church. The Reformers (and the Anglican Articles) defined the limits of the church somewhat more vaguely in terms of the proper preaching of the word and administration of the sacraments. The Anabaptists limited the church to those who were truly regenerate.

Some theologians, notably Anglicans, have argued that communion not with the bishop of Rome but with a bishop standing in the apostolic succession is an essential element in the definition of the limits of the church.[21] Other theologians have argued that apostolic succession belongs to the *plene esse* or fullness of the church rather than to its *esse* or essence. On the basis of the Bible it would seem that the best way to define the limits of the church is in terms of baptism, confession of faith in Christ, and participation in the eucharist. This shifts the debate to the essential nature of baptism, the confession of faith, and the eucharist.

If the limits of the church are defined in some such way, a crucial question arises in regard to the nature of the unity of the church. The New Testament (see Eph. 4:4f) and the creeds affirm the unity of the church, that there is but one church. The one God has called the one church into being to proclaim to the world the gospel of atonement, literally at-one-ment, in order that the world may be reconciled to God and may be at unity in itself. Yet it follows from our conclusions above about the limits and the visible character of the church that the church is divided, that there are in fact many churches which are not at unity or in communion with one another. This means that there is a contradiction between the essential unity of the church and its empirical disunity.

There are some theologians who deny the disunity of the church or who deny that this disunity contradicts God's will for the church. In the free church tradition there is a view that the unity of the church is entirely spiritual and invisible and does not need to be manifest visibly and organically. The unity of spirit and purpose which God wills for the church is not threatened or contradicted by the divisions of the church. Unity is an attribute of the invisible church, and the diversity of the visible church is not a threat to this unity.

There is another approach which denies the disunity of the church and which can be called the sectarian view. Here it is asserted that a part of the church is in fact the one and only true church and that the others are not really part of the church at all. Consequently the church can never be divided, because any group which separates itself from the one true church thereby ceases to be a part of the church.

Our conclusions above about the visibility and limits of the church undercut the validity of these views which deny the disunity of the church. Thus we are left with the contradiction between the essential unity and the emphical disunity of the church. To see how these are related we must explore the nature of the unity of the church.

The unity of the church can be understood in terms of the four approaches to the nature of the church in the New Testament. The idea of the congregation of the faithful implies that there is a unity based on the common object of the church's faith, a common affirmation of the one God. Moreover when people enter into a faith relationship with God, they thereby enter into a closer relationship to each other.

As we have noted above, Paul uses the body metaphor to explain the nature of the unity of the church. Because the church is like a human body, each member or part has a function to perform for the well-being of the whole body. Any dismembering or disunity in the body is a threat to its life and existence. The phrase "fellowship of the Spirit" means literally the commonness of the Spirit, common participation in the Spirit. And it is the main work of the Spirit of God to create communion or unity among people and between God and people.

The Johannine author affirms that the unity of the church is based on that between the Father and the Son and that the purpose of the unity of the church is that the world may believe that the Father has sent the Son (Jn. 17:11, 21). Thus the unity of the church is part of its mission to the world, and the disunity of the church casts doubt upon the validity of the gospel. This is confirmed by the fact that the deep concern for the unity of the church has come from those who are prosecuting its mission. So we conclude that the church as the community of hope means that the church now possesses only fragmentarily the unity to which it is called. But this foretaste is the promise and guarantee that the church's hope for the perfection of its unity will be fulfilled.

It is sometimes asserted that we are now in a post-ecumenical era, a period in which the problem of the unity of the church as it has been conceived in the modern ecumenical movement is no longer of any significance. On one level this means that many Christians have become bored with the problems of church unity and the progress of the Consultation on Church Union, for example. It means that Christians are more and more assuming the unity of the church in the sense of acting, studying and worshipping together with little or no concern about the divisions of the church or the reasons for them. This can be seen in the phenomenon of the "underground church." It often takes place around certain public issues such as peace, poverty and civil rights. On a deeper level this phrase means that the most significant divisions in the church are not those between the traditional denominations but rather the divisions between Christians who are people of color and white, rich and poor, liberal and conservative, third-world and western. This means that new kinds of unity and disunity are emerging in the church. So the task of the church today is to heal the old divisions while not allowing the new tensions to divide the church further.

Questions for Discussion

1. *What is the relation of the church and the reign of God?*
2. *What image, metaphor, or view of the nature of the church is most appropriate to the present American cultural situation?*
3. *What is the best way to state the purpose of the church today? To what extent is your decision based on the Bible, tradition, or the contemporary social-cultural situation?*
4. *Is the church primarily a visible group with specific names and addresses, or is it essentially an invisible group known only to God? Why?*
5. *How would you define the limits of the church? That is, how would you determine who is a member and who is not?*
6. *Is the church essentially an event or a continuous body? Is it primarily a vertical or horizontal reality? Can it be both?*
7. *Is the church essentially an institution? Can it avoid being an institution?*
8. *Do the traditional marks of the church (one, holy, catholic, apostolic) constitute a sufficient statement of the nature of the church?*
9. *What are the possible meanings of "catholic" and "apostolic" in reference to the church? Which meanings are essential to the church? Why?*
10. *What is the nature of the unity of the church? Does it necessarily involve organizational or organic unity or only spiritual unity?*
11. *In what sense, if any, do we live in a post-ecumenical age?*
12. *In the light of your view of the nature and purpose of the church, what is the nature of the church's responsibilty for the following: evangelism, education, medical care, the struggle for justice and freedom, scientific and technological advance, art? Which have priority over the others? Why?*

13. *Why is there such a thing as the church? What is its reason for being?*
14. *Is church polity a theological problem or only an organizational problem? Why?*
15. *What is the relation between the theological and the sociological approach to and understanding of the reality of the church?*
16. *Is there salvation outside the church? Is there salvation outside (apart from) Christ? What do your answers mean for the definition of the church?*
17. *Assuming that its members are sinful, is the church also sinful? If so, how then is it holy?*
18. *Is it possible to be a Christian without being a member of the church or vice versa? Are they identical? Why?*
19. *Is God present in other communities and/or institutions besides the church? If so, is God's presence difference from that in the church?*
20. *Is the purpose of the church manifested more clearly in its worship or its mission?*
21. *"All persons who have received the Sacrament of Holy Baptism with water in the name of the Father, and of the Son, and of the Holy Ghost, and whose baptism has been duly recorded in this Church, are members thereof" (Constitution, Title I, Canon 16,1). Assess this statement theologically.*

18

Sacraments

According to the theological tradition the salvation which God has accomplished in the Christian events is made available in the present by means of the word and the sacraments. They are the means by which the individual and the church participate in salvation, and thus they are the basis of the continuation of the Christian life in the individual and the church. In Article XIX the church is defined in terms of the presence of the word and the sacraments.

"Word" here refers primarily to the preaching of the gospel and the reading of the Bible publicly and privately (see pp. 21, 30f, 35). The word involves concepts, images and metaphors which have an impact upon the whole person. But it is addressed primarily to the mind, and its aim is to be understood. The sacraments involve words but they also employ acts and objects which impinge on the other senses and also upon the unconscious. Thus word and sacraments are interdependent.

> The very difference between word and sacraments makes each of them necessary to the other. The word needs the concreteness and breadth of the sacraments, while the sacraments need the conceptual and intelligible structure afforded by the word.[1]

In the Bible there is no explicit theological reflection on the sacraments in general, but the basis of the development of particular sacraments is fairly clear. In the Old Testament the covenant is the basis of such sacraments as circumcision, the passover festival, and the sacrificial cultus. In the New Testament Christian baptism is based on the baptism of John and Jesus' baptism, while the eucharist is obviously based on the Last Supper. There is some further teaching on individual sacraments but none on the sacramental idea in general. The basis of later sacramental doctrine in the biblical understanding of God, creation and humanity will be discussed below.

Tradition

Although there was little systematic doctrine on the sacraments until Augustine, there was a growing consensus in East and West that a sacrament could be defined as "a visible sign of an invisible grace" (Augustine). By the fifth century there was general agreement on certain points. First, in the administration of the sacraments God or Christ is the principal agent, the priest being merely God's instrument. This was clarified in the controversy with the Donatists who taught that the validity of the sacraments depended upon the worthiness of the minister. Against this the Catholics argued that the sacraments derive their validity from God and not from the priest.

Secondly, the efficient cause which links the spiritual gift with the outward sign is understood to be the presence of God which is invoked by the formula spoken by the priest, namely, the trinitarian formula in baptism and the words of institution in the eucharist. Augustine made a further distinction when he asserted that the sacraments administered by the Donatists were valid but not efficacious. The Donatists should not be rebaptized or reordained, but their baptism and ordination did not in fact convey the grace which they did in the Catholic Church.

The developed medieval Catholic doctrine of the sacraments, exemplified in Aquinas, included the following points: There are seven sacraments all of which were instituted by Christ. They not only signify but also impart or cause grace. They confer grace *ex opere operato*, that is, by virtue of what they are and by virtue of being done, when the requisite conditions are present. This means that they are not dependent upon the character of the priest or the faith of the recipient. The three necessary elements of a sacrament are the sensible sign or matter, the words or form, and the minister. If any one of these is lacking or defective, there is no sacrament. For example, the minister must be in regular standing and must have the intention to carry out the purpose of the church. The sacraments confer grace on those who receive them worthily or set up no obstacle to them, such as contempt for or positive disbelief in them, or the presence of unforgiven mortal sin. The sacraments of baptism, confirmation and ordination are not repeatable, because they confer an indelible character upon the soul.[2]

Luther's view of the sacraments was based on his new understanding of justification (see pp. 180f). The church exists where the word is preached and the sacraments are duly administered. The same Word of God is manifest in preaching and the sacraments. They belong together, and there is to be no administration of the sacrament without preaching. The sacraments are essential, but they do not offer a special grace which is not imparted in preaching.

Calvin's teaching was similar to Luther's and dependent upon that of Augustine. He held that the sacraments are seals or confirmations of the promises of God to mankind in Christ. They are secondary and supplementary to the word and were given to us because of our weakness. With Luther he stressed the necessity of faith in the reception of the sacraments.

It is sometimes said that the main issue at the Reformation was that the Catholics emphasized the objective efficacy of the sacraments, while the Reformers emphasized the necessity of the subjective condition of faith in the recipient. But this is misleading if left unqualified, since the Catholic teaching held that there must be no obstacle in the soul, and the Reformers affirmed the objective reality of the divine presence in the sacraments and the necessity of their being properly administered. There were, however, fundamental differences of approach and emphasis. The Reformers attacked what they took to be the Catholic overemphasis on the efficacy of the sacraments *ex opere operato*, the idea that grace is infused into the soul if the requisite conditions are present. The Catholics attacked the Protestant emphasis on the word and faith, and argued that the Protestant view implied that the sacraments were not necessary for salvation.

The Articles of Religion contain two articles on the sacraments in general, one on baptism, and four on the eucharist. The first two are taken largely from the Lutheran Confession of Augsburg and are formulated to combat the views of the Anabaptists and the Zwinglians. Article XXV defines the sacraments as "effectual signs of grace," distinguishes the two gospel sacraments from the other five, and stresses the necessity of worthy reception. A condemnation of the theory of grace *ex opere operato*, which was included in 1553, was withdrawn in 1563. Article XXVI combats the Anabaptist view that the personal holiness of the minister was a necessary condition for valid preaching and sacraments.

In the seventeenth century in reaction to the religious intolerance of the various orthodoxies, there appeared the Society of Friends whose central affirmation was the doctrine of the Inner Light, namely the inner experience of the presence of Christ by the Spirit. On the basis of this doctrine the Friends denied the necessity of any of the outward forms of Christianity, including sacraments, creeds, liturgies and ordained ministers.

The theology of the sacraments was at the center of the debates in the Oxford Movement. In the preface to the first volume of *Tracts for the Times* it was asserted that "Sacraments, not preaching, are the sources of divine grace." Sacramental theology has also been central in the discussions aroused by the ecumenical and liturgical movements of this century. In the former attention has focussed on the problems of intercommunion and the mutual recognition of ordination. Apart from the movements the theology of the sacraments has not been a main concern of the neo-orthodox, existentialist, liberation, or process theology. There has been a revival of interest in sacramental theology in the Roman Catholic Church as a result of Vatican II and the work of Karl Rahner.[3]

Technical Terminology[4]

Certain technical terms have been developed in the Catholic tradition which are occasionally useful in clarifying aspects of the doctrine and pastoral use of the sacraments. According to the traditional definition a sacrament has two aspects, the "outward and visible sign" and the "inward and spiritual grace" (BCP, p. 857). The former is constituted by two elements called "matter" and "form." The *matter* of a sacrament is the material substance used, for example, water in baptism and bread and wine in the eucharist. It is important to note in this connection that the matter of a sacrament is not arbitrary but constitutes what has been called an intrinsic symbol. This means that the attributes of the matter are not incidental but essential to its function of signifying in the sacrament.[5] The *form* of a sacrament consists of the ritual action, for example, washing in baptism, and taking, blessing, breaking and pouring, eating and drinking in the eucharist, and the officially specified formula of words.

The "inward and spiritual grace" is what is conferred on the recipient in the sacrament, fundamentally, the saving presence of God through Christ by the Holy Spirit. Sometimes a distinction is made in this aspect between the *symbolic reality* which interprets the recipient's participation in salvation history culminating in the death, resurrection and reign of Christ and the gift of the Spirit, often referred to as the "paschal mystery," and the *benefits* conferred by this participation.[6] For example, in baptism the symbolic reality is dying and rising with Christ, regeneration or rebirth into the new life, and adoption as a child of God, and the benefits conferred are the forgiveness of sin, membership in the church, the gift of the Holy Spirit, and inheritance of the Kingdom of God (BCP, p. 858; Article XXVII). In the eucharist the symbolic reality is partaking of the body and blood of Christ and being united with Christ in his sacrifice (BCP, pp. 369, 859), and the benefits conferred are "the forgiveness of our sins, the strengthening of our union with Christ and one another, and the foretaste of the heavenly banquet which is our nourishment in eternal life" (BCP, pp. 859f).

A sacrament is said to be *regular* "if it is performed in accordance with general rules laid down by competent authority for the due administration of the sacraments."[7] In the Episcopal Church this refers to the Constitution, national and diocesan canons, and local episcopal instructions. Irregularity may be justifiable), for example, lay baptism in emergency, or unjustifiable, for example, lay baptism when a priest is available. Regularity is a matter of church discipline and not doctrine or theology.

A sacrament is said to be *valid* when "the specially appointed conditions constituting the sacrament are duly and intentionally fulfilled."[8] Validity means that when the appointed sign has been duly performed, the promised gift or benefit is believed to be conferred. Thus validity is at least in part a matter of doctrine and not simply discipline. The "specially appointed conditions" are usually said to be proper matter, form and minister, to which is sometimes added proper intention and subject (see below). Matter and form have been discussed above.

The proper *minister* varies with the sacrament. For example, the proper minister in ordination is a bishop, in the eucharist a bishop or priest, in baptism a bishop, priest, or in emergency, a baptized lay person (BCP, p. 313). The western Catholic tradition allows any person to baptize in emergency including the unbaptized and unbelieving. But Anglicanism does not follow this.

> The recognition of baptisms administered by persons who are not members of the Church tends to obscure the vital principle that the sacraments involve representative action on behalf of the Church as well as of Christ himself; and this principle would seem to be of special force in the case of the sacrament whereby a new member is incorporated into Christ's Body.[9]

The western Catholic tradition also holds that the qualification of the minister of a sacrament remains as long as the person lives because ordination is "indelible." Therefore a minister who is apostate, deposed, or separated from the church can perform a sacrament validly if the other conditions are fulfilled. But Anglicanism has not followed this, although it does not require reordination for those who have been deposed.

> The power to administer valid sacraments depends upon a commission, received in ordination, to act in the name Christ in the Church; and we cannot affirm that this commission is unaffected by the severance of the minister from the Church's body as represented at least by some congregation of baptized and faithful Christians. [10]

This is why the Lambeth Conference of 1920 refused to accept as valid the ordinations performed by isolated bishops acting apart from the authorization of any Christian body.

One aspect of the "proper minister" condition which is sometimes listed separately is called *intention*. This is usually defined as the minister's intention "to do what the church does" in the sacrament. It is held to be "sufficiently declared by his outward acts in administering or celebrating what publicly appears and purports to be the sacrament of the Church,"[11] and does not involve the Roman Catholic doctrine of interior intention.

A sacrament is said to be *efficacious* "in so far as it actually effects the purpose for which it was instituted,"[12] that is, mediating grace or the saving presence of God to the recipient. This is distinct from the validity of a sacrament.

> Since "God is not bound by His sacraments," a rite, which is not a valid sacrament, may result in a reception of grace which is not distinguishable from that of which the sacrament is appointed to be the means; and in that case the rite in question may be said to have the efficacy of the sacrament in so far as the spiritual effect in the recipient is concerned.[13]

There is no difficulty here when it is a case of minor aspects of validity. However, if it is asserted that the grace of a sacrament can be conferred apart from any of the conditions of validity, then we are not dealing with sacramental theology but rather with the freedom of God to carry out the divine will apart from the Christian dispensation. God can do what God wills, whenever, wherever, and however God wills, but knowledge of what this might mean is not given in the Christian revelation.

One condition of efficacy, which is sometimes given as an additional element in validity, is a proper *subject*, that is, a recipient in whom there is no serious obstacle such as lack of faith or serious sin. Sometimes the concept of proper subject is limited to its objective aspect, when, for example, it is (erroneously) argued that women cannot be ordained, or (correctly) argued that the unbaptized cannot be ordained. Many of these technical terms entered into the debate on the ordination of women to the priesthood and especially the debate over the validity of the ordination to the priesthood of eleven women in Philadelphia in July, 1974, before the consent of the General Convention in 1976.[14]

The *number of sacraments* affirmed in the church varied from two to twelve or more up through the early medieval period. The number seven became generally accepted by the late twelfth century. Luther usually affirmed three sacraments, including penance, and Calvin two. Article XXV distinguishes the two sacraments of the gospel from the other five which are "not to be counted for Sacraments of the Gospel." Three reasons are given for this distinction which are not entirely clear. They have "grown from a corrupt following of the apostles," which seems to refer to extreme unction. They are states of life allowed (*probati*, approved) in the Scriptures, which applies to orders and matrimony. They do not have "any visible sign or ceremony ordained of God." This seems to refer to all five in the sense that there is no indication in the New Testament that Jesus both commanded something and connected a sign or ceremony with it in regard to confirmation, penance, matrimony, ordination and extreme unction. The question of Jesus' institution of the sacraments will be discussed further below.

Reconstruction

The theology of the sacraments is based on various Christian doctrines: God, creation, humanity, Christ, history and church. The general sacramental principle is that there is a relation between a reality which can be perceived by the senses and a reality which cannot be so perceived, or, to use the traditional terminology, between the material and the spiritual. The material refers to the realm of space, time, objects and events. The spiritual was defined in chapters 5 and 8, following Tillich, as the level or dimension of reality in which there is a unity of power and meaning, which is manifest in human life, and which is applied analogically to God. According to the sacramental principle, the relation between the material and the spiritual is one of significance or expression and instrumentality. The spiritual expresses itself in and through the material, and the spiritual acts or operates in and through the material.

The Christian view of the relation of the material to the spiritual stands over against the two other great theories of this relation, namely, materialism, naturalism, or realism, and spiritualism or idealism. The materialist view sees reality as essentially matter in motion, and it sees the spiritual as only the incidental epiphenomenon or by-product of matter in motion. It doubts the reality and significance of the spiritual. The spiritualist view on the other hand sees reality as essentially mind or spirit, and it sees matter as simply the outward form of spiritual reality or perhaps its accidental by-product. It doubts the reality and goodness of the material.

As against materialism the Christian sacramental view denies that matter is the ultimate reality and sees it as the expression of spiritual reality (God). And as against the spiritualist view Christian sacramentalism affirms the reality and goodness of the material, and it asserts that the source of evil lies in the spiritual realm (sin). In the Christian sacramental view the spiritual expresses itself by acting in and through the material and not by ignoring or suppressing it. And the material acts as the vehicle, the expression, and the instrument of the spiritual and not as its enemy.[15]

In Christian theology the most general or extensive sacramental relation is that between God and the world, between creator and creature. The creator expresses the divine reality, will, and purpose, in and through the creation and its whole history from beginning to end. The creator also acts or effects the divine will and purpose in and through the creation. In this sense the world is a sacrament of God (see Ps. 19:1, Rom. 1:20).

This sacramental relation between God and the world is reflected in the constitution of human nature. There is a sacramental relation between a person's inner life and outward life. The person or self expresses itself, its feelings, attitudes, intentions and ideas, in and through the body and its movements. Persons also act or operate through their bodies. This expression and instrumentality takes the form of word and action. In this sense the body and its movements are the sacrament of the person. This sacramental relation is the basis of all interpersonal relations and human social life. It is applied analogically to God in the assertion that God expresses the divine being and purpose in the events of the history of Israel, old and new, and in the words of the prophets and apostles (see p. 21).

The most intensive sacramental relation in Christian theology is that between God and Jesus. God expresses the divine reality, will, and purpose, most fully in and through Jesus. God also acts or effects the divine will and purpose in and through Jesus. Thus Jesus is the sacrament of God (see 2 Cor. 4:4, Col. 1:15, 2:9, Jn. 1:14, Heb. 1:3). On the basis of Christology there is a sacramental relation between God and the church. The church is called to be the visible expression of the will and purpose of Christ (the body of Christ) and thus of God and the reign of God. And the church is called to be the instrument or means by which the will and purpose of Christ and of God are effected in the world. Vatican II refers to the church as "the primordial sacrament." On the basis of the foregoing there is a sacramental relation between God and various things and actions in the church, especially in its worship: architecture, painting, sculpture, windows, music, lights, ornaments, vestments and gestures. Finally and most specifically, there are in the life of the church certain combinations of words, actions and materials which are called sacraments in the special sense, namely, unique expressions and instruments of the will and purpose of God.

Temple summarizes this in the following way:

> In truth the Church is itself the permanent sacrament; it is an organized society possessed (though not always availing itself) of a supernatural life—the life of God—which united humanity with itself in Jesus Christ. But all of this again was only possible because the universe itself is an organ of God's self-expression. Thus we have the following background of the sacramental worship of the Church: the universe is the fundamental sacrament, and taken in its entirety (when of course it includes the

Incarnation and Atonement) is the perfect sacrament extensively; but it only becomes this, so far as our world and human history are concerned, because within it and determining its course is the Incarnation, which is the perfect sacrament intensively—the perfect expression in a moment of what is also perfectly expressed in everlasting Time, the Will of God; resulting from the Incarnation we find the "Spirit-bearing Body," which is not actually a perfect sacrament, because its members are not utterly surrendered to the spirit within it, but none the less lives by the Life which came fully into the world in Christ; as part of the life of this Body we find certain specific sacraments or sacramental acts.[16]

The essential character of the sacraments can be seen most clearly not simply as arbitrary examples of a sacramental universe but as rites grounded in the crucial turning points of salvation history. The ancient baptismal liturgy recalled the passage of Israel through the Red Sea (1 Cor. 10:2), the baptism of Jesus, and his death and resurrection (Rom. 6:3f, Col. 2:12). The ancient eucharistic liturgy looked back to the passover meal, the manna in the wilderness, and especially to the Last Supper. Calvin made this point by stating that "there is never any sacrament without an antecedent promise of God, to which it is subjoined [attached] as an appendix, in order to confirm and seal the promise itself, and to certify and ratify it to us." [17]

But the sacraments are also eschatological in that they also point forward to the fulfillment of salvation history. The gift of the Spirit in baptism is an earnest and guarantee of the fullness of salvation (Eph. 1:13, 4:30). The eucharist is an anticipation of the heavenly banquet in the reign of God (Mk. 14:24f). It is "a perpetual memory of . . . his precious death and sacrifice, until his coming again" (BCP, p. 334). And in the context of this recalling of past encounters with God in Christ and this hope for the future final meeting, the sacraments mediate the presence of God in the present. In this sense the sacraments are temporary. They belong to the time of the church, between the times of the inauguration of the reign of God and its fulfillment. The eucharist is called *esca viatorum*, food of wayfarers (Hymn 192). In the kingdom there will be no need of sacraments to mediate the presence of God, for the kingdom means being in the immediate presence of God (1 Cor. 13:12, see Rev. 21:22).

One of the problems in the relation of the sacraments to salvation history is posed by the fact that all the classical definitions of a sacrament include the assertion that it was instituted by Christ (see Article XXV, also BCP, p. 857). Article XXV distinguishes baptism and the eucharist as "Sacraments of the Gospel" from the other "five commonly called Sacraments" on the basis of institution by Christ, among other reasons. What if Jesus did not institute the sacraments of baptism and the eucharist in Calvin's sense of making a promise and attaching a sign or seal to it? From a historical critical point of view the institution of the sacraments by Jesus is a matter of only lower or higher probability.

The question of the dominical institution of the sacraments, as it is called, is parallel to the question of whether or not and in what sense Jesus founded the church. Did Jesus intend to found the church, and if so, when did he do it? At the calling of the twelve? At Peter's confession? Historically speaking the church was founded by Jesus in the sense that it was the historical result of the events culminating in the life, ministry, death and resurrection of Jesus. Likewise we can say that the sacraments of baptism and the eucharist were instituted by Jesus in the sense that they were the historical result of the Christian events. There is no evidence of the absence of baptism or the eucharist in the primitive church.

In understanding and interpreting the way in which the sacraments express and effect the will and purpose of God and mediate the divine presence it is important to use personal rather than sub-personal analogies. Many of the problems and debates in traditional sacramental theology derive from the use of sub-personal analogies and images, such as Ignatius' description of the eucharist as the "medicine of immortality" and the use of concepts such as infusion. We have noted above (p. 200) the corrective value of the analogy of infusion, but the presence of God mediated by the sacraments can be interpreted most clearly by means of the analogy of personal presence mediated by word and action (see pp. 20f). Then such problems as what happens in baptism, how the presence of Christ is related to the consecrated elements in the eucharist, and how sacramental grace generally is to be understood, become easier to resolve. For example, the debate about the nature of the real presence of Christ in the eucharist in terms of transubstantiation, consubstantiation, virtualism and receptionism can be clarified. Also the debate at the Reformation as to whether the sacraments are only the signs of God's grace or also effective signs or instruments can be clarified. The personal analogy suggests that the sacraments are both signs and instruments, even as outward signs of human friendship and love, such as a handshake or a kiss, are both expressions and instruments of these attitudes. They both express them and effect them. The fundamental reason for the importance of the personal analogy is that God is personal and that grace is nothing other than the personal presence of God (see p. 81).

Individual Sacraments

Many aspects of the individual sacraments have been discussed above. A treatment of the biblical basis, historical theological interpretation, and systematic analysis of all of the sacraments cannot be undertaken here. All that can be done is to discuss some theological aspects of the individual sacraments which have been under debate.

A major theological and ecumenical issue concerning *baptism* is the question of infant baptism. It is argued against infant baptism that infants cannot fulfill the conditions for baptism: renunciation of evil, repentance, and faith, not to mention being sinners. In favor of infant baptism it is argued that the sponsors can fulfill these conditions since according to the Bible God acts in response to the faith of sponsors and representatives (Mt. 8:5-13, Mk. 2:3-12, 9:14-29). It is further argued in favor of infant baptism that the Holy Spirit can be received unconsciously as well as consciously, that the infant is involved in original sin in the sense of a tendency toward self-assertion, and that infant baptism symbolizes the fact that God's love and grace are prevenient and unmerited (see Mk. 10:15).[18] In any case infant baptism has been practiced and affirmed in the Catholic, including the Anglican, tradition from the beginning.

Confirmation was originally an element in baptism which constituted its completion. When it is separated from baptism, as it is in *The Book of Common Prayer*, its theological meaning changes to that of a mature reaffirmation of baptismal vows and prayer for the increase of the Holy Spirit. The matter in confirmation is the imposition of hands; the form is prayer for the gift of the Holy Spirit; and the minister is a bishop. The only theological question concerns the relation between the gift bestowed in confirmation and that in baptism. Although some have argued that the Holy Spirit is given for the first time in confirmation (see Acts 8:14-17, 19:6), the Anglican consensus is that the Spirit is given in baptism and increased in confirmation.

Although during the patristic period there was almost no argument over the doctrine of the *eucharist*, controversy broke out in the ninth century and increased in the medieval and reformation periods. The main topic of debate was the doctrine of the real presence of Christ.[19] The Thomist doctrine of transubstantiation held that the substances of the bread and wine in the eucharist, that which makes them essentially what they are, are changed by the consecration into the substances of the body and blood of Christ, while the accidents of the bread and wine, their sensible properties or qualities, remain. The Lutheran doctrine of consubstantiation asserted that through the eucharistic consecration the substances of the body and blood of Christ are added to the substances of the bread and wine so that both are present.

The doctrine of transubstantiation is condemned in Article XXVIII on the grounds that it cannot be proven from Scripture, that it is repugnant to Scripture, that it overthrows the nature of a sacrament, and that it has given rise to superstition. By the third point the Article apparently means that, since the essence of a sacrament is the use of material things as effectual signs of grace, if the substance of the material things is removed, then the material thing no longer functions sacramentally. If the substance of bread is removed, then it is no longer bread and its accidents thereby veil rather than manifest its reality and thus the reality of the body of Christ.

In any case the Thomistic doctrine of transubstantiation asserts that the real presence of Christ in the eucharist is spiritual and not material, that Christ's body is not present locally.[20] Furthermore, the concept of substance has largely disappeared from modern metaphysics apart from neo-Thomism. Temple asserts that if substance is defined as value, as he believes it should be, then transubstantiation is made more acceptable and consubstantiation is exactly correct.[21]

The three main views of the presence of Christ in the eucharist which have been held in Anglicanism are called real presence, receptionism and virtualism. The real presence view holds that the bread and wine really become the body and blood of Christ in some sense, whether understood as transubstantiation, consubstantiation, or in some other way. Receptionism affirms that the presence of Christ is found in the hearts of the faithful recipients rather than in the elements prior to reception. Virtualism holds that the bread and wine become the body and blood of Christ not in substance but in spiritual effect, power, or virtue.

It is characteristic of Anglicanism to affirm the real presence of Christ in the eucharist while avoiding any official declaration of some particular metaphysical interpretation of this presence. When God's presence in the world through Christ by the Spirit is interpreted on the analogy of personal presence, then some form of virtualism would seem to be the most adequate interpretation. Temple puts it this way:

> "My body" is that part of the physical world which moves directly in response to my will, and is thus the vehicle and medium whereby I effect my purposes. . . . In precisely this sense (I suggest) the Eucharistic Bread is the Body of Christ. . . . As through the physical organism which was His Body He revealed in agony and death that utter obedience of Humanity in His Person to the Father, which is the atoning sacrifice, so through the broken Bread He shows it still and enables us to become participants therein.[22]

Finally the modern liturgical understanding of the eucharist sees the real presence of Christ mediated through the whole liturgical action of offertory, consecration, fraction and communion and as focussed in but not limited to the elements and their reception.

Two of the sacraments, ordination and marriage, confer what the Article refers to as "states of life." In the sacrament of *ordination* the matter is the imposition of hands, the form is prayer expressing the intention to ordain and asking for the appropriate gifts of the Holy Spirit, and the minister is a bishop. Further issues in the theology of ordination will be taken up in chapter 20.

One aspect of the traditional doctrine of ordination, which it shares with baptism and confirmation, is that it is believed to confer what has been called an "indelible character." The concept of character is derived from the biblical idea of the seal of the Spirit given in baptism (2 Cor. 1:22, Eph. 1:13. 4:30). This is a metaphorical use of the idea of a wax seal on a document which ratifies and confirms the document as authentic. The concept of character was taken up by Augustine and the medieval theologians and applied to the concept of the soul understood as a substance upon which a certain character could be impressed indelibly. Thus character is defined by the Council of Trent as "a sign, that is, a certain spiritual and indelible mark" "imprinted on the soul."

If, however, soul or spirit is understood not in neo-Platonic or Aristotelian terms but rather in personal and relational terms, then the concept of indelible character can be interpreted on the analogy of the results in the person of particular decisions, encounters and commitments. Certain long-term commitments, such as those concerning vocation and marriage, as well as certain human encounters which constitute fundamental turning points in a person's life, can have decisive and permanent effects upon a person. Likewise a person's encounter with God through Christ by the Spirit in the decision and commitment of baptism, confirmation and ordination, can be understood to produce a particular and permanent effect upon a person. Macquarrie elaborates this on the analogy of moral character.[23]

Marriage is the only sacrament which is also a natural covenant and institution. Although the institution of marriage and its significance has a solid basis in the Bible (Gen. 1:27f, 2:24, Hos. 2:19f, Ezek. 16, Mk. 10:6-9 par, Eph. 5:21-33), the sacrament of its initiation has little or none. Likewise most of the issues surrounding marriage today fall in the area of ethics, moral theology, and canon law, and they are concerned with the institution rather than with the sacrament.[24] The matter of marriage varies in different cultures, but in the Prayer Book it is the joining of hands and the giving of a ring or rings. The form is the exchanging of vows in the presence of witnesses. The minister is the couple themselves. The blessing by a bishop or priest is not necessary to the sacrament. The "inward and spiritual grace" is the gift of the Holy Spirit to enable the couple to keep their vows.

The sacrament of *penance* has as good (or better) grounds for having been instituted by Christ as the other sacraments (see Mt. 16:19, 18:18, Jn. 20:23). It is the sacrament of the forgiveness of sins which is the heart of the Christian gospel. "Forgiveness is the greatest and most incomprehensible miracle of God's love. . . . The Church is the basic sacrament of this word of God's forgiveness." Therefore, "what happens here in the sacrament of penance is an actualization of the Church's own essence."[25]

In spite of this it was widely held in the early church through a misinterpretation of Hebrews 6:4-8 that sins committed after baptism could not be forgiven. Thus baptism was often postponed until the approach of death. In the third century, however, a rigorous system of public penance was established. This broke down after the establishment of the church, and a private penitential system was developed in the early medieval period which was made compulsory in the thirteenth century. The Anglican Prayer Books made confession and absolution public and part of the regular services, and made provision for private penance only in connection with the ministry to the sick. The American Prayer Book provided forms for penance for the first time in 1979.

Penance is essentially a ministry of the word which, because it is addressed to the concrete situation of an individual, is also an event and thus a sacrament.[26] God always forgives those who truly repent, whether privately or in public worship, but for those who cannot quiet their consciences and need assurance of forgiveness the church provides private penance.

The matter of penance is usually defined as repentance, and the form is absolution, while the minister is a bishop or priest. Traditionally penance is understood to consist of these parts: contrition, confession, absolution and satisfaction or penance. The latter is something assigned by the priest to be done by the penitent, usually a psalm, hymn, prayer, or action as a sign of penitence or an act of thanksgiving.

The sacrament of *unction* has a solid foundation in the New Testament. One third of the material in the synoptic gospels deals with Jesus' ministry of healing. Mark's account of the mission of the twelve includes anointing of the sick (6:13), and this practice was followed by the apostles (Jas. 5:14f). Jesus used healing as a sign and symbol of salvation (Mk. 2:17 par) and the words for healing and salvation are cognate in most languages.[27] Anointing and laying hands on the sick with prayer for healing became common in the early church.

In the early medieval period unction of the sick became limited to preparation for death and was called extreme unction. It was restored, however, to its original usage in the Anglican Prayer Books, with the exception of 1552. In the 1979 American Prayer Book the matter is the laying on of hands to which anointing may be added, and the form is prayer for healing. The minister is a bishop or priest, but in emergency a deacon or lay person may anoint using oil blessed by a bishop or priest.[28]

Questions for Discussion

1. In light of the testimony of the Society of Friends, are sacraments a necessary part of the Christian faith and life? Why?
2. How would you assess theologically the doctrine that the sacraments confer grace "ex opere operato"?
3. Are baptism and the eucharist "generally [universally] necessary to salvation?" as stated in old catechism? Why?
4. If it should become the consensus of historians that it is highly probable that Jesus did not institute baptism and the eucharist, how would this affect the theology of the sacraments? Why?
5. According to the Catholic tradition the conditions of a valid and efficacious sacrament are proper matter, form, minister, and no obstacle in the soul of the recipient. How would you assess theologically these conditions? Why?
6. What is the theological relation between the word (Bible preaching) and the sacraments?
7. If repentance, faith, and renunciation of Satan are required for baptism (BCP, p. 858), can infant baptism be justified theologically?
8. What happens between God and the recipient in baptism? How do you know?
9. What is the theological difference between two children of Christian parents, one of whom has been baptized in infancy and the other not yet baptized, according to Baptist custom?
10. If Christ is "at the right hand of God," how can Christ be "really present" in the eucharist?
11. What place, if any, does the concept of sacrifice have in the theology of the eucharist?
12. Do conformation, matrimony, unction, penance and orders fall under the definition of a sacrament? If so, how? If not, what are they?

19

Worship

As suggested in the chapter on the doctrine of the church, chapters 17-20 constitute the theological basis of the various parts of practical theology and the practice of the church. In particular, the chapters on sacraments and worship constitute the theological basis of the discipline of liturgics. The fundamental theological question which must be posed about each of these areas of practical theology and the practice of the church is: What is the reason or ground for this particular activity or function? Is it essential to the nature and purpose of the church such that without it the church would cease to be the church? Or is it not essential but helpful or occasionally necessary to the church? Why?

Occasionally, the term "worship" is used in a very broad sense to refer to the whole of the Christian life or even to the being of the whole of creation. But such inflated use of language is too vague, and whatever truth it may contain will be explored later. This lecture deals with worship as the conscious turning of the attention toward God in an attitude of praise and thanksgiving. More specifically, it deals with Christian public corporate worship in the New Testament sense of assembly or gathering (see Mt. 18:20, Acts 20:7f, 1 Cor. 11:17f, 14:23, 26).

Bible

In the Old Testament the nature of worship is made clear by the contrast between the worship in Israel and that in other ancient New Eastern religions. In the latter, the fundamental purpose of worship is to serve the gods, to enable them to lead a carefree divine life. In ancient Mesopotamian religion, for example, the main purpose of humanity and the state is to support the cult which, in turn, supports the gods economically and frees them to function in the universe. In this sense, the cult contributes to the maintaining and perpetuation of the cosmos. Th. C. Vriezen describes this as follows:

Here the cult is a service to and for the gods in order that this world and the state, so closely linked with these gods, should survive. Here the cult ensures in principle the existence of the gods and therefore of the cosmos and of the state itself. The cult is the all-important means to preserve God, the world, and man.[1]

Beside the state cult, there is also the personal cult in behalf of the deities which individuals have chosen as their gods. The object of the personal cult is to gain the favor of the deity, particularly in times of distress, when the anger of the deity manifests itself.

In contrast to this situation, worship in the Old Testament exists on the basis of the covenant of grace and for the sake of the covenant. In no sense is worship carried out in order to maintain God or the world, to do something for God, or to get something from God. The purpose of worship is to maintain and purify the relation between God and Israel which has been established by God in the covenant. Vriezen again:

> In Gen. 1, 28 man is given a cultural task at the Creation, not a cultic assignment; Yahweh does not need a cult in the ancient Eastern sense of the word. The cult has no cosmic or natural significance, but has a purely *religious* meaning. *Israel's God does not demand a cult from which He could reap benefit, but on the contrary He gives His people a cult that enables them to maintain communion with Him by means of atonement.*[2]

Thus, worship in the Old Testament is the focal point of communion between God and Israel, the medium of God's revelation, forgiveness, and demands, and of Israel's response in confession, supplication and praise. The temptation of Israel was to fall back into the kind of worship exemplified in the ancient New Eastern religions. This was the cause of the passionate anti-cultic oracles of Isaiah and Amos and the denial by some of the prophets that God had required sacrifices as part of the covenant (Amos 5:21-25, Jer. 7:22). The prophetic protest was probably not against the cult per se but against the perversion of the cult from what it was supposed to be as the visible expression of the faith of Israel.

By the first century A.D., the attitude toward the temple cultus had tended to become legalistic in the sense that it was performed because it was commanded by God in the Law. It had also apparently fallen back occasionally into the attitude that the proper performance of the cultus accomplished or assured salvation for the participants. But our knowledge of this period is partly colored by Christian polemic.

Jesus and his disciples apparently attended the synagogue and occasionally the temple. Beside this, there is no reference in the gospels to their participation in corporate worship. Jesus' teaching about worship is primarily concerned with private prayer rather than with public corporate worship. Its central theme is a negative one directed at legalistic ritualism. It is a protest against the idea that the will of God is expressed in the written Law and in the tradition which interprets it, and against the idea that detailed fulfillment of the law's stipulations, both moral and ritual, will win God's favor and secure a reward. It is a protest against the failure to distinguish morality from ritual and against formal obedience to law because it is given as divine law.

Jesus' teaching is that the relation between God and humanity is not a legal one but is based on grace, upon the giving of the reign of God or upon the gracious invitation to enter this reign freely. On the basis of this relation, God lays a radical demand upon humanity which requires total obedience from the heart to God's will of love for the neighbor. In Jesus' teaching, all cultic and ritual regulations are excluded from this demand, including laws about the sabbath, alms, prayer, fasting and ritual cleanness. Worship is no longer understood as required by God. The result is that the positive significance of worship is not drawn out explicitly in the gospels.

It is quite clear, however, that Christian corporate worship developed soon after the resurrection and took the form of parts of synagogue worship plus the Lord's Supper. This worship was understood to be offered through or in the name of Jesus Christ and in or by the Holy Spirit. It is offered through Jesus Christ in the sense that it is done on the basis of the relationship to God established by God in Christ. It is done in the Spirit in the sense that it is a response to God which is inspired by the Spirit (see Col. 3:17, Eph. 5:20, Rom. 8:15, 26).

According to Bultmann, a fateful transition takes place in the theology of worship in the New Testament itself. Bultmann begins by defining "cult" as human action which is for the purpose of influencing the deity, disposing the deity graciously toward the congregation and making the divine power effective for it, which takes place at holy times and places and according to holy rules, and which is performed by holy persons who mediate between the deity and the congregation. Bultmann asserts, "If this is what cult means, then the *meetings and services of the Christian Congregation* obviously *cannot be termed cultic.*"[3]

The original understanding of Christian worship involved the abolition of cult and ritual as the way to salvation. God's grace cannot be won by offering sacrifices of any kind. The sacrifice of Christ makes God's grace operative once and for all. Christ is the one true high priest of the Christian church (Heb. 2:17, 3:1, 4:14, etc.). For this reason human priesthood and sacrifice are asserted only metaphorically, and we find references to the whole church as a royal priesthood which offers spiritual sacrifices of praise, thanksgiving, doing good, and sharing with those in need (1 Pet . 2:5, 9, Rom. 12:1, Heb. 13: 15f, Rev. 1:6). Thus, there is no essentially holy time, place, building, or person. These are matters of expediency and convention.

This theme is explicated most clearly in the Johannine treatment of Jesus' saying about the destruction of the Temple and his building of another temple in three days. The Johannine author explains that Jesus was speaking of "the temple of his body" (Jn. 2:21). This means that in the death and resurrection of Jesus, the Jewish temple is supplanted as the true holy place of worship where God is uniquely present to the people of God. The new temple, the new place where God is present to the people is the risen Lord and the Spirit of Christ. The new place of worship is where God in Christ is present to the believer by the Spirit (Jn. 4:21-24). For Paul also the temple of God is the Christian community, because it is indwelt by the Spirit of Christ (1 Cor. 3:16f).

The implication is that there is no clear distinction in the New Testament between the worship, the mission, and the moral life of Christians and the church. This can be seen in Paul's use of Jewish cultic terminology to describe his missionary activity and the whole of the Christian moral life (Phil. 2:17, Rom. 12:1, 15:16). But these terms are never used to describe Christian worship in the narrower sense. This implies that the whole of the Christian life is worship and that there is no worship in the narrower sense required of Christians which is distinct from the rest of the Christian life. The only passage in which Christians are told not to neglect corporate worship is Hebrews 10:25.

F. W. Young describes this situation as follows:

> In the cultic sense the early Christians had nothing to do with worship. Unlike the Jews with their cultic service (*lateria, leitourgia*) well defined by Torah, the Christians had none. What they were to do in response to God, Christ had done. . . . Worship meant responding to that deed of Christ in one's total existence.[4]

We have seen, however, that worship in the narrower sense did develop in the early Christian community. Insofar as it was understood in the light of the New Testament insights which have been mentioned above, it was a recalling and celebration of the "total deed of Christ" in praise and thanksgiving and thus pointed away from itself to this deed and to the Christian response in mission and service of the neighbor. Bultmann argues, however, that cultic elements existed in Christian worship from the beginning, and that these were developed more and more until Christian worship came to be understood completely in a cultic manner.

Tradition

"It is a remarkable fact that in Christian history theologians have offered doctrines of sacraments but not a doctrine of worship."[5] The theological issues which have been discussed above in connection with the view of worship in the Bible were discussed only at the Reformation. In his doctrine or justification, Luther criticized the cultic understanding of the sacraments in medieval theology (see pp. 180f). His teaching is reflected in Article XXXI which was influenced by the Augsburg Confession. Apart from this, these issues have been treated only indirectly and implicitly.

One way in which these issues have been debated in Christian history is in terms of the contrasting themes of the vision of God and the love of neighbor. K. E. Kirk in his book *The Vision of God* argues that the vision of God is the ultimate goal or end of human life and that therefore worship is the primary human activity. He claims that the idea of the vision of God dominates the teaching of Jesus, Paul, Plato, Aristotle, Neoplatonism, and the early Christian authors. He argues that worship and contemplation aiming at the vision of God are more selfless and disinterested than service of the neighbor, and that only worship can save service from lapsing into the spirit of patronage.

> Service here on earth is no more than a preparation for the contemplation of heaven, and in heaven contemplation is the only service required of the redeemed. In earthly worship man does not merely secure for service that which alone can make it serviceable; he anticipates the essential and all-engrossing activity of eternal   life.[6]

A. Nygren in his book *Agape and Eros* addresses himself to the same issue, surveys the same historical material, and comes to exactly the opposite conclusion. His thesis is that of the fundamental theme of Christian faith and life is *agape*, God's love for humanity in Christ, and in response humanity's love for their neighbors. Thus, service of the neighbor is humanity's primary activity. The theme of *agape* is in fundamental contradiction at every point to what he calls the *eros* tradition, exemplified in the doctrine of the vision of God.

Nygren argues that the *agape* motif is fundamental and pervasive in the Bible, but that it was gradually lost in early Christian thought under the influence of Hellenism. He interprets the history of Christian thought as a story of the conflict, compromise and synthesis between these two fundamentally contradictory ideas. He sees Augustine's doctrine of *caritas* as an example of such synthesis and Luther's teaching as the renewal of the *agape* motif. He summarizes the contrast between these two traditions as follows:

Religion is fellowship with God. But two different conceptions are possible of the way in which this fellowship is brought about. It can either be thought of as achieved by the raising up of the human to the Divine— and that is the contention of egocentric religion, of Eros; or else it is held to be established by the gracious condescension of the Divine to man— and that is the contention of theocentric religion, of Agape.[7]

It can be argued that the continuing debate between the vision of God and the love of neighbor themes is implicitly a debate about the theology of worship. The vision of God tradition suggests that worship is the highest and most important Christian activity, since it leads humanity directly toward its final goal. As Kirk says, it is a preparation for and an anticipation of human fulfillment. The implication is that worship is more important than love of neighbor and that we should spend as much time, energy, talent and resources as possible in worship.

The *agape* tradition argues that loving service of the neighbor is the highest and most important Christian activity, since it is the one and only thing required of humanity by God. It is also a preparation for and an anticipation of the fulfillment, namely, the reign of God. The implication is that love of neighbor is more important than worship of God. Worship is essentially praise of God for the divine love manifest in Christ, but it is not the way humanity achieves salvation. Salvation does not have to be achieved, because it has already been granted freely in Christ. Furthermore, any time, energy, talent and resources spent in worship are taken away from the Christian's main responsibility which is love of neighbor. Therefore, worship is placed in a questionable situation.

Reconstruction

It is clear from our consideration of the Bible and the theological tradition that Christian worship cannot be understood as something directed toward God to win divine favor and to gain salvation. As Brunner puts it, "The cultus as the means of bringing us into touch with God . . . is abrogated, in principle by the sacrifice of Christ."[8] In other words, we have no religious or moral duties toward God which are distinct from our moral duty toward our neighbor. Our relation to God cannot be understood as part of the moral realm.

> The command to love God is not a moral command; it is not on the same level as the love of man, but it indicates the root of all morality. . . . Therefore our relation to God cannot itself be placed within the sphere of the moral [for it is] the presupposition of all that is moral. Our relation to God has been constituted by the act of Christ and

does not need to be established by any action of ours. Henceforth, our action does not take the form of striving *after* God, rather it springs from our life *in* God.[9]

Brunner expands on this theme in another passage:

No longer do we need to propitiate God nor to win His favour. The repetition of the Sacrifice in the Mass . . . betrays some doubt about that which God has done once for all. Where the sacrifice of Christ is taken seriously, no action is offered directly to God, and thus there is no cultus. The delimitation of a sacred zone of life alongside the secular sphere, of a religious form of action alongside the secular, the distinction between "duties toward God" and "duties toward man" or "duties within the world," which is characteristic of all non-Christian religion, has been abolished. All that is secular is holy, and all that is holy has become secular.

This change is due to the fact that the whole direction of life has been altered: henceforth, it is man's duty and privilege to live as one whose whole life springs *from* God—the days of his anxious striving *after* God are over; he now knows only the God whose Face is turned towards the world. God does not wish us to offer Him any special sacrifice, intended for Himself alone; when a man turns to Him, desiring to serve Him, God directs his attention to the world and its need. It is His will that our service of Him should be expressed as our service of the world—through him, and for His sake. For us there are no holy places, times, persons, acts. There are no special "religious" regulations. The cultus, divine service, our turning towards God, is to be found in life itself.[10]

Thus, there is no religious action as distinguished from moral or secular action, no religious sphere beside a secular sphere. If there were a religious sphere and religious actions, they would have to be considered to be more important than the secular. And the ideal of the religious life would be to live full time in the religious sphere, doing religious actions, fulfilling religious duties toward God. And this has usually been the result in other religions and in the "vision of God" tradition as seen in monasticism.

But where does this leave worship? It seems to leave it in the highly ambiguous and paradoxical situation of properly belonging everywhere, "at all times, and in all places" (BCP, p. 333), and also properly belonging nowhere. Since our whole life is based on our relationship to God in Christ and since this relationship comes to conscious awareness and is made explicit in worship, then it would seem to follow that worship should be universal, that in one sense we should do nothing but worship. Brunner makes this point in regard to prayer:

It is characteristic of the place of prayer in the Christian life that it is not placed alongside of other forms of action, but that it per God all our action is to take place in the presence of God, that is, it is to fiow from union with God in prayer. From the point of view of principle prayer ought not to be something alongside of other things, just as God is not something alongside of the world.[11]

On the other hand, since our relationship with God has been established in Christ, and since God's only command is that we should love our neighbors, then it would seem to follow that we need spend no time, energy, talent, or resources on our relationship to God, but only on our service to our neighbor.

This paradoxical situation is summed up in two New Testament passages: "Rejoice always, pray constantly, give thanks in all circumstances; for this is the will of God in Christ Jesus for you" (1 Thess. 5:16f; see Phil. 4:4, Eph. 5:20, 6:18). "And I saw no temple in the city, for its temple is the Lord God the Almighty and the Lamb." (Rev. 21:22; see the Johannine view of the temple discussed above.) These passages imply that worship should be at all times and in all places and yet at no particular time or place.

The solution of the paradox appears when we perceive that the city in which there is no temple is the heavenly city, the reign of God. We have worship which is distinct from the rest of life because the heavenly city is not yet. We are in history, in frailty and sin, and not in the reign of God. Tillich puts it this way:

> Why, then, the difference [between a religious sphere and a secular sphere]? The answer can only be that the Kingdom of God has not yet come, that God is not yet all in all, whatever this "not yet" may mean. Asked what the proof is for the fall of the world, I like to answer: religion itself, namely, a religious culture beside a secular culture, a temple beside a town hall, a Lord's Supper beside a daily supper, prayer beside work, meditation beside research, caritas beside *eros*.[12]

In other words, Christian worship is a sort of "eschatological time out," a foretaste of the end, but of an end in which there will be no distinction of worship and life. Brunner makes this same point in regard to the sabbath:

> Yet if . . . we are bidden to keep the Sabbath, that is, if we are bidden to observe fixed times for prayer, this is a concession to our human frailty, lest the exhortation to "pray without ceasing" come to mean—for us— that we "never" stop to pray at all. In the New Testament in principle the Sabbath is abrogated; but as a means of securing order, as a necessary method of training, as a God-given means of discipline, we, too, have our

special "Lord's Day," with its special forms of worship. Still we are free to determine how, and when, and how often these special observances are to take place, according to our experience.[13]

Thus, Christian worship is provisionally necessary in the Christian life because we are in history, in sin, and in the body. Apart from worship, we would tend to forget and distort the foundation of the Christian life in God's act in Christ. So the fundamental purpose of Christian worship is to make explicit what is the implicit basis of the whole of the Christian life. It is to recall the salvation given to us by God in Christ and to praise and thank God for this. Because of our sin, worship will involve confession of sin. Because we are called to love our neighbors, it will involve intercession for them. But the detailed retirements of worship are *adiaphora*, (see Rom. 14:5-9), and will be determined by expediency and tradition (see 1 Cor. 14:26, 40; Article XXXIV). "Expediency" here includes such considerations as aesthetic judgment and psychological insight as well as what is helpful and what edifies (1 Cor. 14:23).

At the heart of Christian worship are the word and the sacraments, the means by which the church participates in the salvation which God has accomplished in Christ, and the means by which persons are initiated into the church and nurtured in the Christian life. In particular Christian eucharistic worship is the thankful recital of the events culminating in Christ through which God has brought the people of God into being. It is the church's characteristic act of self-identification in which it receives again its identity as the people of God and through which it continues its history with God. Thus, worship is the focus of the edification, upbuilding, or constitution of the church. Tillich describes the constitutive function of the church as consisting of receiving, mediating and responding to the source of the church's being.[14] Barth asserts that the work of upbuilding or construction of the church is its common worship. "It is not only in worship that the community is edified and edifies itself. But it is here first that this continually takes place. And if it does not take place here, it does not take place anywhere."[15]

Questions for Discussion

1. *How would you define worship theologically? What is its relation to the doctrines of salvation and church?*
2. *Is or is not corporate worship essential to the life of the church, something without which the church is not the church? Why?*
3. *"My bounden duty [as a member of the church] is . . . to worship God every Sunday in his Church." Discuss this statement from the old Offices of Instruction indicating how you interpret it, whether or not you agree with it, and why.*

4. What kinds of criteria should be involved in making liturgical decisions? In what ways might theology be involved? Give some examples.
5. "Worship is the duty which the creature owes the creator." Assess this statement theologically.
6. Why is not private prayer all that is required from a Christian?
7. Which is the more essential or fundamental theme or manifestation of the Christian life, worship of God, or service to the neighbor? Why?
8. "The cultus as the means of bringing us into touch with God is abrogated in principle by the sacrifice of Christ." (Brunner) Assess this statement theologically.
9. Do we have any moral or religious duties toward God which are distinct from our moral duty toward our neighbors?
10. Is worship a means to another end or an end in itself? Why?
11. What is the essential to the theological character of preaching?
12. Is or is not preaching essential to the life and purpose of the church, something without which it would not be the church? Why?
13. Is worship only provisionally necessary because we are in sin and history and not in the kingdom, or is it absolutely necessary as the means by which salvation is made available in the present?

20

Ministry

The doctrine of the ministry can be considered as an aspect of the doctrine of the church. In its broadest sense it is a description of the calling of all members of the church. In its narrower sense it concerns the office and function of certain members of the church. In the latter sense it constitutes part of the basis of such disciplines of practical theology as parish ministry, pastoral counseling, liturgics and homiletics. The main question about the doctrine of the ministry in the narrower sense is whether or not it is a doctrine, that is, whether it is properly a question of theology or a question of social organization.

New Testament

In the New Testament all ministry in the general sense of mission and service derives from the Christian events, that is, from Jesus' mission and ministry, his teaching and actions, his death and resurrection, and the gift of his Spirit. Jesus is depicted in many passages as describing himself as one who is sent by the Father (Mk. 9:37, Mt. 15:24, Lk. 9:48; see Jn. 3:17, etc.). He also chooses and sends out the twelve apostles (Mk. 3:14, 6:7 par; see Jn. 4:38) and the seventy (Lk. 10:1) and gives them power and authority to act in his name in preaching, teaching and healing (Mt. 10:40).

The twelve or the eleven plus Matthias held the highest position in the ministry of the church. They performed all or most of the functions on which the primitive church depended for its existence: preaching, teaching, appointing elders, settling disputes, pastoral care, and presumably presiding at the eucharist. Paul and the author of Luke-Acts, however, apply the term "apostle" more widely than the twelve. They define an apostle as a witness to the resurrection of Christ (1 Cor. 9:1, Acts 1:23).

Two New Testament passages support the idea of the divine appointment of apostles and other ministers in the church. In 1 Corinthians 12:28 Paul states "God has appointed in the church first apostles, second prophets, third teachers," and other kinds of functionaries. In Ephesians 4:7f the author states that the gifts of the ascended Christ to the church are "that some should be apostles, some prophets, some teachers." Paul's other emphasis is the inspiration of various gifts of ministry by the Holy Spirit. In 1 Corinthians 12 he lists prophecy, the utterance of knowledge and wisdom (teaching), and other functions as gifts of the spirit, but not apostleship. However, the difference between divine appointment by God or the risen Christ and inspiration by the Spirit are only matters of emphasis, since it is the "same Lord" and the same God" who inspires them all.

All of these gifts, functions and offices are occasionally referred to by the term ministry (*diakonia*) and by the verb meaning to serve or minister (1 Cor. 12:5). Beyer in Kittel defines *diakonia* as "all significant activity for the edification of the community." The importance of this idea is derived from the example of Jesus and his teaching that the true measure of greatness is service or ministry (Mk. 10:43f, Lk. 22:27). Paul often refers to his work in the service of the gospel and the church as a ministry (Rom. 11:13, 2 Cor. 5:18, 6:3f).

But all of these "varieties of service" or ministry are gifts of the Spirit (*charismata*). This was true whether the particular ministry was derived from human appointment, as in the case of the seven appointed to serve tables (Acts 6:1-6) and the elders appointed by the apostles, or arose spontaneously by the inspiration of the Spirit, as in the case of prophecy. Furthermore, these varieties of ministry refer primarily to functions rather than to offices. Particular individuals exercised several kinds of ministry or function. For example, Paul was not only an apostle but also exercised the function of teacher, spoke in tongues, had oversight, and probably prophesied.

However, we do see in the New Testament a tendency toward the coalescing of certain functions with certain more permanent offices of human appointment, namely, bishops, elders and deacons. Following the pattern of the synagogue, the apostles appointed elders (*presbuteroi*) in local churches who exercised authority in all matters and all forms of ministry (Acts 14:23, 20:17, 28). This apparently involved the laying on of hands and prayer (Acts 6:6, 1 Tim. 4:14, 2 Tim. 1:6).

The references to bishops and to the function of oversight seem to overlap with the office and functions of elders. (Acts 20:28, 1 Pet. 5:1-4, Tit. 1:5-7). It may be that in each local church some elders were bishops and some were not. Or it may be that the elders were simply a class, the senior members of the congregation, whereas bishops were appointed elders. Deacons were apparently a subordinate office and primarily assistants to bishops and elders (Phil. 1:1, 1 Tim. 3).

Although the term "priest" is derived from the Greek *presbuteros* which is translated "elder" in the New Testament, it is the Greek term *hiereus* which is translated "priest." Although the terms "priest" and "priesthood" are applied to the Jewish offices in the New Testament, they are never applied to any Christian individual or office but only to Christ. Sacrificial language is applied to Jesus and especially his death throughout the New Testament. According to the Letter to the Hebrews Jesus is the one sinless victim and high priest who has performed the one complete sacrifice for sin once for all and now intercedes for us. The whole Jewish system of priesthood and sacrifice was fulfilled and brought to an end in Jesus. The only sacrifice for Christians to make is one of praise and thanksgiving to God and of mission and service to others (Heb. 13:15f, Rom. 12:1). Thus the church is referred to as a holy and royal priesthood and a kingdom of priests (1 Pet. 2:5, 9, Rev. 1:6, 5:10, 20:6).

Tradition

By the early second century the monarchical episcopate and the threefold ministry had emerged. This involved one bishop in each town, a presbyter in charge of each house church, and deacons assisting the bishop and perhaps the presbyters. There are two theories about how the monarchical episcopate arose. Lightfoot holds that bishop and elder were originally synonymous terms and that the episcopate arose out of the presbyterate by the elevation of one of their number to a new and higher order. Sohm and Lowrie argue that bishops and elders were originally distinct, bishops being appointed elders. Then in the rise of the monarchical episcopate the bishop delegated to some of the elders certain ministerial functions such as presiding at the eucharist.

A clear picture of the nature of ordination and succession in authority does not emerge until the beginning of the third century in the *Apostolic Tradition* of Hippolytus. Here bishops are ordained by other bishops, presbyters by bishops with the assistance of presbyters, and deacons by bishops alone. There was little theologizing of this in the early centuries, but the implicit assumption was that the fullness of apostolic authority and function resided in the bishops who delegated some of this to presbyters and deacons. Bishops and presbyters were occasionally called priests by the late second century, but it was not until the middle of the third century that Cyprian referred to presbyters regularly as priests (*sacerdotes*).

Cyprian asserted the absolute authority of the bishops, transmitted in succession from the apostles. The bishops owe their appointment to God and not to human beings, therefore the bishop is wholly independent of other clergy and laity. The church is founded on the bishops: where the bishop is, there is the church. Augustine asserted that the sacrament of ordination not only conveys grace but also imparts a permanent character which cannot be lost. This was the basis of his view that the ordinations of the Donatists were valid. In the medieval period the grace conferred by ordination was understood to be that which enables the clergy validly to administer the sacraments.

Luther offered a radical critique of this traditional doctrine of ordination and ministry. According to him the ordained ministry is not a necessary mediation between God and humanity, because all Christians are priests to each other, that is, mediators of grace and love. Luther expressed this in his doctrine of the priesthood of all believers. This described the relationship of Christians to each other and their common direct relationship to God. It meant positively that each Christian is involved in a humanly unmediated relation to God through Christ and that Christians are called to pray for their fellows, to serve them, teach them, and give witness to God for them. It meant negatively that there is no difference of theological status between clergy and laity, that ordination is not a higher calling than the lay Christian life. It is simply a rite by which the church chooses its ministers of the word.

This does not mean for Luther, however, that an ordained ministry is superfluous. The faithful proclamation of the word and administration of the sacraments requires time, talent and industry, and therefore a special and educated ministry is essential for the well-being of the church. But this is a distinction of function and not theological status. The Anabaptists went further and denied even the functional distinction between clergy and laity. No Christian has any special status or function which is not shared by all.

Two of the Articles of Religion deal with the ordained ministry. Article XXIII is directed against the Anabaptist view that an internal call was all that was necessary for the practice of the ordained ministry and that an external call or authorization by the church was not required. The vagueness of the article is a result of the fact that it was a compromise between Anglicans and Lutherans who agreed in opposing the Anabaptist view but could not agree on how to describe the external call. Article XXXVI was included to deny the claims of the Puritans that the Anglican ordinal contained superstitious elements and the claims of the Roman Catholics that the orders conferred by the ordinal were invalid.

The Church of England and the Episcopal Church have always held that an inward call was necessary, as indicated in the question in the Ordinal: "My *brother*, do you believe that you are truly called by God and his church to this priesthood?" (BCP, p. 531; see pp. 517, 543). This inward call must be supplemented by the outward call of the church, namely, the process of selection, recommendation, and presentation involving both clergy and laity (see BCP, pp. 513, 514, 526, 538).

These inward and outward calls are completed by ordination by a bishop which involves authorization for the duties of the office, prayer for the gift of the Spirit for the exercise of these duties, and the laying on of hands. But this ordination has been interpreted in different ways. On the one hand it has been interpreted as an authorization to perform certain functions in the church plus prayer for the gift of the Spirit to assist in the exercise of these functions. On the other hand it has been interpreted to include beside this the actual conveying of a special grace which confers an indelible character.

The question of the nature of the ordained ministry has been at the center of attention in the ecumenical movement of this century. Debate has focused on two issues. One is that mentioned above as to whether ordination involves simply authorization for a function or also conveys a special theological status. The other is whether any particular kind of order is essential to the church. Some argue that while ordained ministers are essential to the church, no particular order is essential. Others argue that the Catholic order of bishops, priests and deacons is essential. Some of the latter also argue that this order must include the apostolic succession of bishops from the apostles. There is a growing consensus that Catholic or at least episcopal order should be maintained in order to signify the continuity and unity of the church but that this should not cast doubt upon the efficacy of non-episcopal orders such as the presbyterian and congregational. There is also some consensus that in view of the disunity of the church all orders are lacking the fullness of authority and validity.

Reconstruction

There have been two main approaches to the doctrine of the ordained ministry in Christian history. They can be called the hierarchical and the vocational. The hierarchical view is based on the thesis that God in Christ granted full authority in regard to sacraments, teaching and government in the church to the apostles and thus to the bishops in succession and by them to the lower orders of ministry. The vocational view is based on the thesis that God in Christ calls individuals to the ordained ministry and the church accepts their call and authorizes them to function in the church in this capacity.

This is one aspect of the tension between the horizontal-continuity and the vertical-event character of the church (see pp. 236f). These approaches must be held together because, if separated, they tend to become distorted. The hierarchical view alone would tend to allow the church to go astray if not constantly judged and corrected by the vocational view. The vocational view alone would tend to lead to endless division in the church if not corrected by the hierarchical view. The following reconstruction is an attempt to indicate how these two views can be integrated.

The first principle of the doctrine of the ministry is that Christian ministry is modeled on and is a continuation of the ministry of Christ and is enabled by the Spirit of Christ. This means that it is a ministry of testimony to God and loving service of the neighbor which is inspired, guided and empowered by God the Holy Spirit. The second principle is that this ministry belongs to the whole church and is the calling of each member of the church. It is aimed at both the edification or inward renewal of the church and also the service of the world in testimony to God and in work for the fulfillment of the divine purposes.

Within this ministry of all Christians there are varieties of gifts, service and function, but each is carried out for the whole community (1 Cor. 12:4f). Those functions specially related to the mediation of God's presence, the word and the sacraments, and to oversight in the church are delegated to particular persons by ordination. All these functions are usually delegated to one order of ministry, but in the Catholic tradition some of these functions are also delegated by this order to lower orders. These ordained ministries, like all the other functions, are carried out for the whole community and are representative in character. That is, they are exercised in, by, and for the whole church through the agency of these ordained persons. Their exercise apart from the church or its delegation is an anomaly.

The rite of ordination is, therefore, essentially an acceptance by the church of the call of God in Christ to the ordinand, the authorization of this person by the church to perform certain functions for the church, and an act of prayer for the assistance of God in the performance of these functions. Ordination is carried out by those who have been ordained as representatives of the whole church and as a sign of the visible unity and continuity of the church. The division of the church means that all ordinations are lacking somewhat in validity in that they are not explicitly authorized by and for the whole church.

As was stated at the beginning, the main question about the doctrine of the ministry in the special sense of ordained ministry is whether it is properly a question of theology or only a question of social organization. Some theologians hold that the question of the ordained ministry is in no sense a theological issue. For example, V. A. Harvey in his *Handbook of Theological Terms* has no entries on such topics as ministry, ordination, or priesthood, whereas A. Richardson, ed., *A Dictionary of Christian Theology* has more than ten entries. G. D. Kaufman does not mention these topics at all in his *Systematic Theology*. Brunner and Bultmann assert that the whole idea of office, ordination and priesthood, represents the fatal transformation of the primitive community of the church into the Catholic sacramental institution. The implication is that the ordained ministry can be considered a theological question only as a result of a theological error.

At the other end of the spectrum are many theologians who affirm that the nature of the ordained ministry is a theological issue and must be understood theologically. Many Roman Catholic, Orthodox, Anglican and Reformed theologians take this point of view. K. E. Kirk in *The Apostolic Ministry* argues that Jesus commissioned the apostles to be his plenipotentiaries in the church with the sole power to ordain and thus to transmit his commission to their successors. This commission has been passed on in unbroken succession of the bishops. Apart from this succession the church does not exist. This view, however, has been held in Anglicanism only since the Oxford Movement.

More recently Macquarrie has asserted that episcopacy "is nothing less than the embodiment of a fundamental note of the church," namely, the note of apostolicity. He describes the ordained ministry as "relatively independent" of the church. "The Church and its ministry are equally primordial, the ministry belonging to the very structure of the Church." He affirms the idea of "grades of fullness in the ministry" and asserts that the "clergy have a fuller ministry" than the laity.[1]

A theological question is one whose solution involves a judgment about some aspect of the relation between God and the world. The resolution of an organizational question would not involve such a judgment. The nature of the ordained ministry is understood as a theological question when ordination is interpreted as imparting a special grace and an indelible character which thus involves a unique relation to God, or when ordination is interpreted as presupposing a unique internal call from God which is distinct from the calling of all Christians to the Christian life and to particular kinds of work.

The nature of the ordained ministry is interpreted as an organizational question when it is understood that any Christian may preach or preside at the eucharist, and when the choice of who actually does these things is a matter of ability, interest and expediency. Here ordination involves authorization and prayer for God's assistance in performing these functions, but it does not involve a special grace or theological status or a divine call which is distinct from that of other Christians performing other important and useful functions in church and society.

Another way to state this issue is: What is essential to the church and what is not essential but perhaps contributes to the well-being or fullness of the church? It is quite clear on the grounds of Bible and tradition that the functions of preaching the gospel and administration of the sacraments are essential in the life of the church. It can be argued on the basis of some parts of the tradition but not from the Bible that these functions should be carried out only by those persons who have been authorized in a particular way to do so. Such authorization or ordination is therefore not essential, but it may contribute to the visible unity and continuity of the church and its faithfulness to be apostolic tradition. Thus, the existence of such an order is of secondary or instrumental theological significance. But the particular form of the order is not of theological significance except in so far as one form may be more conducive to unity, continuity, and faithfulness than another.

Tillich makes this point in the following way. At first he seems to agree with Bultmann and Brunner.

> If the functions of the church [constitution, expansion, and construction] are of its very nature, they must always be present where there is a church. . . . However, they are not always organizationally present; functions and institutions are not necessarily interdependent. The institutions are dependent on the functions they serve, but the functions may exist even where no institutions serve them, and this is often the case. . . . No institution, not even a priesthood or ministry, special sacraments or devotional services follow necessarily from the nature of the church, but the functions for the sake of which these institutions have come into being do follow from it. They are never completely missing.

> No church office, not even those which existed in the apostolic churches, is a result of a direct command by the divine Spirit. But the church is, and its functions are, because they belong to its nature. The institution and offices serving the church in these functions are matters of sociological adequacy, practical expediency, and human wisdom.[2]

But then he continues as follows:

> However, it is right to ask the question whether differences in constitution are not of indirect Spiritual significance since interpretations of the relation of God and man are involved in the form of leadership (monarchic, aristocratic, democratic). This would make the problems of constitution indirectly theological, and it would explain the struggles and divisions of the churches about constitutional forms. Considering the problem of constitution both theologically and sociologically, one can first point to the ultimate theological principles implied in the differences of constitutions, for example . . . the Protestant principle of the "priesthood of all believers" and the consequent protest against a priesthood which is separated from the laymen and which represents a sacred degree in a divine-human hierarchical structure. Such principles are matters of ultimate concern.[3]

Thus we can conclude that the functions performed by the ordained ministry, the word and the sacraments, are to be understood theologically. Also the setting aside of particular persons to perform these functions is to be interpreted as theological, since it involves the recognition of a divine call and also prayer for the gifts of the Spirit for the fulfillment of these functions. However, the particular form of this ordained ministry, whether episcopal or presbyterian, for example, is only indirectly a theological question in so far as it implies a particular type of divine-human relationship and also symbolizes and effects the unity and continuity of the church in a particular way.

Another aspect of this issue is that one of the main problems in the life of the church today is clericalism, the identification of the church with the clergy. Clericalism both causes confusion about the clergy and undercuts the mission of the church. If ordained ministers are understood to have a higher theological status than lay people, then the ministers are often understood to be the typical or ideal Christians. Thus the serious lay people will try to model their life and activity on that of the minister. They will want to do the same kind of things as the minister; they will be layreaders, church school teachers, members of the vestry and so forth.

But ordained ministers are not the typical or ideal Christians. Their main functions are focussed in corporate worship and the gathered church. But the main purpose of the church is its mission to the world, even as God's concern is with the whole world (Mt. 5:13f, 2 Cor. 5:19, Jn. 3:16). And it is lay people who have daily contact in depth with the world outside the church. So lay people are the typical Christians, for the mission of the church is manifest more clearly in their life than in that of the ordained ministers. Since the ordained ministers are in this sense the only atypical Christians, if lay people model their Christian life on that of the minister, they are subverting the mission of the church. Thus an understanding of the ordained ministry in terms of function rather than status will go a long way toward avoiding clericalism and its attendant problems.

Questions for Discussion

1. *What is the nature of the ministry which is shared by all Christians? Are all called to carry out this ministry? Is it a ministry to the members of the church, or to those outside, or both? Why?*

2. *What is the theological difference between a lay person and an ordained minister?*

3. *Is the question of the nature of the ordained ministry a theological question or an*

organizational question? Why?

4. *Can a minister be properly ordained by a congregation or only by those who have otherwise been ordained? Why?*

5. *What is the relation between the priesthood of Christ, the priesthood of all believers, and the priesthood of the ordained minister?*

6. *Is the ordained ministry a profession? Why?*

7. *Is the ministry of the ordained directed toward the members of the church, to those outside, or to both?*

8. *Does the authorization confer an indelible character on the recipient? Why?*

9. *Are the validity and regularity of ordination theological or legal questions?*

10. *Are there any theological reasons for maintaining the threefold ministry? Are there non-theological reasons?*

11. *In ordination what is from God and what is from the church?*

12. *Is a minister ordained by and for the whole church through the ministers of the whole church, or only by and for a part of the church by ministers of that part of the church?*

13. *Is the inward call to ordination essentially different from the inward call of a Christian to any kind of service or work?*

14. *Does the authorization of an ordained minister come from God, the whole church, that part of the church of which he is a member, his own congregation, or from all or some of these.*

15. *Does an ordained minister "speak for the church" in a way that a lay person does not? Why?*

16. *If a lay person can baptize, why do we need an ordained minister to celebrate the euchrist?*

Notes

1 INTRODUCTION

[1] *Nature, Man and God* (New York: Macmillan, 1951), p. 497.

[2] *Theology of the New Testament*, 2 vols. (New York: Scribner, 1951-55), p. 2:237f.

[3] *William Temple's Philosophy of Relgion* (London: SPCK, 1961), ch. 16.

[4] *Systematic Theology*, 3 vols. (Chicago: Chicago University Press, 1951-63), I, pp. 18, 130. (Hereafter *S.T.*).

[5] See my book *Science Challenges Faith* (New York: Seabury Press, 1967).

[6] See my essay "Psychology and Theology on the Nature of Man," *Pastoral Psychology* 13 (1962), pp. 41-46.

[7] *S.T.*, I, pp. 54f.

[8] *God Was in Christ* (New York: Scribner, 1948), ch. 5.

[9] For the debate between Barth and Tillich on this point see my essay, "Barth and Tillich: A Conversation in Contemporary Theology," *Religion in Life*, 32 (1963): 508-20.

[10] See my essay on Barth and Tillich for their debate on this issue; also my essay "Barth on Non-Christian Knowledge of God," *Anglican Theological Review*, 46 (1964): 261-85.

[11] See essay by J. W. Woelfel in *New Theology No. 2*, ed. Martin E. Marty and Dean G. Peerman (New York: Macmillan, 1965).

[12] See B. Mitchell's essay in *New Essays in Philosophical Theology,* ed. Antony Flew and Alasdair Macintyre (London: SCM, 1955) and John Wilson, *Language and Christian Belief* (New York: Macmillan, 1958). The place of experience in making theological judgments will be treated in the chapter on authority.

[13] See K. Stendahl, "Biblical Theology, Contemporary," *Interpreter's Dictionary of the Bible*, 4 vols. (Nashville, TN.: Abingdon Press, 1962), 1:418-32. (Hereafter *I.D.B.*)

[14] See my essay on Barth and Tillich for their consensus on this point.

[15] See my essay "Some Issues in Theological Education," *Theological Education*, 5 (1969): 346-56.

[16] For an elaboration of this point see my essay "Where Are We in Theology?" *New Theology, No. 9*, ed. Marty and Peerman (New York: Macmillan, 1972).

[17] See *S.T.*, 1:12

[18] For an introduction to this process of conceptual analysis, I recommend John Wilson, *Thinking With Concepts* (Cambridge: Cambridge University Press, 1963).

[19] For further exploration of this task see my essay "Where Are We in Theology?" and K. Stendahl, "Biblical Theology, Contemporary." In the near future, I hope to publish a volume in which treatment of specific theological questions is explored and exemplified more fully.

2 REVELATION

[1] See Wolfhart Pannenberg, ed., *Revelation in History* (New York: Macmillan, 1968); Langdon B. Gilkey, "Cosmology, Ontology, and the Travail of Biblical Language," *Journal of Religion* 41 (1961): 194-205; James Barr, " Revelation Through History in the Old

Testament and Modern Theology," *New Theology No.1,* ed. Marty and Peerman (New York: Macmillan, 1964); F. Gerald Downing, *Has Christianity a Revelation?* (London: SCM, 1964); and Frank B. Dilley, "Does the 'God Who Acts' Really Act?" *Anglican Theological Review* 47 (1965): 66-80.

[2] *The Christian in Philosophy* (Faber, 1949), p. 34.

[3] (New York: Scribner, 1946), ch. 5.

[4] See also Temple, *Nature, Man and God,* pp. 123ff.

[5] See pp. 6f. above.

[6] See my essay "Psychology and Theology on the Nature of Man."

[7] *Op. cit.,* p. 198.

[8] *Op. cit.,* pp. 200ff.

[9] *Nature, Man and God,* pp. 317, 322.

[10] *Our Knowledge of God,* pp. 42f.

[11] See, for example, John B. Cobb, Jr., *A Christian Natural Theology* (Philadelphia: Westminster, 1965); and John Macquarrie, *Principles of Christian Theology* (New York: Scribner, 1966) ch. 2.

[12] *Chrisitian Apologetics* (New York: Harper, 1947), p. 112.

[13] See, C.H. Dodd, *The Bible Today* (New York: Macmillan, 1947) p. 114; J. Ballie, *The Idea of Revelation in Recent Thought* (Columbia, 1956), p. 132.

[14] See my essay "Barth on Non-Christian Knowledge of God."

[15] See Emil Brunner, *Revelation and Reason* (Philadelphia: Westminster, 1946), pp. 63f.

[16] *S.T.* 1:139.

[17] For a somewhat different interpretation of the relation between general and special revelation, see Schubert M. Ogden, "Our Revelation," in *Our Common History as Christians,* ed. John Deschner, et al. (Oxford: Oxford University Press, 1975).

[18] *Nature, Man and God,* p. xxiv.

[19] *Op cit.,* p. 70. See also his essay "Revelation in History," *I.D.B.* suppl. vol.

[20] For a discussion of recent views of revelation and a presentation of the symbolic approach see Avery Dulles, *Models of Revelation* (Garden City, N.Y.: Doubleday, 1983).

[21] *The Servant of the Word* (New York: Scribner, 1942), p. 19.

[22] See Kierkegaard's discussion of this problem in *Philosophical Fragments* (Princeton: Princeton University Press, 1944), ch. 4.

[23] For a good rationale and analysis of preaching as exposition, see Paul Van Buren "The Word of God in the Church," *Anglican Theological Review* 39 (1957): 344-58.

[24] *S.T.,* 1:131. See Temple, *Nature, Man and God,* pp. 323f.

[25] For a brief discussion of these criteria, see Kent Bendall and Frederick Ferré, *Exploring the Logic of Faith* (Association, 1962), sectn. 10.

[26] Tillich, *S.T.,* 1:102.

3 AUTHORITY

[1] See *Church Dogmatics,* 13 vols. (Edinburgh: T. & T. Clark, 1936-69), I/2: 522f, 532f. (Hereafter *C.D.*) For a discussion of the spectrum of evangelical views on inerrancy, see Robert K. Johnston, *Evangelicals at an Impasse: Biblical Authority in Practice* (Atlanta: John Knox Press, 1979), ch. 2.

[2] Brunner, *Revelation and Reason,* p. 276.

[3] John H. Leith, *Creeds of the Churches* (Garden City,N.Y.: Doubleday, 1963), pp. 456f.

[4] *Dogmatic Constitution on the Church,* XII, 18, 25.

[5] See *Infallible ? An Inquiry* (Collins, 1971). For the ensuing debate see John J. Kirvan, ed., *The Infallibility Debate* (Ramsey, N.J.: Paulist Press, 1971).

[6] *The Christian Faith,* Nos. 15, 29.

[7] See, for example, Langdon Gilkey, *Naming the Whirlwind* (Bobbs-Merrill, 1969), pp. 296-304, 417-21; and Tom Faw Driver, *Patterns of Grace: Human Experience as Word of God* (New York: Harper & Row, 1977).

[8] Tillich, *S.T.,* 1:42.

[9] See *Articles of Religion,* VI, VIII, XX, XXI, XXII.

[10] Tillich, *S.T.*, 1:35.

[11] Eusebius, *Church History*, III, 39.

[12] Wolfhart Pannenberg, *Basic Question in Theology,* 2 vols. (Philadelphia: Fortress Press, 1970-71), 1:9.

[13] See Barth, *C.D.*, I/2: 485-92 for a detailed analysis of this question.

[14] See Kurt Aland, *The Problem of the New Testament Canon* (London: Mowbray, 1962), pp. 4f.

[15] The centrality of the Old Testament in the canon has been presented in a somewhat different way by Harvey H. Guthrie Jr., in his book *Theology as Thanksgiving: From Israel's Psalms to the Church's Eucharist* (New York: Seabury Press, 1981). The status of the Old Testament in the canon has been raised in a new way by Bultmann and his views are debated in Berhard W. Anderson, ed., *The Old Testament and Christian Faith* (Herder, 1969).

[16] But see Paul J. Achtemeier, *The Inspiration of Scripture* (Philadelphia: Westminster, 1980).

[17] Aland, *op. cit.,* p. 18.

[18] Aland, *op. cit.,* pp. 23f.

[19] See *Theology as Thanksgiving*, ch. 6.

[20] Leith, *op. cit.,* p. 402.

[21] On this issue, see the essay by Heiko A. Oberman, " Quo Vadis? Tradition from Irenaeus to Humani Generis," *Scottish Journal of Theology*, 16 (1963): 225-55.

[22] John H. Leith, ed., *Creeds of the Churches*, is recommended in this connection.

[23] SPCK, 1938, pp. 36f.

[24] Paul Elmer More and Frank Leslie Cross, eds., *Anglicanism* (London: SPCK, 1951), p. 186.

[25] On this issue see S.W. Sykes, *The Integrity of Anglicanism* (London: Mowbrays, 1978)

4 TRINITY

[1] G. Ernest Wright, "The Faith of Israel," *Interpreter's Bible*, 12 vols, ed. George Arthur Buttrick (Nashville, TN.: Abingdon, 1952-57), 1:366f. (Hereafter *I.B.*).

[2] See G.A.F. Knight, *A Biblical Approach to the Doctrine of the Trinity* (Oliver and Boyd, 1957.)

[3] Wright, *I.B.*, 1: 362a.

[4] See especially J.N.D. Kelly, *Early Christian Doctrines* (New York: Harper, 1958). chs. 4, 5, 10; and Jaroslav Pelikan, *The Christian Tradition*, 5 vols. (Chicago, 1971), 1: ch. 4.

[5] The later developments can be studied in such books as Claude Welch, *In This Name* (New York: Scribner, 1952), and Edmund J. Fortman, *The Triune God* (Hutchinson, 1972).

[6] See Barth, *C.D.*, I/2: 126f.; Emil Brunner, *The Mediator* (New York: Macmillan, 1934), pp. 173f; Tillich, *S.T.*, 1: 157n, 2:140f, 3:287.

[7] See pages 148, 228, 356, 380 and 464.

[7a] Claude Welch, *In This Name: The Doctrine of the Trinity in Contemporary Theology* (New York: Charles Scribner's Sons, 1952).

[8] (New York: Scribner, 1944) See also his work *For Faith and Freedom*, 2 vols. (Blackwell, 1956-57), 2: appendix.

[9] *God Was in Christ*, p. 141; see pp. 133ff.

[10] Welch, *op. cit.,* pp. 282ff.

[11] *On the Trinity*, V, 9.

[12] Welch, *op. cit.,* pp. 64f., 116ff., 194f., 224f.

[13] (Nashville, TN.: Abingdon, 1958). The discussion was continued by Richardson and Welch in *Religion in Life* 29 (1958-59): 7-31.

[14] (New York: Harper & Row, 1964), ch. 10.

[15] (New York: Harper & Row, 1981).

5 GOD

[1] *Naming the Whirlwind, p. 5*

[2] See *"The Problem of a New Testament Theology," Journal for Theology and the Church,* 1 (1965): 169-85.

[3] "God and the Theologians," *The Honest to God Debate,* ed. David L. Edwards (New York: Westminster, 1963), pp. 215ff.

[4] See W. Hamilton, "The Death of God Theologies Today," in *Radical Theology and the Death of God* by Thomas J. J. Altizer and William Hamilton (Indianapolis: Bobbs-Merrill, 1966).

[5] *The Secular Meaning of the Gospel* (New York: Macmillan, 1963) pp. 64f, 98f.

[6] H. Gollwitzer, *The Existence of God* (London: SCM,1965), pp. 132, 195.

[7] Tillich, *S.T.,* 1:249.

[8] See Knight, *A Biblical Approach to the Doctrine of the Trinity,* pp. 36ff; Barth, C.D., II/1: 265ff; Tillich, *S.T.,* 1:249F, 3:21f, 111f; Temple, *Nature, Man and God,* lect. 19.

[9] Gollwitzer, *op. cit.,* pp. 188f.

[10] Gollwitzer, *op. cit.,* pp. 196f; Barth *C.D.* II/1: 284ff.

[11] See Phyllis Trible, *God and the Rhetoric of Sexuality* (Philadelphia: Fortress Press, 1978).

[12] See Rosemary Ruether, *New Woman/New Earth: Sexist Ideologies and Human Liberation* (New York: Seabury Press, 1975), and Mary Daly, *Beyond God the Father* (Boston: Beacon Press, 1973).

[13] *The Humanity of God* (Atlanta: John Knox, 1960), p. 42.

[14] *The New Man,* (London: SCM, 1956), p. 65; see ch.5.

[15] (SCM, 1963), p. 44.

[16] Schubert M. Ogden, ed. *Existence and Faith* (Meridian, 1960), p. 15. See Reinhold Niebuhr, *The Nature and Destiny of Man,* 2 vols. (New York: Scribner, 1946), 1:161f.

[17] See Gordon W. Allport, *Becoming* (New Haven, CT.: Yale University Press, 1955), pp. 36f, 54f.

[18] *Christian Faith and Natural Science* (New York: Harper & Row, 1953).

[19] Paul Tillich, *The Protestant Era* (Chicago, 1948) pp. 229f.

[20] See C.H. Dodd, *The Johannine Epistles,* (New York: Harper & Row, 1946), pp. 109f.

[21] See Tillich, *S.T.,* 1:279f.

[22] *S.T.* 1:283.

[23] See, for example, for Maurice Wiles, *Working Papers in Doctrine* (London: SCM, 1976), ch. 11.

[24] See Kierkegaard, *Philosophical Fragments,* p. 25.

[25] See my essay "Being and Some Theologians," *Harvard Theological Review* 70 (1977): 137-60.

[26] For the best introduction to process theology and guide to its literature see John B. Cobb, Jr. and David Ray Griffin, *Process Theology: An Introductory Exposition* (Philadelphia: Westminster Press, 1976. See also Norman Pittenger, *Process-Thought and Christian Faith* (New York: Macmillan, 1968).

[27] See *Nature, Man and God,* lect. 10. For other criticism of process theology, see Cobb and Griffin, *op. cit.,* Appen. B, to which should be added Robert C. Neville, *Creativity and God: A Challenge To Process Theology* (New York: Seabury Press, 1980).

6 CREATION

[1] *Maker of Heaven and Earth* (Garden City, NY.: Doubleday, 1959), p. 210. See Athanasius, *On the Incarnation of the Word of God,* 1. I am indebted to Gilkey for several of the following points.

[2] *Against Hermogenes,* ch. 9.

[3] See Origen, *Against Celsus,* VI, 62, 65.

[4] See William H. Poteat, " Birth, Suicide and the Doctrine of Creation: An Exploration of Analogies," *New Essays on Religious Language,* ed. Dallas M. High (Oxford: Oxford University Press, 1969).

[5] Quoted by Gilkey, *op. cit.,* p. 73.

[6] See, for example, Gordon D. Kaufman, *Systematic Theology* (New York: Scribner, 1968), p. 275.

[7] *Nature, Man and God*, p. 37

[8] *Op. cit.,* p. 258

[9] See Rudolph Bultmann, "Faith in God the Creator," *Existence and Faith*, ed. Ogden, p. 171-82.

[10] See Casserley, *The Christian in Philosophy*, pp. 45, 50, et passim.

[11] See my book *Science Challenges Faith*, ch. 7; Ian G. Barbour, *Issues in Science and Religion* (Englewood Cliffs, N.J.: Prentice-Hall, 1966), pp. 44-50; John Baillie, *Natural Science and Spiritual Life* (New York: Scribner, 1952); H. Butterfield, *The Origins of Modern Science* (New York: Macmillan, 1960).

[12] See Lynn White Jr., "The Historical Roots of our Ecologic Crisis," in *Western Man and Environmental Ethics* ed. Ian G. Barbour (Reading, Mass.: Addison-Wesley Publishing Co., 1973), pp. 25, 27. White's essay is followed by two critiques and White's response to them.

7 PROVIDENCE

[1] *God Was in Christ*, p. 110.

[2] See, for example, pp. 229, 258.

[3] See, *C.D.*, III/3

[4] "The Concept of Providence in Contemporary Theology," *The Journal of Religion*, 43 (1963): 171-92.

[5] See John Hick, *Evil and the God of Love* (New York: Macmillan, 1977): and David R. Griffin, *God, Power, and Evil: A Process Theodicy* (Philadelphia: Westminster, 1976).

[6] See Richard L. Rubenstein, *After Auschwitz* (Indianapolis: Bobbs-Merrill, 1966).

[7] See Ulrich E. Simon, *A Theology of Auschwitz* (London: SPCK, 1978).

[8] *Christianity and the Problem of History* (New York: Scribner, 1953), pp. 248.

[9] Tillich, *S.T.*, 1:116.

[10] *C.D.*, III/3: 129, 161.

[11] See my book *God's Activity in the World* (Chico, CA.: Scholars Press, 1983).

[12] *Summa Theologiae*, Ia, 103-105.

[13] See, for example, Etienne Gilson, *The Christian Philosophy of St. Thomas Aquinas* (New York: Random House, 1956), pt. 2, ch. 3.

[14] *Jesus Christ and Mythology* (New York: Scribner, 1958), p. 65.

[15] See, for example, Maurice Wiles, *Working Papers in Doctrine* ch. 11; and James A. Pike, *A Time for Christian Candor* (New York: Harper & Row, 1964), chs. 7, 8.

[16] "Science and God's Action in Nature," in *Earth Might Be Fair*, ed. Ian G. Barbour (Englewood Cliffs, N.J.: Prentice-Hall, 1972), p. 39.

[17] See G. Ernest Wright, *God Who Acts: Biblical Theology as Recital* (London, SCM, 1952).

[18] See Compton, *op. cit.,* for an explication of this approach.

[19] See David R. Griffin, " Relativism, Divine Causation, and Biblical Theology," *Encounter* 36 (1975): 207-22; reprinted in my book *God's Activity in the World*; and Daniel Day Williams, "How Does God Act?: An Essay in Whitehead's Metaphysics," in *Process and Divinity*, ed. William L. Reese and Eugene Freeman (Lasalle, Ill.: Open Court, 1964).

[20] *Nature, Man and God*, p. 290.

[21] *Ibid.,* p. 267.

[22] *Chance and Providences: God's Action in a World Governed by Scientific Law* (New York: Scribner, 1958).

[23] *Man in God's World* (New York: Harper & Row, 1963), p. 136.

[24] See above for Tillich; see Bultmann, *Faith and Understanding* (New York: Harper & Row, 1969), ch. 10.

[25] Tillich, *S.T.*, 1: 117.

[26] *Ibid.,* p. 112.

8 HUMANITY

[1] See Emil Brunner and Karl Barth, *Natural Theology* (Geoffrey Bles, 1946).

[2] See, for example, Schubert M. Ogden, *Christ Without Myth* (New York: Harper & Row, 1961), pp. 150-53.

[3] See Harvey Cox, *The Secular City* (New York: Macmillan, 1965), pp. 61f, 79f.

[4] See Roger L. Shinn, *Man: The New Humanism* (Philadelphia: Westminster, 1968).

[5] See Karl Rahner, *Foundation of Christian Faith* (New York: Seabury, 1978), chs. 1, 2; also *Hearers of the Word* (New York: Herder, 1969).

[6] See Rosemary Radford Ruether, ed. *Religion and Sexism: Images of Women in the Jewish and Christian Traditions* (New York: Simon and Schuster, 1974).

[7] For an analysis of this issue see Emil Brunner, *Christianity and Civilization* (New York: Scribner, 1948-49), pt. 1, ch. 6.

[8] See, for example, Edward O. Wilson, *Sociobiology* (Belknap, 1975).

[9] See pp. 6f. and my essay referred to there.

[10] See Gilkey, *Maker of Heaven and Earth*, ch. 6.

[11] See Cuthbert A. Simpson, *I.B.*, 1:504, 512.

[12] See Emil Brunner, *Dogmatics*, 3 vols. (Philadelphia: Westminster, 1950-60), 3:385f.; Barth, *C.D.*, III/2: 587f.

[13] See my essay "Psychology and Theology on the Nature of Man," ad fin.

[14] See Kelly, *Early Christian Doctrines*, chs. 7, 13, for a discussion of the influence of Platonist and Stoic views of humanity, Origen's theory of the preexistence of souls and their embodiment as a punishment for sin, the struggle with Manichaeism, the problem of the origin of the soul [creationism vs. traducianism], and the theory of human mortality as the result of sin.

[15] See also *The Book of Common Prayer*, pp. 260-845.

[16] See Emil Brunner, *Man in Revolt* (Lutterworth, 1939) Appen. I. This question will be discussed further in the next chapter.

[17] *S.T.*, 1:259.

[18] *C.D.*, III/1: 186.

[19] *Dogmatics*, 2:60.

[20] See the careful study by Marianne Cline Horowitz, "Image of God in Man— Is Woman Included?" *Harvard Theological Review* 72 (1979): 175-206. For an attempt to restore the balance in the doctrine of the image of God see Marianne H. Micks, *Our Search for Identity: Humanity in the Image of God* (Philadelphia: Fortress, 1982).

[21] For an introduction to these theologies see Robert McAfee Brown, *Theology in a New Key: Responding to Liberation Themes* (Philadelphia: Westminster, 1978), and André Dumas, *Political Theology and the Life of the Church* (Philadelphia: Westminster, 1978).

[22] *The Nature and Destiny of Man*, 1:293.

9 SIN

[1] See Herbert W. Richardson, *Toward an American Theology* (New York: Harper & Row, 1967), ch. 5.

[2] See Shinn, *Man: The New Humanism*, ch. 16.

[3] On the oppressive results of the myth of the fall see Mary Daly, *Beyond God the Father*, ch. 2.

[4] Kelly, *Early Christian Doctrines*, chs. 7, 13, should be consulted for the development of the ideas of sin and the fall through Augustine: Ireneaeus' view of the fall of Adam, Origen's theory of the precosmic fall, Tertullian's traducianist theory of inheritance of Adam's sin, the struggle with Gnostic and Manichaean ideas of sin, the Pelagian-Augustinian debate, and the Western settlement.

[5] As against Kaufman, *Systematic Theology*, pp. 335-61.

[6] *Psychotherapy and a Christian View of Man* (New York: Scribner, 1950), p. 104.

[7] See *op. cit.*, pp. 95f.

[8] See *The Nature and Destiny of Man*, 1:255f.

[9] *Pensees*, 434.

[10] See *S.T.*, 2:36ff.

[11] *Op. Cit.*, pp. 106ff.

[12] William Temple, *Christianity and Social Order* (New York: Seabury Press, 1976), p. 60. See *Nature, Man and God*, lects. 14, 20.

[13] See my book *William Temple's Philosophy of Religion*, ch. 13.

[14] Robinson, *Honest to God*, p. 118.

[15] See Brunner, *Revelation and Reason*, pp. 383f.

[16] See *op. cit.*, 1:186ff., 228ff. See Tillich, *S.T.*, 2:47f.

[17] "The Human Situation: A Feminine View," in *Womanspirit Rising: A Feminist Reader in Religion*, ed. Carol R. Christ and Judith Plaskow (New York: Harper & Row, 1979), p. 37.

[18] *Sex, Sin and Grace: Women's Experience and the Theologies of Reinhold Niebuhr and Paul Tillich* (Washington: University Press, 1980), p. 2.

10 CHRIST

[1] *The Christology of the New Testament* (Philadelphia: Westminster, 1959), pp. 2f. For an argument against the centrality of Christology, see Richardson, *Toward an American Theology*, ch. 5.

[2] *The Person and Place of Jesus Christ* (Independent, 1909), p. 346.

[3] Cullman, *op. cit.*, pp. 3f; see Reginald Fuller, *The Foundations of New Testament Christology* (New York: Scribner, 1965), p. 15.

[4] Tillich, *S.T.*, 2:168.

[5] A brief introduction to these questions can be found in Reginald H. Fuller, *The New Testament in Current Study* (SCM, 1963).

[6] For a somewhat different outline, see Van Austin Harvey, *The Historian and the Believer* (New York: Macmillan, 1966), pp. 265-68.

[7] *Jesus and the Word* (New York: Scribner, 1958), p. 8.

[8] For the best analysis of these issues, see Harvey, *op. cit.*, and also Leander E. Keck, *A Future for the Historical Jesus* (Nashville, TN.: Abingdon, 1971).

[9] *Revelation and Reason*, p. 283.

[10] *S.T.*, 2: 113.

[11] See G. Ebeling, *Word and Faith* (Philadelphia: Fortress Press, 1963), ch. 1.

[12] *Op. cit.*, p. 8.

[13] The discussion of this issue is summarized by Fuller, *The New Testament in Current Study*, pp. 53ff.

[14] The history of the development of Christology in the first five centuries can be reviewed in Kelly, *Early Christian Doctrines*, chs. 6, 9, 11, 12, and Pelikan, *The Christian Tradition*, 1: ch. 5. These can be supplemented for later periods by the works of Cave, Mackintosh and Ottley.

[15] Temple, *Christus Veritas* (New York: Macmillan, 1962), p. 134.

[16] *Op. cit.*, p. 8.

[17] *Op. cit.*, p. 247f.

[18] Temple, *op. cit.*, p. 127.

[19] See Casserley, *The Christian in Philosophy*, pp. 256ff. For a recent analysis of the difficulties of traditional Christology, see Schubert M. Ogden, *The Point of Christology* (New York: Harper & Row, 1982), pp. 5-11.

[20] pp. 161, 378, 864f.

[21] *S.T.*, 2:94.

[22] *Ibid.*, p. 109f.

[23] *Ibid.*, p. 148. For an elaboration of Tillich's Christology see George H. Ravard, *Paul Tillich and the Christian Message* (New York: Scribner, 1962), ch. 8.

[24] *Christus Veritas*, p. 147n.

[25] For a view similar to Tillich's, see James A. Pike, *A Time for Christian Candor* (New York: Harper & Row, 1964), p. 113.

[26] *Christus Veritas*, p. 113.

[27] *The Problem of Christ in the 20th Century* (Oxford: Oxford University Press, 1950), pp. 64, 67, 70.

[28] *Ibid.,* pp. 70f.

[29] G.W.H. Lampe and K.J. Woolloombe, *Essays on Typology* (London: SCM, 1957), p. 29.

[30] *Soundings,* ed. A.R. Vidler (Cambridge: Cambridge University Press, 1962) ch. 7.

[31] See F. G. Healey, ed. *Prospect for Theology* (Nisbet, 1966), ch. 6.

[32] See *God Was in Christ,* pp. 117f, 129f; *The Word Incarnate* (Nisbet, 1959), pp. 241ff.

[33] *Op. cit.,* p. 144.

[34] See quotation from Matthews above, pp. 152f.

[35] For views similar to that of Hick, see Robinson, *Honest to God,* p. 76, and Bultmann, *Essays Philosophical and Theological* (London: SCM, 1955), p. 287.

[36] *Op. cit.,* pp. 47-55.

[37] *Op. cit.,* p. 48.

[38] See the discussion of this issue by Wolfhart Pannenberg, *Jesus—God and Man* (Philadelphia: Westminster, 1968), pp. 33-37.

[39] See *Theological Investigations,* vol. 13 (New York: Seabury Press, 1975), pp. 213-23.

[40] New York: Seabury Press, 1978.

[41] Garden City, N.Y.: Doubleday, 1976.

[42] *Jesus: An Experiment in Christology* (New York: Seabury Press, 1979) and *Christ: The Experience of Jesus as Lord* (New York: Crossroads, 1981). See also his *Interim Report on the Books Jesus and Christ* (New York: Crossroads, 1981).

[43] *Christology at the Crossroads: A Latin American Approach* (Maryknoll, N.Y.: Orbis Books, 1978).

[44] See Mary Daly, *Beyond God the Father* (Boston: Beacon Press, 1973), ch. 4.

[45] *To Change the World: Christology and Cultural Criticism* (New York: Crossroads, 1981).

[46] *A Black Theology of Liberation* (Philadelphia: Lippincott, 1970), pp. 28, 32, 204.

[47] See *God of the Oppressed* (New York: Seabury Press, 1975), ch. 6.

[48] *Christ in a Pluralistic Age* (Philadelphia: Westminster, 1975).

[49] See *A Process Christology* (Philadelphia: Westminster, 1973).

[50] ed. John Hick (London: SCM, 1977).

[51] See Michael Green, ed. *The Truth of God Incarnate* (London: Hodder & Stoughton, 1977); Michael Goulder, ed. *Incarnation and Myth: The Debate Continued* (London: SCM, 1979); and Durstan R. McDonald, ed., *The Myth / Truth of God Incarnate* (Wilton, CT.: Morehouse-Barlow, Co., 1979).

[52] Pannenberg, *Jesus—God and Man,* pp. 141ff; Brunner, *Dogmatics,* 2:352ff.

[53] *C.D.,* I/2; 172-202.

11 SALVATION

[1] John Macquarrie, *Principles of Christian Theology* (New York: Scribner, 1977), p. 247. See discussion of the unity of revelation on page 36.

[2] See *Toward an American Theology* (New York: Harper & Row, 1967), ch. 5.

[3] See pp. 11ff.

[4] *Atonement and Psychotherapy* (Philadelphia: Westminster, 1966), p. 26. See Tillich, *S.T.,* 2:166-68.

[5] See my essay, "Barth and Tillich: A Conversation in Contemporary Theology."

[6] *S.T.,* 1:4.

[7] See Tillich, *S.T.,* 1:49, 2:165ff; Pannenberg, *Jesus—God and Man,* ch. 2, pp. 198ff.

[8] *The Significance of the Cross* (Philadelphia: Westminster, 1944), pp. 137f.

[9] *Ibid.,* p.130.

[10] *The Christian Understanding of Atonement* (Philadelphia: Westminster, 1968), p. 27.

[11] *Systematic Theology,* p. 51.

[12] See pp. 19ff.

[13] Dillistone, *The Christian Understanding of Atonement,* p. 278.

[14] *God Was in Christ,* pp. 173f.

[15] See Pannenberg, *op. cit.,* pp. 258ff.

[16] See Kaufman, *op. cit.,* pp. 401ff.

[17] See Alan Richardson, "Salvation Savior," *I.D.B.,* 4:168-81.

[18] *God of the Oppressed* (New York: Seabury Press, 1975), pp. 141-44.

[19] *The Point of Christology* (New York: Harper & Row, 1982), p. 166. See his distinction of redemption and emancipation within the concept of liberation in *Faith and Freedom: Toward a Theology of Liberation* (Nashville, TN.: Abingdon, 1979), pp. 36f, 82-99. Gustavo Gutiérrez, one of the foremost Latin American liberation theologians, tends to overlook this distinction. See *A Theology of Liberation* (Maryknoll, N.Y.: Orbis Books, 1973), pp. 151, 158, 176.

12 JUSTIFICATION

[1] See Leith, ed., *Creeds of the Churches*, p. 407-24.

[2] For a recent study of Hooker's doctrine of justification see Lee W. Gibbs, "Richard Hooker's *Via Media* Doctrine of Justification," *Harvard Theological Review* 74 (1981): 221-39.

[3] p. 304.

[4] *The Protestant Era*, pp. xivf.

[5] *Word and Faith* (Philadelphia: Fortress Press, 1963), pp. 55ff.

[6] *Kerygma and Myth,* ed. Hans Werner Bartsch (New York: Harper & Row, 1961), pp. 210f.

[7] For illuminating interpretations of justification, see Bultmann, *Essays Philosophical and Theological*, chs. 3, 9; Tillich, *The Shaking of the Foundations* (New York; Scribner, 1950), ch. 19.

[8] *S.T.,* 2:178.

[9] *Ibid.,* pp. 178f.

[10] *S.T.,* 3:224.

[11] *The Renewal of Man* (New York: Doubleday, 1955), p. 107.

13 ELECTION AND PREDESTINATION

[1] See Paul Van Buren, *Discerning the Way* (New York: Seabury Press, 1980)

[2] *The Epistle to the Romans* (New York: Harper & Row, 1932), pp. 158f.

[3] *City of God*, xv, 1.

[4] *Summa Theologiae*, I, 23, 3.

[5] *Institutes*, III, 21, 5.

[6] Leith, *Creeds of the Churches*, pp. 198f.

[7] See my book *Attitudes Toward Other Religions* (New York: Harper & Row, 1969).

14 HOLY SPIRIT AND SANCTIFICATION

[1] See Kelly, *Early Christian Doctrines*, ch. 10; Pelikan, *The Christian Tradition*, 1:211-19.

[2] *C.D.* I/1:541-57 (1936 edn.).

[3] See Michael Hamilton, ed., *The Charismatic Movement* (Eerdmans, 1975).

[4] See *S.T.*, 3:221ff.

[5] *God Was in Christ,* ch. 5.

[6] *S.T.,* 3:231ff.

[7] *Toward an American Theology*, pp. 146f.

[8] See Brunner, *Dogmatics*, 3:293-95.

[9] *C.D.*, IV/2: 511f.

[10] See the treatment of general revelation in chapter 2.

[11] See especially the quotations from Temple, p. 114f.

15 HISTORY

[1] See Rudolph Bultmann, *History and Eschatology* (New York: Harper & Row, 1957); Pannenberg, et. al.;, *Revelation as History*; and Carl E. Braaten, *History and Hermeneutics* (Philadelphia: Westminster, 1966).

[2] *Systematic Theology*, p. xii.

[3] *Basic Questions in Theology*, 1:15.

[4] See Hans Conzelmann, *The Theology of St. Luke* (New York: Harper, 1960).

[5] For the main points in the history of this doctrine see Lloyd G. Patterson, *God, and History in Early Christian Thought* (New York: Seabury Press, 1967); Karl Löwith, *Meaning in History* (Chicago, 1949); and Roger L. Shinn, *Christianity and the Problem of History*. All three treat Augustine's doctrine of history.

[6] See Löwith, *op. cit.*, Appen, I.

[7] See John Baillie, *The Belief in Progress* (New York: Harper & Row, 1951).

[8] I am indebted to Braaten for this outline.

[9] See *Christ and Time* (London: SCM, 1951), and *Salvation as History* (New York: Harper & Row, 1967).

[10] *History and Eschatology*, p. 155.

[11] *Theology of Hope* (New York: Harper & Row, 1967), p. 16.

[12] *Ibid.*, p. 329.

[13] *The Household of God* (Friendship, 1954), pp. 157f.

[14]. *S.T.,* 3:397f.

[15] See, for example, the discussion of this in John B. Cobb Jr., *A Christian Natural Theology*, pp. 161-63.

[16] See my book *Attitudes Toward Other Religions*, ch. 9, by H. Küng.

[17] New York: Harper, 1951.

16 ESCHATOLOGY

[1] John A.T. Robinson, *In the End God* (New York: Harper & Row, 1968), p. 47f.

[2] *Principles of Christian Theology*, p. 318.

[3] *Op. cit.*, p. 136.

[4] See Robinson, *op. cit.*, pp. 62f.

[5] *Op. cit.,* pp. 63f.

[6] Robinson, *op. cit.*, p. 109.

[7] *Op. cit.*, p. 130.

[8] But see Kenneth E. Kirk, *The Vision of God* (Longmans, Green, 1931).

[9] See pp. 253, 481, 488.

[10] See *C.D.*, IV/1:334ff.

[11] See *Kerygma and Myth*, ed., Bartsch, pp. 39ff.

[12] John A.T. Robinson, *I.D.B.*, 4:48a.

[13] For an analysis of recent historical and theological studies of the resurrection of Christ, see Peter Selby, *Look for the Living* (Philadelphia: Fortress, 1976).

17 CHURCH

[1] *The Christian Faith*, No. 2.

[2] See my essay "Some Issues in Theological Education," *Theological Education,* 5 (1969): 346-56.

[3] I am indebted to J. E. L. Newbigin for this outline.

[4] Harper & Row, 1977.

[5] See Theodore O. Wedel, *The Coming Great Church* (New York: Macmillan, 1945), p. 1; Colin W. Williams, *The Church* (Philadelphia: Westminster, 1968), pp. 11f.

[6] *The Church* (Shead and Ward, 1967), pp. 119f.

[7] For a good statement of this theme, see Küng, *op. cit.*, pp. 130f.

[8] See Martin E. Marty, *Second Chance for American Protestants* (New York: Harper & Row, 1963).

[9] *Op. cit.*, p. 174., note 13.

[10] See Harvey Cox, *The Secular City* (New York: Macmillan, 1965), ch. 6.

[11] See Gibson Winter, *The Suburban Captivity of the Church* (Garden City, N.Y.: Doubleday, 1961).

[12] *Models of the Church* (Garden City, N.Y.: Doubleday, 1974), p. 183.

[13] See K. Barth, *Church Dogmatics*, IV/1: 650ff.

[14] *The Misunderstanding of the Church* (Lutterworth, 1952), p. 17.

[15] *His Body the Church* (Morehouse-Gorham, 1945). p. 15.

[16] See *Institutes*, IV, 1, 7.

[17] *The Household of God*, p. 21.

[18] *Treasures in Earthen Vessels: The Church as a Human Community* (New York: Harper & Row, 1961), p. 110.

[19] *The Church in the Power of the Spirit*, p. 21.

[20] See Horton Davies, *Christian Deviations* (London: SCM, 1972).

[21] See Kenneth E. Kirk, ed., *The Apostolic Ministry* (New York: Harper & Row, 1966).

18 SACRAMENTS

[1] Macquarrie, *Principles of Christian Theology*, p. 399.

[2] For further details see Pelikan, *The Christian Tradition*, 3: 184-214.

[3] See his book *The Church and the Sacramental* (Burns & Oats, 1963).

[4] In this section I am indebted to Robert D. Hughes, III, for many valuable suggestions.

[5] See Tillich, *S.T.*, 3:123; Rahner, *The Church and the Sacraments*, pp. 34-40.

[6] The term "symbolic reality" has a somewhat different meaning in the Roman Catholic tradition. See Bernard Leeming, *Principles of Sacramental Theology* (Newman, 1960), ch. 8.

[7] *Doctrine in the Church of England*, pp. 131f.

[8] *Ibid.*, p. 131.

[9] *Ibid.*, p. 133.

[10] *Ibid.*, p. 134.

[11] *Ibid.*, p. 135.

[12] *Ibid.*, p. 131.

[13] *Ibid.*, p. 131.

[14] See Michael P. Hamilton and Nancy S. Montgomery, eds., *The Ordination of Women: Pro and Con* (Wilton, CT.: Morehouse-Barlow, n.d.)

[15] For an elaboration of this thesis see William Temple, *Nature, Man and God*, lects. 5, 8, 10, 11, 19.

[16] Temple, *Christus Veritas*, p. 234.

[17] *Institutes*, IV, 14, 3.

[18] But see Karl Barth's radical criticism of all these arguments for infant baptism in *C.D.*, IV/4:164-94.

[19] See Pelikan, *The Christian Tradition*, 3:74-80, 184-204.

[20] See *Summa Theologiae*, III, 76, 5.

[21] See *Christus Veritas*, pp. 15, 247f.

[22] *Christus Veritas*, p. 251.

[23] See his essay "Priestly Character," in *To Be a Priest: Perspectives on Vocation and Ordination*, ed., Robert E. Terwilliger and Urban T. Holmes, III (New York: Seabury, 1975), ch. 17.

[24] But see Rahner, *The Church and the Sacraments*, pp. 107-12.

[25] Rahner, *Foundations of Christian Faith*, p. 421f; *The Church and the Sacraments*, p. 94.

[26] See *Doctrine in the Church of England*, p. 192; Rahner, *Foundations*, p. 423.

[27] See Tillich, *S.T.*, 2:166; also *The New Being* (New York: Scribner, 1955), ch. 5.

[28] For a discussion of some of the theological problems involved in spiritual healing, see Tillich, *S.T.*, 3:275-82.

19 WORSHIP

[1] *An Outline of an Old Testament Theology* (Blackwell, 1958), p. 279.

[2] *Ibid.*, p. 281. For a more detailed analysis of this point see Harvey H. Guthrie Jr., *Theology as Thanksgiving: From Israel's Psalms to the Church's Eucharist* (New York: Seabury Press, 1981), ch. 1.

[3] *Theology of the New Testament*, 1:121.

[4] *Worship in Scripture and Tradition*, ed., Massey H. Shepherd Jr., (Oxford: Oxford University Press, 1963), pp. 89f.

[5] Richard M. Speilmann, *History of Christian Worship* (New York: Seabury Press,

1966), p. 161.

  [6] Kenneth E. Kirk, *The Vision of God* (London: Longmans, Green, 1931), p. 451.

  [7] *Agape and Eros* (London: SPCK, 1953), pp. 206f.

  [8] *The Divine Imperative* (Lutterworth, 1937), p. 310; see Article XXXI.

  [9] *Ibid.,* pp. 309f.

  [10] *Ibid.,* p. 189.

  [11] *Ibid.,* p. 311.

  [12] *The Protestant Era,* p. 59; see *S.T.,* 1:80.

  [13] *Op. cit.,* 311.

  [14] *S.T.,* 3:188-93.

  [15] *C.D.,* IV/2:638.

20 MINISTRY

  [1] *Principles of Christian Theology,* pp. 379f.

  [2] *S.T.,* 3:188f, 207.

  [3] *Ibid.,* pp. 207f.

Selected References

1 INTRODUCTION

Doctrine Commission of the Church of England. *Believing in the Church: The Corporate Nature of Faith.* New York: Morehouse-Barlow, 1981.
——. *Christian Believing: The Nature of the Christian Faith: Its Expression in Holy Scripture and Creeds.* London: SPCK, 1976.
Ferré, Frederick. *Language, Logic and God.* New York: Harper & Row, 1961.
Gilkey, Langdon. *Naming the Whirlwind.* Indianapolis: Bobbs-Merrill, 1969.
Macquarrie, John. *God-Talk: An Examination of the Language and Logic of Theology.* New York: Crossroad, 1967.
Tracy, David. *Blessed Rage for Order.* New York: Seabury Press, 1975.
——. *The Analogical Imagination.* New York: Crossroad, 1981.
Wall, James M., ed. *Theologians in Transition.* New York: Crossroad, 1981.

2 REVELATION

Ballie, John. *The Idea of Revelation in Recent Thought.* New York: Columbia University Press, 1956.
——. *Our Knowledge of God.* New York: Scribner, 1959.
Brunner, Emil. *Revelation and Reason.* Philadelphia: Westminster, 1946. Pt.1.
Downing, F. Gerald. *Has Christianity a Revelation?* London: SMC, 1964.
Dulles, Avery. *Models of Revelation.* Garden City, N. Y.: Doubleday, 1983.
Niebuhr, H. Richard. *The Meaning of Revelation.* New York: Macmillan, 1941.
Pannenberg, Wolfhart, ed. *Revelation in History.* New York: Macmillan, 1963.
Rahner, Karl, and Ratzinger, Joseph. *Revelation and Tradition.* Herder, 1966.
Temple, William. *Nature, Man and God.* New York: Macmillan, 1951.
Wolf, William J. *Man's Knowledge of God.* Garden City, N.Y.: Doubleday, 1955.

3 AUTHORITY

Achtemeier, Paul J. *The Inspiration of Scripture.* Philadelphia: Westminster, 1980.
Aland, Kurt. *The Problem of the New Testament Canon.* London: Mowbray, 1962.
Barr, James. *The Bible in the Modern World.* New York: Harper & Row, 1973.
Brunner, Emil. *Revelation and Reason.* Chs. 9, 10.
Farley, Edward. *Ecclesial Reflection.* Philadelphia: Fortress Press, 1982.
Johnson, Robert C. *Authority in Protestant Theology.* Philadelphia: Westminster, 1959.
Kelsey, David H. *The Uses of Scripture in Recent Theology.* Philadelphia: Fortress Press, 1975.
Reid, J.K.S. *The Authority of Scripture.* Methuen, 1957.

4 TRINITY

Fortman, Edmund J. *The Triune God.* Hutchinson, 1972.
Hodgson, Leonard. *The Doctrine of the Trinity.* New York: Scribner, 1944.
Moltmann, Jürgen. *The Trinity and the Kingdom.* New York: Harper & Row, 1981.

Rahner, Karl. *The Trinity*. New York: Seabury Press, 1970.
Richardson, Cyril C. *The Doctrine of the Trinity*. Nashville, TN.: Abingdon, 1958.
Welch, Claude. *In This Name*. New York: Scribner, 1952.

5 GOD

Cobb, John B. Jr. *A Christian Natural Theology*. Philadelphia: Westminster, 1956. Chs. 4, 5.
Cone, James H. *God of the Oppressed*. New York: Seabury Press, 1979.
Daly, Mary. *Beyond God the Father*. Boston: Beacon Press, 1973.
Farley, Edward. *The Transcendence of God*. Epworth, 1958.
Gollwitzer, Helmut. *The Existence of God*. London: SCM, 1965.
Hartshorne, Charles. *The Divine Relativity*. New Haven, CT.: Yale University Press, 1948.
Kaufman, Gordon D. *God the Problem*. Cambridge: Harvard University Press, 1972.
King, Robert H. *The Meaning of God*. Philadelphia: Fortress Press, 1973.
Macquarrie, John. *Thinking about God*. New York: Harper & Row, 1975.
Moltmann, Jürgen. *The Crucified God*. New York: Harper & Row, 1975.
Ogden, Schubert M. *The Reality of God*. New York: Harper & Row, 1963.
Robinson, John A.T. *Explorations into God*. Stanford, 1967.

6 CREATION

Barbour, Ian G. *Issues in Science and Religion*. Englewood Cliffs, N.J.: Prentice-Hall, 1966. Ch. 12.
Evans, Donald D. *The Logic of Self-Involvement*. Herder, 1963.
Gilkey, Langdon. *Maker of Heaven and Earth*. Garden City, N.Y.: Doubleday, 1959.
Heim, Karl. *The World: Its Creation and Consummation*. Oliver and Boyd, 1962.
Young, Norman. *Creator, Creation, and Faith*. Collins, 1976.

7 PROVIDENCE

Barbour. *Issues in Science and Religion*. Ch. 13.
Bultmann, Rudolph. *Jesus Christ and Mythology*. New York: Scribner, 1958. Ch. 5.
Farmer, H.H. *The World and God*. Nisbet, 1935.
Hazelton, Roger. *God's Way With Man*. Nashville, TN.: Abingdon, 1956.
Pollard, William G. *Chance and Providence*. New York: Scribner, 1958.
Thomas, Owen C., ed. *God's Activity in the World*. Chico, CA.: Scholars Press, 1983.
Wiles, Maurice, ed. *Providence*. London: SPCK, 1969.

8 9 HUMANITY AND SIN

Brunner, Emil. *Man in Revolt*. New York: Scribner, 1939.
Cairns, David. *The Image of God in Man*. London: SCM, 1953.
de Chardin, Pierre T. *The Phenomenon of Man*. New York: Harper & Row, 1959.
Cherbonnier, E. Lab. *Hardness of Heart*. Garden City, N.Y.: Doubleday, 1955.
Cobb. *A Christian National Theology*. Chs. 2, 3.
Jewett, Paul K. *Man as Male and Female*. Eerdmans, 1975.
Micks, Marianne H. *Our Search for Identity: Humanity in the Image of God*. Philadelphia: Fortress Press, 1982.
Niebuhr, Reinhold. *The Nature and Destiny of Man*, 2 vols. New York: Scribner, 1941-43.
Owen, D. R. G. *Body and Soul*. Philadelphia: Westminster, 1956.
Plaskow, Judith. *Sex, Sin and Grace*. University Press. 1980.
Rahner, Karl. *Hearers of the Word*. Herder, 1969.
Roberts, David. E. *Psychotherapy and a Christian View of Man*. Scribner, 1950.
Shinn, Roger L. *Man: The New Humanism*. Philadelphia: Westminster, 1968.
Smith, Ronald Gregor. The Whole Man. Philadelphia: Westminster, 1969.

10 CHRIST

Baillie, D. M. *God Was in Christ*. New York: Scribner, 1948.
Cobb, John B., Jr. *Christ in a Pluralistic Age*. Philadelphia: Westminster, 1975.

Cullmann, Oscar. *The Christology of the New Testament.* Philadelphia: Westminster, 1959.
Goulder, Michael, ed. *Incarnation and Myth.* London: SCM, 1979.
Griffin, David R. *A Process Christology.* Philadelphia: Westminster, 1973.
Hick, John, ed. *The Myth of God Incarnate.* London: SCM, 1977.
Knox, John. *The Humanity and Divinity of Christ.* Cambridge: University Press, 1967.
Moule, C.F.D. *The Origin of Christology.* Cambridge: University Press, 1977.
Ogden, Schubert M. *The Point of Christology.* New York: Harper & Row, 1982.
Pannenberg, Wolfhart. *Jesus—God and Man.* Philadelphia: Westminster, 1968.
Pittenger, W. Norman. *The Word Incarnate.* New York: Harper, 1959.
Rahner, Karl, and Thüsing, Wilhelm. *A New Christology.* New York: Seabury Press, 1980.
Robinson, J.A.T. *The Human Face of God.* London: SCM, 1973.
Ruether, Rosemary R. *To Change the World: Christology and Cultural Criticism.* New York: Crossroad, 1981.
Schillebeeckx, Edward. *Christ: The Experience of Jesus as Lord.* New York: Crossroad, 1981.
Sobrino, Jon. *Christology at the Crossroads.* Maryknoll, N.Y.: Orbis Books, 1978.
Temple, William. *Christus Veritas.* Macmillan, 1924.
Teselle, Eugene. *Christ in Context.* Philadelphia: Fortress Press, 1975.

11 SALVATION

Aulen, Gustaf, *Christus Victor.* New York: Macmillan. 1951.
Brown, Robert M. *Theology in a New Key.* Philadelphia: Westminster, 1978.
Browning, Don S. *Atonement and Psychotherapy.* Philadelphia: Westminster, 1966.
Cone. *God of the Oppressed.*
Dillistone, F.W. *The Significance of the Cross.* Philadelphia: Westminster, 1968.
Gutierrez, Gustavo. *A Theory of Liberation.* Maryknoll, N.Y.: Orbis Books, 1973.
Ogden, Schubert M. *Faith and Freedom: Toward a Theology of Liberation.* Nashville, TN.: Abingdon, 1979.
Knox, John. *The Death of Christ.* Nashville, TN.: Abingdon, 1958.
Lochman, Jan M. *Reconciliation and Liberation.* Philadelphia: Fortress Press, 1980.
Taylor, Vincent. *The Atonement New Testament Teaching.* Epworth, 1946.
Wolf, William J. *No Cross, No Crown.* Garden City, N.Y.: Doubleday, 1957.

12 JUSTIFICATION

Cox, David. *Jung and St. Paul.* Association, 1959.
Küng, Hans. *Justification.* Philadelphia: Westminster, 1964.
Hordern, William. *Living by Grace.* Philadelphia: Westminster, 1975.
Lampe, G.W.H., ed. *The Doctrine of Justification by Faith.* London: Mowbray, 1954.
Luther, Martin. *The Freedom of a Christian.*
Miller, Alexander. *The Renewal of Man.* Garden City, N.Y.: Doubleday, 1955.

13 ELECTION AND PREDESTINATION

Hageman, Howard G. *Predestination.* Philadelphia: Fortress Press, 1963.
Pannenberg, Wolfhart, *Human Nature, Election, and History.* Philadelphia: Westminster, 1975.
Rowley, Harold W. *The Biblical Doctrine of Election.* Lutterworth, 1950.

14 HOLY SPIRIT AND SANCTIFICATION

Barth, Karl. *The Holy Ghost and the Christian Life.* Muller, 1938.
Barclay, William. *The Promise of the Spirit.* Philadelphia: Westminster, 1960.
Come, Arnold B. *Human Spirit and Holy Spirit.* Philadelphia: Westminster, 1959.
Dillistone, F. W. *The Holy Spirit and the Life of Today.* Philadelphia: Westminster, 1959.
Hendry, George S. *The Holy Spirit in Christian Theology.* Philadelphia: Westminster, 1965.
Hulme, William E. *The Dynamics of Sanctification.* Minneapolis, MN: Augsburg, 1966.
Lampe, G. W. H. *God as Spirit.* Clarendon, 1977.
Neill, Stephen C. *Christian Holiness.* New York: Harper & Row, 1960.
Richardson, Herbert H. *Toward an American Theology.* New York: Harper & Row, 1967.

Robinson, H. Wheeler. *The Christian Experience of the Holy Spirit.* Nisbet, 1928.

15 HISTORY

Baillie, John. *The Belief in Progress.* Oxford: Oxford University Press, 1950.
Braaten, Carl E. *History and Hermeneutics.* Philadelphia: Westminister, 1966.
Bultmann, Rudolph. *History and Eschatology.* New York: Harper & Row, 1957.
Butterfield, H. *Christianity and History.* Collins, 1957.
Cullmann, Oscar. *Christ and Time.* London: SCM, 1962.
Gilkey, Langdon. *Reaping the Whirlwind.* New York: Seabury Press, 1976.
Guthrie, Harvey H. Jr. *God and History in the Old Testament.* New York: Seabury Press, 1960.
van Leeuwen, Arend Th. *Christianity in World History.* New York: Scribner, 1964.
Löwith, Karl. *Meaning in History.* Chicago, 1949.
Niebuhr, Reinhold. *Faith and History.* New York: Scribner, 1949.
Pannenberg, Wolfhart, *Theology and the Kingdom of God.* Philadelphia: Westminster, 1969.
Patterson, Lloyd G. *God and History in Early Christian Thought.* New York: Seabury Press, 1967.
Shinn, Roger L. *Christianity and the Problem of History.* Bethany, 1953.
Tillich, Paul. *The Interpretation of History.* New York: Scribner, 1936.

16 ESCHATOLOGY

Baillie, John. *And the Life Everlasting.* New York: Scribner, 1948.
Brunner, Emil. *Eternal Hope.* Philadelphia: Westminster, 1954.
Caird, G.B., ed. *The Christian Hope.* London: SPCK, 1970.
Hick, John. *Death and Eternal Life.* New York: Harper & Row, 1976.
Heim. *The World: Its Creation and Consummation.*
Moltmann, Jürgen. *The Theology of Hope.* New York: Harper & Row, 1967.
Pittenger, W. Norman. *The Last Things in Process Perspective.* Epworth, 1970.
Rahner, Karl. *On the Theology of Death.* Herder, 1961.
Ramsey, A.M. *The Resurrection of Christ.* Collins, 1961
Robinson, John A.T. *In the End God.* New York: Harper & Row, 1968.
——. *Jesus and His Coming.* Nashville, TN.: Abingdon, 1957.
Schillebeeckx, Edward, and Willems, Boniface. *The Problems of Eschatology.* Ramsey, N.J.: Paulist Press, 1969.
Selby, Peter. *Look for the Living: The Corporate Nature of Resurrection Faith.* Philadelphia: Fortress Press, 1976.
Stendahl, Krister, ed. *Immortality and Resurrection.* New York: Macmillian, 1965.

17 CHURCH

Brunner, Emil. *The Misunderstanding of the Church.* Lutterworth, 1952.
Dulles, Avery. *Models of the Church.* Garden City, N.Y.: Doubleday, 1979.
Hoekendijk, J.C. *The Church Inside Out.* Philadelphia: Westminster, 1964.
Knox, John. *The Church and the Reality of Christ.* New York: Harper & Row, 1962.
Küng, Hans. *The Church.* Sheed and Ward, 1967.
Moltmann, Jürgen. *The Church in the Power of the Spirit.* New York: Harper & Row, 1977.
Newbigin, Lesslie. *The Household of God.* Friendship, 1954.
Welch, Claude. *The Reality of the Church.* New York: Scribner, 1958.
Williams, Colin W. *The Church.* Philadelphia: Westminster, 1968.

18 SACRAMENTS

Baillie, Donald M. *The Theology of the Sacraments.* New York: Scribner, 1957.
Baillie, John. *Baptism and Conversion.* New York: Scribner, 1963.
Clark, Neville. *An Approach to the Theology of the Sacraments.* London: SCM, 1956.
Clemens, R. E. et al. *Eucharistic Theology Then and Now.* London: SPCK, 1968.
Doctrine Commision of the Church of England, *Christian Initiation.* Church Army, 1971.
——. *Thinking about the Eucharist.* London : SPCK, 1972.
Ganoczy, Alexander. *Becoming Christian: A Theology of Baptism as the Sacrament of Human History.*

Ramsey, N.J.: Paulist Press, 1976.
Powers, Joseph M. *Eucharistic Theology*. Herder, 1967.
Quick, Oliver C. *The Christian Sacraments*. Nisbet, 1932.
Rahner, Karl. *The Church and the Sacraments*. Burns and Oates, 1963.
Schillebeeckx, Edward. *Christ The Sacrament of the Encounter with God*. Sheed and Ward, 1963.
Stookey, Laurence. *Baptism: Christ's Act in the Church*. Nashville, TN: Abingdon, 1982.
Temple, *Nature, Man and God*. Lect. 19.
Vaillancourt, Raymond. *Toward a Renewal of Sacramental Theology*. Liturgical Press, 1977.
Wainwright, Geoffrey. *Christian Initiation*. Atlanta: John Knox, 1969.

19 WORSHIP

Von Allmen, J.J. *Worship: Its Theology and Practice*. Oxford: Oxford University Press, 1965.
Davie, Charles. *Liturgy and Doctrine*. Sheed and Ward, 1960.
Guthrie, Harvey H., Jr. *Theology as Thanksgiving*. New York: Seabury Press, 1983.
Hahn, Wilhelm. *Worship and Congregation*. Lutterworth, 1963.
Hardin, H. Grady, et al. *The Celebration of the Gospel*. Nashville, TN: Abingdon, 1964.
Micks, Marianne H. *The Future Present*. New York: Seabury Press, 1970.
Moule, C.F.D. *Worship in the New Testament*. Atlanta: John Knox, 1961.
Nichols, William. *Jacob's Ladder: The Meaning of Worship*. Atlanta: John Knox, 1958.
Shepherd, Massey H. Jr., ed. *Worship in Scripture and Tradition*. Oxford: Oxford University Press, 1963.
White, James F. *The Wordliness of Worship*. Oxford: Oxford University Press, 1967.

20 MINISTRY

Carey, Kenneth M., ed. *The Historic Episcopate*. Philadelphia: Westminster, 1964.
Congar, Yves M.J. *Lay People in the Church*. Philadelphia: Westminster, 1957.
Cooke, Bernard. *The Ministry to Word and Sacraments*. Philadelphia: Fortress Press, 1976.
Hanson, Anthony T. *The Pioneer Ministry*. London: SCM, 1961.
Holmes, Urban T. III. *The Future Shape of Ministry*. New York: Seabury Press, 1971.
Jenkins, Daniel T. *The Protestant Ministry*. Faber, 1958.
Kirk, Kenneth E., ed. *The Apostolic Ministry*. London: Hodder and Stoughton, 1957.
Kraemer, Hendrik. *A Theology of the Laity*. Philadelphia: Westminster, 1958.
Manson, Thomas W. *The Church's Ministry*. London: Hodder and Stoughton, 1948.
Neill, Stephen C, et. al. *The Ministry of the Church*, Canterbury, 1947.
Terwilliger, Robert E., and Holmes, Urban T., III, eds. *To Be a Priest: Perspectives on Vocation and Ordination*. New York: Seabury Press, 1975.

SYSTEMS OF THEOLOGY

Aquinas, Thomas. *Summa Theolgiae*.
Barth, Karl. *Church Dogmatics*, 13 vols. Edinburgh: T. & T. Clark, 1936-69.
Brunner, Emil. *Dogmatics*, 3 vols. Philadelphia: Westminster, 1950-60.
Calvin, John. *Institutes of the Christian Religion*.
Schleiermacher, Friederich. *The Christian Faith*. Edinburgh: T. & T. Clark, 1928.
Tillich, Paul. *Systematic Theology*, 3 vols. Chicago: Chicago University Press, 1951-63.

SURVEYS OF THEOLOGY

Aulen, Gustaf. *The Faith of the Christian Church*. Muhlenberg, 1960.
Barth, Karl. *Credo*. New York: Scribner, 1962.
——. *Dogmatics in Outline*. New York: Harper & Row, 1959.
——. *The Knowledge of God and The Service of God*. New York: Scribner, 1939.
Berkhof, Louis. *Systematic Theology*. Eerdmans, 1941.
Bicknell, E. J. *A Theological Introduction to the Thrity-Nine Articles*. Longmans, Green, 1953.
Bloesch, Donald G. *Essentials of Evangelical Theology*, 2 vols. New York: Harper & Row, 1978-79.
Burnaby, John. *The Belief in Christendom*. London: SPCK, 1959.
Cobb, John B., Jr. and Griffin, David R. *Process Theology: An Introductory Exposition*. Philadelphia:

Westminster, 1976.
DeWolf, L. Harold. *A Theology of the Living Church.* New York: Harper & Row, 1960.
Doctrine Commission of the Church of England. *Doctrine in the Church of England.* London: SPCK, 1938.
Fackre, Gabriel. *The Christian Story.* Eerdmans, 1978.
Gore, Charles. *The Reconstruction of Belief.* New York: Scribner, 1926.
Hall, Francis J. *Theological Outlines.* Morehouse-Gorham, 1933.
Horton, Walter M. *Christian Theology: An Ecumenical Approach.* New York: Harper & Row, 1955.
Kaufman, Gordon D. *Systematic Theology.* New York: Scribner, 1968.
Macquarrie, John. *Principles of Christian Theology.* New York: Scribner, 1977.
Prenter, Regin. *Creation and Redemption.* Philadelphia: Fortress Press, 1967.
Quick, Oliver C. *Doctrines of the Creed.* Nisbet, 1938.
Rahner, Karl. *Foundations of Christian Faith.* New York: Seabury Press, 1978.
(This volume can be supplemented by *A Rahner Reader,* ed. Gerald A. McCool. New York: Seabury Press, 1975.)
Wainwright, Geoffrey. *Doxology.* Oxford: Oxford University Press, 1980.
Whale, J.S. *Christian Doctrine.* New York: Macmillan, 1941.

BIBLICAL THEOLOGY

Bauer, Johannes B., ed. *Encyclopedia of Biblical Theology.* New York: Crossroad, 1981.
Buttrick, George A., ed. *Interpreter's Dictionary of the Bible,* 4 vols. & Suppl. Nashville, TN: Abingdon, 1962-76.
Léon-Dufour, Xavier, ed. *Dictionary of Biblical Theology.* New York: Seabury Press, 1973.
Richardson, Alan, ed. *A Theological Wordbook of the Bible.* New York: Macmillan, 1953.
Old Testament: Eichrodt, Jacob, Knight, von Rad, Vriezen.
New Testament: Bultmann, Conzelmann, Grant, Richardson.

HISTORY OF THEOLOGY

Dillenberger, John, and Welch, Claude. *Protestant Christianity.* New York: Scribner, 1954.
Fisher, George P. *History of Christian Doctrine.* New York: Scribner, 1896.
Gonzales, Justo. *A History of Christian Thought,* 2 vols. Nashville, TN: Abingdon, 1970.
Kelly, J. N.D. *Early Christian Doctrines.* New York: Harper & Row, 1960.
Leith, John H., ed. *Creeds of the Churches.* Garden City, N.Y.: Doubleday, 1963.
McGiffert, Arthur C. *A History of Christian Thought,* 2 vols. New York: Scribner, 1932-33.
Pelikan, Jaroslav. *The Christian Tradition,* 5 vols. Chicago, 1971.
Tillich, Paul. *A History of Christian Thought.* New York: Harper & Row, 1968.

THEOLOGICAL DICTIONARIES

Halverson, Marvin, and Cohen, Arthur A., eds. *A Handbook of Christian Theology.* Meridian, 1958.
Harvey, Van A. *A Handbook of Theological Terms.* New York: Macmillan, 1964.
Rahner, Karl, and Vorgrimler, Herbert. *Theological Dictionary.* Herder, 1965.
Rahner, Karl, et. al., eds. *Sacramentum Mundi,* 6 vols. Herder, 1968-70.
Richardson, Alan, ed. *A Dictionary of Christian Theology.* Philadelphia: Westminster, 1969.

Indexes

Names

Abelard, 166, 175
Aland, K., 48 n. 14, 50 n.17&18
Anselm, 4,9, 165, 173*f*
Aquinas, T., 14, 21,72, 93, 102, 113, 179, 190, 207, 224, 245
Athanasius, 126, 165, 197
Augustine, 9, 14*f*, 65, 67, 71*f*, 74, 93, 125*f*, 131*f* n. 4, 133*f*, 137*f*, 190*f*, 197, 207, 209, 215, 217*f*, 224, 233, 238, 246, 257, 265, 275*f*
Aulen, G., 68, 87,166

Baillie, D.,8, 67*f*, 109, 112, 151, 154, 172, 199
Baillie,J., 6, 20, 25, 27
Barr, J., 19 n.1, 30
Barth, K., 7, 10, 14, 26, 40, 47 n.13, 53, 64 n. 6, 67-70, 74, 80 n.8, 82 n.10, 84, 93, 102, 110, 112*f*, 117, 119, 122 n.12, 124, 159*f*, 163*f*, 168, 174, 181, 187, 191, 197, 201, 209, 220, 226,
237 n.13, 269
Bonhoeffer, D., 19, 77, 84, 119, 129, 151, 215
Browning, D. S.,167, 201
Brunner, E., 3, 20, 28, 29 n.15, 41 n. 2, 64 n.6, 68, 81, 93, 102, 112, 117, 119, 120 n. 7, 122 n.12, 124 n.16, 125, 138 n. 15, 143-46, 159, 179, 187, 191, 200 n.8, 209, 224, 237, 239, 266-69, 276
Buber, M., 9, 20
Bultmann, R., 3*f*, 19, 49 n.15, 77, 85, 112-15, 117, 119, 129*f*, 144*f*, 147, 155 n. 35, 159, 164, 174*f*, 183*f*, 203, 206, 210, 220*f*, 222, 226, 237, 239, 263*f*, 276

Calvin,J., 10, 15, 113, 190*f*, 215, 224, 238, 247, 250, 253
Cappadocians, 64, 70, 126, 197
Casserley, J.V.L., 20, 24, 149, 150 n. 19
de Chardin, P.T., 170, 221
Cobb, J.B., 25 n.11, 94 n.26, 156, 158, 214 n.15

Compton, J.J., 114
Cone, J.A., 156, 158, 176
Cox, H., 120 n. 3,164, 170, 215, 236
Cullmann, O., 90, 143 n. 1, 147, 149, 152, 155, 209
Cyprian, 233, 273

Daly, M., 83, 130 n.3, 156, 158 n.44
Darwin, C., 103, 119
Dilley, F.B., 19 n.1, 32*f*, 112*f*
Dillistone, F.W., 168*f*
Dodd, C.H., 27 n. 13, 49, 89 n. 20, 122, 189, 208
Downing, F.G., 19 n. 1, 22, 24
Driver, T.F.,42 n. 7, 156
Dulles, A., 33 n. 20, 236

Ebeling, G., 146 n.11, 183

Farmer, H.H., 28, 34, 85, 112, 117
Ferré, F., 36 n.25
Forsyth, P.T., 42,56, 143
Freud, S., 119,134
Fuller, R.H., 143 n. 3,144 n.5,147 n.13

Gilkey, L., 19 n. 1, 32*f*,42 n. 7, 77, 98, 102, 110, 112*f*, 115, 122 n.10
Gollwitzer, H., 78 n.6,81 n.9,82 n.10
Gustafson, J.M., 239
Guthrie, H.H., 15,50,262 n.2
Gutiérrez, G.,126,177 n. 19

Hamilton, W., 77, 164
Hartshorne, C., 77, 94
Harvey, V.A., 144 n.6, 145 n.8, 164, 276
Heidegger, M., 119*f*
Heim, K., 86

SUBJECTS

303